Defining Cinema

The Oxford Music / Media Series
Daniel Goldmark, Series Editor

oxford music/media series

Tuning In: American Narrative Television Music
Ron Rodman

Special Sound: The Creation and Legacy of the BBC Radiophonic Workshop
Louis Niebur

Seeing Through Music: Gender and Modernism in Classic Hollywood Film Scores
Peter Franklin

An Eye for Music: Popular Music and the Audiovisual Surreal
John Richardson

Playing Along: Digital Games, YouTube, and Virtual Performance
Kiri Miller

Sounding the Gallery: Video and the Rise of Art-Music
Holly Rogers

Composing for the Red Screen: Prokofiev and Soviet Film
Kevin Bartig

Saying It With Songs: Popular Music and the Coming of Sound to Hollywood Cinema
Katherine Spring

We'll Meet Again: Musical Design in the Films of Stanley Kubrick
Kate McQuiston

Occult Aesthetics: Synchronization in Sound Film
K. J. Donnelly

Sound Play: Video Games and the Musical Imagination
William Cheng

Sounding American: Hollywood, Opera, and Jazz
Jennifer Fleeger

Mismatched Women: The Siren's Song Through the Machine
Jennifer Fleeger

Robert Altman's Soundtracks: Film, Music and Sound from M*A*S*H to A Prairie Home Companion
Gayle Sherwood Magee

Back to the Fifties: Nostalgia, Hollywood Film, and Popular Music of the Seventies and Eighties
Michael D. Dwyer

The Early Film Music of Dmitry Shostakovich
Joan Titus

Making Music in Selznick's Hollywood
Nathan Platte

Hearing Haneke: The Sound Tracks of a Radical Auteur
Elsie Walker

Unlimited Replays: Video Games and Classical Music
William Gibbons

Hollywood Harmony: Musical Wonder and the Sound of Cinema
Frank Lehman

*French Musical Culture and the Coming of
Sound Cinema*
Hannah Lewis

Theories of the Soundtrack
James Buhler

*Through the Looking Glass: John Cage and
Avant-Garde Film*
Richard H. Brown

*Sound Design Is the New Score: Theory,
Aesthetics, and Erotics of the Integrated
Soundtrack*
Danijela Kulezic-Wilson

*Rock Star/Movie Star: Power and Performance in
Cinematic Rock Stardom*
Landon Palmer

*The Presence of the Past: Temporal Experience
and the New Hollywood Soundtrack*
Daniel Bishop

Metafilm Music in Jean-Luc Godard's Cinema
Michael Baumgartner

Acoustic Profiles: A Sound Ecology of the Cinema
Randolph Jordan

*Defining Cinema: Rouben Mamoulian and
Hollywood Film Style, 1929–1957*
Michael Slowik

Defining Cinema

Rouben Mamoulian and Hollywood Film Style, 1929–1957

MICHAEL SLOWIK

OXFORD
UNIVERSITY PRESS

Oxford University Press is a department of the University of Oxford. It furthers the University's objective of excellence in research, scholarship, and education by publishing worldwide. Oxford is a registered trade mark of Oxford University Press in the UK and certain other countries.

Published in the United States of America by Oxford University Press
198 Madison Avenue, New York, NY 10016, United States of America.

© Oxford University Press 2024

All rights reserved. No part of this publication may be reproduced, stored in a retrieval system, or transmitted, in any form or by any means, without the prior permission in writing of Oxford University Press, or as expressly permitted by law, by license, or under terms agreed with the appropriate reproduction rights organization. Inquiries concerning reproduction outside the scope of the above should be sent to the Rights Department, Oxford University Press, at the address above.

You must not circulate this work in any other form
and you must impose this same condition on any acquirer.

Library of Congress Cataloging-in-Publication Data
Names: Slowik, Michael, author.
Title: Defining cinema : Rouben Mamoulian and Hollywood film style, 1929–1957 / Michael Slowik.
Description: New York : Oxford University Press, 2024. |
Series: The Oxford music/media series | Includes bibliographical references and index.
Identifiers: LCCN 2023036443 (print) | LCCN 2023036444 (ebook) |
ISBN 9780197511237 (paperback) | ISBN 9780197511220 (hardback) |
ISBN 9780197511251 (epub)
Subjects: LCSH: Mamoulian, Rouben—Criticism and interpretation. |
Motion pictures—United States—History and criticism.
Classification: LCC PN1998.3.M345 S56 2023 (print) | LCC PN1998.3.M345 (ebook) |
DDC 791.4302/33092—dc23/eng/20230807
LC record available at https://lccn.loc.gov/2023036443
LC ebook record available at https://lccn.loc.gov/2023036444

DOI: 10.1093/oso/9780197511220.001.0001

Paperback printed by Marquis Book Printing, Canada
Hardback printed by Bridgeport National Bindery, Inc., United States of America

*For Emily Hazel Slowik and Everett Graham Slowik
And in memory of Colin Wesley Slowik*

Contents

Acknowledgments   xi

Introduction: Why Mamoulian Matters   1

1. Mamoulian, Art, and Cinema   17

2. Mamoulian and Early Film Sound: *Applause, City Streets, Dr. Jekyll and Mr. Hyde*   53

3. Mamoulian and Rhythm: *Applause, City Streets, Dr. Jekyll and Mr. Hyde, We Live Again, High, Wide, and Handsome, Golden Boy, The Mark of Zorro, Blood and Sand*   90

4. Mamoulian and the Musical: *Applause, Love Me Tonight, The Gay Desperado, High, Wide and Handsome, Summer Holiday, Silk Stockings*   124

5. Mamoulian and Color: *Becky Sharp, Blood and Sand, Summer Holiday, Silk Stockings*   177

6. Mamoulian and Filmmaking under Censorship: *Applause, Dr. Jekyll and Mr. Hyde, The Song of Songs, Queen Christina*   204

Conclusion: Mamoulian's Legacy   247

Appendix 1: Completed Films Directed by Mamoulian   251
Appendix 2: Plays Directed by Mamoulian   253
Appendix 3: Additional Films Consulted   255
Notes   261
Bibliography   293
Index   299

Acknowledgments

It has been my great fortune to work with outstanding mentors for as long as I've been studying film, and this book is especially indebted to their guidance and encouragement. I must first of all thank my former teacher and later colleague Jeanine Basinger, who initially suggested the book's topic to me, continued to nudge me to pursue it, and later devoted countless hours sharing her thoughts on Mamoulian and lending me her encyclopedic knowledge of film history. Rick Altman, my adviser back when I was a PhD candidate at the University of Iowa, offered vital early feedback on my ideas and later gave my written proposal a careful read. Scott Higgins, another teacher-turned-colleague at Wesleyan University, offered invaluable advice and assistance as I navigated the project, which included providing a close reading of the chapter on color.

Among the many other scholars who have offered their thoughts on the project in its various stages, I must thank especially Daniel Weigand, who organized an early sound-era conference and provided me with new insights into Mamoulian's relationship to other theorists, and Lea Jacobs and Martin Barnier, both of whom caught important omissions and helped me think through some tricky questions. Sharon Carnicke was a valuable resource on the state of Russian theater during the first few decades of the twentieth century, and John Belton offered kind assurances when they were most needed.

My research trips to the Library of Congress, the Young Research Library at UCLA, and the Margaret Herrick Library were funded by grant money provided by Wesleyan University. My sincere thanks to Wesleyan and to all the wonderful assistants at those archives. I must also profusely thank Rebecca Gates-Coon and Rick Coon for helping me plan my DC trips and offering me their generous hospitality.

On a daily basis, the faculty and staff of the College of Film and the Moving Image at Wesleyan University have given me the stimulating and supportive environment needed to write this book. I thank especially Steve Collins, Marc Longenecker, and Richard Parkin for their conversations about Mamoulian, and Lea Carlson for timely and vital administrative assistance along the way. Many others associated with the college also deserve recognition for helping in ways large and small: Joe Cacaci, Rich Contrastano, Lisa Dombrowski, Anuja Jain, Randall MacLowry, Joan Miller, Lisa Mingione, Sal Privitera, Mirko Rucnov, Sadia Shepard, and Tracy Heather Strain.

At Oxford University Press, I could not have asked for a better editor than Norm Hirschy, whose warmth, assistance, timely replies, and flexibility were all invaluable. Both Norm and Daniel Goldmark have been steadfast in their belief in this project, and I thank them for their support. During this book's production phase, Egle Zigaite and Hemalatha Arumugam guided the project and helped me through some hiccups. Timothy DeWerff provided careful copyediting and saved me from a number of gaffes.

Portions of chapters 1 and 4 appear in an issue of *The Soundtrack* (12.1), and portions of chapter 2 appear in an edited collection titled *Aesthetics of Early Sound Film* (Amsterdam University Press). My thanks to Claus Tieber, Anna Windisch, and Daniel Wiegand for inviting me to contribute to these collections, and for their sharp editorial eyes.

Finally, this project could never have been completed without my family. My parents, John and Lynn, and my brother, Jay, have been enthusiastic and constant sources of encouragement. Much of this book was written during the COVID pandemic, a time of both joy and loss for my family, and my wife and children have been my anchor throughout this project. Thank you, Emily and Everett, for your sense of humor, resiliency, and good cheer. Finally, words cannot adequately express my gratitude to my wife, Amy, who has sacrificed much and has provided me with nearly twenty years of unwavering love and support.

Introduction
Why Mamoulian Matters

In August 1932, *American Cinematographer* published an article by William Stull providing tips for amateur filmmakers. After running through various considerations, Stull instructed readers to study productions directed by "artists of the highest order" to gain a full grasp of filmmaking techniques. The directors Stull suggested spanned the globe and included figures lionized today: René Clair, Sergei Eisenstein, Ernst Lubitsch, and Fritz Lang. First on Stull's list, however, was a filmmaker whose work has largely receded from view: Rouben Mamoulian.[1]

Far from an idiosyncratic choice, Stull's selection of Mamoulian as one of the world's premier directors was consistent with how Mamoulian was regarded across the industry and among critics, particularly from his debut film—*Applause* (1929)—through his 1941 feature *Blood and Sand*. At the peak of his prestige in the late 1930s, he commanded possibly the highest salary of any director in Hollywood.[2] In 1941, Stull, now serving as editor of *American Cinematographer*, mentioned the "well known" fact that Hollywood's top producers and directors—David O. Selznick, Cecil B. DeMille, George Cukor, and Mamoulian—generated sizable audiences by their names alone.[3]

Mamoulian was held in such high regard in large part because his work was strikingly innovative during these years. He was responsible for some of the most groundbreaking films of the early sound era (*Applause, City Streets* [1931], *Dr. Jekyll and Mr. Hyde* [1931], and *Love Me Tonight* [1932]), he directed the first three-strip Technicolor film—*Becky Sharp*—in 1935, and he directed stylistically rich films into the 1940s, with *Blood and Sand* winning an Academy Award for the color design that he conceptualized. Remarkably, had an article comparable to Stull's been written about *stage* directors, Mamoulian's presence on the list would have been even more likely, especially if the article had been written in the 1940s. Among many other plays, Mamoulian directed the influential *Porgy* (1927), the Gershwin musical *Porgy and Bess* (1935), and the original productions of *Oklahoma!* (1943) and *Carousel* (1945).

After the 1940s, Mamoulian continued to be championed by film historians for a time, but in the 1960s, his status fell considerably. Arthur Knight's influential 1957 book *Film: The Liveliest Art* pinpointed Mamoulian as the single most important early sound-era filmmaker "to transform the talking picture into a genuinely cinematic art."[4] The rise of auteurism, however, marked a decline in attention toward Mamoulian that persists today. The auteur theory—popularized especially by Andrew Sarris and Peter Wollen in the United States in the late 1960s—held that the films most worthy of attention were those that displayed stylistic and thematic consistency across a director's body of work.[5] Directors like Alfred Hitchcock, Howard Hawks, and John Ford were elevated and praised for their ability to inject their personalities and interests into their films. Mamoulian, a thematically eclectic filmmaker by inclination, amounted to little more than—in Sarris's memorable words—an "innovator who ran out of innovations."[6] To date, although a few biographies of Mamoulian exist, the only book-length analysis of his films was written over fifty years ago, and the lone book focused on analyzing his directorial efforts on the stage centers on a single production: *Porgy and Bess*.[7] Scholars have singled out individual films—mainly *Applause*, *Dr. Jekyll and Mr. Hyde*, *Love Me Tonight*, and *Queen Christina* (1933)—for close attention, but Mamoulian's films have not been treated collectively as the product of a director who took a singular and unified approach to his work. Today, Elia Kazan—not Mamoulian—is more widely recognized as the paragon of an elite stage director who transitioned successfully to filmmaking.

As a result, Mamoulian's identity as an artist—what mattered to him and how he conceptualized his craft—and his precise contributions to film history remain murky. If we refocus our attention on Mamoulian's creative ideas, his style, and the historical context within which he worked, however, we see a filmmaker of startling originality who remains badly undervalued and insufficiently understood. A close look at Mamoulian reveals a largely untold story of a director who possessed a consistent and ambitious vision of cinema throughout his career. Mamoulian's innovations might initially seem technical and disparate (early sound-era camera movement, two-track recording, the voice-over, synthetic sound, color design, and various contributions to the musical genre), but they were the result of a director who, through his extensive theoretical writings as well as his films, sought to do something grand and cohesive: test and define the basic potentials of sound cinema aesthetics. Mamoulian offered broad and foundational ideas pertaining to early sound and image strategies during the transition to sound, the achievement of rhythm and pacing in early sound film, the development of the musical genre, color filmmaking, and filming strategies under industry censorship. Arriving near the beginning of the early sound era, when many techniques and approaches had yet to harden, Mamoulian was nothing short of a pivotal player in their formation. Focusing on Mamoulian is vital not just for better understanding the work of a neglected filmmaker, but for anyone who cares about the history of Hollywood filmmaking.

This book is an in-depth study of Mamoulian's films, the ideas behind them, and their place within the history of sound cinema. The book also pays substantial attention to Mamoulian's stage work to help explain his stylistic contributions to film, but in the interest of maintaining a manageable scope, cinema is the book's main focus. The book's attention to a single director might, on the surface, give the appearance of yet another auteurist study, but in my view, a study of Mamoulian mandates several key deviations from this traditional approach. First, this book's focus is not on determining a consistent thematic "worldview" in Mamoulian's films in line with Hawks's professional male group, Douglas Sirk's undercutting of American culture, or Ford's emphasis on the community. Mamoulian's central preoccupation rested not with particular themes, but with the form of cinema itself: its properties, potentials, and opportunities for stylization. It is this underlying concern that drives much of the book's focus.

Second, auteur studies frequently come under fire for failing to adequately situate a director's films historically, resulting in a constrained approach that ignores pertinent contexts. A close analysis of Mamoulian's work, however, requires a radically different approach because it is impossible to grasp the significance of his films without a thorough understanding of the typical filmmaking methods taken by the industry when Mamoulian was active as a director. For each topic covered in the book—early synchronized sound techniques, film rhythm and pacing, the musical genre, color, and censorship—I compare Mamoulian's films to prevailing industry practices at the time. To do so, I have consulted relevant scholarship when possible, but I also draw regularly upon my own viewing of 217 films that are pertinent to these contexts (see Appendices). Doing so enables a better-informed assessment of the newness of Mamoulian's specific "innovations," but more important, it helps us better grasp the broader aesthetic significance of Mamoulian's movies at the time of their release.

Third, auteur approaches have long been criticized for ascribing a level of agency to directors that cannot be proved. Though the increasing availability of archival materials has changed the situation somewhat, the issue of directorial agency often remains uncertain. In the case of Mamoulian, however, less guesswork is needed, because in 2009, the Library of Congress opened for public use the Rouben Mamoulian Papers, which constitute approximately 59,000 items from his personal collection. These materials are a treasure trove for anyone wishing to better understand Mamoulian's artistic contributions to film and theater. To my knowledge, they have been used extensively for only one book: Joseph Horowitz's *On My Way*, a study of Mamoulian's work on the stage musical *Porgy and Bess*. Of central importance for *Defining Cinema* are Mamoulian's personal screenplays and playscripts, because in many cases they contain extensive annotations in Mamoulian's handwriting that reveal in detail his thought processes and contributions to the films and plays he directed. This—combined with production records and a vast collection of interviews, speeches, and writings (both published and unpublished)—offers unparalleled insights into this neglected director. The analyses throughout this book make extensive use of the Mamoulian collection, along with censorship records, production files, and screenplays found at the Margaret Herrick Library and UCLA. Mamoulian's marginal notes do not constitute iron-clad evidence, since Mamoulian's annotations could have been written on the advice of others, but as I discuss below, their consistency across different production circumstances and personnel makes it likely that most of the annotations were his idea. Any historical account necessarily requires a degree of gap filling, but for Mamoulian, archival evidence helps piece together an unusually precise account of a director's contributions.

The book's argument is as follows: when Mamoulian entered filmmaking in 1929, he did so at a time that was chaotic for the US film industry, but quite fortuitous for him. Hollywood committed to making only 100 percent talking films in 1929. Yet while the industry understood that sound cinema was there to stay, its filmmakers lacked a firm idea of what this nascent form would look and sound like. Aesthetically speaking, the definition of cinema was up for grabs, and the door was open for rampant experimentation. Mamoulian was well positioned to play a pivotal role in the definition of sound cinema for several reasons. First, his artistic philosophy was geared toward ignoring boundaries in favor of pursuing one's own ideas. Mamoulian viewed a theater or film director less as a collaborator and more as someone whose personal vision, no matter how idiosyncratic, should be faithfully executed. Second, Mamoulian's writings reveal that he entered filmmaking already equipped with a well-formed theory of where an artist's focus should be directed. For Mamoulian, an artist working in any form should (1) home in on the properties essential to that medium and (2) stylize those properties to express the author's viewpoint on the material. Mamoulian's artistic stance thus mandated that he saliently explore the elements that he felt defined cinema. Third, and somewhat paradoxically, Mamoulian was also well versed in a broad array of other art forms—including drama, literature, music, dance/movement, painting, and sculpture—and he was interested in applying concepts from these areas to film. Film was, from its inception, a deeply intermedial form, and this was arguably never more the case than when sound arrived. Hollywood looked toward theater, music, and other forms to establish sound cinema's identity. Mamoulian's diverse range of knowledge made him exceptionally suited to capitalize on sound cinema's potential and enabled the industry to better see fruitful interchanges between these forms.

The films from Mamoulian that followed displayed an array of cinematic methods that had been underutilized or—in some cases—may have been genuinely new. In particular, Mamoulian's early sound techniques demonstrated the value of prioritizing camera movement during directly recorded sound sequences, constructing narratively expressive soundtracks, harnessing sound to character subjectivity, achieving crisper pacing, and heavily stylizing the musical genre. Even after the early sound era, Mamoulian continued trailblazing work, offering the first three-strip Technicolor film, directing a prototype for what Rick Altman calls the "folk" musical in the 1937 film *High, Wide, and Handsome*, and exploring color film's relationship to painting (*Blood and Sand*) and character subjectivity (*Summer Holiday* [1948]). Accompanying many of these films were writings, speeches, and interviews that clearly articulated his methods and the broader philosophies that underpinned them. This book's title, *Defining Cinema*, may seem grandiose, but it is nothing short of what Mamoulian—as both a practitioner and theorist—sought to do. Through his films and writings, Mamoulian aimed to define what sound cinema, as an art form, could be.

In making the case for Mamoulian's historical importance, I remain aware of the danger of falling into a Great Man approach, which attributes substantial historical change to (often male) individual "geniuses" who proved uniquely capable of understanding the "true" potential of an object or art form. The pitfalls of such an approach can be substantial, including insufficient attention to the context within which the Great Man worked, and the assumption that new art forms contain merely a fixed array of potentials for the Great Man to discover. Mamoulian, we should note, was himself an active contributor to this historiography. As I discuss in chapter 1, Mamoulian never provided a full account of his early theater training in Russia, instead presenting his ideas as if they came from his thinking alone. Mamoulian's intellectual influences can thus be difficult to decipher, a matter I address more fully in chapter 1. Likewise, it can be challenging to gauge the precise extent to which his writings and films influenced others. What *can* be more concretely determined, thanks to film availability and extensive scholarship, is the extent to which his cinematic methods were—or were not—unusual. Yet even here, we will see that the story is often complex. Some of his approaches, based on existing evidence, had no clear precedent, but for other areas, I will at various times suggest that Mamoulian somewhat overstated his originality, that his approach was not so much new as an unusually forceful embrace of expressive silent-era strategies, and that Mamoulian was likely thinking in parallel with other innovative creators.

Still, whether or not he was the absolute "first" to do something, I will argue that Mamoulian frequently used approaches that were cutting-edge, prescient, and foundational to how later filmmakers would approach sound cinema. Mamoulian's films, we should note, explored *certain* potentials, not the *only* ones. Yet even after consulting archival evidence, examining the contributions of his collaborators, and situating him within the period's prevailing filmmaking strategies, I believe Mamoulian remains highly notable for the level of responsibility he had for his creations and the significance of the cinematic ideas he put into practice. Like anyone else, Mamoulian was affected by technological, economic, and social forces, but his theories, his stylistic methods, and the creative power he enjoyed in many of his films make him a crucial figure in the history of film as an art form.[8]

Mamoulian is also worth celebrating as an individual contributor because as an Armenian immigrant from Russia, his background was unlike any other Hollywood director at the time. Immigrants, of course, were hardly anathema in Hollywood during the 1920s and 1930s. Founding figures Louis B. Mayer (MGM), Harry Warner (Warner Bros.), and Adolph Zukor (Paramount) had all—like Mamoulian—been born in eastern Europe. When Mamoulian moved to Hollywood in late 1930, a number of European-born directors already worked there. Many were German (Ernst Lubitsch, F. W. Murnau, William Wyler, and the lesser-known Gus Meins and Lothar Mendes), but several others were born in eastern Europe, including Michael Curtiz (who emigrated from Hungary), and Russian-born directors Lewis Milestone, John M. Stahl (who moved to the United States as a young child), and Robert Milton. Other important directors born in the Russian Empire would arrive as the 1930s progressed, including Richard Boleslawski, Gregory Ratoff, and Anatole Litvak. Still, Hollywood's directors were *mostly* native-born Americans, and with the possible exception of Milestone, no other Russian-born filmmaker would enjoy as much prestige and acclaim during the studio years as Mamoulian.

Mamoulian was also, to my knowledge, the only Armenian employed as a director during the years of the Hollywood studio system. Though Mamoulian grew up in a wealthy Armenian family in Russia, Armenians were a minority group within the Russian Empire with a history of persecution. During World War I and the Russian Revolution, Mamoulian's family lost nearly all their assets and were forced into a nomadic existence, and in nearby Turkey, a mass genocide of Armenians was taking place. As a Hollywood director, Mamoulian was thus a formerly persecuted, doubly marked minority (a minority in his home and adopted country) who learned English as his seventh language and who worked at a time when considerable discrimination against eastern European immigrants existed in the United States. That a man with this background—and with no contacts in the film industry until he was first approached to direct movies in 1928—became one of the world's top directors alone makes an analysis of his filmmaking and his level of creative agency worthwhile.

Outline of Chapters

Because Mamoulian's importance as a filmmaker is tied predominantly to how he probed and innovated within certain spheres of sound cinema, a topic-based—rather than chronological—approach will best enable us to grasp his thought processes and importance. In chapter 1, I examine Mamoulian's philosophies of art and how his ideas played out via specific techniques that recurred across his films. Mamoulian came to cinema with firm ideas about medium specificity and stylization already in place that would inform his approach to a wide array of filmmaking topics and challenges. Chapter 1 thus examines Mamoulian's overarching views about art and cinema, and how these viewpoints resulted in such repeated techniques as shadow play, forced framings, and elaborate transitions.

Chapters 2–6 then examine individual areas where Mamoulian's style was at its most innovative. For each topic, I describe Mamoulian's stated ideas about the subject, analyze how these ideas played out stylistically in his films, and assess their level of innovation within the context of filmmaking at the time. Chapter 2 examines Mamoulian's sound and image strategies during Hollywood's transition to synchronized sound. Focusing on *Applause*, *City Streets*, and *Dr. Jekyll and Mr. Hyde*, I discuss ways in which Mamoulian surmounted significant technological obstacles and announced sound film's potential as a visually and sonically expressive form. At a time when many filmmakers used sound cinema as a dispassionate recording medium, Mamoulian's *Applause* instead demonstrated how a filmmaker might focus on devices specific to cinema—particularly camera movement and selective and manipulated sound—to articulate narrative ideas. Mamoulian often claimed that he invented two-track recording for *Applause*, the voice-over in *City Streets*, and synthetic sound in *Dr. Jekyll and Mr. Hyde*. Through archival evidence and my own viewing of films from the period, I attempt to gauge the validity of these claims and offer an assessment of Mamoulian's historical importance in terms of the broader idea of manipulating the soundtrack for expressive purposes.

Chapter 3 then examines Mamoulian's approach to film rhythm, a concept I define broadly as a film's general sensation of pace and energy. Rhythm was probably Mamoulian's most prized concept in film *and* theater, and the chapter thus begins by exploring his prior experiments with rhythm on the stage. I then turn to his films, focusing on how Mamoulian found cinematic ways to further his explorations with rhythm. First, I examine specific methods Mamoulian used to give his early sound films a sense of momentum and vitality at a time when many industry professionals were complaining about the era's turgidly paced films. The chapter's second half then examines Mamoulian's pacing methods beyond the early sound period, including the literal use of an on-set metronome and conductor's baton, and the employment of musical performance within many of the non-musicals that he directed.

With Mamoulian's approaches to the soundtrack and music as key background, chapter 4 explores probably Mamoulian's single most important contribution to the stage and screen: the musical genre. Mamoulian shuttled between stage and screen musicals throughout his career, applying principles from one medium to the other, and ultimately offering innovative and influential approaches to the genre in both forms. Chapter 4 takes a chronological look at each of his stage and screen musicals, examining in particular how his work anticipated subsequent trends and reflected values and aims he highly prized. I analyze Mamoulian's contributions to the three film-musical subgenres identified by Rick Altman—the "show," "fairy-tale," and "folk" musical—and show how and why his interests in stylization, rhythm, folk-music traditions, narrative-number integration, and community enabled him to produce such pioneering work.

Chapters 2–4 are tightly bound by such concerns as sound, rhythm, and music. Chapters 5 and 6 shift gears somewhat by addressing two less closely related topics that were nevertheless of great interest to Mamoulian: color and censorship. Chapter 5 examines the four Technicolor films Mamoulian directed: *Becky Sharp*, *Blood and Sand*, *Summer Holiday*, and *Silk Stockings* (1957). Color long fascinated Mamoulian, and he devoted numerous essays to its potential. The chapter focuses especially on the industry's inaugural three-strip Technicolor film, *Becky Sharp* (which Mamoulian had little time to prepare), *Blood and Sand* (which featured an elaborate color plan that was Mamoulian's primary interest during filmmaking), and *Summer Holiday* (which contained a prominent experiment with subjective color). Through these films and his accompanying writings, Mamoulian laid out important early ideas for color control, color expressivity, painting-based color, and subjectivity.

The final chapter returns to the early sound era to address one domain that would not prove to be as influential: stylistic methods for conveying sexual content under censorship. *Applause*, *Dr. Jekyll and Mr. Hyde*, *The Song of Songs* (1933), and *Queen Christina* were among the most sexually explicit films made in Hollywood prior to the more stringent application of industry self-censorship in mid-1934. In *Applause*, *Dr. Jekyll and Mr. Hyde*, and *The Song of Songs*, Mamoulian explored ways in which film style could accentuate his viewpoint on the conventional dynamics of the male look and the female body. Disgusted by certain types of sexual display yet captivated by others, Mamoulian—whether rightly or wrongly—showcased methods by which film style could alternately condemn crass sexual display or encourage audiences to share a male character's aroused or excited state. *Queen Christina*, in contrast, featured a different method of stylization to convey the glories of sexual experience from a female character's perspective. The arrival of enhanced censorship after *Queen Christina* put a stop to these experiments, but while they lasted, Mamoulian charted an aesthetic course for a sexually permissive and emotionally powerful mode of sound filmmaking.

Two additional notes of explanation are in order here—one pragmatic, the other conceptual. First, for the sake of readability, the subtitles for chapters 2–6 include a list of films discussed in each chapter. This is intended to make it easier for readers to quickly turn to analyses of specific films, but one should note that many of Mamoulian's plays are covered in some depth as well, including *Porgy* in chapters 1 and 3; *Sister Beatrice* (1926) and *Wings over Europe* (1928) in chapter 3; *Porgy and Bess*, *Oklahoma!*, *Carousel*, *St. Louis Woman* (1946), and *Lost in the Stars* (1949) in chapter 4; and *Sadie Thompson* in chapter 6. Second, throughout the book, I use the word "expressive" when discussing Mamoulian's stylistic devices, by which I mean techniques designed to articulate or accentuate narrative ideas. As I discuss in the next chapter, the term is important because while Mamoulian's style could sometimes be flashy, he strongly believed that even the most unconventional creative moves should serve story purposes.

A Brief Chronology of Mamoulian's Career

Though all six chapters address portions of Mamoulian's biography, the book's topical layout means that this biography remains piecemeal. Thus, in what follows, I provide a brief chronology of Mamoulian's life and career from beginning to end, followed by a discussion of Mamoulian's recurring relationships with professional collaborators and supervisors.

Mamoulian was born in 1897 in the city of Tiflis. At the time, Tiflis was part of the Republic of Russia, but it is now called Tbilisi and is located in Georgia. Mamoulian's parents were wealthy Armenians, and while relatively little information is available about his early years, historians do know that Mamoulian played violin as a boy and that his mother performed in the local theater. Sometime during Mamoulian's youth, the family moved to Paris for a spell, though the dates and reasons remain unclear.[9] After returning to Russia, Mamoulian attended Moscow University to study criminal law. Theater was a far greater interest, however, and he studied for a short time at the Moscow Art Theatre with notable theater director Evgeny Vakhtangov. World War I and the Russian Revolution, as previously noted, caused the Mamoulians to lose much of their money. Mamoulian's father was recalled to fight in the tsar's army, and Mamoulian, his mother, and his sister, Svetlana, were displaced from Tiflis and led a dangerous, nomadic existence during this period. During the war, Mamoulian's sister met and married an officer, and Mamoulian eventually moved to London, where his sister now resided with her husband. Thanks apparently to his first-hand knowledge of the Russian Revolution, Mamoulian was invited to direct his first play, a Russian Revolution-set drama titled *The Beating on the Door*, in London in 1922.

Likely on the recommendation of Russian émigré Vladimir Rosing,[10] George Eastman hired Mamoulian to travel to Rochester, New York, to co-direct with Rosing an opera training program at the Eastman School of Music at the University of Rochester. At the behest of Rosing, Eastman was in the process of launching the Rochester American Opera Company as an effort to provide English-language opera productions, and he wanted young innovators to help progress this vision. Despite possessing no formal training in opera, Mamoulian thrived in Rochester, where he directed scenes from operas and—on occasion—full operas from 1923 through 1926. Mamoulian also conceived of, and started, the Eastman School of Drama and Dramatic Action in 1925. A record of Mamoulian's written theories of artistry in the theater first appears at this time. It was here that Mamoulian, who had apparently seen relatively few films, first became interested in them. Mamoulian had access to Eastman film stock and movie cameras, and he enjoyed filming and reviewing rehearsals for stage productions.[11] Mamoulian also began directing movie prologues (live performances that preceded feature-length films) at the Eastman Theatre in downtown Rochester, then a movie palace.[12]

Mamoulian's direction of *Sister Beatrice*—his favorite production while at Rochester—captured the attention of members of the Theatre Guild in New York City. The Theatre Guild hired Mamoulian to first teach, and shortly thereafter to direct plays. From 1927 to 1929, Mamoulian directed six Theatre Guild plays: *Porgy, Marco Millions* (1928), *These Modern Women* (1928), *Congai* (1928), *Wings over Europe*, and *The Game of Love and Death* (1929). Of these productions, his first—*Porgy*—was by far the most important. It was a sensational hit and a critical darling, and it would be difficult to overstate its importance for Mamoulian's subsequent theater and film work. The play—a slice-of-life portrait of an impoverished black community in Charleston, South Carolina—was notable simply for its focus on African American life, but its critical and commercial success also assured Mamoulian of an important career on Broadway and attracted the attention of the film industry. The publicity surrounding *Porgy* emphasized the play's artistry, a quality that Mamoulian would embrace for the remainder of his career. Mamoulian's decision to tackle a play with a nearly all-black cast was somewhat unusual at the time, and it helped define him as an offbeat director who possessed integrity. Many interviews and articles touted him as a young genius. Other articles pointed to the idea that an Armenian man directing a play set in the black South seemed a stretch, and Mamoulian would repeatedly select projects that seemed far afield from his actual life experiences. Perhaps most important, the press labeled Mamoulian an innovator, a mantle that would influence Mamoulian's approach to filmmaking.

Porgy, it should be noted, would come under fire for racially stereotyped depictions of black characters, especially in the 1950s, when Hollywood adapted George and Ira Gershwin's musical version into a film.[13] In particular, commentators pointed to the association of black culture with drugs, sex, gambling, and violence. This critique—and debates that ensued—remain important, but there is little to suggest that Mamoulian altered story material to enhance these depictions. Mamoulian, as chapter 4 notes, did struggle in rehearsals with his grasp of black culture, but his primary focus was on how to stylize the existing material. Still, the controversy surrounding this property deserves to be remembered.

Thanks largely to *Porgy*'s fame, Jesse Lasky and Walter Wanger of Paramount Pictures approached Mamoulian and asked him to serve as a dialogue director for synchronized sound films that the studio was shooting on their lot in Astoria, New York. Mamoulian had, in fact, refused an earlier contract tendered by Paramount to relocate to Hollywood and direct in February 1928.[14] Mamoulian refused Lasky and Wanger's initial dialogue-director offer as well and instead negotiated to work as sole director of *Applause* (1929), a film that proved financially disappointing but was widely admired by the industry for its innovative early sound techniques. Both Wanger and Lasky appear to have been looking to hire an innovator, and they were willing to step back and allow Mamoulian to experiment with sound and image strategies. Paramount was ultimately impressed with *Applause* but reluctant to rehire a potentially unprofitable director, so Mamoulian returned to the stage, directing *R.U.R. (Rossum's Universal Robots)*, *A Month in the Country*, *Die glückliche Hand (The Hand of Fate)*, *A Farewell to Arms*, and *Solid South* for the Theatre Guild in 1930 before Paramount lured him to Southern California, first with a single-film offer to direct *City Streets* (1931) and then with a multiyear contract.[15]

Mamoulian settled in Beverly Hills, his primary residence for the remainder of his life. He quickly sent for his parents (his sister had died of tuberculosis in the mid-1920s), who lived with him until Mamoulian's marriage to Azadia Newman in 1945. During his years at Paramount, there is ample evidence that the studio saw Mamoulian as a prized talent and largely gave him free rein. It is there that he directed some of the most stylistically inventive movies of his career: the gangster film *City Streets*, *Dr. Jekyll and Mr. Hyde* (1931), the Maurice Chevalier–Jeanette MacDonald musical *Love Me Tonight* (1932), and *The Song of Songs* (1933), Marlene Dietrich's first American film made for a director other than Josef von Sternberg. Little is known about the specifics of his contract for *City Streets*, but on his next two films—*Dr. Jekyll and Mr. Hyde* and *Love Me Tonight*—Mamoulian served as his own producer, and by this point, his contract stipulated that he could be supervised by no one but the studio head.[16]

Given this enviable arrangement, it may seem surprising Mamoulian left Paramount after *The Song of Songs*, but Mamoulian's biographer Mark Spergel speculates that it was Mamoulian's old friend Walter Wanger who helped lure him to MGM to direct Greta Garbo in *Queen Christina*.[17] It also bears mentioning that *The Song of Songs* had largely been forced upon Mamoulian by Paramount, which may have further prompted Mamoulian to become a freelancer. Whatever the reasons, for the remainder of the 1930s Mamoulian worked under a series of one-off contracts that still seem to have given him substantial control. Mamoulian joined *Queen Christina* when it was already in development, but he helped shape the screenplay and was apparently able to argue successfully with MGM head Louis B. Mayer against the happy ending that Mayer wanted.[18] Mamoulian then directed *We Live Again*—an adaptation of the Leo Tolstoy novel *Resurrection* (1899)—for independent producer Samuel Goldwyn in 1934. Little is known about the precise arrangement between Mamoulian and Goldwyn on this film, but the screenplay had been developed before Mamoulian's arrival. Mamoulian then stepped in as director for the RKO-released *Becky Sharp* (1935) when its initial director, Lowell Sherman, died unexpectedly. Spergel points out that *Becky Sharp* producer Kenneth Macgowan had worked with Mamoulian on the stage play *These Modern Women*, one possible reason why Mamoulian was selected.[19] Though Mamoulian was an emergency replacement, his clout was such that he was allowed scrap the existing footage and rethink the color design.

After traveling back to New York City to direct George and Ira Gershwin's musical *Porgy and Bess* (1935)—which was based on the Mamoulian-directed *Porgy*—Mamoulian returned to Los Angeles and directed three more films in the 1930s: a bizarre musical comedy titled *The Gay Desperado* for producers Mary Pickford and Lasky (now an independent producer) in 1936, the Paramount musical *High, Wide and Handsome* for producer Arthur Hornblow in 1937, and the drama *Golden Boy* under Columbia head Harry Cohn in 1939. *The Gay Desperado* was fully controlled by Mamoulian, who was permitted to dictate everything from screenplay to final editing. The contract situation for *High, Wide and Handsome* is less clear. As chapter 4 discusses, Mamoulian arrived after the screenplay was written, but at the very least, he commanded an extraordinarily high salary for his work.[20] Little is also known about his contract for *Golden Boy*, but archival evidence demonstrates that Mamoulian personally shaped the film from the screenplay onward. During these years, Mamoulian was also a founding member of the Screen Directors Guild, which was formed in 1936 and was eventually renamed the Directors Guild of America.

At the end of 1939, Mamoulian began working for Twentieth Century-Fox, first on a single-film contract (which yielded *The Mark of Zorro* [1940]) and then under a two-film contract (*Blood and Sand* [1941] and *Rings on Her Fingers* [1942]).[21] *The Mark of Zorro* and *Blood and Sand* were vehicles for top box-office star Tyrone Power, while *Rings on Her Fingers* was a screwball comedy. Twentieth Century-Fox production head Darryl Zanuck, archival evidence reveals, played a greater role in the creative process than Mamoulian was accustomed to. Zanuck appreciated Mamoulian's artistic aspirations, but Zanuck's pragmatism and attention to detail could frustrate Mamoulian. Still, in spite of some major ups and downs, the duo appears to have generally gotten along fairly well during the production of these films. For *The Mark of Zorro*, Zanuck and Mamoulian collaborated on screenplay revisions, and the commercial appeal of the finished film led Zanuck to offer Mamoulian the two-film contract. *Blood and Sand* was controlled almost exclusively by Mamoulian, leaving Zanuck somewhat leery of Mamoulian after it failed at the box office. Zanuck became further frustrated when Mamoulian subsequently rejected numerous films that Zanuck felt would be good fits for the second movie in his contract.[22] Time stretched on, and Mamoulian eventually took a leave of absence and left for the desert, apparently due partly to an unspecified illness.[23] Perhaps because his leave was unpaid, Mamoulian eventually agreed to direct *Rings on Her Fingers*, but he viewed it as merely a routine assignment, and it remained his least favorite film.

Following *Rings on Her Fingers*, Mamoulian saw his film and stage career move in opposite directions. With several planned film projects failing to reach fruition, Mamoulian returned to New York City and directed the original stage production of *Oklahoma!* in 1943, a hit of unprecedented proportions and one of the most influential stage productions in American theater history. Then, he returned to Hollywood, only to be fired by Zanuck as director of *Laura* (1944) and replaced by Otto Preminger. The firing occurred because Zanuck, upon viewing the early rushes, felt that Mamoulian lacked the correct feel for the material. He objected in particular to the way that Dana Andrews, under Mamoulian's guidance, was portraying Detective MacPherson. Zanuck, in his own words, sought a "hard boiled cynical copper" character in MacPherson that would dramatically contrast with Laura's "sophisticated Park Avenue" crowd, whereas the rushes showed MacPherson as a "rather clean cut" "agreeable schoolboy." Increasingly believing that Mamoulian did not grasp this essential dynamic between MacPherson and Laura, Zanuck removed Mamoulian from what would ultimately become one of the most admired films of the 1940s.[24]

Likely due to the reputation of *Oklahoma!*, Mamoulian directed almost entirely musicals for the remainder of his career. First, he returned to New York City, where he directed the stage musicals *Sadie Thompson* (1944), *Carousel* (1945), and *St. Louis Woman* (1946). Also in 1946, Mamoulian directed the film musical *Summer Holiday* (released two years later in 1948) for producer Arthur Freed at MGM. Mamoulian had essentially complete creative control over this expensive film, yet it failed badly with critics and the public. This, coming on the heels of *Laura*, badly damaged his reputation, and Mamoulian increasingly became known as both costly and headstrong. With his star having fallen in Hollywood, Mamoulian directed three more stage productions in New York

City—*Leaf and Bough* (1949), *Lost in the Stars*, and *Arms and the Girl* (1950)—but he was gaining a reputation for being difficult on the stage as well.

After *Arms and the Girl*, the only production that Mamoulian directed to completion for the remainder of his life was the Freed-unit film musical *Silk Stockings* in 1957. Prior to that movie, Mamoulian was notably *not* chosen to direct the film adaptations of *Oklahoma!* (Fred Zinnemann, 1955) and *Carousel* (Henry King, 1956). Though the reasons are not entirely clear, it seems most likely that the industry saw Mamoulian as too big a risk, instead favoring Zinnemann (hot off of *High Noon* [1952] and *From Here to Eternity* [1953]) and King (who could boast a decades-long track record of successfully directing prestige films).[25] Freed still admired Mamoulian's artistry, however, and once he was able to branch fully into independent production, he hired Mamoulian to direct *Silk Stockings*. Though Mamoulian had limited creative power on that film (see chapter 4), it was a critical and commercial success.

At first, it seemed that *Silk Stockings* had revived Mamoulian's career. However, Mamoulian was then unable to complete two high-profile Hollywood productions, and these aborted efforts nailed home the fact that Mamoulian lacked the power and esteem he had earlier enjoyed. Goldwyn, who had worked with Mamoulian back in 1934 on *We Live Again*, hired Mamoulian to direct the movie adaptation of *Porgy and Bess*. Mamoulian was not his first choice, however, and he remained uneasy about handing the reins to a director with an uneven history who still sought creative control. *Porgy and Bess* was a passion project for the nearly eighty-year-old producer, and he had a vested interest in seeing it done his way. After eight months of preparation on Mamoulian's part, the *Porgy and Bess* set burned down in the early morning before the first scheduled day of shooting, likely by an arsonist who was politically opposed to the film. The subsequent delay caused Goldwyn to rethink his options, and he fired Mamoulian before shooting began (with Preminger again replacing Mamoulian, to Mamoulian's humiliation). A lengthy and acrimonious legal battle over screen credit ensued, but outside of the casting, the finished film appears not to bear Mamoulian's direct imprint.[26]

Seeking to rebound, Mamoulian signed once again with producer Wanger to direct *Cleopatra* (1963), which would prove to be one of the most troubled productions of the entire century. Mamoulian quickly found himself enmeshed in a project of unprecedented scope where key decisions were made by producers who did not always bother to notify him. Substantial and costly pre-production work was done before a viable screenplay had been written, and the script seemed to only deteriorate in subsequent versions. Mamoulian spent months scouting locations in Italy, only to learn on a trip to England that the producers had changed their minds about the location and had been building sets in London. Shooting was delayed because key leading roles had yet to be cast, was stalled further by bad weather, and then stopped entirely due to Elizabeth Taylor's illness. Wanger accepted Mamoulian's resignation in January 1961, and private correspondences indicate that Mamoulian was genuinely relieved to be rid of this troubled production.[27] Lucid well into his eighties, Mamoulian spent the remainder of his life traveling, giving interviews, and championing his artistic ideas until his death at the age of ninety in 1987.

From this thumbnail history, several patterns emerge regarding Mamoulian's relationships with co-workers that serve as key background for the chapters that follow. First, because Mamoulian bounced so frequently between studios and production companies, he never completed more than a handful of films with the same technicians or craft workers. At Paramount in the early 1930s, three films contained writing by Samuel Hoffenstein and set designs by Hans Dreier (*Dr. Jekyll and Mr. Hyde*, *Love Me Tonight*, *The Song of Songs*), while the latter two featured Victor Milner as cinematographer. Dreier would return for *High, Wide and Handsome*, while Hoffenstein would later write *Laura*. *The Mark of Zorro* and *Blood and Sand* contained much of the same crew (as well as cast). Bess Meredyth did a rewrite of *Queen Christina* and later co-adapted *The Mark of Zorro*. Alfred Newman provided music for *The Gay Desperado* as well as two of the Fox films. Leo Birinski co-wrote *The Song of Songs* and later wrote *The Gay Desperado*. Garrett Fort adapted *Applause* for the screen and co-adapted *The Mark of Zorro*. These recurrences are notable, but their quantity is nowhere near those of many other premier studio-era directors. It thus seems unlikely that the recurring ideas and techniques covered throughout this book were heavily influenced by individual collaborators. Mamoulian's concerns, the nature of his screenplay annotations, and the resulting techniques in his films remained extremely consistent even amid his near-constant shifts in studio and personnel. I will, in the chapters that follow, note instances where authorship questions or complications arise, but on the whole, there are good reasons to believe that Mamoulian was heavily responsible for the ideas and experiments examined in this book.

The importance of producers and studio heads, however, was probably more substantial. Though Mamoulian seldom acknowledged it, his ability to innovate was likely tied closely to *whom* he was working for. Mamoulian moved briskly between producers as well as craft workers, but there *were* several recurring supervisors, and they tended to be people who admired experimentation and were pre-inclined to grant directors autonomy. Wanger, Lasky, and Freed all worked with Mamoulian multiple times (Lasky, in fact, also attempted to convince Warner Bros. to let Mamoulian direct his production of the Gershwin biopic *Rhapsody in Blue*[28]), and all were known for this tendency. Conversely, when Mamoulian encountered supervisors who chafed at his efforts to seize control or disliked it when he pontificated about film artistry, the relationship could be more fraught (Mayer on *Queen Christina*) or end badly for Mamoulian (Goldwyn on *Porgy and Bess*). Landing somewhere between these poles was Zanuck, who was willing to grant Mamoulian leeway if he thought the result would enhance box-office returns. In interviews, Mamoulian enjoyed narrating tales in which his brilliant ideas always won over the skeptics, but his biography suggests that he actively sought out—and flourished under—supervisors who were *already* inclined to step back and cede control.

If certain production circumstances enabled Mamoulian to innovate, so too did prior box-office success. Mamoulian's most stylistically daring films are arguably *Applause, Dr. Jekyll and Mr. Hyde, Love Me Tonight, Blood and Sand,* and *Summer Holiday,* and each was made in the immediate wake of a substantial stage or screen hit. *Porgy* caused Mamoulian to be tapped for *Applause, City Streets* (Mamoulian's first commercially successful film) led to producer status on *Dr. Jekyll and Mr. Hyde* and *Love Me Tonight, The Mark of Zorro* enabled Mamoulian to enjoy considerable freedom on *Blood and Sand,* and the musical *Summer Holiday* was shot shortly after stage hits *Oklahoma!* and *Carousel.* On the flip side, Mamoulian's box-office failures remind us that being an experimenter was a risky endeavor, and his résumé gaps after certain films—*Applause* and especially *Summer Holiday*—show what could happen when innovations failed to click with audiences.

Those creative ideas, and their manifestation in his films, are the subject of this book. To grasp the nature of Mamoulian's contributions, we must turn first to Mamoulian's broad theories of artistry and their application to the medium of cinema.

1
Mamoulian, Art, and Cinema

Art is not a mirror of life[1]

I'm a great believer in theory.[2]

—Rouben Mamoulian

In an industry where top-tier talents like John Ford, Frank Capra, and Alfred Hitchcock took some time to reach what many consider to be their most mature and celebrated period of filmmaking, Mamoulian is notable among studio-era Hollywood directors for "finding" his style and offering it nearly full blown upon his first feature-film outing. With the exception of Orson Welles, it would be difficult to name another studio-era director who burst so strikingly onto the film scene with an approach that seemed to redefine stylistic expectations. Certainly, temperament helped—Mamoulian was ambitious, confident, and eager to follow his artistic instincts. Mamoulian was also fortunate to begin his career at Paramount, a studio known for giving its directors more autonomy than the norm, at the precise moment when the arrival of sound film threw the parameters and definition of cinema into question. But equally important, Mamoulian was able to announce himself as a filmmaker with such daring and assurance in *Applause* (1929) because he had spent the previous half-dozen years thinking deeply about art and how it should be used.

In this chapter, I examine Mamoulian's theory of film as an art form and how this mindset translated into a series of recurring stylistic devices in his movies. Though scholars and critics writing about Mamoulian's films often move quickly into a discussion of his innovations, doing so can obfuscate a full understanding of *why* Mamoulian was intent upon playing a defining role in sound cinema techniques, and *how* his theory of art helped him became such a pivotal player in 1920s, 1930s, and 1940s cinema. The chapter begins by outlining Mamoulian's theory of art in general and film in particular. I then turn to an examination of three techniques—shadow play, forced framings, and elaborate scene transitions—that recur across his work and reflect in various ways the broader theories of film and artistry that he embraced. By tracing Mamoulian's theory of film and its practical applications, we can begin to understand how a young, inexperienced Armenian immigrant became a key figure in the formation of sound cinema aesthetics.

Mamoulian on Art and Film

In addition to being a renowned director of theater and film, Mamoulian was an unabashed intellectual. In a studio system where even top-shelf directors like Howard Hawks or Otto Preminger generally avoided any tinge of intellectualism when publicly discussing filmmaking, Mamoulian embraced theory as an instrumental part of his creative process, even suggesting that a solid grounding in theory was necessary for the successful creation of a work of art.[3] From his early years in the theater through the remainder of his life, Mamoulian presented copious ideas in articles, speeches, and interviews about art, theater, film, and how a creative artist should use certain tools to achieve specific effects. Indeed, had he not enjoyed a successful directorial career, Mamoulian might have made a good living as a journalist or critic. The essays he wrote were published in the most important professional magazines of the day, including *Variety* and *American Cinematographer*, and many were reprinted numerous times. His recollection of the differing performance styles of Sarah Bernhardt and Eleonora Duse remains a definitive account of these two stage icons.[4]

Sifting through Mamoulian's statements on film, however, presents a challenge because it requires being on guard against the distortions and even falsehoods that crop up in his writing. As he aged, Mamoulian became increasingly obsessed with his image as an innovator, and this led him to exaggerate the novelty of some of his techniques.[5] Moreover, as Spergel has pointed out, Mamoulian was fond of telling formulaic behind-the-scenes stories in which he would advance a daring idea that was met by skepticism by those in power—such as George Eastman, Eugene O'Neill, Greta Garbo, or the entire studio brass and technicians at Paramount—only to win them over by showing them the result of his outstanding idea.[6] Mamoulian's determination to narrate so many of his experiences through the repetitive lens of a genius whose brilliance dazzled the critics led him to periodically fudge facts, and his stories sometimes take on the sheen of a performance rather than a historical account. If one is willing to sift through these nervous tics, however, what remains is a thoughtful and extensive array of ideas about the nature of art and how an artist should use his or her tools. Though one could argue that these theories are also unreliable "performances" aimed at creating a particular self-image, the consistency of his ideas across seven decades—combined with their clear application in his film and theater work—suggests a largely earnest account of art and its potential.

Mamoulian's earliest efforts at theorization were directed not at cinema, but at his first creative endeavor: the theater. Theater had been an interest of Mamoulian's since his childhood. As discussed in the Introduction, his mother performed in a theater group in his hometown of Tiflis, and Mamoulian had studied briefly at the Moscow Art Theatre (MAT) in the 1910s and tried his hand at theater directing as a young man in London in the early 1920s.[7] It was not until Mamoulian was hired by George Eastman to direct live opera performances for the Rochester American Opera Company in Rochester, New York, in 1923, however, that a paper record emerges of Mamoulian's intellectualism toward art.

Unfortunately, the influences behind Mamoulian's early theories of art remain unclear. As mentioned in the Introduction, Mamoulian was loath to admit an intellectual debt, and because he rarely discussed his years in Russia, it is difficult to pin down the precise nature of Mamoulian's exposure to Russian theater, which surely occurred during a formative period in his life. Mamoulian did acknowledge, in interviews, that he studied briefly with Yevgeny Vakhtangov at the MAT in the mid-1910s.[8] This presumably means that Mamoulian studied at the First Studio within the MAT, since Vakhtangov worked there at the time. Mamoulian apparently met Konstantin Stanislavski, but there is no evidence that he ever studied with him.[9] Still, Stanislavski had created the First Studio in 1912, and he was a towering figure in Russian theater, thus making him another potential influence.

According to Mamoulian, the MAT was important primarily for pushing him toward a creative approach that he later broke away from completely. Vakhtangov and others, by Mamoulian's account, were, in the mid-1910s, heavily under the sway of Stanislavski's conceptions of naturalism, so when Mamoulian was eventually tasked with directing his first play—*The Beating on the Door* (1922)—he used the naturalist approach he had been taught. Believing that naturalism made the play fall flat, Mamoulian claimed that he then developed an opposing theory of stylization over the next several years that drove the rest of his work.[10]

Though Mamoulian's claim is likely true in part, his time in Moscow probably affected his later theories more than he ever admitted. Joseph Horowitz raises the possibility that Mamoulian's later devotion to stylization—along with his interests in integrated musical theater, a meticulous attention to detail, and a devotion to rhythm—stemmed from his encounters with Vakhtangov, including the latter's concept of "fantastic realism."[11] This is plausible, though there is also evidence to suggest that Vakhtangov—as Mamoulian would assert when the topic was raised in interviews—was still under the sway of naturalism in the mid-1910s.[12] Given Stanislavski's pervasive influence at the time, it may, in fact, be Stanislavski who was the more dominant force on Mamoulian's thinking. Unlike Mamoulian, Stanislavski is commonly associated with realism, but like Mamoulian, he was an extensive pre-planner who thought musically about his productions. Stanislavski originally intended to be an opera singer, and he never lost sight of this musical orientation. From his landmark 1898 direction of Anton Chekhov's *The Seagull* (1898) onward, Stanislavski thought about the "score" for his plays in the same way he thought about music, which included the breaking down of his scripts into rhythmic beats. Moreover, Stanislavski could be quite versatile. In 1905, he started the Studio Theatre on Povarskaya Street with Vsevolod Meyerhold to experiment with music and symbolism, a form that—like Mamoulian's work—favored stylization over realism.[13] Horowitz has also pointed out that Stanislavski's MAT troupe apparently once stayed at Mamoulian's home when he was a boy, an experience that Mamoulian said "was subconsciously ingrained in me."[14] In short, though Mamoulian always portrayed himself as someone who simply broke free of his earlier training, many of his theories outlined in these chapters—stylization, rhythmic integration, narrative-number integration—likely had some grounding in the Stanislavski-influenced period of Russian theater in which he studied.

Whatever the influences, shortly after he arrived in Rochester in 1923, Mamoulian began delivering lectures on theater that were aimed at determining theater's essential qualities. In these lectures, Mamoulian argued that the key to understanding any art form was to identify the elements that needed to be present in order for the art form to be recognizable. In theater, Mamoulian argued, at various times certain elements had been successfully eliminated, including music, scenery (in Shakespeare's time), playwriting (in improvisational theater), dialogue (in pantomime theater), or acting (in puppet theater). What could *not* be eliminated, Mamoulian concluded during his Rochester years, was action and movement. If these elements were removed, one would merely have a reading of a play rather than something recognizable as a theater production. Thus, Mamoulian concluded, to capture the essence of theater, a director should focus on movement above all else.[15]

This overarching theory bears similarities to what has been—in more recent years—called "medium specificity." Like other medium-specific art theorists, Mamoulian sought to identify a medium's basic attributes and explore its potentials in those areas. Yet Mamoulian never argued—as other medium-specificity theorists sometimes did—that a medium's essential elements were automatically unique to that art form. Rather, Mamoulian sought to locate and explore the elements that enabled an art form to be called by its name. The notion of medium specificity has become contentious in more recent decades, both for its validity as a concept and for the notion that an art form's essential elements should necessarily be the most impactful.[16] What matters here is not whether Mamoulian was "correct" to take this approach, but rather the fact that even before he visited his first film studio, Mamoulian's philosophy toward any art form *necessitated* an interrogation of its definition.

After several years in Rochester, Mamoulian was hired by the New York City–based Theatre Guild, a group dedicated to producing innovative plays. Thanks to this position, Mamoulian could put his artistic ideas into practice in a far more prominent and prestigious venue. On the strength of the plays he directed for the Theatre Guild—particularly *Porgy* (1927)—Mamoulian caught Paramount's eye, and he directed his first film for Paramount in 1929. Thus, when Mamoulian began making films, he had not only already developed a medium-specific theory of art, but he had also seen his theory repeatedly validated in the theater capital of the United States. It is thus not surprising that when Mamoulian began discussing and publishing theories of film in the early 1930s, his focus was on film's essential qualities.

As with his prior writings on theater, the question of what influenced Mamoulian's film theories looms over his work, and once again, the answer is difficult to determine. Mamoulian does not appear to have been particularly interested in film prior to his arrival in the United States in the mid-1920s.[17] Mamoulian could read Russian, French, and German, and thus he might—in the late 1920s or early 1930s—have read a range of film theorists who wrote in those languages and stressed aspects of medium specificity and stylization, such as Rudolph Arnheim, Béla Balázs, many of the French Impressionists, writers for *Close Up*, and the Russian montage theorists.[18] I am unaware of any conclusive evidence, however, and Mamoulian's philosophies of film are so similar to his prior ideas about theater that it may have been primarily his own established methodology that drove him to define cinema in the ways he did.

In one of his first publicly articulated theories of film—a lecture given to the American Society of Cinematographers in 1932—Mamoulian immediately focused on the medium-specificity issue, stating, "each and every art has its own vital element which distinguishes it from all other arts," before proceeding to argue, "in the art of motion pictures, that vital element is obviously the camera."[19] One might critique the "obviousness" of such a claim (editing, for instance, seems conspicuously absent, though as discussed later, Mamoulian's subsequent writing would embrace it). But his claim remains important because it affirms not only that Mamoulian transferred his essence-based approach to cinema, but that he conceptualized cinema as a *visual* art form. Mamoulian's prioritization of the image in many of his writings may come as a surprise to people aware of his sophisticated use of film sound, and I will suggest in chapters 2, 3, and 4 that in certain ways, Mamoulian actually undervalued his contributions in this area. Yet Mamoulian's belief that visuals were central to cinema remained clear and resolute across his writings. Mamoulian even went so far as to repeatedly say that the mark of a good film was that it could be understood by a deaf person.[20]

If the camera constituted the essence of cinema, how should it be used? For Mamoulian, no matter the medium, an aesthetic of *stylization* represented the greatest potential for art. Mamoulian saw any effort to record life simply as it existed to be a creative dead end, since it necessitated that a filmmaker move inexorably toward a single point: the reproduction of reality. Mamoulian felt that doing so closed off artistic avenues and, if true realism was somehow reached, closed off creativity entirely.[21] Instead, Mamoulian drew upon his extensive knowledge of art forms across history—including sculpture, painting, and music—to argue that the best artistic works in history endured because they successfully and meaningfully *transformed* real life into art. The camera, for Mamoulian, should try to achieve the same ends. And the goal, for Mamoulian, was to use the camera in ways that expressed a particular viewpoint. As Mamoulian wrote in *The American Cinematographer*, "It is not only the action that is important, but the way in which the camera sees that action."[22] For Mamoulian, stylization offered limitless possibilities because the human imagination itself was limitless.[23]

Whose viewpoint should the camera reflect? Though Mamoulian seldom put it bluntly, his writings repeatedly demonstrate his belief that the camera should express the point of view of the filmmaker. In an unpublished 1938 essay, for instance, Mamoulian contrasted the role of the scientist, who objectively presents facts, with an artist, who transforms those facts by creating new values out of them. This necessarily meant that artistry was highly personal, and that the new values the artist achieves would be colored by the artist's subjective perspective.[24] The artist's goal, then, was to seek a *personal* truth, and a truth that—in words Mamoulian used in a lecture around the same time—articulates "imaginative reality or the imaginative truth of things."[25] The camera would thus become, for Mamoulian, the eye, interpreter, and guide for the audience.

At first blush, such a theory might seem to favor self-indulgent films that prioritize personal style and expression at the expense of story. Mamoulian, however, did not advocate this philosophy. For Mamoulian, every device should have a specific story function, and its purpose should be to express what the artist saw as the inner truth of some aspect of that story rather than merely show off the capabilities of the cinema or highlight the inner life of the director. In Mamoulian's view, a flashy device that distracted from story or character was a failed device.[26] Proper experimentation, for Mamoulian, occurred only when the artist said, "The conventional way isn't strong enough, isn't eloquent enough."[27] Mamoulian's cinematic theories are classical at heart—favoring values like order, purpose, clarity, and beauty—and his professed belief that style should serve the story resonated with a film industry that, by the late silent era, prioritized what David Bordwell has called a relatively low level of "self-conscious" narration.[28] Mamoulian's preference for classical-style filmmaking is especially clear in interviews Mamoulian gave after the French New Wave began in the late 1950s. Mamoulian admired the New Wave's sense of rebellion and experimentation, but he decried it for, in his view, destroying existing forms of film art without adding any substantial new values. For Mamoulian, "chaos, obscurity, and disorder" were the "antithesis of any art."[29]

Taken together, Mamoulian's writings, speeches, and interviews on film constituted a series of ideas about art that were remarkable for their thoughtfulness, coherence, and consistency. Still, we should note at this point two general contradictions that would emerge when Mamoulian translated his theories into practice. First, while many of Mamoulian's theorizations were aimed at defining cinema in opposition to the theater, his love of theater and his fame on Broadway encouraged him to transfer some of his theatrical aims—including a rhythmic approach to drama and the close integration of music and narrative—to cinema. Such transfers from theater to film fit his view that art should be stylized, but they did not always mesh with his belief that the artist should focus on the essential qualities of each medium. Second, Mamoulian's status as an upstart innovator—solidified nationally with his sensational production of *Porgy*—encouraged him to periodically engage in directorial flashiness that stood in tension with his professed belief that techniques should unobtrusively convey story ideas. Such stylistic saliency helped mark him as a notable innovator, but it sometimes placed him on the outskirts of a Hollywood style that more commonly hid its construction. Mamoulian's films thus do not adhere to every aspect of his theories at all times. However, as I show in the upcoming chapters, Mamoulian's embrace of a range of values—stylization, classicism, medium specificity, theatrical influences, innovation—helped place him on the cutting edge of sound-cinema aesthetics in the late 1920s through the 1940s.

Elucidating Mamoulian's theories of art and film is useful in the abstract, but to fully grasp how Mamoulian's artistic principles translated into practical filmmaking decisions, we must turn to some of his recurring techniques. The three techniques I discuss below epitomize various aspects of the kind of film artistry his theories espoused. It is not my intention to argue that these techniques were original to Mamoulian, or that they are the *only* recurring techniques one could select. Rather, my aim is to pin down in concrete terms a cinematic sensibility and attitude that would put Mamoulian in a strong position to make substantial contributions to a Hollywood film industry wrestling with sound, rhythm, the musical, genre, censorship, and color filmmaking.

Shadow Play

Despite his avowed commitment to exploring the essence of cinema, one of the most salient visual techniques across Mamoulian's oeuvre was not especially cinematic in conception or impact. In nearly every Mamoulian film, one finds at least one pronounced instance of human figures abstracted into silhouettes. Borrowing from Stephen Prince, I call this silhouette technique "shadow play."[30]

Though Mamoulian's use of shadow play was likely influenced by such German Expressionist films as *The Last Laugh* (1924)—which Mamoulian frequently cited as a favorite—there was a more proximate influence: his own stage work. Prior to *Applause*, Mamoulian had incorporated cast shadows into numerous theatrical productions. An example of shadow play can be found as far back as Mamoulian's Rochester production of *Faust* (1923), where Mamoulian threw a gigantic shadow of Mephistopheles against the back wall of the stage to make him appear more imposing.[31] It was Mamoulian's production of *Porgy* in New York City, however, that brought him widespread acclaim for this device.

As subsequent chapters will explore, critics were blown away by numerous aspects of *Porgy*—including its use of rhythm, music, and choreography—and Mamoulian would prize these values in his film work. What demands attention here, however, is Mamoulian's decision to use cast shadows during a wake for a murdered man name Robbins in which the African American mourners try to raise enough money to give him a proper burial. In reviews of *Porgy*, the shadow play in this scene was almost universally recognized and praised. Nearly every reviewer—even those skeptical of the value of the overall play—singled out the wake as a highlight (if not *the* highlight) of the production. And while not every reviewer mentioned the shadows specifically, many did. One reviewer praised the "weird and extravagantly proportioned shadows on the dingy walls" and called the scene a "thrilling moment."[32] Another described the "myriad of dancing, swirling, leaping shadows" as the best part of the play.[33] Yet another described the scene as reaching "one of the most exciting climaxes I have ever seen in the theatre."[34] One particularly ebullient reviewer marveled at the scene's craftsmanship and response elicited from the audience before writing, "certainly a more unusual and characteristic scene has rarely been staged. It was something new to most of us—may I say, to all of us."[35]

Because of this level of attention—and the frequency with which he would reuse shadow play in his films—it is worth closely examining what it looked like in *Porgy*. One of the more detailed accounts comes from Mamoulian himself in a later interview:

> Spiritual singing at a wake—a group of blacks and a coffin—this spiritual builds and builds. I have them sitting down. A man comes in with a lantern and puts it in the center of the forestage. At the same time, I have three baby spots come up in front. I had the set about twice as high as you would ordinarily have on the stage. I had the mourners moving toward the footlights as they sang, so their shadows grew on the tree walls until it became gigantic.[36]

Mamoulian's playscript collection at the Library of Congress leaves little doubt that this was his personal contribution. Dorothy and DuBose Heyward's typed playscript makes no reference to shadows; the only references are extensive penciled-in marginal notes in Mamoulian's handwriting. Mamoulian's annotations also elaborate on the extent to which he sought a realistic justification for the "building" of expressive shadows in the scene. After the undertaker agrees to bury Robbins for the small amount of money the mourners are able to raise, for instance, the spiritual singing builds and a handwritten Mamoulian note reads, "Lamp on mantel flickers and goes out as spot in foots comes up."[37] Thus, not only do the shadows get bigger as the scene progresses, but the extinguishing of the lamp—presumably more poignant for the audience because it is tied to the extinguishing of a life—motivates the more prominent casting of shadows on the back wall, thus creating a further sense of "building" up to the point when the curtain falls.

Shadow play was so meaningful to Mamoulian that he would quickly return to it again on the stage. The *New York Times* review of his play *Marco Millions* (1928) makes reference to "dark, brooding silhouettes against the sky."[38] For his Vietnam-set production of *Congai* (1928), Mamoulian simulated the presence of hundreds of soldiers by having several performers march in circles backstage next to a spotlight that threw their shadows against the rear of the set, a technique affirmed by the light plot for *Congai*.[39]

On the stage, shadow play would have been appealing because it functioned in similar ways for spectators sitting anywhere in the theater. When used in film, however, the device is not particularly dependent upon a specific camera position, and it thus fails to fully adhere to Mamoulian's belief that a film artist should focus on the properties of the camera. Why, then, was Mamoulian so drawn to the technique in his movies? Though his regular reuse of the device was surely an effort to stamp his personal signature across media,[40] Mamoulian was also eager to reuse shadow play because it fit so strongly with his idea of stylization. In particular, Mamoulian liked the idea that cast shadows could become bigger than the characters themselves, elongating people whom one could not—on a literal level—physically stretch.[41] Doing so, for Mamoulian, intensified the viewer's experience while retaining a connection to human beings and, by extension, to reality itself. Moreover, Mamoulian saw cast shadows as an opportunity to give the space of his images visual depth. Mamoulian was never particularly disposed toward deep-focus cinematography, but his interviews indicate that he liked the idea that cast shadows could imply a sense of space across or—if the shadow source was offscreen—beyond the frame.[42]

Mamoulian's shadow play offers a particularly vivid example of the balancing act Mamoulian struck between theatrical and medium-specific experiments in cinema, and between flashy flourishes and story-based functionality. Mamoulian first used shadow play in *Applause*, a film whose gritty story might not—on the surface—seem inclined toward any sort of stylized treatment. *Applause* opens with an outdoor parade for a burlesque troupe that has arrived in a small town. When we see the actual burlesque performance in the following scene, however, it is presented as a cheap, tawdry, and exploitative affair. During this performance, the star of the show—Kitty Darling (Helen Morgan)—is taken ill and unexpectedly gives birth in her dressing room (the father, we learn, is about to be executed by the state). The film then jumps forward five years. Kitty, who lives in New York City, feels that her five-year-old daughter, April, should no longer be exposed to the burlesque business, and she decides to send April to a convent in Wisconsin.

The film then moves forward eleven years to paint a grim picture of Kitty's life. Where her previous male partner was caring, her new boyfriend—Hitch Nelson (Fuller Mellish Jr.)—abuses the vulnerable Kitty and cheats on her with another burlesque performer. Learning that Kitty has a daughter, Hitch forces Kitty to bring her daughter back to New York City so that she can make some money for the family. April (Joan Peers) returns to New York City knowing virtually nothing about her mother's line of work, and she is devastated by the male catcalls and other inhumane behavior directed at Kitty when she performs. Making matters worse, Hitch tries to groom April for the burlesque business and sexually harasses her in the process. One night, to escape Hitch, April meets a young sailor from Wisconsin named Tony (Henry Wadsworth) on the street. The two fall in love during a first date that lasts from night until morning. April and Kitty's fortunes then diverge sharply: April and Tony plan to be married and live in Wisconsin, while Hitch abandons Kitty, who has been told that she is too old and unattractive to perform. Not wishing to leave her mother, April breaks off the engagement with Tony, who announces he will return to his soon-to-be departing ship. Yet unbeknownst to April, Kitty—feeling useless and not wishing to be a burden—has deliberately overdosed on poison. Believing her mother to be merely drunk, April takes Kitty's place as the lead performer of the burlesque show. As she exits the stage after her first starring performance, she discovers that Tony is waiting in the wings—he has decided to try again for April's hand in marriage. April admits that her concern for her mother drove her to break off their engagement, and Tony tells April that Kitty can simply live with them in Wisconsin. The film ends with the duo happily embracing, unaware that Kitty has now died of her overdose.

Mamoulian's decision to heavily stylize this downbeat story stemmed partly from visits he made to burlesque houses as research for the film. He quickly developed strong opinions about burlesque that he wished to convey via style. "Frankly it made me sick in the stomach, this kind of titillation," Mamoulian would later say about the strip acts that constituted burlesque's entertainment by the late 1920s. "The audiences were ugly. The girls were bored. The whole thing was tawdry, shoddy, unworthy of a human being, woman or man."[43] Mamoulian thus opted to use shadow play—among other devices—to condemn male dominance and the objectification of women.

We see two kinds of human silhouettes in *Applause*. The first type, which matches the kind of shadow play found in *Porgy*, occurs when a light throws a character's shadow against a wall. In *Applause*, this "cast-shadow" technique is almost always tied to Hitch and his identity as a domineering, dangerous presence for Kitty. We first see this technique early in the film when Hitch forces Kitty to write a letter insisting that her daughter, April, leave the convent and come home. Hitch and Kitty walk over to a table against the wall, and the camera tracks with their movement to frame them in a two-shot. Kitty then sits down in a manner that presses her into the right corner of the frame. Hitch steps just out of frame on the left and instructs Kitty as his elongated shadow is thrown against the wall (Figure 1.1). As Hitch makes sharp hand gestures for emphasis, his right hand periodically enters the frame. As with the wake scene in *Porgy*, shadow play provides a heightened sense of presence, but here the emphasis is on the oppressive *power* Hitch enjoys over Kitty. Graphically, Hitch is both a large menacing shadow and a "double" power because his sharpest gestures are seen twice: once with his actual hand and once with his shadow. Movement as well as size thus help visually amplify Hitch's controlling nature and set the stage for his conflict with April.

The second type of shadow play, which I will call "through the screen," is used in *Applause* mainly to represent female burlesque performers. For this

Figure 1.1 Two types of shadow play in *Applause*. Hitch's cast shadow displays his power over Kitty...

technique, a person stands on the other side of a screen and a light on that side casts a shadow against the screen. This technique first appears early in the film when Kitty goes into labor in the burlesque house. In the background of several backstage shots, Mamoulian shows the silhouettes of women behind screens preparing to go onstage. Later, after April arrives in New York City and waits in a dressing room with Hitch while her mother performs, Mamoulian rack focuses away from April and Hitch to a screen in the background behind which we can see only the silhouette of Kitty offering cheap, provocative dancing to the (unseen) customers (Figure 1.2).

Taken together, *Applause*'s two forms of shadow play signal a specific "point of view" on the story that is sharply critical of the burlesque business and its impact on women. For the behind-the-screen female performers, the device abstracts and de-personalizes the female shape in a way that seems to comment on the dehumanizing nature of burlesque. Mamoulian is careful to frame female silhouettes only in the background of his shots, thus making them seem unmenacing and more like mere objects—a reflection of the status of these performers in the burlesque world. Hitch's cast shadow, in contrast, looms large, a stylized reminder of male power and female vulnerability in this environment.

Figure 1.2 ... while a more objectifying through-the-screen shadow depicts Kitty's onstage burlesque performance.

With the exception of a through-the-screen silhouette of Amelia (Frances Dee) in *Becky Sharp* (1935), Mamoulian would use only cast shadows for the remainder of his film career, and he would often tie them to moments involving power. In his follow-up film *City Streets* (1931), for instance, Mamoulian casts the shadows of gangster Blackie (Stanley Fields) and his bodyguard Pop Cooley (Guy Kibbee)—who plans to kill Blackie—against the back wall as the two men walk down the hallway. By angling the characters' mostly lateral walk imperceptibly away from the camera, Mamoulian—who noted this shadow-play plan in the margins of his screenplay[44]—allows Cooley's shadow to grow in size as Blackie's becomes smaller. Shadow play thus comments on both the danger Cooley poses and Blackie's own state of unease, since Blackie then whirls around and asks for Cooley's gun. In *Love Me Tonight* (1932), Mamoulian shunts three spinster aunts who cast a spell (Macbeth style) and "summon" Maurice (Maurice Chevalier) to the castle into the bottom half of the screen, thereby allowing the shadows they cast on the back wall to become larger than the characters themselves. Here, shadow play suggests the authorial power of the aunts, whose spell seems to set the rest of the plot into motion. And in *Becky Sharp*, Mamoulian changed the script he was given by adding cast-shadow shots of Napoleon, whose escape from Elba breaks up the ritzy Richmond Ball that serves as the film's centerpiece.[45] Here, shadow play also solved a plot problem for Mamoulian, who feared that any flesh-and-blood representation of Napoleon might inadvertently render a man of Napoleon's historical stature comedic.[46]

Though less common, shadow play in Mamoulian's hands could be reworked as comedy if the material called for it. In the farcical *The Gay Desperado* (1936), opera singer Chivo (Nino Martini) is supposed to be executed by a bandito firing squad. Chivo changes everyone's mind by singing, and Mamoulian takes advantage of the fact that firing squad executions commonly occur against a wall by providing the cast shadows of the executioners. Yet rather than use shadow play to express menace or danger, Mamoulian uses a comedic composition by having each executioner's shadow be bigger than the previous one (Figure 1.3). Consequently, the image looks silly: the executioners' shadows create a perfect diagonal-line composition, while Chivo's shadow looks absurdly diminutive.

Whether on stage or in film, Mamoulian found in shadow play a key device for expressive stylization. Grounded in both the imagination of the director and the real-world figures whose presence motivated the shadows, shadow play to Mamoulian was an ideal way to stylize the image in accordance with story and theme. As subsequent chapters will demonstrate, Mamoulian would also use the device to address problems relating to early sound film rhythm and the stylization of musical numbers. Yet regardless of purpose, the device was foundational to Mamoulian's filmic approach because it fused his theatrical interests with the opportunity to exercise graphic control of the cinematic image.

Figure 1.3 Comedic shadow play in *The Gay Desperado*.

Forced Framings

If shadow play epitomizes the stylization that Mamoulian admired and sought, many of his other recurring "stylized" visual devices are closer to Mamoulian's interest in what he saw as film's essential, camera-driven, non-theatrical qualities. Among the more frequent camera-based devices Mamoulian favored was what I will call "forced framings." As a stage director, Mamoulian had been tasked with presenting entertainment that would appeal to spectators in any seat in the theater. When Mamoulian entered film, he immediately embraced the fact that the movie camera presented images from a singular optical viewpoint. In an article comparing the stylistic potentials of stage and screen, Mamoulian practically bubbled about this potential:

> The spectator has at his disposal a magic flying carpet, as comfortable as a loge seat. On this he flies up and down, from one side to another, through a rich selection of the most advantageous points of view and angles pre-arranged by the camera.[47]

Of course, any camera position necessarily involves a singular ocular viewpoint on the action. By "forced framings," I refer to moments when the camera, through its positioning, *overtly* structures the spectator's perception of the space. Forced framings were hardly unique to Mamoulian—Soviet montage filmmakers, for instance, often used striking and carefully composed extreme angles. Yet because forced framings were so vital to Mamoulian's conception of cinema, a brief look at his favored methods can help us grasp the ways in which Mamoulian conceptualized himself as a stylist whose techniques denoted attitudes toward narrative, character, or theme.

Early in Mamoulian's career, the most salient forced framings involved extreme camera angles and obtrusively restricted views. Both types appear in Mamoulian's first film. *Applause* features an astonishing number of high angle shots for the period, including a "top shot" of a burlesque performance that resembles (and precedes) the Busby Berkeley–choreographed *Whoopee!* in 1930 and his better-known 1933 musical numbers for Warner Bros. (Figure 1.4). Yet as a story-oriented classicist, Mamoulian took pains to *pattern* such forced framings to ensure that they would reflect particular ideas about the story. For instance, Mamoulian reserves many of his high-angle shots in

Figure 1.4 In isolation, the "top shot" from *Applause* might seem to show off the performance. However, . . .

Applause for moments when Hitch takes advantage of the control he enjoys over Kitty and images of onstage burlesque performers. These moments, combined with crucial dressing-room high-angle shots of Kitty at the beginning and end of the film, allow Mamoulian to equate the burlesque world with death. During the first burlesque performance, as Kitty lies backstage in labor with her daughter, Mamoulian uses high-angle shots to depict backstage performers rushing onstage, performing a disheveled chorus-line number, and later filing backstage to see Kitty and meet the new baby. The latter is especially striking, with Mamoulian providing a bird's-eye view of Kitty and her baby lying side by side in a bed and basket, respectively, with a clown and a line of chorus girls slowly filing past (Figure 1.5). The shot is reminiscent of a funeral service, with Kitty and her baby lying in their "caskets." This high-angle reference to death becomes even more pronounced at the conclusion of the film, when another high-angle dressing-room shot shows Kitty slowly dying from an overdose. Yet by tying other high-angle shots to burlesque performers and the immoral Hitch's interactions with Kitty, Mamoulian equates high angles not only with death, but with the sense that Kitty has been "killed" specifically by burlesque and male exploitation. Thus, while the top shot in *Applause* may

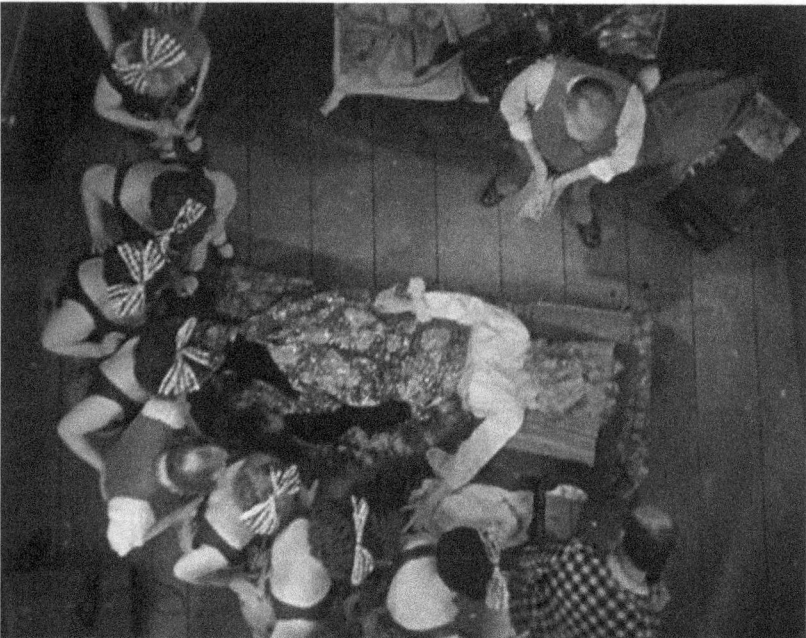

Figure 1.5 . . . *Applause* consistently associates high-angle shots with female exploitation and disempowerment in the burlesque world, including a casket-like shot of Kitty and her baby.

visually anticipate Berkeley's work, its function is quite different. If Berkeley generally aimed to use top shots to render women as objects in a grand display, Mamoulian integrates the top shot into a larger stylistic pattern that *critiques* the display of women.[48]

Mamoulian's other striking framing decision in *Applause* occurs when he elects to train the camera on characters' feet and legs rather than their upper halves. The most sustained example occurs when April first meets Tony. In a single shot lasting a minute and forty-five seconds, April leaves the sexually abusive Hitch and tries to walk home at night in New York City. As she begins walking down the street, dialogue indicates that numerous men try to pick up the unwilling April, but we cannot see this happening. Instead, Mamoulian tilts the camera down to April's legs and feet as she tries to stride by the men. She is halted by a man who apparently—based on the leg movement we see—grabs her and twists her around. Tony's legs then appear in the frame as he confronts the other man and appears to punch him to the ground, though once more the camera remains trained only on legs. The camera then tilts up in a two-shot of April and Tony to reveal the face of April's rescuer. However, when April tells Tony she does not want to be bothered and Tony responds, "did you say *bother*?," the camera again tilts down and follows April's and Tony's legs as Tony pursues her. Only when it starts to seem that Tony might not be such a bad guy after all does the camera tilt back upward to their faces for good.

This extended shot appears nowhere in writer Garrett Fort's screenplay for the film, making it highly likely that it was a Mamoulian addition. Like Mamoulian's high-angle work, the device is showy yet integrated into the film's narrative. Taken in isolation, the idea behind the framing decision seems fairly simple: men see April as merely a "pair of legs," and initially, Tony's similar framing reflects April's suspicion that he is yet another creep on the street. Yet Mamoulian has carefully built toward this moment by using the camera to emphasize legs and feet at earlier points in the story. The film's first burlesque performance begins with a shot that frames only the mechanically kicking legs of the chorus line. In the next scene, Mamoulian introduces the five-year-old April performing a dance for Kitty and her boyfriend by training the camera only on April's feet before tracking back and tilting up to reveal Kitty playing piano for April and giving her instructions. The conversation that ensues indicates that the young April would be sexually vulnerable and warped if raised within the burlesque business, and this discussion prompts Kitty to send her to a convent. A few scenes later, the camera isolates Hitch's feet as he enters Kitty's room after sleeping with another woman, a fact that Kitty is sadly oblivious to. Thus by the time Mamoulian's bravura leg shot occurs, the isolation of legs and feet has been tied to female objectification, April's vulnerability, and male predatory behavior—all ideas that are highly relevant to this scene.

Though Mamoulian's flashy forced framings in *Applause* serve the story by articulating key ideas embedded within it, they remain rather self-conscious by studio-era Hollywood standards, and Mamoulian would never again use high angles or feet framings in such overt ways. In later interviews, Mamoulian often mentioned that the disappointing box-office results of *Applause* led him to believe he had employed a too-audacious style.[49] Perhaps for this reason, as Mamoulian's career progressed he settled on a somewhat less flamboyant but still camera-based technique: framing *objects* from specific vantage points that enabled them to function as highly active players in the creation of meaning.

The final shot in *Applause* offers an early example of such "forced-object" framings. As April and Tony hug backstage for what they believe is an unambiguously happy reunion (they will marry and Kitty will live with them in Wisconsin), the camera tracks backward to include not just April and Tony, but a large and glamorized (and dated) promotional poster of Kitty on the wall behind them. Initially, this shot is not entirely dependent upon camera position—the poster is so large that one would theoretically be able to see it clearly from multiple vantage points. However, Mamoulian then exploits the camera by tracking forward and shunting April and Tony to the lower edge of the frame so that the poster becomes the dominant feature in the shot (Figure 1.6). Camera positioning forces us to remember what April and Tony do not know: Kitty has committed suicide partly because she is no longer deemed attractive enough to star in burlesque, and partly to free April to marry Tony. Mamoulian's forced framing thus undercuts the "happy" ending and amplifies a sense of irony and tragedy: we see an image of a vital, living star that simultaneously evokes the stillness of the now-dead Kitty. Thanks to this framing, Mamoulian seems to suggest that Kitty has become a specter that haunts the couple's future.

This final shot exemplifies Mamoulian's theory of film artistry in several respects. Most simply, it exploits the singular perspective of the camera. But equally important, the framing feels especially pronounced because it matches not what the characters have noticed, but what Mamoulian has independently chosen. The forced framing thus provides an added commentary that operates separately from character perception or comprehension, thereby enabling Mamoulian to more forcefully express his "point of view" on events. Furthermore, forced framings for Mamoulian reflected what he saw as a key definitional difference between stage and screen. Whereas on the stage, in Mamoulian's words, "background is subservient to the actor," in cinema the camera could frame the background to be at least as expressive as the actor.[50] For Mamoulian, film was a graphic art most akin to painting, which meant that there was no implicit hierarchy between actor and object. Consequently, as Mamoulian once wrote, the screen could sometimes "tell a more dramatic story by the use of inanimate objects than with animate ones."[51]

Figure 1.6 A forced-object framing in *Applause* devotes more attention to the poster behind the couple than the couple itself.

Mamoulian was in a good position to understand cinema's ability to render objects expressive because early in his theatrical career, he had attempted to make expressive use of statuary on the stage. In his 1929 production of *The Game of Love and Death*, Mamoulian had—during a lengthy and static dialogue scene between two friends on opposite sides of the French Revolution—placed on the mantelpiece "the famous bust of Voltaire, by Houdin ... smiling at the ironies of human nature, which was softly lighted" by a nearby candle.[52] Such use of statuary might well have augmented the impact of the discussion on the stage, but Mamoulian still viewed the statue as a necessarily secondary element in the theater. In cinema, however, Mamoulian saw the camera as an instrument for rendering inanimate objects expressive.

Framing objects to assert a directorial—rather than character-oriented—viewpoint constituted a risky move in the classical style of Hollywood because it threatened to direct attention away from the story and toward the hand of the nondiegetic filmmaker.[53] Throughout his work, Mamoulian addressed this problem by making sure that his forced framings conveyed ideas that fit closely with story, character, and theme. Before a bullfight in *Blood and Sand* (1941), for instance, Mamoulian positioned his camera so that a stuffed bull's head, mounted on the back wall, appears just above and to one side of master bullfighter Juan's (Tyrone Power) head in the midground when he admits his fear of the bull (Figure 1.7). The bull's head thus becomes Juan's veritable thought bubble—an effect derived by framing the scene from one particular vantage point—and thus remains fully grounded in storytelling concerns.

A lifelong lover of art, Mamoulian was especially inclined toward using paintings, portraits, and busts in his forced-object framings. Consider, for instance, scenes from *Golden Boy* (1939) that take place in the home of Mr. Bonaparte (Lee J. Cobb). An Italian American, Mr. Bonaparte wants his son, Joe (William Holden), to pursue the aesthetic beauties of a violinist's life rather than the brutal, crass commercialism of a boxing career. Mamoulian's personal screenplay features numerous annotations that detail precisely which artworks in the family home should be visible in the background at which points. Early in the film, for instance, Mr. Bonaparte enters his home to hear Joe playing a violin that Mr. Bonaparte bought for him. As he listens to Joe's music, a painting that somewhat resembles Raphael's *Sistine Madonna* appears in the mirror just to the right of Mr. Bonaparte. Joe turns while playing to face his father, and Mamoulian positions the camera so that the illuminated Madonna is just to the left of Joe's head. Then, when Mr. Bonaparte walks over to Joe, the two-shot frames them

Figure 1.7 The precise framing of bullfighter Juan and a bull's head in *Blood and Sand* shows that fear of bulls is on his brain.

so that *both* artworks are visible in the gaps between the characters (Figure 1.8). Through these precise framings, the consistently Italian artwork helps convey a key narrative idea: that the Bonaparte home is a cloistered, safe space within which one can be true to oneself, and by extension, to the beauties of one's culture. Such esteemed art objects stand in stark contrast to the sports memorabilia and sleek modernism found in places like boxing manager Tom Moody's (Adolphe Menjou) office, thus furthering the sense that they convey old-world ideas like nurture, love, and parental protection. Later in the film, in a decision again penciled into the screenplay, Mamoulian frames Joe not just with the *Sistine Madonna* in the background, but also with busts of Napoleon and Beethoven, thereby conveying the warring geniuses of violence and music that constitute Joe's central conflict in the film.

The forced framings described above articulate either earnest connections between framed artwork and story ideas (*Blood and Sand*, *Golden Boy*) or tragic irony (*Applause*). But if the film's material suggested it, Mamoulian could modify the device to convey a sense of fun and play. In *The Gay Desperado*, Mamoulian introduces an immoral, unscrupulous American gangster in a medium shot seated at his desk. A portrait of Abraham Lincoln—a man with as little in

Figure 1.8 A forced-object framing in *Golden Boy*. When Bonaparte and Joe occupy the same shot, the framing makes the Sistine Madonna (*left*) and the Madonna statue (*center*) seem almost attached to the characters.

common with the gangster as possible—hangs directly behind him on the wall. Though this visual joke could theoretically occur on a stage, the framing begins by positioning the gangster's head only halfway up the frame, which allows the entire Lincoln portrait, whose size is roughly equivalent to the gangster's, to be seen clearly. The joke then unfolds via a track back, which reveals that the noble Lincoln portrait is bracketed by pictures of scantily dressed showgirls.

At their most salient, Mamoulian's forced-object framings could evoke the sense that societal forces mold the fates and decisions of individuals. *We Live Again* (1934) explores two conflicting institutional forces: the callous power enjoyed by the Russian aristocracy, and Christian teachings of sacrifice and penance. In the film, Dmitri (Fredric March), a nobleman in Tsarist Russia, impregnates and abandons the unwed farm girl Katusha (Anna Sten), an action that leads to her banishment from the farm and, eventually, being sentenced to hard labor in Siberia due to a clerical error that no one in the legal system cares to correct. During the legal scenes, Mamoulian repeatedly articulates the oppressive nature of Russian law, and the extent to which the ruling system props up the undeserving, through framings of several large paintings that hang behind representatives of the law. During the trial scene, for instance, Mamoulian places a gigantic portrait of Tsar Alexander III behind the seated judges and frames it so that the entire painting is visible, thus squashing the judges into the very bottom of the frame. Such framings, which recur to portray other members of the legal profession and a prison warden, suggest both the power of the governmental institution they represent and, implicitly, the sheer artifice upon which their authority rests—two key ideas that drive the film. To reflect the contrasting influence of Christian teaching, an Easter mass scene earlier in the film contains repeated, prominent framings of emblems of Jesus' crucifixion, including a recurring high-angle shot from behind the altar that features two crosses jutting diagonally into the foreground of the frame and enveloping the worshippers. Such framings encourage us to read Christianity as a powerful competing presence and help explain Dmitri's final decision to pursue a moral existence.

As with his use of shadow play, Mamoulian's forced framings often toed the line between subordinating style to story and self-consciously drawing attention to craft. In doing so, Mamoulian forged a style that both demanded attention *and* remained within the parameters of studio-era acceptability. Though the saliency of this device sometimes opened him up to charges of pure "symbolism," forced-object framings remained central to Mamoulian's belief in film as an art form because they exploited the camera's ability to compel viewers to see things from only one position and enabled him to mold the image with the care and fussiness of a painter. For Mamoulian, forced framings demonstrated that cinema was as legitimate an art form as the artworks he wove into the visual design of his films.

Scene Transitions

Mamoulian was a meticulous shot planner and composer, and his forced framings were hardly his only recurring camera device. The most frequently penciled-in technique in Mamoulian's personal screenplays, for instance, was the pull back (or, in Mamoulian's words, the "truck back"). Particularly for the opening shot of a scene, Mamoulian routinely crossed out typed screenplay instructions indicating other camera set-ups and denoted a pull back. It is likely that Mamoulian favored the pull back because it allowed him to capitalize on cinema's ability to isolate objects even in shots designed to establish a scene's space more broadly. In his 1932 lecture to the American Society of Cinematographers, Mamoulian detailed various functions of camera movement, including the fact that it could "concentrat[e] interest on a single point."[54] Mamoulian also seems to have liked the pull back's ability to give the audience a keener feeling about the scene—its emotional content and focus—before moving outward into a more impersonal establishing shot.[55] More generally, the pull back functioned as a less obtrusive way to assert directorial control. While any camera distance constitutes some kind of narrowing down of the field of vision, to begin close range is to insist upon framing something from an especially restricted and controlled perspective, while the ensuing track back implies that the guiding hand of the narrator is choosing when and what a viewer will see.

Though a favorite Mamoulian technique, pull backs—even lengthy ones—were common during Hollywood's studio era. Some of Mamoulian's most unusual and elaborate recurring devices resided not in the realm of cinematography, but in editing. Though Mamoulian enjoyed trumpeting the potentials of cinematography in his early writings, his theory of cinema as it emerged in the 1930s also included editing. In particular, Mamoulian placed great value on something impossible to achieve on the stage: carefully thought-out transitions between one scene—or space—and the next. Mamoulian saw cinematic transitions as important opportunities to layer stylization over what would otherwise be an ordinary, objective movement from one scene to the ensuing one. Mamoulian once remarked in an interview, "You know, the most boring or routine thing is a transition. What do you do with a transition? To go from one room to another, you have to step over a threshold. Well, there is a great excitement in making that threshold more eloquent than the scene itself; it suddenly becomes a highlight."[56]

For convenience, we can divide Mamoulian's transitions into two categories: the sustained split-screen transition, and the dissolve-based transition. Both devices for Mamoulian are fundamentally comparative in nature, and they often convey authorial attitudes toward the films' subject matter. However, they reflect different modes of engagement with the material and different levels of saliency. Of the two, Mamoulian's split screens are far more self-conscious and far less common in his work. Split screens appear in only three Mamoulian films: *Applause*, *Dr. Jekyll and Mr. Hyde*, and *Love Me Tonight*. The device deserves close attention, though, not just because of its audaciousness, but because it reflects with particular clarity the value Mamoulian found in stylizing his films through image juxtapositions and his belief that even the most overt stylistic decisions should be anchored to storytelling.

The sustained split screen appears only once in *Applause*,[57] but it occupies considerable screen time and comes at an unexpected and meaningful moment in the film. As Kitty moons over a photograph of Hitch in the bottom-right corner of the screen and softly sings Jay Gorney and E. Y. Harburg's "What Wouldn't I Do for That Man?," a slow diagonal wipe beginning from the top left of the screen reveals Hitch having an affair with a woman who resides just down the hall from Kitty. In later discussions of his work,[58] Mamoulian took great pride in what happens next: the wipe *pauses* midway for several seconds, thus allowing the audience to meditate on the comparative implications of the two actions (Figure 1.9). Mamoulian positioned the camera at similar distances from the characters in both shots, which creates the sense that Kitty, Hitch, and the other woman almost occupy the same room. Yet the similar distances only serve to highlight the disparity in knowledge between Kitty and Hitch.

Figure 1.9 In *Applause*, a wipe pauses mid-frame to compare Kitty mooning over Hitch's photograph to Hitch kissing another woman....

By holding both shots simultaneously, Mamoulian presents a stark picture of infidelity, vulnerability, and exploitation. The audience is encouraged to reflect upon Hitch's dishonesty and callousness and Kitty's blindness, attributes that will drive and explain what happens in the rest of the film. Even Mamoulian's placement of the characters holds significance. Occupying a higher position in the frame, Hitch is implicitly the dominant one, while Kitty occupies a more marginalized space. As with the earlier shadow-play shot (Figure 1.1), Kitty is stuffed into the bottom corner of the frame, as if pushed to the ground and already discarded by Hitch.

It is worth pausing here to note the sheer boldness of this split-screen device. An annotated screenplay in the Mamoulian collection clearly reveals the split screen to be Mamoulian's decision. In the original typed screenplay, the image was to have dissolved from Kitty holding Hitch's photograph to the shot of Hitch cheating on her. In the margin, Mamoulian penciled in the split-screen technique—indicated via a box with a diagonal slash running through it—found in the finished film (Figure 1.10). Mamoulian's markings even specify "Hitch on left" during the split screen, thus ensuring that Hitch would remain in a higher position in the frame.[59] Though used during the late silent era,[60] the split screen, to my knowledge, did not appear in any US all-talking film prior to *Applause*. Moreover, the device was a major technical challenge. Optical printers—which permitted films to be duplicated with little deterioration in quality—would not be in use for another year. Thus, as Barry Salt has pointed out, any wipe in 1929 needed to be performed in-camera by filming one shot with a masking device moving across the camera, rewinding the film, and then filming the other shot while attempting to move the masking device "at precisely the same speed, and starting from exactly the same frame."[61] Indeed, by Mamoulian's account:

> There was no mechanism for [the wipe] at all. . . . I cut out of a cardboard a big triangle, put it on a circle, marked regular intervals on it, like a dial of a clock, and placed it in front of the glass window behind which the camera was hidden. Of course, it was quite a trick to make the line on the screen come out precisely from one top corner and stop between the two corners in the middle. The square of the lens is so tiny, and the glass in front of it was so huge. . . . I remember, one man held a second-watch in his hand; he kept pinching my leg to indicate every second, and I kept moving the fan-shaped cardboard down, so the movement would be smooth and correctly timed.[62]

In addition to timing-based concerns (see chapter 3), the sustained wipe in *Applause* shows Mamoulian's eagerness to innovate, as well as the value he placed on techniques rooted in what he saw as defining features of cinema: camera placement and image juxtaposition. The resulting device is showy but not *purely*

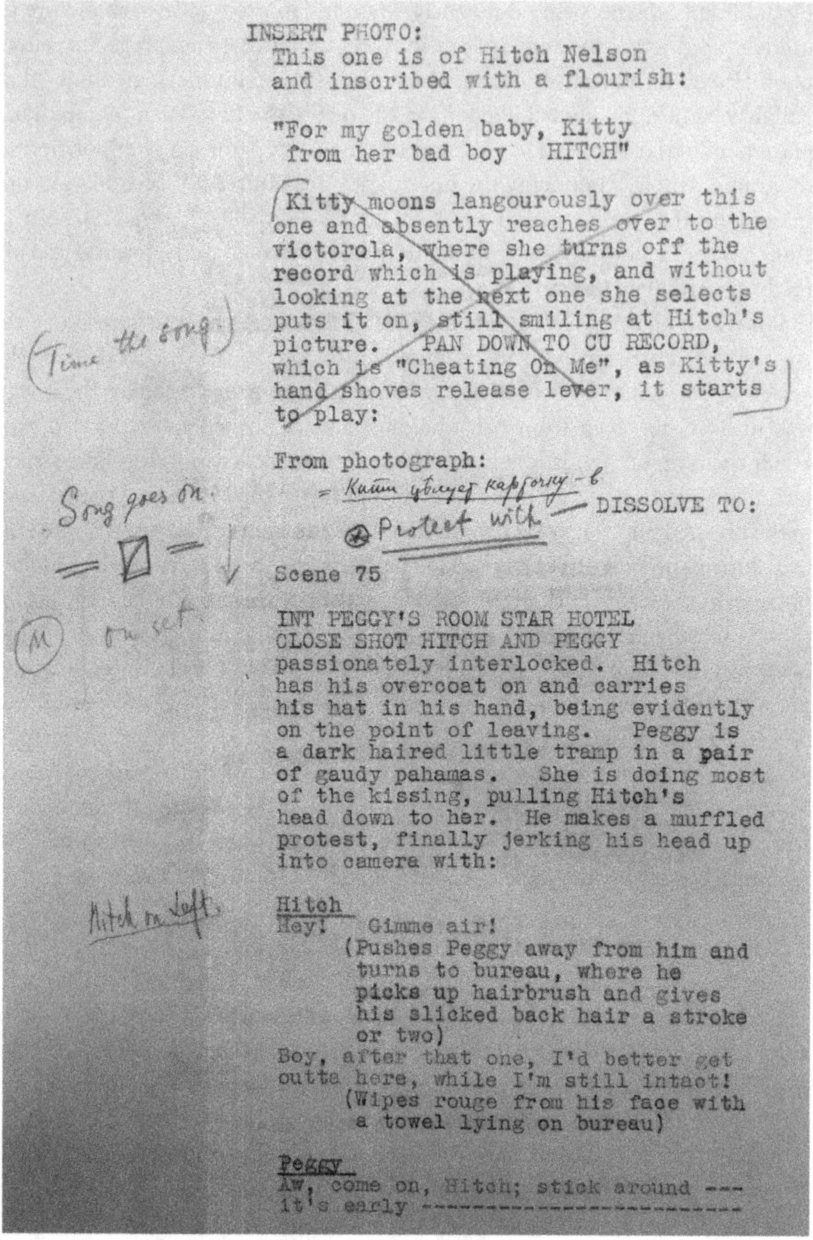

INSERT PHOTO:
This one is of Hitch Nelson
and inscribed with a flourish:

"For my golden baby, Kitty
from her bad boy   HITCH"

Kitty moons langourously over this
one and absently reaches over to the
victorola, where she turns off the
record which is playing, and without
looking at the next one she selects
puts it on, still smiling at Hitch's
picture.   PAN DOWN TO CU RECORD,
which is "Cheating On Me", as Kitty's
hand shoves release lever, it starts
to play:

From photograph:

= Katun ybueyer kapporsuy - b
① Protect with   DISSOLVE TO:

Scene 75

INT PEGGY'S ROOM STAR HOTEL
CLOSE SHOT HITCH AND PEGGY
passionately interlocked. Hitch
has his overcoat on and carries
his hat in his hand, being evidently
on the point of leaving.   Peggy is
a dark haired little tramp in a pair
of gaudy pahamas.   She is doing most
of the kissing, pulling Hitch's
head down to her. He makes a muffled
protest, finally jerking his head up
into camera with:

Hitch
Hey!   Gimme air!
        (Pushes Peggy away from him and
        turns to bureau, where he
        picks up hairbrush and gives
        his slicked back hair a stroke
        or two)
Boy, after that one, I'd better get
outta here, while I'm still intact!
        (Wipes rouge from his face with
        a towel lying on bureau)

Peggy
Aw, come on, Hitch; stick around ---
it's early ----------------------------

(Time the song)

Song goes on:
= ∅ =

Ⓜ on set

Hitch on left

Figure 1.10 In his personal screenplay, Mamoulian handwrote his revision to this scene, including the split-screen effect, character positioning, and timing.

a show-off move, accentuating as it does the inequitable relationship of Kitty and Hitch.

Though flamboyant, the wipe in *Applause* was a mere prelude to the sustained wipes Mamoulian would use two films later in *Dr. Jekyll and Mr. Hyde*. By now, Paramount possessed a mechanical device for split-screen wipes,[63] and Mamoulian—tasked with directing a story about a split identity—seized upon this thematic justification to use the sustained wipe in more daring and complex ways. Once again, the archive leaves little doubt that Mamoulian conceived of and orchestrated the wipes—as with *Applause*, the wipes appear not in the typed screenplay, but in Mamoulian's handwriting in the screenplay margins.

As in *Applause*, in *Dr. Jekyll and Mr. Hyde* Mamoulian sometimes exploits graphic similarities during wipes, but here he finds more elaborate ways to make the two shots within the wipe seem to "fit" together as a single shot. This is clearest in the first split-screen wipe, which also functions as the film's introduction to Jekyll's upper-class fiancée Muriel (Rose Hobart). As Jekyll (Fredric March) attends to an elderly woman in the sick ward, he asks his friend Lanyon (Holmes Herbert) to inform Muriel's family that his work will prevent him from attending Muriel's dinner. With Jekyll standing in medium long shot in the left part of the screen at the woman's bedside (Figure 1.11), a slow diagonal wipe—anchored

Figure 1.11 The first wipe in *Dr. Jekyll and Mr. Hyde* begins with Jekyll attending to a sick woman in the charity ward before . . .

on the bottom left of the screen—begins from the top-left corner. It wipes away Jekyll to reveal Muriel standing in a similar position. Midway through its movement, the wipe briefly pauses to show Muriel—wearing an expensive white dinner dress—in the left part of the screen, and the sick woman lying in bed on the other side of the wipe (Figure 1.12). A moment later, the wipe continues and concludes by revealing the butler to whom Muriel is speaking about dinner-party arrangements.

As in *Applause*, Mamoulian has carefully matched camera distance. Though the first shot is a bit closer range than the second, the difference is negligible, and the characters in the two shots appear roughly the same size on the screen. Here, however, other methods further the sense of a singular space across shots. When the wipe pauses midway, for instance, the wall in the newer shot is the same shade of gray, and a chair behind Muriel is positioned as if it were pulled up to the bedside of the older woman. More precise still, Jekyll's hands—still visible in the shot—are framed as if extensions of Muriel's hands. Specific elements of the decor in both shots also match each other. One of the vertical rungs of the charity-ward headboard continues in Muriel's shot as a candlestick, and a ridge on the wall of the charity ward appears, in the split screen, to continue as the

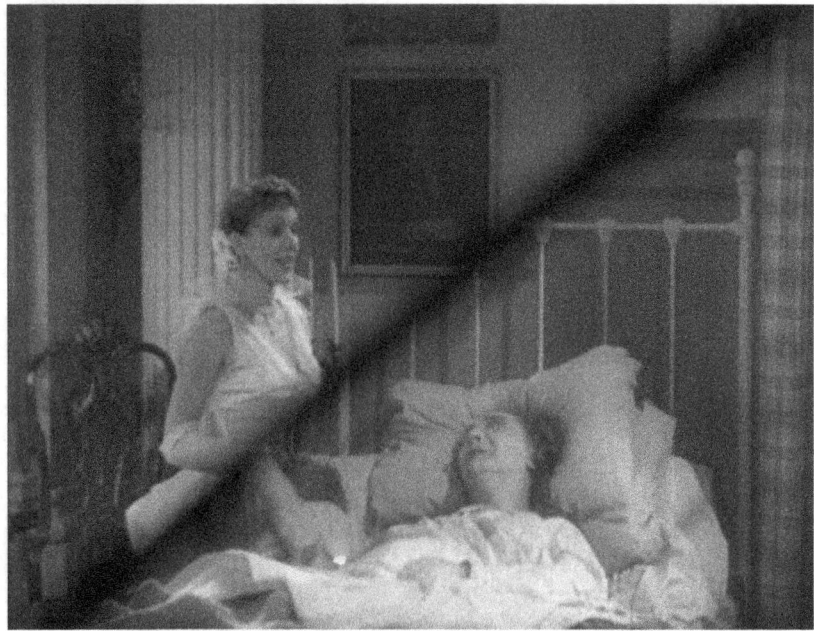

Figure 1.12 ... Mamoulian wipes to Muriel and holds the wipe mid-frame, with similarities between the shots helping to present a somewhat-unified space.

picture frame on the wall of Muriel's home (this is later revealed to be a part of the fireplace, but the illusion is initially present nonetheless).

Of course, the idea is not to fool the audience into thinking that Muriel and the older woman occupy the same space—the self-conscious wipe ensures this does not occur. Rather, Mamoulian is finding more visually compelling ways to accentuate difference within graphically similar shots. The contrast between the beleaguered older woman's face in the drab charity ward and the young, freshly made-up face of Muriel in her opulent home emphasizes the differing fortunes of rich and poor, a topic that will be important for understanding bar singer Ivy's (Miriam Hopkins) predicament later in the film. Yet at the same time, in the context of the story (we learn in this scene that Muriel loves Jekyll's devotion to the charity ward), one could also argue that Mamoulian uses these graphic matches to suggest that Jekyll and Muriel might be the right "match" for each other, right down to the hands of Jekyll seeming to complete the body of Muriel.

If this early graphic match across a split screen suggests optimism, however, that attitude fades with Mamoulian's subsequent uses of the device, which more heavily stress graphic difference and incompatibility. The second split screen occurs much later in the film when Jekyll vows to stop transforming into Hyde due to Hyde's abusive relationship with Ivy, a promise he proves unable to keep. As Ivy stands in medium long shot on the left side of the screen talking with her landlady, who is seated on the bed in the bottom-right corner of the frame, a wipe begins that replaces the landlady with Muriel. When the wipe pauses, the viewer can see Jekyll from only the torso down—his head is blocked from view by the wipe (Figure 1.13). On the film's terms, the wipe overtly contrasts polar opposites Muriel (Jekyll's upper-class fiancée) and Ivy (Hyde's working-class mistress). Furthering the sense of contrast, there is now little in the decor to suggest unity between these two spaces, with objects like curtains abruptly cut off at the wipe line.[64] Mamoulian also finds psychological meaning in this sustained wipe by laying Ivy's image *over* Jekyll's as we begin to hear Jekyll apologizing for his lengthy absence and telling Muriel he needs her. Ivy's overlaid image articulates the looming presence that Hyde/Ivy still has in Jekyll's life and implicitly questions whether he can rid his sexual obsession with Ivy from his consciousness.

The most complex use of the device, however, occurs when Jekyll irrevocably separates from a life with Muriel by unexpectedly turning into Hyde without taking any potion. When Jekyll—on his way to a dinner party to announce his engagement to Muriel—changes into Hyde, he hustles away from the park chair where he transformed and toward the back left of the image. Mamoulian then begins a diagonal wipe from the bottom right of the frame (anchored again at the bottom left of the image) to reveal the dinner party. When the wipe line pauses midway through, the camera moves across the room in high angle to reveal

Figure 1.13 A later wipe in *Dr. Jekyll and Mr. Hyde* makes far less effort to visually blend together the shots.

Muriel seated and looking worried in extreme long shot. As the camera starts moving closer to her, the wipe slowly begins to erase the rest of the park image, yet because Jekyll is continuing to walk away in the top-left corner of the frame, he remains on the screen until nearly the end of the wipe (Figure 1.14). The visual characteristics of this wipe again stress contrast and separation—the open-field milieu of the park offers no graphic match with the lavish interior of Muriel's home—but here, Mamoulian also finds expressive potential in the *pacing* of the wipe. By slowing down the wipe near the end of the transition, Mamoulian lingers on the idea of erasure, a concept that matters because, as a later conversation will emphasize, if Jekyll can no longer control his transformation into Hyde, he can no longer have Muriel. The flashy split-screen wipe thus functions as a visual way to emphasize that Jekyll has permanently "wiped out" his future with Muriel via his inability to restrain Hyde. Mamoulian even incorporates character movement into the wipe and the separation it implies—as he once pointed out in an interview, the wipe portrays Hyde effectively "running away" from the reception.[65]

The choreography of this wipe is notable for its range of expressive tools, but Mamoulian isn't done. A mere ten seconds after the wipe is completed,

MAMOULIAN, ART, AND CINEMA   47

Figure 1.14 In *Dr. Jekyll and Mr. Hyde*, Mamoulian slows the wipe near its conclusion to emphasize the departing Jekyll/Hyde's erasure from the engagement party and his life with Muriel. . . .

Mamoulian begins a new wipe that manages to provoke both broad-scale contemplation and suspense. The wipe begins from the top left of the frame to reveal Ivy drinking champagne in celebration of her belief that she will never see Hyde again. Once more, Mamoulian holds the wipe midway through, so that both Ivy and Muriel are visible on the screen (Figure 1.15). In one sense, this split-screen image seems a simple repetition of the previous juxtaposition of "bad" Ivy and "good" Muriel, but Mamoulian's choice of a split screen holds additional meaning. First, pausing the wipe midway emphasizes that both women are set to celebrate under false pretenses: Ivy because she thinks she is rid of Hyde, Muriel because she expects to be married to Jekyll. That we are forced to simultaneously watch both sadly mistaken women encourages us to reflect upon the extraordinary extent to which Jekyll's actions have wrecked both women's lives. Second, we are aware, while Ivy is not, that Hyde is almost surely coming for her. Showing Ivy in a split screen thus helps amp up tension, making her brutal murder more emotionally charged.

With the sustained wipe, Mamoulian embraced what his theory called for: an intricately planned and stylized method for commenting on the narrative that exploits the properties of cinema. However, aside from a sustained split-screen

Figure 1.15 Then, during the same transition, Mamoulian holds a split screen to compare Ivy and Muriel.

wipe in *Love Me Tonight*—which I discuss in chapter 4—Mamoulian never returned to the device. Perhaps the studios Mamoulian subsequently worked for expected a more reined-in approach, or perhaps Mamoulian himself came to view the device as being too intrusive. Yet although the sustained wipe vanishes from Mamoulian's later films, he never lost his broader interest in fastidiously crafting scene transitions, albeit via a more conventional dissolve-based approach.

The care Mamoulian devoted to such transitions is evident from his first film onward, but it was not until a 1936 article that he articulated a theory of cinematic art that reflected his interest in the meaningful accumulation of images. In an article strenuously devoted to defending film as an art form, Mamoulian offered the following definition of cinema: "a dynamically and rhythmically organized *series* of moving images expressing a story, character, or mood in a dramatic way which appeals to our sense of the beautiful" (emphasis is mine).[66] Where Mamoulian's dissolve-based transitions are concerned, the "sense of the beautiful" is a key component of this definition. All Mamoulian transitions are notable for the graphic attention lavished on the image as well as their functionality in the story. In an industry whose style was characterized by formal elegance,[67] this value meshed nicely with classical Hollywood aims.

Mamoulian's heightened attention to transitions is evident from the first scene in *Applause* onward. At the end of this scene—which depicts ballyhoo for the arriving burlesque troupe—Mamoulian provides a close-up of a drum that the Zenith Band is playing. The image then dissolves to a beating drum inside the burlesque house played in the orchestra pit. As a graphic match of circular imagery, the transition is aesthetically striking, and one gets the sense of a theater director delighting in something he could not produce on the stage. Yet the transition is also meaningful within the context of the film because it provides an early undercutting of burlesque entertainment. As presented in the opening scene, the Zenith Band drum represents the music that has drawn everyone in to see the show. The transition to the drum during the performance is graphically similar, but it also plays up one key difference: placed in the foreground—and propped on the drummer's music stand—is a mug of beer. By using graphic disparity to emphasize that burlesque performance is lubricated by alcohol, Mamoulian immediately marks burlesque as a crass, low-taste entertainment.

In addition to object-based matches, Mamoulian's dissolve transitions sometimes exploited character-action matches to make story-based points. A harrowing example can be found late in *Applause*. When April sacrifices herself for her mother by sending Tony away, Mamoulian shows April drinking the last of her beverage. In close-up, the camera follows her hand as she puts down her empty glass, and then provides a brief dissolve to a graphic match of her mother's hand, who back in her apartment is putting down *her* empty glass. This match—which the archive reveals was Mamoulian's addition[68]—is poignant: not only does it suggest the bond between mother and daughter that will cause April to reject Tony, but since we know that the mother's glass contains poison, it marks April's action of leaving Tony and engaging in a burlesque career as an alternative form of suicide.

Not always content with graphic matches alone, Mamoulian also periodically added symmetrical camera movements to his transitions. By "symmetrical," I mean camera moves that are either identical across a transition or constitute mirror images of each other. In doing so, Mamoulian even more strongly marked his transitions as opportunities for stylization. In *City Streets*, for instance, Mamoulian begins with a medium close-up of Nan (Sylvia Sidney)—sitting in the police station and facing likely time in jail—staring rightward and up toward the off-screen clock. Mamoulian tilts and pans to follow her gaze until the camera rests upon the clock, which reads 12:05. The image then dissolves to another wall clock, and the camera tilts down and to the right again until it rests in a medium close-up of her romantic interest, the Kid (Gary Cooper), who has been looking at the clock. In effect, the camera movement inscribes a two-thirds triangle, with Nan and the Kid connected at the triangle's upper point by the clock. Once again, archival records indicate that this transitional device was Mamoulian's idea. In the original version, Nan was to look at the clock, followed by an eyeline-match cut to the clock itself. Seeking a more noticeable flourish that could be arranged symmetrically across a transition, Mamoulian changed this to an unmotivated pan.[69] Through this change, Mamoulian placed additional stylistic weight on the clock. The importance of this object is not just that Nan has missed her appointment with the Kid (they were to meet at 12:00), but that their fates are now connected by time and its passage, as the couple must endure a lengthy physical separation (a poignant jail visitation scene shows them unable to kiss through a mesh screen) and cope with the way that time can change a person (Nan exits jail shocked that the innocent Kid has become a gangster).

Another flexible device in the Mamoulian arsenal, the symmetrical graphic match could also be harnessed to comedic situations. At the end of an early scene in *Becky Sharp*, Becky (Miriam Hopkins) writes in her diary, irritably calling her suitor Joseph (Nigel Bruce) a "fat fool" for not yet proposing to her. Then, in medium shot, Becky examines a flower that Joseph presumably gave her before tossing it disgustedly out of the right of the frame. Mamoulian then uses a graphic-match dissolve to a shot of Becky at nearly the same distance sitting on a family-room couch. In a reverse of the previous shot, Joseph, seated to her right, hands her a flower from out of frame, and the camera tracks back to frame Joseph and Becky as Becky declares, "Oh I shall press this one too. I've kept all of your dear flowers." The result is a humorous stylistic gag—it is as if the flower she discarded has magically bounced up and returned to her—while the graphic match plays up the contrast between her private and public behavior.

Not all of Mamoulian's stylized transitions are based on graphic matches. On rare occasions, for instance, Mamoulian instead emphasized the *length* of the dissolves rather than the graphic similarities across images. Doing so likely stretched the boundaries of permissible self-conscious narration in Hollywood, but once again, Mamoulian was careful to find strong narrative reasons for doing so. In *High, Wide and Handsome*, a slow dissolve occurs after the villainous railroad baron Walt Brennan (Alan Hale) offers Peter (Randolph Scott) a chance to join forces so that only a select few will profit from Peter's discovery of oil. After Peter angrily refuses and leaves, Mamoulian provides a close-up of Brennan laughing at Peter. The shot constitutes one of Mamoulian's more notable over-the-shoulder forced framings, since the statue of a black cat, mouth open to expose its sharp teeth, rests just behind Brennan's right shoulder (a clear comment on Brennan's vicious business practices). Mamoulian then begins dissolving to an image of Peter walking in the rain, and he holds the dissolve for around ten seconds—far past any conventional length of time. Though flashy, this extended dissolve helps suggest that Brennan is etched inexorably in Peter's mind, which justifies Peter's lengthy and increasingly maniacal behavior for the rest of the film as he begins to sacrifice everything he has—wife, home, money—in his effort to beat Brennan.

Mamoulian did not, we should note, invent graphic matches or lengthy dissolves any more than he did the other devices analyzed in this chapter. In the late silent era, 1920s filmmakers at Fox influenced by F. W. Murnau sometimes offered dissolves based on graphic matches. In *7th Heaven* (1927), for instance, Frank Borzage had emphasized the spiritual connectedness of two physically separated lovers by dissolving from one similarly framed lover to the other. At Paramount in the early sound era, Josef von Sternberg regularly utilized lengthy dissolves during scene transitions, especially in his early sound films *Morocco* (1930) and *Dishonored* (1931). These filmmakers, in turn, may have been influenced by prior French examples. Nevertheless, dissolve-based transitions were especially important to Mamoulian's style because they enabled him to do what he treasured: artfully manipulate cinema-specific elements to express story ideas.

Conclusion

Armed with a theory of art before he ever set foot in a movie studio, Mamoulian—from the beginning of his film career to the end of it—seized upon his conception of cinema's essence to provide a stylized approach aimed at reflecting and amplifying the narrative, character, and theme-based traits inherent in the material. Deeply versed in a wide array of classic art forms yet open to the artistic possibilities of a contemporary mass medium, Mamoulian saw cinema as a serious art form that was just as capable of experimentation, expression, and beauty as theater, painting, or sculpture. Sometimes drawing overtly upon stage-based ideas, sometimes reveling in the new tools that cinema offered him, Mamoulian's films—though eclectic in genre, subject matter, and even level of self-conscious style—display a remarkably unified effort to put his theories into practice.

Shadow play, forced framings, and stylish scene transitions are notable simply for their frequent recurrence, but when viewed in terms of their relationship to Mamoulian's writings, we gain a fuller picture of a filmmaker determined to probe what cinema was and what it could become. Far from being a mere hotshot experimenter, Mamoulian is best understood as a stylist who performed a balancing act between showing off his techniques and remaining mindful of Hollywood's expectation that style would be subordinate to story. Because Mamoulian took pains to tie even his most salient techniques to narrative ends—and because he had the good fortune to be dropped into sound filmmaking when its identity was still quite fluid—Mamoulian's methods yielded a style that was well suited for illuminating key potentials of sound cinema. As subsequent chapters will demonstrate, when tackling questions specific to sound techniques, pacing, the musical genre, color, and filmmaking under censorship, Mamoulian would similarly look for methods that would express narrative ideas. This insistence upon tying his devices to story, character, or theme enabled him to present viable, long-term solutions to challenges faced in the first few decades of sound filmmaking.

To understand Mamoulian's more innovative approaches, however, we must now look closely at the contexts within which he made his films and assess the originality and significance of his contributions. In each of the chapters that follow, I historically contextualize a key challenge that Mamoulian faced and examine how Mamoulian used his theories of artistry and his theatrical background to address it. In doing so, we can see with much greater clarity how and why Mamoulian sought to play a defining role in sound filmmaking.

2
Mamoulian and Early Film Sound
Applause, City Streets, Dr. Jekyll and Mr. Hyde

> When sound came in, I couldn't have gotten away with what I did if it weren't for the fact that they were all caught with their pants down.[1]
> —Rouben Mamoulian

In October 1929, only a few months after the American film industry had committed to producing exclusively all-talking films, Paramount Pictures premiered Mamoulian's debut movie, *Applause*, which featured expressive camera movements and sounds that would later seem years ahead of their time. A year and a half later, Paramount released Mamoulian's second film, *City Streets*, which contained an early example of the voice-over, now a common filmmaking device. Eight months later, Mamoulian's third film—*Dr. Jekyll and Mr. Hyde*—provided an unconventional re-recorded conglomeration of overlapping sounds that existed nowhere in reality, an instance of post-production manipulation that anticipated later ways in which entire genres would construct fantastical or horrific soundtracks.

From a present-day vantage point, the innovations of these films can be difficult to recognize. Because these techniques resonate closely with later sound cinema methods, it is easy to miss how unusual they were when they appeared in Mamoulian's films. As a result, the broader historical significance of these devices—and the conception of sound-cinema artistry that lay behind them—remains challenging to grasp.

This chapter aims to recapture Mamoulian's sonic intentions and delineate the ways—and extent to which—his approaches stood out and anticipated later Hollywood values and techniques. Drawing upon archival records, Mamoulian's interviews, and viewings of many other extant early sound-era films, I explore how *Applause*, *City Streets*, and *Dr. Jekyll and Mr. Hyde* reflected Mamoulian's valuation of medium specificity and demonstrated his belief that a sound filmmaker should expressively manipulate sound and image at a time when doing so was far from typical. As we shall see, through his films and writings, Mamoulian sought to do nothing less than chart a course for how the nascent form of sound cinema could exist as an independent and narratively effective art form.

Understanding what made Mamoulian's approach to early synchronized sound unusual and prescient requires us to address a variety of basic sonic questions. What were the prevailing methods for microphoning speech in the earliest years of film sound? How often was background sound used, how loud was it likely to be, and what was the logic behind these decisions? When—and how often—was re-recording used, and for what purposes? When did filmmakers start using voice-overs in fiction film? Although a number of scholars have addressed aspects of these questions, a comprehensive account of sound filmmaking in the early sound era remains to be written. In what follows, I have attempted to break new ground not just on the significance of Mamoulian's sound techniques, but also on the broader history of early sound-era aesthetics.

In assessing Mamoulian's early sound work and its resemblances to later approaches, I do not wish to suggest that Mamoulian "perfected" sound and its "proper" use before others did. Other filmmakers, as I will indicate, were also exploring some of these avenues, and we should note that the early sound era was rife with promising experiments that could have—but ultimately did not—endure. Such paths are also deserving of close study. Mamoulian's efforts, however, often *did* anticipate subsequent sound filmmaking, and that story is equally important.

The first half of this chapter examines Mamoulian's stylistic methods in *Applause* within the context of early sound technologies and the period's most common filmmaking strategies. Because synchronized sound posed visual as well as sonic challenges, I begin by examining how Mamoulian approached cinematography in *Applause*, particularly camera movement. I then turn to Mamoulian's use of sound. Mamoulian's artistic beliefs led him to conceptualize sound cinema not as a neutral recording of on-screen performers and sounds—a widespread approach at the time—but rather as an opportunity for filmmakers to discover and utilize an expanded and narratively expressive toolkit. For Mamoulian, the path for sound cinema lay in a filmmaker's enhanced ability to *manipulate* sounds and images to emphasize narrative ideas and directorial viewpoints. Consequently, where many films from the period prioritized stage-based techniques or emphasized cinema's sheer ability to capture synchronized sounds, *Applause* stood out for the extent to which it sidestepped technological challenges and aggressively announced a different set of priorities.

The second half of the chapter examines Mamoulian's sound strategies for his subsequent films, in terms of both innovation and consistency. By the time Mamoulian shot his next two films in 1931 (*City Streets* and *Dr. Jekyll and Mr. Hyde*), the industry had moved closer to what we find in *Applause*, yet Mamoulian's continued interest in constructed and expressive sound resulted in additional innovations, particularly in the domain of sonic subjectivity. I conclude with a brief assessment of Mamoulian's films beyond the early sound era, which demonstrates that Mamoulian remained devoted to sonic construction, distortion, and subjectivity throughout the remainder of his career.

Just how directly Mamoulian's work influenced later sound practices is difficult to determine, a matter I address later in the chapter. What *is* clear, however, is that Mamoulian—in thought and practice—was prominently engaged in the vital process of defining sound cinema aesthetics in the late 1920s and early 1930s. The conclusions he reached offered an early model for an industry wrestling with the fundamental question of how sound cinema should look and sound.

Sound Technologies, Representational Assumptions, and Mamoulian

From the beginning, Mamoulian's career in filmmaking was tied closely to sound. In the late 1920s, the American film industry—mindful of the massive profits reaped by early synchronized "all-talking" films like *The Lights of New York* (July 1928) and part-talkies like *The Singing Fool* (September 1928)—looked to the stage for personnel and properties. In Long Island, Paramount reopened their Astoria studio specifically to take advantage of Broadway talent.[2] Mamoulian was among Astoria's acquisitions.

The contract Mamoulian eventually struck with Paramount apparently allowed him to direct one film as soon as he felt he had learned enough by observing filmmaking on the Astoria lot.[3] According to Mamoulian, after only five weeks of watching films being made and peppering film technicians with "silly questions" about cinema technology, Mamoulian—who always fancied himself a quick study—surprised Paramount by declaring himself ready to direct his feature film.[4] Mamoulian's diaries affirm this basic timeline, though Mamoulian may have slightly exaggerated the brevity of his training at Astoria. Diary entries show Mamoulian taking trips to Astoria as early as January 24, 1929, and evidence of his work on *Applause* does not appear until April of that year.[5] This would be a period longer than five weeks, though Mamoulian did spend all of February rehearsing for his upcoming stage production of *The Game of Love and Death* and presumably had little time for Astoria in that month. Regardless, Paramount apparently honored the agreement, because by June 1929, Mamoulian—after working together with Garrett Fort on the screenplay—began shooting *Applause*.

When Mamoulian visited Astoria in early 1929, he witnessed a form of filmmaking that was substantially affected both by available technologies and by assumptions about what sound cinema should offer. Filmmakers generally used a condenser microphone to record dialogue on the set, a largely omnidirectional device that easily picked up stray noises, including the whirring of the motion picture camera.[6] When Mamoulian began his visits, filmmakers were already experimenting with wrapping the camera in soundproof materials, but the prevailing method—and the one apparently used at Astoria—was to soundproof the camera by placing it inside a large booth with a single glass wall through which the camera could shoot scenes.[7] The substantial weight of the booth made camera movements—outside of the mild pans and tilts that the glass wall would allow—far more difficult than had been the case in the silent era.[8]

An added issue for filmmakers in 1929 was the difficulty of editing together multiple strips of sound onto a single soundtrack. At Warner Bros. in Hollywood, technicians had devised a method for sound-on-disc editing whereby sound information from as many as eight different records could be re-recorded together during post-production to yield a single, composite track.[9] Though such a method was apparently regularly used at Warner Bros.,[10] the other studios—including Paramount—were far more reluctant to re-record soundtracks in post-production, at least partly because of the loss in audio quality that occurred. There is evidence that Paramount engaged in some degree of re-recording, but as Lea Jacobs has noted, Paramount—along with RKO and MGM—did not seem to view it as an important element of post-production.[11] With sound editing difficult, many filmmakers in 1929 chose multiple-camera shooting, in which filmmakers used more than one camera at a time (often between two and six) to film a scene. These cameras would run while lined up side by side, with various focal-length lenses used to replicate the close- and long-range shots that characterized late silent-era scene dissections.[12] The scene would be shot all in one take, and the single soundtrack the filmmakers obtained would be, in John Belton's words, the "measure against which the image was assembled" using footage from the various cameras in the post-production editing room.[13] Though multiple-camera shooting resulted in a lot of unused film stock, the technique prevented filmmakers from having to edit the soundtrack, thus making it easier for the series of shots that constituted a scene to remain synchronized with the soundtrack during post-production.

For a variety of reasons, these technological factors resulted in a substantial reduction of camera and character movement when dialogue was recorded on the set. Not only did the use of booth-enclosed multiple-camera shooting substantially limit camera movement, but the nature of the microphone made character movement more challenging as well. The fact that the microphone was omnidirectional meant that an actor generally needed to stand close to the microphone to ensure that dialogue would be intelligible.[14] Microphones were also relatively immobile—they were quite heavy in 1929, and while makeshift "boom" mics appear to have been utilized on occasion, they would not enjoy regular usage until 1930.[15] Thus, if dialogue was to be heard from multiple spaces within the frame, technicians commonly hung multiple microphones above the frame line (or sometimes hid them in props). Characters might walk around the set *between* their lines of dialogue, but if they moved while they were speaking, filmmakers risked creating a vocal record that would fade in and out to a degree they felt was unacceptable.[16]

Such a technological situation was formable for filmmakers wishing to tell vibrant and engaging stories, but these restrictions did not, by themselves, *mandate* the period's sizable reduction of movement. In theory, a scene could be shot silent, with sound recorded at another time added later. For such an approach, a filmmaker might use what Rick Altman has called "semi-sync" sound, which refers to sound—such as generalized crowd noise—that appears to emerge from the space of the scene but contains no salient visual "sync point" to match particular sounds.[17] The option of shooting without sound (also known as shooting "wild") was not a secret. It can be found in films from 1926 onward featuring music and sound effects only. Once the industry moved to synchronized dialogue, shooting wild so as to retain character or camera movement was common knowledge, possible especially when there was no dialogue or when the speaking character's lips could not be easily seen. A big advantage of this method in the earliest sound years was that no on-set microphone was needed to record the sound, thus enabling characters and camera to be more mobile.

Yet despite this advantage, in nearly all extant films marketed as "all-talking" in 1928 and 1929, the vast majority of shots and scenes feature directly recorded dialogue, with semi-sync sound often used intermittently as only a one-shot flourish. In single shots from *In Old Arizona* (January 1929) and *The Letter* (March 1929), for instance, semi-sync hubbub accompanies a camera that tracks a short distance through a barroom, yet such moments serve as only brief respites from the visually static, directly recorded dialogue that soon follows. Such shots in *The Letter* and *In Old Arizona*—as well as in many other pre-*Applause* films— also contain no narrative development; they serve instead as establishing shots before an ensuing series of images conveys the story largely through directly recorded dialogue. In some instances, shots or scenes filmed wild are a bit more central to a sound film, such as certain outdoor gags in Laurel and Hardy's 1929 short films or the use of post-synchronization for musical numbers like "The Wedding of the Painted Doll" in *The Broadway Melody* (February 1929) or "Turn On the Heat" in *Sunny Side Up* (October 1929).[18] Yet even in these films, the overwhelming majority of the film's running time features directly recorded sound.

The industry's reluctance to offer extensive semi-sync sound in full-talking films likely stemmed from its belief that to justify the introduction of sound, filmmakers needed to frequently display the technology's ability to record sound directly and play it in synchronization with the image. There is also substantial evidence that the industry saw sound cinema as being more closely connected to theater, a form where spectators remained fixed in their seats and viewed entire scenes in real time.[19] Warner Bros. initially conceptualized synchronized sound film as a substitution for the live onstage performances that preceded feature-length films in many large theaters in the United States, and by 1929, Hollywood was rushing to produce cinematic versions of Broadway stage properties.[20] It also bears mentioning that smash hits like *The Lights of New York* and *The Singing Fool* were relatively static affairs, and they may have suggested to other filmmakers that the lack of movement in the films was permissible to audiences.

Still, "all-talking" films had been produced for less than a year when Mamoulian began directing *Applause*, so the use of direct sound with relatively little camera or character movement was common but hardly set in stone. What was a sound film? What should it look like? What should it sound like? The possibilities were vast, and sound cinema's definition remained in question.

As Richard Koszarski notes, Paramount appears to have hired Mamoulian, already known as a flashy Broadway talent, partly in the hopes that he would help take sound cinema *away* from static filmmaking, a desire that was likely communicated to Mamoulian.[21] Even if Paramount had not been looking for an innovator, however, Mamoulian's theoretical orientation all but mandated that he push cinema in a different direction. As chapter 1 discussed, Mamoulian was a fervent believer in medium specificity, and he felt strongly that a medium's essential tools should be manipulated to express story ideas. Thus, when he entered his first film studio, Mamoulian was excited by the opportunity not to reproduce plays on the screen using multiple-camera shooting (thus resulting in a "third rate carbon-copy of a stage play," as he would later put it[22]), but to explore cinema-specific devices. This, for Mamoulian, included not just camerawork, but also microphone placement, background music, sound effects, and sound editing. Sonically as well as visually, Mamoulian sought a style that would emphasize what film could do that theater could not, and a style that would also aid the story being told.

The repercussions of this goal were considerable. As Donald Crafton has pointed out, the prevailing conception of film as a vessel for theater plays in 1929 assumed that sound cinema was only "a medium, not an art in its own right."[23] By aiming to saliently present cinema-specific techniques, Mamoulian was instead offering an approach that positioned sound cinema as a distinct artistic form. But how, exactly, could Mamoulian mold his first sound film into a stylized, narratively expressive piece of cinema?

Cinematography and Sound: To Semi-Sync or Not to Semi-Sync?

Among the more anomalous features of *Applause* is the sheer quantity of shots and scenes featuring semi-sync sound. One of the only extant "all-talking" films from 1928–1929 that exceeded *Applause* in this regard was King Vidor's *Hallelujah!* (August 1929), which was not released until after *Applause* was filmed. Due to a delay in outdoor recording equipment, Vidor opted to shoot the film's numerous exterior scenes silent, which enabled an unusual degree of camera and character movement for a film from this period.[24] *Applause*, however, appears to have been planned from the beginning to feature many shots and scenes with semi-sync sound, and Mamoulian used these instances to consistently attain a level of visual expressivity more akin to the late silent era than the early sound years. For instance, the opening scene from *Applause*—which was shot outdoors on the Astoria back lot[25] and depicts the arrival of Kitty and her troupe at a Midwestern town—was shot silent, despite the presence of musical instruments in the scene. To direct the audience's attention away from prominent sync points that would give away the shooting method, Mamoulian began the scene by training his camera not on the arriving band—whose distant sound gets progressively louder—but on trash drifting in the breeze and mobs of townspeople rushing toward the (offscreen) sound of the band. Never stationary, the camera pans and sometimes tracks during the opening eight shots, often to follow the blowing trash. Because no precise synchronization was needed, Mamoulian could point the camera anywhere he wished and move it in any manner he felt was narratively relevant. Here, he uses semi-sync as an opportunity to immediately condemn burlesque by tying it to trash and the herd-like mentality of the masses.

Other scenes similarly showcase Mamoulian's effort to harness semi-sync sequences to expressive visuals. When April must travel from her sheltered convent life in Wisconsin to the bustle of New York City, Mamoulian's semi-sync shooting enables his camera to *show* her dialogue-free journey, which includes the convent's interior and exterior, as well as her shot-on-location arrival at New York City's busy Pennsylvania Station, her efforts to hail a cab, the cab ride itself, and her arrival at her mother's hotel. Due to the difficulties of location shooting, a dialogue-heavy direct-sound sequence in this period likely would have conveyed this information by having characters *talk* about the journey while standing in a single space. By instead opting for a semi-sync approach, Mamoulian could place his camera in a variety of locations along the journey, thereby emphasizing the geographic distance between Wisconsin and New York City, the burden of having to travel between them, and April's sense of culture shock when she arrives in the chaotic, bustling metropolis. Mamoulian was certainly not the only filmmaker aware of semi-sync's possibilities, but his use of semi-sync in *Applause* is remarkably frequent and adept. In these and other scenes, Mamoulian employed semi-sync not as a quick flourish or for a single musical number, but rather as a lengthy opportunity for framing, camera movement, and a multitude of spaces to convey key ideas about the story.

Direct Sound and Camera Movement

Even an iconoclast like Mamoulian could not get away with shooting an entire "all-talking" film with semi-sync sound, however. The bulk of *Applause* still features directly recorded, dialogue-driven sound. On occasion in these scenes—such as the segment when April introduces Tony to her mother—Mamoulian *did* use the static, multiple-camera shooting method he wished to avoid.[26] Far more commonly, however, Mamoulian broke from conventional practice by shooting directly recorded dialogue scenes with only a single camera, and that camera typically moves at least once during the scene.

In the context of 1929, the nature of *Applause*'s camera movement during direct-dialogue sequences may be its most unusual visual feature. It received considerable attention at the time, and it has been the subject of critical commentary in more recent decades.[27] Still, it is important to clarify what would have made the movements stand out. As Patrick Keating has detailed, the popularity of the German films *The Last Laugh* (1924) and *Variety* (1925) initiated a vogue for camera movement—both flashy and subtle—in US silent films of the late 1920s.[28] Extant films indicate, however, that once synchronized sound arrived, the camera was almost always stationary during directly recorded dialogue shots in late 1928 and the first few months of 1929. Shots filmed *without* sound were another matter—bravura camera moves continued to be used for "wild" shots in 1929. In the part-talkie *The Shakedown* (March 1929), for instance, William Wyler mounted the camera on an industry crane as the protagonist is raised and later lowered to the ground, while Paul Fejos's *Broadway* (May 1929) features swooping camera moves courtesy of Universal's enormous—and just-built—crane.[29] For direct-sound shots, however, the camera was nearly always stationary in the earliest months of sync-sound shooting. Prominent films containing a total absence of tracking movements during direct-sound shots include *The Lights of New York*, *The Singing Fool*, *The Canary Murder Case* (February 1929), *The Letter*, and even *The Wild Party* (March 1929), which is sometimes credited with an early use of the boom mic.[30] At best, the camera might sneak forward or back by a mere foot or two—as is the case during a directly recorded dialogue scene late in *In Old Arizona*—but this appears to have been quite rare during a sync-sound shot.

By May 1929, however—one month before *Applause* started shooting—one sees evidence that this situation was slowly beginning to change. In *The Cocoanuts* (May 1929)—also filmed at Paramount's Astoria studio—cinematographer George Folsey, who later shot *Applause*, tracks inward twice (from long shot to medium-long shot, and then to medium shot) to reframe a dialogue scene between miscreants Penelope (Kay Francis) and Harvey (Cyril Ring). In the following scene, Folsey again tracks forward—this time from long shot to medium shot—during a directly recorded conversation and song by lovers Polly (Mary Eaton) and Bob (Oscar Shaw). In *The Last of Mrs. Cheyney* (July 1929), the camera rolls a greater distance—around fifteen to twenty-five feet—during two directly recorded dialogue scenes to move from extreme long shot to medium-shot framing.[31] By *Applause*'s premiere in October, the camera was loosening further, with prominent direct-sound examples occurring in such major releases as *Marianne* (September 1929), *Rio Rita* (September 1929), *Disraeli* (October 1929), and *Sunny Side Up* (October 1929). The last-named film is especially notable for its opening direct-sound shot, which tracks and cranes around a New York City tenement block as the soundtrack captures the generalized cacophony of the street along with individual on-screen voices and sounds in a variety of spaces.

Mamoulian was thus not the only one interested in moving the camera movement in 1929. Still, extant films indicate that *Applause*'s sync-sound camera movements would have stood out in at least four respects: the moving camera's *proximity* to the speaking characters, the *frequency* of its movements, the persistent narrative *expressivity* of its movements, and the narrative *patterning* of these movements across the larger film.

A useful starting point for examining these features is the lullaby scene between April and Kitty, which Mamoulian would later highlight in interviews. As I discuss in a later section, it is likely that some of the mother's singing in this scene was obtained at another time, but the dialogue itself was plainly recorded on the set. In this scene, April, who feels psychologically shattered after seeing her mother perform on the burlesque stage, is eventually soothed to sleep in her bed by Kitty, who sings her a song. Rather than deploying multiple cameras for the directly recorded five-minute conversation, Mamoulian used only a single camera in one long take, with the camera periodically tracking toward and away from the characters. At the beginning of the shot (Figure 2.1), April's early acknowledgment that she feels "funny . . . all mixed up inside" causes Kitty to sit down near April on the bed, and the camera, which begins in extreme long shot, slowly tracks inward for twenty-five seconds before resting on a medium close-up that frames the duo (Figure 2.2). After staying in place for over a minute, the camera moves even further inward to a close-up as mother and daughter hug, their faces pressed together (Figure 2.3). April then reclines in bed after the embrace, and the camera tracks backward again to a medium shot as Kitty begins singing her song (Figure 2.4). April starts praying while Kitty continues to sing, and Mamoulian tracks forward once more to a close-up of April's face (Figure 2.5). Upon the completion of her prayer, the camera executes its final trackback, eventually resting on a long shot of Kitty and April in the foreground and Kitty's boyfriend's looming shadow in the background (Figure 2.6).

62 DEFINING CINEMA

Figure 2.1 In/out camera movements (and re-recording) during a directly recorded dialogue scene in *Applause*. The camera begins in extreme long shot as Kitty stands at the dresser and sings a song that was likely recorded at a different time. . . .

Figure 2.2 The camera tracks inward to a medium close-up as Kitty and April converse in a directly recorded conversation . . .

Figure 2.3 ... and then further inward to an intimate close-up, which continues to feature directly recorded dialogue....

Late in life, Mamoulian began asserting that he was personally responsible for two "firsts" in this scene: the first to use a tracking shot in a sound film, and the first to put wheels on the soundproof bungalow that housed the camera.[32] Both claims are false: even the earliest soundproof booths—including those at Astoria—already came mounted on wheels so that the booth could be moved *between* shots,[33] and as we saw, direct-sound camera movements occurred prior to *Applause*, including in Astoria's own *The Cocoanuts*. Still, the shot stands out for the distance the camera travels and how close it gets to the characters in a direct-sound shot. Whereas cameras generally moved very little in direct-dialogue sequences prior to *Applause*—a long shot to a medium-long shot, for instance—Mamoulian's camera in the lullaby scene at one point moves from a long shot to a close-up of only April's face.

Merely on a technical level, moving the camera so close to the actors was notable. Not only did it require a careful pulling of focus, but there was a substantial risk that the microphone would record the camera noise, since noise from even semi-silenced cameras could be picked up by microphones located ten feet away (careful ears can, in fact, detect multiple clanks when the camera is moving close to April's face).[34] Probably more significant, however, is Mamoulian's determination

Figure 2.4. The camera tracks back to a medium shot as Kitty begins to sing, part of which appears to have been recorded later. . . .

to make his moving camera an expressive player during directly recorded dialogue by closely coordinating camera movement with the scene's emotional flow and focus. April and Kitty's interaction begins casually and is accompanied by the more impersonal long shot (Figure 2.1). At the precise moment when April begins describing her emotions and Kitty becomes concerned, the camera denotes this shift by moving to a more intimate framing, eventually resting on a close-up of the characters' faces (Figure 2.3). Later, Mamoulian trains the camera on only April's face, thus centering attention on the driving force behind the scene: April, her fears, and her feelings about the burlesque world her mother inhabits (Figure 2.5). Then, when April finally falls asleep, Mamoulian's final track back redirects our attention to the outside world that troubles her, an idea enhanced by the exploitive Hitch's shadow, which appears at the conclusion of the shot (Figure 2.6).

Through these in-and-out movements, Mamoulian's camera expresses both the intimacy of the moment and the characters' vulnerability to their surrounding environment. Though such an expressive function may seem unremarkable today, moving-camera shots in direct-dialogue scenes seldom correlated with narrative ideas in such clear terms. Films contemporaneous with *Applause*—such as *Marianne*, *Disraeli*, and *Rio Rita*—generally use

Figure 2.5. The camera then tracks forward to another close-up as April murmurs a prayer while her mother sings offscreen, with volume levels adjusted in post-production to match each other....

camera movements to reframe characters or provide slow track-ins or -outs from considerable distances, with little apparent coordination with the emotional beats of the scene. Occasionally, more expressive camera movements in sync-sound dialogue sequences do crop up, suggesting that Mamoulian was not alone in seeking to regain this quality in sync-sound shots. Two different scenes from *The Last of Mrs. Cheyney*, for instance, harness camera movement to characters' psychological shifts. Midway through the film, jewel chief Cheyney (Norma Shearer) waffles over whether to proceed with a planned heist, and two lengthy tracking movements correspond precisely to her reversals in decision. Then, in the film's final scene, director Sidney Franklin—who had skated across a set while holding a camera for a bravura moving camera shot two years earlier in the silent film *Quality Street* (1927)—uses camera movement to accompany the uniting of lovers: as they talk and move closer together, the camera slowly tracks inward to further accentuate the couple's growing physical closeness.[35] Such timing of camera movement to the emotional shifts in a direct-sound shot, however, appears to have been very uncommon in the late 1920s.

Figure 2.6. The five-minute shot concludes by tracking back again, with Hitch's shadow conveying the dangers of the outside world.

Not only does Mamoulian use overtly expressive camera movement, but he also *patterns* such camera movements across *Applause*'s entire running time. Every film released prior to *Applause* that I have consulted uses a static camera for the vast majority of its direct-dialogue shots, thereby making any moving-camera patterning impractical. *Applause*, in contrast, frequently and consistently weaves camera movements into the emotional ideas and themes of the larger film. The inward-then-outward camera movements found in the lullaby scene, for instance, are regularly reused throughout the film to reflect the efforts of the film's central characters—April, Tony, and Kitty—to forge a space of closeness and comfort within a harsh and unfeeling outside world. With one possible exception, all are direct-sound shots. In an early scene, Mamoulian conveys the emotional stakes behind Kitty's decision to send five-year-old April to a convent for her protection by tracking in on Kitty and April (this shot was probably shot silent, as the frame line is below Kitty's mouth when she starts speaking) before cutting and then tracking back in a direct-sound shot of a nun speaking to April at the convent. These two shots show parallel images of love and nurture, thereby articulating the maternal concern that drives Kitty's decision. One shot later, a direct-sound shot shows the deteriorated Kitty lying on the floor, singing, and taking comfort in a letter written by April. Mamoulian tracks in toward Kitty and then—after an insert shot of the letter—tracks back outward. Well after the lullaby scene, when April decides to break up with Tony to save her mother, Mamoulian tracks in to Kitty and April as they embrace during their direct-dialogue scene, followed by a track back when April tells Kitty she will "fix it up" with Tony. Mamoulian patterns April's hopeful relationship with Tony with similar track in/track out shots during direct-sound moments, including their conversation on the Brooklyn Bridge and their embrace in the film's final shot (Figure 1.6).

It seems likely that Mamoulian, who greatly admired *The Last Laugh*, was aiming to return cinema to its more fluid late silent-era phase. Still, within the context of mid 1929, *Applause* was exceptional for demonstrating the narrative power of camera movement during directly recorded dialogue shots. Believing the camera to be a defining element of cinema itself, Mamoulian laid down a key idea at an early date: that direct-sound shots—major selling points for sound film—could also regularly utilize camera movements to enhance narrative emotions and ideas. Thus, a filmmaker could simultaneously satisfy the audience's appetite for direct sound *and* retain late silent-era visual expressivity and artistry. In laying down this principle, Mamoulian was vigorously probing the basic potentials of sound cinema itself.

Sound Theory and *Applause*

Advanced publicity for *Applause* trumpeted Mamoulian's camera movements.[36] Sound techniques were far less frequently noted.[37] *Applause*'s use of sound, however, was arguably more unusual than its visual strategies. Mamoulian's extensive sync-sound camera movements at least resonated with those in the late silent era. For sound, however, Mamoulian had no clear proximate model to draw upon. Mamoulian did not wish to replicate stage sound, and there is little evidence to suggest that Mamoulian drew from the aesthetics of phonograph recordings or the nascent medium of radio. Instead, Mamoulian found his approach by applying his broad notions of artistry to the particular problem of film sound. To understand how this worked, we must turn briefly to Mamoulian's writings on sound, which reveal a director who was quite sensitive to sound's expressive possibilities.

The clearest articulation of Mamoulian's sound theory can be found in an unpublished two-part position paper he wrote in 1938 following the shooting of *High, Wide and Handsome*. The first paper, discussed briefly in chapter 1, is a philosophical treatise on artistry and the reasons why, in Mamoulian's view, an artist should favor stylization over realism. As we saw, Mamoulian differentiated between a scientist, who aims to state facts in an impersonal manner, with an artist, who should strive to transform facts so as to express his or her viewpoint on the subject matter.[38] Mamoulian's second paper—titled "The Psychology of Sound"—uses this framework to consider an artist's role with respect to film sound. If an artist, Mamoulian argued, seeks to transform rather than reproduce, the artist's job is "to select, to organize, [and] to sharpen" any element that can be used to express ideas.[39] To determine how this general philosophy applied to film sound, Mamoulian drew a contrast between human ears and a microphone. Ears, Mamoulian asserted, are highly critical and selective instruments: they decide what to attend to versus what to merely hear. The microphone, in contrast, picks up sounds indiscriminately. Thus, since the microphone is an impersonal instrument more akin to science, a true film artist must, in essence, transform the microphone into a critical device akin to the human ear by consciously *selecting* the components of the soundtrack for the audience member.[40]

In truth, Mamoulian's claims about the microphone were not fully accurate. Microphones *are* selective instruments—they record only certain sound waves—and by the early 1930s, the rise of directional microphones had made them more selective still. But Mamoulian was not aiming at a theory of technology. Rather, his point was that microphones (outside of their recording capabilities) make no decisions; they collect rather than organize. To Mamoulian, it was thus incumbent upon the film artist to perform the essential tasks of selection and manipulation. "No matter what the natural sounds of a scene may be," Mamoulian argued in "The Psychology of Sound," "it is up to [film artists] to select them—to subdue, eliminate, exaggerate, and otherwise distort these sounds, in complete defiance of Nature."[41] Any noise that one takes for granted in life, Mamoulian argued, should not be present in film at all. Each sound should instead be chosen with rigorous care to convey the emotional implication and mood of the scene. In short, film sound should not be a casual or accidental capturing of reality. Rather, as in art in general, "everything should be done according to a consciously controlled artistic and dynamic pattern."[42] As with stylization in general, Mamoulian felt that for film sound, "the more completely and successfully an artist battles realism, the more real will be the result to the audience spectator."[43]

It would be difficult to overstate how strongly at odds with the mainstream this philosophy would have been when Mamoulian made *Applause* in 1929. During the earliest years of synchronized sound, many films open with precisely what Mamoulian rails against: the presentation of a wide range of noises that showcases the technology's ability to capture and reproduce sounds irrespective of any expressive function within the story. Such stretches are often narrative-less and centered on the sounds of a particular space, from the din of Tin Pan Alley (*The Broadway Melody* [February 1929]) or the New York City streets (*Sunny Side Up*), to the western frontier (*The Virginian* [November 1929], *The Big Trail* [October 1930]). Many films also dwell on the presentation of accents and stuttering, even when irrelevant to the story. Song plugging—the repetition of a song to drum up sheet music sales—often takes priority over narrative coherence.[44] Crafton has pointed to the 1928–1929 season, in particular, as insistently featuring a " 'you can't miss this!' approach to sound."[45] Film sound in the earliest years often seemed less about being integrated expressively into a formal system of meaning, and more about offering noises as discrete, unaltered attractions.

Mamoulian wrote "The Psychology of Sound" in 1938, when filmmaking had drifted away from such approaches, and one might be tempted to argue that his essay reflected this shift. Mamoulian's sound work in *Applause*, however, hews closely to the principles he would later lay out. Whether tackling foreground dialogue or background environmental sounds, Mamoulian's focus was on the *expressive construction* of the soundtrack, with every element functioning as an artistic tool that Mamoulian could select, alter, and manipulate to better narrate the story. In doing so, Mamoulian was defining a sound filmmaker as an artist who creates and expresses, rather than a fieldworker who documents existing sounds or a showman who presents them as discreet attractions.

This conception of the soundtrack—and filmmakers' relationship to it—would anticipate the film industry's increased interest in treating the soundtrack as a constructed entity as the 1930s progressed.[46] As the next four sections—which focus on foreground and background sound—demonstrate, *Applause* regularly displays Mamoulian's commitment to expressive construction at a time when few US filmmakers were heavily prioritizing it.

The Foreground Voice and Sound Construction

We can begin to recognize how Mamoulian expressively manipulated sound in *Applause* by considering his handling of foreground voices. In general, Mamoulian's approach in this domain was conventional for 1929, as he appears to have simply used on-set vocal recordings with minimal post-production manipulation. One key scene, however, deviates sharply from this tendency, and it indicates the lengths Mamoulian could go to in order to provide expressive sound. That scene is—once again—April and Kitty's five-minute lullaby sequence. The sonically expressive moment occurs near the conclusion of the scene. Kitty sings and hums a lullaby version of a burlesque number she performed in the prior scene—"Give Your Little Baby Lots of Lovin' " (by Joseph A. Burke and Dolly Morse)—while April simultaneously murmurs a prayer to help herself fall asleep.

The idea of overlapping these two voices on the soundtrack was almost certainly Mamoulian's—it appears not in the typed script but in Mamoulian's handwritten annotation in his copy of the screenplay.[47] Overlapping voices were not especially unusual in 1929, but the method used for obtaining and reproducing them *was* significant. Ordinarily, a 1929 sound technician tasked with miking two physically close speaking characters would hang a single microphone above the actors. Such a setup, however, would have caused Kitty's singing to overwhelm April's murmured prayer, an unacceptable result to Mamoulian's mind. For Mamoulian, the voices needed to be heard at the same volume level so as to express the larger clash between the burlesque and convent worlds that the film dramatizes.

To attain equal volume levels, Mamoulian would later claim to have used a method that, as best I can tell, was similar—but not identical—to what was actually used. By Mamoulian's account, two microphones were used on the set: one near Kitty for her singing, and one under April's pillow as she prays.[48] The two microphones, according to Mamoulian, recorded onto two different tracks (that is, onto two different strips of sound film). These two tracks were then re-recorded together onto a single strip in post-production, with the volume of April's prayer raised to the same volume level as Kitty's song.[49]

The omnidirectional nature of 1929 microphones, however, likely would have made such an on-set arrangement impossible.[50] Kitty sits very close to April for much of the scene (Figure 2.4), including when April prays, making it doubtful that microphones could have isolated Kitty or April's voices. Multiple tracks *do* appear to have been used, however, as one can detect an increase in ground noise as April prays and a simultaneous reduction in the volume level of Kitty's singing. Moreover, at least one track was surely recorded live, since the clanks of the moving camera bungalow can be heard on a few occasions. It thus seems mostly likely that April's prayer and much of Kitty's spoken dialogue were recorded on the set, while most of Kitty's singing was recorded either beforehand or afterward. The camera's proximity to April as she prays necessitates tight lip synchronization that would be difficult unless miked live, and at one point in the conversation, Helen Morgan—who plays Kitty—accidentally interrupts the nearby April and must repeat her line, which could have occurred only if both actresses were recorded live at that moment. For her humming and singing, however, Kitty is frequently off camera, and when she is visible, her humming does not require lip synchronization (Figure 2.5). If Kitty's humming/singing was, indeed, recorded at a different time, this opens up the possibility that the beginning of the scene—which features Kitty singing in near darkness across the room from April and being interrupted by April—also used re-recorded vocal tracks (Figure 2.1).

Whether or not both microphones were located on the set, the most historically significant aspect was not—as Mamoulian would later assert—the mere fact that he used two microphones to record two different voices.[51] A number of films prior to *Applause* feature characters who speak too far away from each other for a single omnidirectional microphone to catch their words, making it all but certain that multiple microphones were hung to catch their dialogue.[52] Re-recording was also not, as I have indicated, entirely new.[53] The scene's originality stems instead from Mamoulian's decision to use *separate* dialogue tracks, re-record those tracks in post-production, and *expressively adjust* their volume levels. As Lea Jacobs has demonstrated, studios in the early sound era shied away from re-recording dialogue because they feared that the re-recording process would ruin its intelligibility.[54] Filmmakers also generally avoided raising the volume level of an already recorded track in post-production because doing so often noticeably increased ground and surface noise.[55]

The simple decision to record voices on separate tracks may seem like a mere technical matter, but it has broad ramifications for a filmmaker's role with respect to recorded sound. In June 1929, when Mamoulian opted to use two microphones, the expectation would have been that he would mix both microphones onto the same track during shooting, with technicians determining the microphones' volume levels prior to filming the scene. Yet on-set sound mixing lacked precision. Once the information from two microphones was recorded onto a single soundtrack, a filmmaker could not separate back out sound from the two microphones to further adjust volume levels.[56] Mamoulian instead pushed for the method that would give him the most control in post-production, and therein lies a key assumption about film sound's potential. *Through two-channel recording, Mamoulian was conceptualizing directly recorded sound—including dialogue—as an object for filmmaker manipulation.* As commonsensical as this notion may seem in filmmaking today, in 1929—and indeed, for a number of years afterward—filmmakers regularly prioritized (and even showcased) the apparatuses' ability to *faithfully reproduce* the sound record of a given space. Jacobs notes that as late as 1932, the industry felt strongly that the volume levels of on-set dialogue shouldn't be tampered with in post-production, and not until the mid-1930s did the re-recording of dialogue become commonplace.[57]

Also crucial to this recording method is Mamoulian's prioritization of what he saw as the unique properties of cinema. Part of what appealed to Mamoulian about raising April's voice to Kitty's level was that he *couldn't* do it in a medium like the theater, where Kitty's onstage singing would have drowned out April's near whisper.[58] The scene further separates itself from the stage through Mamoulian's decision to raise the volume level of April's voice in coordination with the camera's in/out movements. April's prayer occurs when the camera has moved quite close to April, eventually resting on a close-up of only her (Figure 2.5). The elevated volume of April's voice thus adheres to the auditory perspective of the camera, a coordination of sound and image that only cinema could provide. Moreover, re-recording itself, as Jacobs has pointed out, was in the late 1920s distinctive to cinema.[59] The scene thus stands as an early testament to Mamoulian's belief that cinema-specific image *and* sound manipulation should work hand in hand to accentuate vital aspects of story and character.

Warped Sound: The Music of Burlesque

Mamoulian's handling of his actors' voices in the lullaby scene reflected his belief that sound should be expressively manipulated rather than faithfully reproduced. A similar attitude prevails in Mamoulian's handling of background or environmental sound, which I am defining here as the sounds heard in a character's surroundings other than foreground dialogue (such as sound effects, diegetic music, and background hubbub). For Mamoulian, background sound, too, was a tool for expressive selection and modification. Unlike the foreground voice, however, Mamoulian expressively manipulated background sound for the near entirety of *Applause*.

For the larger industry in the late 1920s and early 1930s, how to handle background sound appears to have been among the most unsettled of aesthetic questions. Films from these years generally display a dizzying—and often inconsistent—array of decisions surrounding the basic question of whether to provide background sound at all. Depending on the film—or even particular shots within a single scene—one finds everything from the inclusion of apparently every background sound to a complete absence of background noise, even when sound-producing elements appear clearly in the background of a shot. Though seemingly every possible conceptualization of background sound can be found in this period, probably the most frequent is what Rick Altman has called the on/off switch approach, in which some element—such as an open versus closed door, or an onscreen versus offscreen producer of sound—dictates the presence or absent of background sound. A closed door might eliminate loud music entirely—as it does repeatedly in *The Lights of New York*—or nearby sounds might be heard only when visible in the frame, as is frequently the case for *The Big Trail*.[60] Even in these instances, however, inconsistency remained the norm, with rules seemingly established in one shot or scene quickly jettisoned in the following shot or scene.

In *Applause*, Mamoulian's spatial rule for handling background sound *is* fairly consistent, and it falls under what we might call perceptual realism, a fairly uncommon approach in the late 1920s. In general, Mamoulian provides background sounds whenever they could plausibly be heard, regardless of their onscreen visibility. Moreover, as Lucy Fischer has pointed out, he consistently adjusts volume and reverberation levels in accordance with the distance between camera and sound source (an approach that may have also made use of re-recording).[61] Such an approach might appear merely naturalistic, but it gave Mamoulian the opportunity to (1) *select* sounds that would be especially expressive and (2) expressively *manipulate* these sounds if their distance from the camera might plausibly result in sonic distortion.

A quick consideration of *Applause*'s background burlesque music reveals how Mamoulian tied perceptual realism to his expressive aims. *Applause*'s numerous scenes set inside burlesque houses feature the constant sounds of onstage burlesque performances. This includes scenes taking place in the wings of the stage and the theater's dressing rooms. Mamoulian paid particular attention to the presence of music in such spaces, often writing the letter "M" with a circle around it (denoting music) in the margins of his screenplay for *Applause*, along with the song name and when—and for how long—the song should be heard.[62] Such music's prevalence, alone, conveys the sense that burlesque indelibly molds every facet of its central characters' lives, but Mamoulian also uses the reverberant nature of these spaces to transform burlesque music into grotesque noise.[63] Early in *Applause*, when the chorus line files into Kitty's dressing room to visit Kitty and the newborn April, Mamoulian offers an onstage rendition of Irving Berlin's "Turkey Trot" that is so reverberant that the singer sounds as if she is shouting or even barking the lyrics. It is this extraordinarily "bad," ear-ringing music that hangs over April and Kitty in this scene, and it establishes in vivid terms their relationship to burlesque. Later in the film, when the grown April watches the conclusion of her mother's burlesque performance from backstage in dismay, Mamoulian again uses a high level of reverberation. Here, because the song—Art Fitch, Kay Fitch, and Bert Lowe's "Doin' the Raccoon"—is performed so quickly and with a balance level favoring the instrumental accompaniment, the reverberation warps the performance into a jumbled mess of unintelligible and nearly tuneless singing. In both scenes, sonic distortion helps present burlesque as an overbearing presence for the female performers who toil within it. By consistently allowing offscreen music to bleed into backstage shots of Kitty and April, Mamoulian uses background sound and distortion as expressive elements at a time when most filmmakers were grappling simply with whether to use background sound at all.

Cacophony and Quietude: Selective On-Location Sound

Just how strongly Mamoulian prioritized selective, constructed, and narratively expressive environmental sound can be further gleaned by examining scenes from *Applause* shot—at least partly—on location in urban New York City. Because shooting direct-sound scenes in urban space in 1929 was technically difficult and extremely rare,[64] Mamoulian would have felt considerable pressure to showcase the technology's ability to merely capture and present these new sounds. Moreover, location sound often involved less control over the soundtrack thanks to unpredictable environmental factors and the hazards of omnidirectional microphones, making the use of expressive sound more difficult.

Applause's location scenes do show off the technology's capabilities to a certain degree, but Mamoulian also labored to select and emphasize only the most narratively meaningful sounds. Mamoulian's decision to shoot April's journey from Wisconsin to New York City using semi-sync sound, for instance, enabled him to choose expressive sounds throughout the spaces of her voyage. A diegetic organ and choral version of Franz Schubert's "Ave Maria" (a song selection that Mamoulian's screenplay indicates was his[65]) plays as April walks through the Wisconsin monastery hallway and its outdoor grounds. To express the jolt April experiences upon her New York City arrival, Mamoulian cuts away from the monastery grounds on what would have been the downbeat of a measure to an image of April disembarking in New York City at Pennsylvania Station. Instead of hearing the downbeat, Mamoulian provides the loud sound of steam escaping as April's train comes to a stop. "Sound of trains," Mamoulian wrote into the margin of the screenplay at this moment,[66] but this noise is only the start of what is to come. A constant muffled roar—likely attained by on-location sound recording at Pennsylvania Station—accompanies Mamoulian's hidden-camera footage of April inside this station. Once April steps outside the station (in a segment again shot on location), a loud horn honk startles the viewer, an effect heightened by the fact that Mamoulian cuts to our first image of a car just as this sharp honk is heard. It is as if we, as audience members, are asked to get out of the way of a car we hadn't seen. Mamoulian then provides a veritable symphony of angry, blaring car horns as we watch April trying to secure a taxi. These honks, along with the loud squeal of brakes and roaring motors, persist until April arrives at her mother's hotel, making the whole sequence a tightly organized symphony of New York City at its most percussive, abrasive, and cacophonous. Through a curated soundtrack of aural contrasts between Wisconsin and New York City, the audience hears New York City as April does: a jarring, confusing, and dangerous space.

It is plausible that Mamoulian, a lover of Murnau's work, was inspired to construct this urban noise symphony after watching Murnau's first US film, *Sunrise* (1927), a silent movie with a synchronized score that similarly features a cacophony of horn honks and other urban noises to indicate that a rural couple is out of place in the big city.[67] The city in *Sunrise*—unlike *Applause*—was a set, but the constructed nature of this moment can still be considered a precursor to Mamoulian's approach. Within the context of 100 percent talking films, however, there was, to my knowledge, little precedent for constructing environmental sound along such narratively and psychologically expressive lines.

Sharply contrasting with these harsh, punctual noises is the soundtrack Mamoulian selects for April's first two dates with Tony, which both include location work. The first occurs atop the Brooklyn Bridge and begins with two shots of the actors walking on the actual bridge, with muffled car noise on the soundtrack that was likely captured on location. Mamoulian then switches to a studio set to shoot them and record their extensive dialogue, and the soothing environmental sounds—distant foghorns and low rumbles of passing cars—are the antithesis of April's prior experiences with urban New York. These environmental sounds are sparse and soft, a sonic expression of the peace and respite that Tony offers April.

The second date, which was shot partly atop the AT&T building in New York City, was—like the Brooklyn Bridge scene—filmed in a location where Mamoulian could not capture directly recorded dialogue. This scene features some dialogue-heavy moments that were filmed in a studio replica of that location, but Mamoulian also managed to insert studio-recorded dialogue into *on-location* shots by placing the camera behind the actors at several points. Doing so obviates the need for precise lip synchronization and enables Mamoulian to provide an expansive New York City backdrop for the couple's conversation (Figure 2.7). As with the Brooklyn Bridge scene, Mamoulian uses the couple's extreme height as a justification for expressive background sounds, with distant, gentle foghorn sounds—along with quiet train whistles—conveying the couple's cocoon-like romance high above the squalid city.

Taken collectively, both date scenes showcase the microphone's ability to capture environmental sounds—as would be expected in the period—while also expressively conveying the comforting quietude of the couple's love space. Perhaps Mamoulian's clearest effort at merging presentational and expressive sound, however, comes at the end of the AT&T scene. When April accepts Tony's proposal of marriage and he shouts, "Hooray!" a low-angle location shot of the lovers shows an airplane swooping close to the couple, its loud engine noise blasting on the soundtrack. It is plausible that an airplane might fly by, but the moment is no coincidence—Mamoulian hired the plane's pilot to fly low in the sky past the lovers, apparently breaking a city law in the process.[68] Mamoulian would later see this moment as a prime example of how a filmmaker could select certain sounds to accent the emotion inherent in the scene—for him, the sound of the airplane was pivotal for expressing the joy of the moment beyond what any actor could convey.[69]

Even Mamoulian's most technically difficult location work—April and Tony's breakup at a subway stop late in the film—features expressive location sound. Purely on a technical level, the scene—filmed in one take by a single camera using directly recorded sound at New York City's Chambers Street subway stop in the middle of the night[70]—is remarkable. Paramount's sound equipment was extremely heavy (likely around 19,000 pounds[71]) and microphones were not

Figure 2.7 In *Applause*, Mamoulian uses dialogue during location shots by placing the camera behind April and Tony and adding dialogue later, thus providing an expansive backdrop and motivating expressively quiet city noises.

yet directional enough to filter out stray sounds, yet Mamoulian and his crew managed to move the camera and provide direct dialogue in two different places during the shot. Due to direct-sound recording, Mamoulian would seem to have few manipulative options at his disposal, yet by timing the couple's breakup with the subway train's arrival and departure, the soundtrack remains expressive. Quiet, soothing sounds had—in the two prior locations scenes—marked the *heights* of April and Tony's romance. The subway scene, instead, conveys the depths to which the couple's relationship has sunk via the deafening roar of the subway train. The shot—which features dozens of extras waiting for the subway—begins with virtually no background sound. While this decision was surely driven by the need to make April and Tony's conversation audible, the quiet background only enhances the loud arrival of the train, a sonic "monster" that threatens to whisk Tony away forever. After the train departs with Tony aboard and April weeps, environmental sound becomes all but nonexistent once more, an occurrence driven by the fact that the train has departed and the subway stop is now nearly empty of people, but one that also underscores the tragedy of the moment. Even when shooting on location, where sonic control was lessened, Mamoulian consistently configured environmental sound as an object to be selected and timed precisely with the narrative beats of the story.

Kitty's Suicide and Expressive Sound

One final—and especially notable—example of *Applause*'s heavy prioritization of expressive environmental sound can be found near the end of the film when Kitty poisons herself. After taking the poison, Kitty sits grimly in her apartment and waits for death. Background sounds, which had previously been quiet, suddenly spring to life. With the camera trained on Kitty, we hear the offscreen sounds of car engines, a ticking clock, trolley bells, traffic-cop whistles, car horns, a nearby couple on an elevator, and an ambulance siren. Near the end of this sequence, which Mamoulian cuts away from once to depict April and Tony's subway breakup, many of these sounds have grown louder and denser. When this din reaches its loudest and densest pitch, Kitty, now teetering on the brink of insanity, shouts, "April!" and rushes out of the apartment.

The specific sounds used in this scene were, according to Mamoulian, carefully planned and layered. The sounds were produced

> in a separate sound room in the studio with about eight property men handling different horns, klaxons, drums and roller skates, while I stood by on a chair conducting this conglomeration, giving [cues], indicating entrances and building up a gradual crescendo. These traffic sounds started low and soft, then kept growing in volume. At the end, the sound of a siren was heard, presumably approaching from a distance, then passing by Helen Morgan's hotel and then, as if tangled up in the traffic, shrieking with a loud urgency and despair.[72]

Through it all, as Mamoulian pointed out, Morgan remains rooted to her chair in a darkened space. Mamoulian was drawn to the idea that "the sound montage was acting for her . . . the clamor of that dramatic, organized traffic, expressed the rise of her emotions. When the siren reached its highest pitch and volume, it was like the agonized cry of Helen Morgan's heart—she jumped up crying out the name of her child 'April!'"[73]

It would be difficult to find a comparable example of such a constructed and narratively expressive use of environmental sound in all-talking films prior to *Applause*. If, for Mamoulian, a film artist's job was to select, arrange, and sharpen only those sounds that had a direct bearing on the mood and implications of the scene, Kitty's suicide scene demonstrated the dividends such an approach might yield for filmmakers interested not in merely capturing and reproducing environmental sound, but in molding a soundtrack toward distinctly narrative ends.

Applause's Impact

In *Applause*, Mamoulian offered goals and methods that deviated from the early-sound norm. Semi-synced sound could be used frequently even in an "all-talking" film to better express key ideas in the story. Direct-sound sequences needn't default to static cameras, but might instead offer regular camera movements incorporated into a patterned system of meaning. The voice needn't be merely captured and faithfully reproduced, but could also be manipulated in ways that expressed narrative ideas. Background noises—whether songs or city noises—could be spatially consistent while simultaneously enhancing the film's emotional qualities and aiding characterization. Mamoulian was not the only filmmaker interested in expressive possibilities (chapters 2–4 address early sound techniques of René Clair, Ernst Lubitsch, King Vidor, and Roland West, for instance). Yet *Applause* stands out as an unusually forceful assertion that the common aesthetic approaches at the time might be inadequate, and that a true sound film artist should manipulate style to express his or her viewpoint on the material and render the story more impactful.

Perhaps most effective in this regard is the way that Mamoulian uses sound to express the idea that burlesque haunts, immobilizes, and even crushes its female performers. We saw earlier that Mamoulian enjoyed distorting burlesque music, but he also tended to emphasize burlesque sounds when Kitty or April are forced into passive positions. Early in the film, Kitty and her newborn daughter lie motionless as a burlesque performer hollers the mangled version of "Turkey Trot." Later, the adult April powerlessly watches her mother onstage as distorted burlesque music invades the soundtrack. Burlesque music and crowd noise then unwillingly seep into her nightmare as she sleeps, which is depicted subjectively via superimposed images of convent life and the New York City burlesque world, and is accompanied by shifts between a convent organ and the sounds of burlesque music and the raucous crowd. In the final sequence, Kitty lies spasming in a dressing room just before her death as the onstage noises of drumrolls and laughter are heard, thus framing her death as a "murder" executed by the institution of burlesque. These moments are among the most powerful examples in early sound cinema of how a selective—and sometimes distorted—soundtrack could communicate a filmmaker's viewpoint on the story.

Yet in spite of its accomplishments, *Applause*'s impact on subsequent sound filmmaking practices remains difficult to pinpoint. Though *Applause* was immediately recognized as a pathbreaking film by critics and the movie industry, it did not perform well at the box office. Many of Mamoulian's methods, as we shall see, would become more common as the 1930s progressed, but filmmakers are not necessarily eager to imitate box-office failures, and it is impossible to assess the precise extent to which Mamoulian's methods in this film were influential or merely prescient. At the very least, the industry took notice of this film, which announced important goals and methods for sound filmmaking at the precise moment when its definition was contentious and fluid.

City Streets and the Voice-over

When Mamoulian began shooting his second film—*City Streets*—in January 1931,[74] sound film had changed substantially on both a technological and stylistic level. Technologically, filmmakers could now more easily accomplish what Mamoulian had labored to do two years earlier. Microphones were gradually becoming more directional, which—along with lighter-weight and more effective soundproof blimps on the camera—reduced the risk that camera noise would be inadvertently recorded.[75] Consequently, cameras could be more easily moved, and could be placed closer to the actors during directly recorded sequences. Microphones were also becoming lighter, and the boom mic—which enabled the capturing of dialogue while characters moved—was now a common tool, thereby permitting greater character mobility during directly recorded dialogue sequences.[76] Incremental improvements were also being made to the microphone's signal-to-noise ratio. This would ultimately encourage a more frequent use of re-recording, though it remained a minority practice at Paramount and many other studios.[77] And with sound editing becoming somewhat easier, multiple-camera shooting was fading from common use.

Thanks in part to these advances, as 1930 progressed, filmmakers increasingly used sound in ways that more closely resembled Mamoulian's efforts in *Applause*. Extant films from 1930 show a marked increase in the quantity and duration of tracking shots, especially in directly recorded dialogue sequences. Earlier camera movements had often appeared to be little more than efforts to generate some extra visual movement, but as 1930 progressed, camera movement seemed increasingly tied to narrative purposes. *All Quiet on the Western Front* (April 1930), a high-profile film that won the Best Picture Academy Award, features a large number of fluid camera movements in semi-sync *and* direct-sound sequences, and extant films from later in the year suggest that other filmmakers followed suit. One also finds an increased use of direct sound for location shooting. *Danger Lights* (November 1930), for instance, utilized new directional microphone technology[78] to provide numerous directly recorded conversations nestled within the din of trains and—at one point—in downtown Chicago. One also finds in 1930 an increased effort to select background sounds that could best convey the emotional qualities of the story. *The Divorcee* (April 1930), for instance, features a scene in which a married couple's happy, private conversation is interrupted by an organ grinder outsider, a sonic event that anticipates the breakup that will

80 DEFINING CINEMA

ensue thanks to the husband's infidelity. And in *All Quiet on the Western Front*, the sonically dense and cacophonous battle sounds in numerous scenes contrast with the film's somber and meditative conclusion, which occurs amid a background of near silence. Film sound, more commonly an attraction-based element at the time Mamoulian shot *Applause*, was being reconfigured as a selective and expressive element of storytelling.

Still, though many of Mamoulian's strategies and goals for *Applause* were becoming more common by the time Mamoulian shot his next film, *City Streets* contains further innovations in sonic manipulation. The film opens with a highly unusual shot sequencing that is driven by sonic as well as graphic matches, including the sounds of machinery and liquids. In the following sequence, Mamoulian experiments with overtly manipulative—and arguably psychological—sound by beginning in near silence in the opening shot of a raucous carnival, which features an extreme close-up of only the eyes and forehead of the young Nan (Sylvia Sidney) looking offscreen. The camera tracks back to reveal that Nan is aiming a gun directly at the camera. After she fires, Mamoulian cuts to reveal that Nan is merely trying to hit a target at a carnival stand to win a prize. Coinciding exactly with the cut, carnival organ music begins along with the gun noises of other happy contestants, followed by crowd noise. Since it is implausible that the entire carnival went silent to watch Nan fire the gun, the moment constitutes a stylized act of sonic manipulation. Later in the film, Mamoulian pushes his lifelong interest in animating artworks by cutting between the images of two cat statues while two human characters converse off camera, as if the *statues* were the ones having the conversation.[79]

The most important of *City Streets*' overt experiments with sonic manipulation, however, is Mamoulian's use of the diegetic voice-over, a subjective filmmaking device that remains a staple of sound filmmaking today. Midway through the film, Nan, who is now serving time in prison as an accomplice to murder and has sworn off gangster life, is visited by her boyfriend (known only as the Kid), who proudly announces that he has joined the "beer" racket (i.e., become a gangster). In the following scene, Nan lies awake in her bed at night, deeply distressed by the news. Beginning with the sound of only her cellmate snoring, the camera tracks into a medium close-up of Nan (Figure 2.8), and we begin to hear on the soundtrack various sounds she is tearfully recalling: the exchange between Nan and the Kid as she learns he has entered the beer business, a recurring bell indicating that the jail's visitation period is over, a matron saying "time is up" and "come along," and—in a scene just *before* Nan had learned that the Kid was a racketeer—Nan's jail mate, Sophie, expressing happiness that the Kid is not a gangster with such lines as "Lucky your boyfriend isn't mixed up in the beer racket" and "Poor Johnnie, that's being Johnnie on the spot all right."

Figure 2.8 Mamoulian provides an early voice-over during a medium close up of Nan in *City Streets*.

Much as he did for camera movement and two-track recording in *Applause*, Mamoulian would later state that this was a "first," asserting in interviews that "in *City Streets*, for the first time, I used spoken thoughts over a silent close up, the sound of other people."[80] As grandiose as Mamoulian's claim may seem, it is—to the best of my knowledge—rather close to the truth where US cinema is concerned, though once again, greater precision is needed. If the supposed invention is simply the voice-over itself, then Mamoulian was not the first, as newsreel voice-overs occur as early as 1930.[81] In US fiction films, diegetic voice-overs representing characters' thoughts *were* quite rare, but at least one film featured this device prior to *City Streets*: William Wyler's *Hell's Heroes* (December 1929). A careful look at *Hell's Heroes* helps remind us that Mamoulian was not the only experimenter in this period while also enabling us to delineate what was probably most unusual about Mamoulian's voice-over in *City Streets*.

Late in *Hell's Heroes*—an adaptation of Peter B. Kyne's novel *The Three Godfathers*—reformed outlaw Bob Sangster (Charles Bickford) treks alone through the desert without water in a desperate effort to keep alive the newborn baby he is carrying. Bob comes upon a waterhole that contains toxic water. Recognizing that he cannot make it to town without a drink, he begins speaking aloud his thoughts to the baby in medium close-up: "It's no use, little fella. I can't go no further . . . without water. I just . . . can't make it. I reckon . . . this is the finish." His eyes then become wider as he stares offscreen at the water. After a shot of the water and an extreme long shot of Bob, the film returns to the same camera setup, and Bob exclaims, "I got it!" The image then cuts back to the water, and we hear a raspier, closer-miked version of Bob's voice saying, "there's just one chance to get through. To fill up on that stuff . . . fill up good and plenty." At this point, an audience member might suspect we have shifted from Bob's spoken words to his internal thoughts, but Wyler does not render this explicit until the next shot, which shows Bob's hand stroking the water before tilting up to his face. As the voice-over proceeds ("it won't get me for an hour. Maybe I can make it. That's it, that's it!"), we see that Bob is not moving his lips. Later in the same shot, Wyler guides us out of the voice-over by having Bob's moving lips pick up this thought, saying, "sure, that's it, that's it!" This moment constitutes an extremely early instance of a diegetic voice-over, and it serves as a powerful evocation of Bob's level of mania and his protectiveness toward the newborn. The voice-over enables viewers to understand his plan and recognize his love for the child (he won't say the plan out loud because he doesn't want the topic of suicide to reach the baby's ears).

Hell's Heroes thus proves that Mamoulian did not "invent" the diegetic voice-over. What *does* seem to have had little precedent, however, are two expressive moves that were likely conscious continuations of ideas found in *Applause*: (1) the use of voice-over *memories*, and (2) the elaborate *construction* and *layering* of multiple voices.

During April's nightmare in *Applause*, we see superimposed images of convent life and New York City. In a sense, these are "flashback" images and sounds, since they reflect things April saw earlier, and—as we noted—they are accompanied by sounds heard in those spaces (the "Ave Maria" for the convent, and "Give Your Baby Lots of Lovin'" for New York City footage). In US cinema from 1928 to 1930, such backtracks in time—even brief ones of this sort—were uncommon, but when they occurred, the typical approach was to *match* visual and aural time frames. *Romance* (August 1930), for example, is a rare early sound film told almost entirely in flashback. In the film's first scene, an elderly bishop begins narrating the tale. The image slowly dissolves to the flashback, and during this dissolve, the volume of the talking bishop similarly recedes, with his voice eventually reduced to virtually a murmur. The effect is awkward to modern ears—we can still see the bishop moving his lips as if he is speaking audibly even as his voice is barely audible on the soundtrack—but it reflects a belief that an image fadeaway from the present to the past must correspond to the fading of its sound. In *The Big Trail*, a brief flashback from wagon scout Breck Coleman's (John Wayne) perspective shows him discovering the murder of his best friend and announcing—out loud—that "renegade whites" killed him. This flashback dialogue occurs only after the image similarly shifts back in time to show Breck onscreen. Likewise, in *Dishonored* (April 1931), spy X-27 (Marlene Dietrich) discovers the hidden location of a vital document after remembering a conversation she witnessed earlier that night. But when the crucial flashback line ("Don't get excited, Colonel. Have a cigarette.") replays on the soundtrack, director Josef von Sternberg also provides a superimposition of the man speaking the line. Three times in *Rio Rita*—and once in *Madam Satan* (September 1930)—we hear the distant singing of a previously performed song while the camera is trained on a character who is thinking about the meaning behind the song. In both films, however, the singing is apparently coming from another character offscreen, thus allowing us to interpret the moment as a mere present-tense reprise of the song. *Big Boy* (September 1930) is possibly the only pre-1931 all-talking US film featuring a moment when the sonic timeframe unambiguously does not match the image. Partway through the film, a mother begins speaking about the past, which triggers a backward leap in visual and aural time. Though her present-day voice stops the instant the image flashes back, we do hear—at low volume—the singing of "Dixie Land" several seconds before the image switches to the past, a rare instance of a sound advance during this period.

Perhaps the industry was too proud of its newfangled synchronized sound technology to provide chronologically mismatched sound/image relationships, or perhaps they were fearful of confusing audiences. Whatever the reason, *City Streets* deserves substantial credit simply for daring to provide lengthy past-tense sound that never corresponds to a jump back in time by the image. Mamoulian appears to have been at least partly responsible, though his personal papers do open the possibility that the film's screenwriters came up with the idea.[82] What we *can* be certain of, however, is that Mamoulian conceptualized and laid out in detail the precise and elaborate *layering* of various flashback voices and sounds heard in this scene. Many of the sounds in the finished film appear only in Mamoulian's handwriting in the marginal notes of his production screenplay, including the repeated ringing of the bell that signals the end of visiting hours, the Kid's repetition of the word "beer," the matron's voice saying "time is up" and "come along," and prior lines from Sophie. By Mamoulian's account, this layered sound montage was accomplished not via re-recording—which Paramount frowned upon—but by having the actors and property men gather around the set. Mamoulian trained the camera on Sylvia Sydney (whose lips do not move) while the actors spoke their lines and the property men generated the bell noises at the precise cues that Mamoulian had designated (Sydney's lines were apparently prerecorded and played back).[83]

Mamoulian's decision to provide live, layered off-screen sounds resonates with his creation of the on-set city-noise montage during Kitty's suicide in *Applause*. The use of a multitude of *flashback*—rather than present-day—sounds, however, had no precursor that I know of. The result was a vivid demonstration of how a constructed array of past-tense sounds could convey Nan's obsessive, dismayed, and even crazed mindset. The Kid's added repetitions of—and vocal emphasis on—the word "beer" drive home the irony that the Kid has joined the gang (earlier in the film, Nan—before going straight—had urged him to do precisely that). The repetitions of the bell and the matron's words "time is up" communicate the apparent finality of the Kid's decision and Nan's powerlessness to stop him while she remains in prison. The recurrence of Sophie's "Johnnie on the spot" line—which refers to a mobster who was killed—emphasizes Nan's belief that the Kid has put his life in danger by joining the mob. All these lines thus tie directly to Nan's feelings, and toward the end of the voice-over, Mamoulian builds to a climax by having fragments of all these sounds occur simultaneously. In a marginal note in the screenplay, Mamoulian described the voice-over as enabling us to "hear what Nan is thinking about and what incessantly is coming back to her mind in connection with her short meeting with Kid,"[84] an apt description of this deeply subjective and possibly unprecedented use of past-tense, layered voice-overs.

Thus, in *City Streets*, Mamoulian continued his efforts to select and manipulate sound to express narrative ideas. In particular, both the voice-over and Nan's introduction at the carnival reveal Mamoulian's interest in subjective sound at a time when few other filmmakers were using it. Subjective sound was a logical avenue of exploration for Mamoulian, who believed that a soundtrack needed to be constructed and stylized for story purposes. This belief, in turn, would next lead him to one of the most audacious subjective-sound experiments of his career.

Dr. Jekyll and Mr. Hyde: "With a Microphone Anything Is Possible"

Dr. Jekyll and Mr. Hyde (December 1931) is, on the whole, less sonically innovative than *Applause* or *City Streets*, but it features one key escalation of heavily constructed subjective sound. Twenty-five minutes into the film, Jekyll first takes the potion and does the impossible: he isolates his animalistic side, thereby turning into a person who—both visually and psychologically—scarcely resembles himself. Mamoulian, by his account, believed that this transformation demanded special stylistic treatment for two reasons. First, Mamoulian wanted to stress that Jekyll's change into Hyde hinged upon a psychological transformation, not just the physical fact that handsome Jekyll had changed into ape-like Hyde. Second, Mamoulian felt that this supernatural event needed to feel plausible and vivid in a manner befitting a sound film, not a silent one.[85] To address both aims, Mamoulian decided to shoot the scene subjectively, thereby emphasizing the psychological aspect of the transformation and convincing audiences of the change by rendering it more palpable.

In the finished film, Mamoulian uses point-of-view camerawork, vertiginous panning, and superimpositions to convey Jekyll's mental state during the transformation. These devices help inject rhythm and energy into the transformation, and I will discuss them in the next chapter. Sonically, Mamoulian—by his account—was initially stumped, as he felt that restricting the soundtrack to noises normally heard in the physical world would shatter the visual illusion. "Finally," Mamoulian would later say, "I got a notion. I thought: 'With a microphone anything is possible.'"[86] "The only way to create a strange, uncanny feeling, to give one sympathetic shivers, so to speak, was by adding to the camera treatment a composition of sounds that was never heard by anybody before."[87] Ultimately, this compilation of sounds included the sonic recording of the light waves emitted by a candle "with various frequencies of intensity," a recording of a gong played backward with the sound of the stick striking the gong removed, and a sonic record of Mamoulian's own heartbeat, elevated by running up and down a flight of stairs. These and other sounds were then re-recorded together to yield a composite track. The production crew playfully dubbed this concoction "Mamoulian's stew," a handy analog to the mixture of liquids needed to create Jekyll's transformative potion.[88]

The resulting "stew" was a closely coordinated blend of sounds, many of which either could not be—or generally were not—heard in the physical world.[89] After a few minutes of Jekyll's near-silent laboratory work—a silence that only magnifies what follows—Mamoulian begins as the *City Streets* voice-over did: with a lone sound from the physical world, here the strained grunts and gasps of Jekyll immediately after he takes the potion. After eighteen seconds of this noise, careful ears might note a sudden change in their quality, indicating the edited-in arrival of the re-recorded Mamoulian stew. As the grunts of Jekyll/Hyde continue and the camera begins its rapid panning, the distorted gong noise enters the soundtrack quietly and slowly increases in volume. A few seconds later, shimmering, ear-ringing recordings of the candle's light waves begin in a similar manner, sneaking in and raising in volume gradually. Then, Mamoulian introduces his own heartbeat and Jekyll/Hyde's slower-paced panted grunts. As the total volume level of the stew continues to increase, we see superimpositions against the still-spinning main image that accompany repetitions of words heard on the soundtrack from prior scenes—Jekyll imploring fiancée Muriel to "marry me," various scoldings from Muriel's father and Jekyll's friend Lanyon about his "positively indecent" and "disgusting" behavior, saloon-singer Ivy's seductive lines, and Jekyll's violent declaration that he could "strangle" Muriel's father—along with additional blurred imagery and Ivy's ever-swinging leg. Eventually, the voices end, the gong and candle noises fade away, Hyde's breathing becomes less rhythmic, and

Mamoulian's heartbeat—the last element of the stew to disappear—gradually recedes in volume and then vanishes when Hyde walks to the mirror to look at himself.[90]

In one sense, this scene was an elaboration of Mamoulian's philosophies and techniques from his prior two films: narratively expressive re-recording (found already in the lullaby scene in *Applause*) combined with the layering of sonic elements, including flashback voices (found in *City Streets*). In *Dr. Jekyll and Mr. Hyde*, these aims yield an extraordinarily complex soundtrack for the period, but as basic strategies they are not new. What *may* have been new is the incorporation of what Mamoulian would later call sounds that "defy" reality.[91] On a practical level, of course, no recorded sound heard in a film is an exact replica of the original sound. Microphones and sound recording apparatuses do not truly capture and preserve sound; rather, they translate and store them in electric signals, which are later boomed back to the audience via electrified speakers in a mediated approximation of the original sound event.[92] Every recorded sound is thus a translation of original sound, not the real item. But what Mamoulian was doing with his "stew" was *abandoning the fiction* that audiences were hearing the physical sounds from a scene and instead showcasing sound technology's ability to fabricate *new* sounds (candle "noise," reversed and edited gong noises) and defamiliarize existing ones (heartbeats). Indeed, as Neil Lerner has pointed out, Paramount's pressbook for the film emphasized the heartbeat sound in terms of the microphone's capability to exceed what one could hear by simply putting an ear over the heart.[93]

In addition to offering unfamiliar sounds, Mamoulian's "stew" demonstrated that mixing together such sounds could create an even more powerful sensation of human psychology and non-naturalistic experience, thereby better transporting audiences into the realm of fantasy and the unknown. By way of comparison, the supernatural horror film *Frankenstein*—released a month before *Dr. Jekyll and Mr. Hyde*—also offers noises that would not exist in reality: static emitting from Frankenstein's life-giving invention, or the pained grunts of a sewn-together body once it is brought to life. However, there is little sense that *Frankenstein*'s filmmakers are trying to do more than approximate how such noises might sound in the real, physical world. By instead allowing sound to exist only within a character's head, Mamoulian aimed to construct a seemingly impossible soundtrack, and then augment this sonic strangeness via overlapping sound.

Beyond the matter of psychological sound, the general strategy found in *Dr. Jekyll and Mr. Hyde* of creating "unnatural" sounds and creatively combining them on the soundtrack would later become quite important, eventually driving the soundtracks of entire genres of filmmaking. We are accustomed to thinking of *King Kong* (1933) as a landmark for the manipulation of sound records and their recombination (famously, Kong's persuasive roar was a combination of a lion and tiger's roar, played backward at different speeds). Yet Mamoulian was performing sonic manipulations to persuade audiences to accept the fantastical a year and a half earlier. The 1960s and 1970s have been justly lauded for the newfound freedom accorded to sound technicians, who in movies like *Star Wars* (1977) used sound technology to record unfamiliar sounds, manipulate those sounds in post-production, and mix them with other sound recordings, thereby better evoking their fantasy or science-fiction narratives. Though such approaches generally do not involve psychological sound, in other ways they find their origins in Mamoulian's "stew" for *Dr. Jekyll and Mr. Hyde*.[94] This moment, as Lerner points out, even looks ahead to experimental music composer John Cage's use of composite recordings a few decades later.[95]

Mamoulian thus deserves credit for hitting upon this approach at such an early date. Still, one must remember that the technique was no mere experimental gimmick, but rather an outgrowth of a coherent philosophy of film artistry. For Mamoulian, the sonic manipulations of his stew were extensions of what any serious filmmaker ought to do: exploit the essential, non-theatrical qualities of cinema and stylize those elements in ways that paradoxically made the film more believable. Creating the Mamoulian stew involved selecting and enhancing only those sounds that would serve narrative ends, principles that had already occupied Mamoulian's attention in *Applause* and *City Streets*. The Mamoulian stew was an unusual venture into sonic unreality, but it remained grounded in basic principles that Mamoulian held dear as an artist.

Conclusion

Though Mamoulian's sound work after *Dr. Jekyll and Mr. Hyde* has received little attention, his belief that a film artist manipulated reality by expressively selecting, organizing, sharpening, and warping sound would continue for the remainder of his career. In the domain of sonic distortion, Mamoulian, in *Love Me Tonight* (1932), played music backward to accompany a slow-motion retreat by the stag-hunt riders, and mocked the castle's three aunts by having their exclamations take on the flat sonic quality of yipping dogs. To amplify the importance of oil rushing through a pipeline at the climax of *High, Wide and Handsome* (1937), Mamoulian added the repeated sound of a reverberating gong run backward with the initial striking sound removed.[96] And in *Blood and Sand* (1941), a recurring song called the "Saeta"—composed by Vicente Gómez—was rendered more haunting by being recorded in an echo chamber.[97]

In the realm of sonic subjectivity, Mamoulian experimented with mismatching sound effects to convey how a character hears a momentous event. In *Love Me Tonight*, a vase crash sounds like thunder to the snobby guests who are shocked that the "baron" is a tailor. In *High, Wide and Handsome*, Mamoulian increased the volume level of a pen-scratching sound as Peter is forced to sign away his treasured marital land. And in *Silk Stockings* (1957), Ninotchka's pounding typewriter sounds like machine-gun fire to the petrified Russian commissars, who fear that her negative review will send them to Siberia.[98] Subjective flashback voice-overs also abound in later Mamoulian films. In *Love Me Tonight*, when Maurice lies in bed asleep, Mamoulian offers a reprise (and then reimagination) of Maurice and Jeanette's romantic conversation in the prior scene. Flashback voices from a happier past appear in two different places in *We Live Again* (1934), and the device is reused in *Blood and Sand* to reflect the magnitude of bullfighter Juan's professional decline. Most experimentally, in *High, Wide and Handsome* a love song—Jerome Kern and Oscar Hammerstein's "Can I Forget You?"—sung by Peter's wife, Sally (Irene Dunne), recurs as Peter sits sadly alone, and the volume even dips when Peter shakes his head in a futile effort to remove it from his mind.

Even the notion of tying sound to particular objects as if they were "speaking," an effort driven by the cinematic ability to match any image with any sound, finds its way into several more Mamoulian films. A bust on the wall—and later, according to the lyrics, the walls themselves—sing the refrain to "The Son of a Gun Is Nothing but a Tailor" in *Love Me Tonight*.[99] In *Blood and Sand*, the voice of a Macarena statue answers back to Carmen (Linda Darnell) when she prays to it. And in *The Song of Songs*, images of a statue trigger flashback voices. Many of these efforts would not have appeared especially striking when the films were released, in part because they were increasingly becoming part of standard film practices, but they remind us that Mamoulian never stopped using the stylized sound principles he introduced in the early sound era.

Because Mamoulian's sonic work increasingly came to resemble emerging sonic norms, one might be tempted to agree with Andrew Sarris that Mamoulian amounted to an "innovator who [ran] out of innovations."[100] Yet innovations by themselves are hardly insignificant, especially at a time when basic sonic rules and potentials are still being explored. Through his early sound-era experiments with expressive sonic construction, Mamoulian was laying groundwork that would *enable* the directors lauded by Sarris to thrive. Nor should the medium-specific nature of Mamoulian's experiments be ignored. Given Mamoulian's stage background and the overwhelming influence of the stage in the early sound era, he could have simply grafted theatrical methods onto film, but this was seldom his approach. In late 1932, for instance, Robert Z. Leonard directed an adaptation of Eugene O'Neill's acclaimed 1928 stage play *Strange Interlude*, which had famously featured lengthy soliloquies that explained the characters' feelings. Leonard and his collaborators shortened these soliloquies for the screen, but otherwise, the filmmakers merely shifted the monologues from soliloquy to voice-over. When Mamoulian filmed *City Streets* a year and half earlier, he would have been familiar with O'Neill's play, which had been produced by the Theatre Guild while Mamoulian was directing plays there.[101] Yet rather than merely imitating a soliloquy in voice-over form, he offered a layered voice-over experience that stage soliloquies could not provide. Similarly, rather than calling upon Fredric March to act out his transformation into Hyde as the camera rolled—as might occur on the stage and did, in fact, occur in the 1920 silent film version starring John Barrymore—Mamoulian used the particulars of electric recording and post-production sound manipulation to express the transformation.

Through his writing and films, Mamoulian set forward an agenda for sound aesthetics centered on sonic construction, medium specificity, and the ways in which such sound could create and enhance narrative meaning. In the next chapter, we turn to Mamoulian's approach to film rhythm and pacing, a pressing matter for many filmmakers and film commentators alike during the early sound era. Achieving rhythm in art was among Mamoulian's most valued principles, and his use of it in cinema, as we shall see, was fundamental to his identity as an artist.

3
Mamoulian and Rhythm

Applause, City Streets, Dr. Jekyll and Mr. Hyde, We Live Again, High, Wide, and Handsome, Golden Boy, The Mark of Zorro, Blood and Sand

Rhythm is truly my favorite principle. I believe in it unconditionally.[1]

I think that perhaps the most important attribute of any film is its rhythmic construction.[2]

—Rouben Mamoulian

In Mamoulian's mind, the peak achievement of "stylization" in the arts lay primarily not with the many techniques and practices he would become most closely associated with in film—sound-era camera movement, re-recording, the voice-over, integrated musicals, three-strip Technicolor—but rather with the concept of rhythm. Mamoulian's written theories on rhythm first pertained to stage opera, but he quickly became convinced of its potential in dramatic, non-musical stage productions as well. In cinema, rhythm would remain at the forefront of Mamoulian's mind from his first film to his last, regardless of the genre he worked in. Thus, to understand Mamoulian as a filmmaker and innovator, we must gain a firm sense of how he conceptualized rhythm, the practical creative choices he made in an effort to control and exploit it, and what he gained from these methods. Understanding Mamoulian's approach and significance also requires us to look closely at the typical methods of cinematic rhythm at the time, especially during the early sound era when movies were frequently criticized for their turgid pace.

The mode of analysis in this chapter derives in part from pioneering work by Lea Jacobs, who—in her book *Film Rhythm after Sound: Technology, Music, and Performance*—lays out a wide array of ways in which stylistic choices can impact the sensation of cinematic rhythm, including music, the "rhythmic qualities of speech," camera and character movement, sound and image editing, and scene lengths.[3] My own analysis of Mamoulian's films in this chapter examines many of these components. Like Jacobs, I use the term "rhythm" not merely in the restricted sense of a steady, repeated beat, but more generally to describe a film's pacing, tempo, and fluidity as a viewer experiences it. This broader conception of film rhythm fits closely with what Mamoulian meant when he spoke about the topic and what he felt the essence of cinema truly was: a medium whose numerous potentials for exploiting movement made it uniquely poised to emotionally affect an audience.

The chapter begins by detailing Mamoulian's early theories of artistic rhythm prior to his entrance into filmmaking in 1929. In his 1920s stage work in Rochester and then on Broadway, Mamoulian saw actor movement as the defining feature of theater, and he sought ways to enhance such movements via close musical accompaniment, precisely choreographed noises, and shadow play. The remainder of the chapter is then divided into two parts. First, I examine *Applause* (1929) within the context of early sound-era rhythm. At the precise moment when commentators were decrying the slow pace of all-talking films, *Applause* displayed Mamoulian's belief that sound cinema contained an unparalleled array of tools for presenting a lively and dynamic art form. *Applause* thus offered early sound-era filmmakers an important set of ideas for how to achieve a stronger sense of rhythm. After briefly analyzing other pacing experiments in his early sound work, the final part of the chapter investigates how Mamoulian's approach in his later non-musical films remained—in many ways—fundamentally rhythmic and musical. I examine especially Mamoulian's use of diegetic music in two films made at Fox: *The Mark of Zorro* (1940) and *Blood and Sand* (1941). When thinking rhythmically, Mamoulian often utilized intricately choreographed set pieces and focused on the musical traditions of particular groups and cultures. Doing so served the purposes of each film he directed, but it also marked him as a director who thought in musical terms even when he was not making musicals.

Stage Rhythm in Rochester

For Mamoulian, rhythmic construction was a natural outgrowth of the "stylization" approach he treasured. Tracing Mamoulian's viewpoint on rhythm thus begins with his first play, *The Beating on the Door*, which he directed in London in 1922. The subject matter of the play—the loss of fortune suffered by the aristocracy during the Russian Revolution—would have hit Mamoulian close to home, as his own family lost much of their wealth during the Russian Revolution.[4] Perhaps for this reason—and influenced also by his experiences with naturalism when he briefly studied theater in Russia in the mid-1910s (see chapter 1)—Mamoulian decided to use a non-stylized approach. When a previously aristocratic family is put to work, for instance, Mamoulian simply had, by his account, "people chopping real wood with real axes and so on; chips flying all over the place."[5] To his dismay, Mamoulian, while sitting in the audience for the show, discovered that this approach gave him "no satisfaction at all."[6] By his account, his disappointment with the production would encourage him to subsequently pursue the stylization approach outlined in chapter 1, which rested on the assumption that an artwork should be overtly molded and adjusted by its creator, rather than slavishly striving to replicate reality.

There is no evidence of Mamoulian homing in on *rhythm* as his preferred method of stylization, however, until he moved to Rochester the following year to direct opera as part of the Eastman School of the University of Rochester. The goal for the school was to use its students to present an act or scene from an opera approximately once a month, which would gradually lead, according to extensive Rochester newspaper coverage on the subject, to a full-fledged "American Grand Opera Company."[7] In Rochester, Mamoulian directed numerous opera scenes—sometimes multiple scenes in a single month. Starting with *Faust* in January 1925, Mamoulian began directing full operas.[8] These opera productions encouraged Mamoulian, who was already interested in unifying the artistic tools of an art form, to begin theorizing in writing how music and character movement, specifically, might best be merged. According to Mamoulian, it was during these productions that he thought of an anecdote told to him as a boy by his physics teacher. "Whenever a regiment of soldiers crosses a bridge," the teacher apparently told Mamoulian, "they are ordered to break their step. If they don't, the rhythmic vibration of their steps can destroy a bridge."[9] To Mamoulian, this account suggested that "if rhythm can destroy a bridge, if it has such a power, then the same power can certainly strengthen and be immensely constructive, especially in theater." Thus, in the case of opera, Mamoulian concluded that the most impactful staging method was to *amplify* the rhythm of the performance by synchronizing performer actions to music.[10]

Though Mamoulian first applied this idea to his opera productions, he quickly became interested in exploring the notion that rhythm was the vital ingredient of *all* stage performances, not just operas. Mamoulian thus arranged for a production of Maurice Maeterlinck's dramatic play *Sister Beatrice* that would be driven by music-based rhythm throughout the performance. To ensure a rhythmic organization to the production, Mamoulian cast students who could act *and* dance, and he arranged to have a score—composed by Otto Luening—written during rehearsals (which lasted an extraordinary four months[11]) to ensure that music merged fully with the dramatic action onscreen. In the show, actors slid from talking to (rhythmic) singing, and with the help of choreographer Martha Graham and her assistant, Esther Gustafson, their movements onstage were arranged not as dancing per se, but what Mamoulian called "dance-action."[12] As befitted this more experimental work, Mamoulian presented *Sister Beatrice* (1926) at the 446-seat Kilbourn Hall at the Eastman School of Music rather than the grand 3,352-seat Eastman Theatre where Mamoulian's operatic productions were performed.

Mamoulian, both at the time and in later interviews, stressed the alleged novelty of this approach. Mamoulian's intellectual influences, as chapter 1 discussed, are difficult to pin down, but it bears mentioning that Stanislavski—a highly influential figure when Mamoulian studied theater in Russia—saw drama and the rhythms of music as "kindred forms" and sometimes timed line readings and the duration of pauses and other actions to musical beats. Stanislavski also, like Mamoulian, saw pure realism as a "dead end."[13] Vakhtangov, as discussed in chapter 1, remains another possible influence, while over in Germany, famed theater impresario Max Reinhardt had experimented with the tight interlinking of music and gesture, most famously in *Sumurun* (1912). It is challenging to determine the precise extent to which Mamoulian's rhythmic ideas were in debt to others, but his belief in rhythm's value was clearly genuine.

The result of his experiments with *Sister Beatrice*, according to both Mamoulian and extant reviews of the performance, was extremely positive. Though a few reviewers questioned Mamoulian's claims for the approach's newness, they praised the production, including what one reviewer called its "genuine impression of sincerity."[14] By Mamoulian's account, despite the inexperience of the actors, the audience cried at the end of the production. Whether or not this account is true, Mamoulian concluded two things from his experience. First, rhythm was uniquely impactful on an emotional level.[15] Second, *Sister Beatrice* worked because he had harnessed rhythm to the quality most essential to theatrical performance: onstage movement. As discussed in chapter 1, Mamoulian saw physical movement as the lifeblood of theater. To exploit movement was thus to more fully engage with theater as an art form. Not just any movement would do, however. If people simply walked around while reciting the playwright's lines, such movement would still be subservient to literature. Theater worked best, Mamoulian believed, when onstage movements served as the *primary* means of expressing a play's ideas and emotions. In essence, by fusing rhythm and movement in *Sister Beatrice*, Mamoulian believed he had killed two birds with one stone: he had exploited rhythm's emotional power while drawing upon a medium-specific property to do so.

Stage Rhythm on Broadway

Within the protective cocoon of a smaller theatrical space in a medium-sized city, Mamoulian in *Sister Beatrice* explored theories of rhythm and medium specificity that would—in various ways—inform all of his subsequent work on Broadway and in the movies. Sitting in Kilbourn Hall to observe *Sister Beatrice* was Theatre Guild cofounder Lawrence Langner, and on the basis of this production, he invited Mamoulian to the Theatre Guild in New York City.[16] Between

1927 and 1929, Mamoulian directed six productions on Broadway: *Porgy* (1927), *Marco Millions* (1928), *These Modern Women* (1928), *Congai* (1928), *Wings over Europe* (1928), and *The Game of Love and Death* (1929). None of these productions were musicals, but many would bear clear marks of Mamoulian's continued interest in rhythm on the stage.

Porgy, the play that established Mamoulian as an elite Broadway director, featured two prominent experiments with how sound and physical movement could be fused into a rhythmic whole. The first—*Porgy*'s noise symphony—has become well known, in part because it would later appear relatively unaltered in two of Mamoulian's famous musical productions: the film musical *Love Me Tonight* (1932) and the original stage production of *Porgy and Bess* (1935). *Porgy*'s rhythmic noise symphony was inspired by a trip Mamoulian took to the all-black Catfish Row quarter of Charleston, South Carolina, where the play was set. By his account, he was struck by the "almost musical fluency and rhythm" that he felt characterized life there.[17] Seeking to stylize what he heard, Mamoulian wrote into the margins of *Porgy*'s playscript a four-minute, wordless opening based entirely upon "strictly rhythmic movements and noises," including percussive sounds like snoring, hammering, and broom sweeps falling on different beats, and visual elements like people opening shutters, emerging from doors, and performing household work, all tightly synchronized to a single rhythmic beat. Mamoulian also injected a sense of musical progression into the scene by gradually increasing the volume and density of the noises, and by starting with traditional on-the-beat noises before moving to syncopated beats and finally "ending up with the buoyant gay rhythm of Charleston (the dance)."[18]

Mamoulian's second rhythmic experiment in *Porgy* involved using shadow play in conjunction with the rhythms of song to escalate the emotional intensity of a scene. As discussed in chapter 1, during a scene in which the inhabitants of Catfish Row hold a wake for a murdered man named Robbins in the hopes of raising enough money to pay for his burial, Mamoulian opted to cast the mourners' shadows against the back wall, thereby enabling the shadows to grow in height and provide an exhilarating climax to the scene. We are now in a position to recognize an additional function of those shadows: the enhancement of stage rhythm via the doubling and elongation of actor movements. In the original playscript that Mamoulian received, rhythm was already a dominant concept. Playwrights Dorothy and DuBose Heyward had spelled out an ebbing and flowing of rhythm and intensity throughout the scene, driven by such details as the specific spiritual songs the mourners would sing; when, how fast, and how loudly they would be sung; when the mourners would sway from side to side; and when they would "shout" ("the term given by the Carolina negroes to the body rhythms and steps which they accompany their emotional songs," the

Heywards asserted in the playscript). At the end of the scene, the rhythm was to have "swell[ed] till the old walls seem to rock and surge into the sweep of it."[19]

Mamoulian's marginal notes indicate that while he adhered to these musical and movement-based instructions, his use of cast shadows—a technique absent from the Heywards' original script—helped enhance the rhythmic qualities of the scene. "Slow sway, Shadows," Mamoulian wrote when the curtain first rises on the singing mourners, making it clear that he tied shadow play to this rhythmic physical action.[20] Then, in the margins throughout the scene, Mamoulian carefully noted the pace of the swaying, a movement that would have been greatly emphasized by the mourners' cast shadows. "Crowd moves from single to double swaying," Mamoulian penciled in when the money for the burial is counted ("double swaying" apparently meant that the crowd would sway at twice its former speed).[21] Later, Mamoulian denoted another rhythmic buildup as follows: "1st rows on each side start double swaying, the rest single. They take up the double [swaying] successively by rows until by last verse everyone is double swaying."[22] When the mourners fear that not enough money has been collected, Mamoulian has the mourners stand "motionless—petrified."[23] When the undertaker finally agrees to bury Robbins, Mamoulian notes that "double swaying" resumes.[24] Then, from back to front, the rows of mourners rise, "shout," and (at least according to Mamoulian's later account[25]), lengthen their shadows by walking toward the footlights just before the curtain falls, thereby building a sense of energy via escalating movement. A good deal of the emotional impact of this widely praised scene likely derived from carefully coordinated and rhythmic physical movement, enhanced by lighting and combined with music.

In *Porgy*, Mamoulian used what he saw as the vibrancy of a community to justify salient experiments with visual and sonic rhythm. Yet Mamoulian also utilized stage rhythm in more restrained ways. Mamoulian's production of *Wings over Europe* the following year, for instance (written by Robert Nichols and Maurice Browne), tells the story of Francis Lightfoot, a nephew of the British prime minister who stumbles upon the secret to harnessing atomic energy. Lightfoot wants to use this secret to ensure world peace, but the British cabinet—believing that humanity is not to be trusted with such power—insists that he instead destroy his secret. The entire play—driven heavily by dialogue—takes place in a single room at 10 Downing Street, with a simple oblong table and Britain's thirteen cabinet members onstage for almost the entirety of the production.

The climax of the play occurs when Lightfoot, now disgusted by humanity, announces that he will blow up the world via an atomic bomb when the clock strikes noon. He departs the stage, leaving the cabinet members alone to process this information. In the ensuing dialogue, the cabinet members quickly become hysterical. Seeking to build to this hysteria more carefully and convincingly, Mamoulian arranged a non-verbal set piece that centered on a ticking clock and the rhythmic choreography of small-scale motions by the cabinet members. Mamoulian—by his account—began with a visual and sonic pause: some cabinet members were sitting and some were standing, but all froze in position when Lightfoot left, and no one said a word. After this pause, Mamoulian brought the scene to life by introducing the sound of an offstage metronome, meant to represent the ticking of an onstage clock that no one had previously noticed but that now occupies all the cabinet members' attention. In conjunction with this sound, Mamoulian staged what he called "chain pacing," in which "one man would get up and walk to a certain spot. Then he would stop and the walk would be taken over by another man—from one man to another—all in rhythm—making an uninterrupted sound of feet pacing the floor."[26] This pacing—which apparently lasted somewhere between three and five minutes[27] —occurred in "counterpoint" to the ticking clock/metronome, which grew louder as the pacing progressed. According to Mamoulian, this rhythmic organization helped build up the intensity of the moment, so that when a cabinet member finally opened a cigarette case, and then snapped it shut, the snapping sound felt like a thunderclap, and the audience gasped out loud.[28] To Mamoulian, this reaction once again served as a testament to rhythm's tremendous power, even during a wordless set piece.

Screen Rhythm and *Applause*

On the stage in the 1920s, Mamoulian repeatedly tied actor movements to rhythmic sounds, including music and a variety of sound effects. When Mamoulian turned to film direction, he remained interested in rhythmic physical movement, in part because it appealed to the aesthete in him. Mamoulian was fond of saying that on stage and screen, the best actors incorporated the qualities of the dog and cat. A strong actor shared the dog's ability to become emotional (and presumably to behave in proscribed ways) at the snap of one's fingers, and the cat's ability to move with grace, sophistication, beauty, and rhythm—attributes that could apply equally to stage and screen performance.[29]

Yet at the same time, Mamoulian felt that cinema possessed exciting potentials for rhythm and movement that exceeded what was possible on the stage. In chapter 2, we saw how Mamoulian overcame many technological restrictions to present visually and sonically expressive cinema. Here, I focus instead on how Mamoulian used many of these same methods to give *Applause* an unusual vibrancy and brisk sense of pace for the period.

As noted in the previous chapter, many practitioners felt that an important value of early sound cinema was its ability to provide a more stage-like experience, including the reconstruction of well-known plays and performances for small-town audiences. Yet as Jacobs has documented, some filmmakers and critics quickly began lamenting the sudden loss of crisp pacing associated with the late silent era.[30] Some pacing concerns stemmed from a dissatisfaction with slow dialogue deliveries, but Jacobs demonstrates that most complaints centered on dialogue's tendency to slow down "action," which could mean either "physical movement within the scene" or "narrative pace."[31] A film did not theoretically have to feature extensive dialogue, but we saw in chapter 2 that filmmakers felt pressured to provide it in films touted as "100% talking." Thus, full-sound films of the late 1920s frequently contained many dialogue-heavy sequences featuring direct sound. This had a range of consequences. As chapter 2 demonstrated, filmmakers in 1929 used bulky cameras for direct sound shots, and their microphones struggled to capture intelligible speech when actors moved, resulting in far less camera or character movement than in the late silent era. The duration of individual shots also lengthened to accommodate dialogue, and the industry was often hesitant to make editing adjustments in post-production.[32] With character and camera movement limited, and shots quite lengthy, dialogue emerged as a key element of pacing. This, according to period commentators, generally meant slower-paced films, partly because the era's measured dialogue deliveries simply felt slow, and partly because filmmakers had few alternatives for controlling pace.[33]

Based on extant 1929 all-talking films, efforts to control the tempo of a film indeed seem to have rested primarily on the ways that actors vary the speed, volume level, and frequency of their dialogue. Other techniques that increase pace do appear in 1929: a character might move between his or her dialogue lines, the camera might move, shot lengths might be quicker than the norm, or background music might affect a scene's tempo (such as a frantic ragtime tune that plays during an attempted abduction scene in *The Wild Party* [March 1929]). None of these techniques seems to have been harnessed to rhythmic ends on a consistent basis, however, and dialogue delivery remained the most common determinator of pace in 1929 films.

Given his interest in—and success with—stage rhythm, it is easy to see why Mamoulian had no interest in imitating these prevailing methods when he began shooting *Applause* in June 1929. Just as he wanted to use cinematic devices for expressive purposes (see chapter 2), so too did he seek cinematic ways to give his films movement and a sense of tempo. Thanks to this sensibility, *Applause* stands out in 1929 for its pacing and energy, and it laid the foundations for Mamoulian's later experiments with screen rhythm. A brief look at four categories of pacing—movement within the frame, camera movement, editing, and sound—demonstrate how Mamoulian continued his stage-rhythm techniques while also seeking cinema-specific ways to further generate a brisk sense of pace.

Film Rhythm and Movement within the Frame

Visually, *Applause* contains far more character movement than most films from 1929. Mamoulian's efforts to move his characters around the frame likely stemmed from both his theater work and his knowledge of late silent-era films, but he was also driven by a fascination with what he saw as cinema's unique ability among the representational arts to *reproduce* movement. For Mamoulian, a sculpture or a painting could merely suggest movement, and a piece of literature could only describe it.[34] Cinema, in contrast, could genuinely provide it. In truth, of course, cinema produces only the illusion of movement—still images are projected so rapidly that they appear to move—but for Mamoulian, the result was close enough to genuine movement to make the form special. To Mamoulian, any use of cinema that did not center on movement was a missed opportunity. As he would say in a later interview, "What is action? Action is life. Life is movement.... And this to me is a tremendous thing to be able to register, to capture, to immortalize, a living moment in action. So therefore I think that [cinema] is the most potent marvelous medium that we have."[35]

As chapter 2 demonstrated, Mamoulian leaned heavily on shooting "wild" and adding sound later, which enabled his characters and camera to move more frequently. Mamoulian also, however, found ways to enhance onscreen movement during directly recorded dialogue shots. Two techniques discussed in chapter 1—close framings of walking feet and shadow play—are among his most salient methods for doing this. *Applause* features several close-range shots of walking feet—most notably April's walk down the street before meeting Tony—during directly recorded dialogue, an unorthodox choice within an industry that was instead showcasing moving-lip synchronization. Doing so not only freed the camera from recording the static images of people standing and speaking, but it also enabled Mamoulian to focus on distinctly *rhythmic* motion, since feet tend to walk at a steady pace.

Mamoulian's use of shadow play in *Applause* is not as beat-by-beat rhythmic as walking feet, but it does affect pacing by enabling Mamoulian to magnify movement. Plenty of cast shadows had been used in the silent era, and they had appeared numerous times in all-talking films prior to *Applause* as well. Yet in extant sound films before *Applause*, shadows were seldom used to enhance *movement* in particular. Instead, they were generally employed either to depict censorable content indirectly or to express a (generally motionless) menace. The former—and more common—use includes silhouettes of a police officer being shot and killed (*The Lights of New York* [July 1928]), a hanging (*The Canary Murder Case* [February 1929]), safe cracking (*Rio Rita* [September 1929]), an attempted rape (the British import *Blackmail* [released in the United States in October 1929]), torture (*Bulldog Drummond*

[May 1929]), and strangulation (*Bulldog Drummond* again). Rarely do the silhouettes in these examples move, and when they do—as in *Blackmail*'s brief shadow play of attempted rape—they occur during moments without dialogue and thus do not escalate rhythm during directly recorded dialogue. Examples of shadows denoting danger to a particular character include a through-the-glass-window silhouette of a police detective that causes a terrified suspect to confess in *Alibi* and the elongated cast shadow of an angry captor at an insane asylum in *Bulldog Drummond*. Such shadows are nearly motionless. One of the only pre-*Applause* moments that stresses the movement of silhouettes is a semi-sync scene that was plainly inspired by Mamoulian's own *Porgy*. In *Hallelujah* (August 1929), King Vidor attempts to convey religious and sexual energy at a black church service by throwing the congregants' moving shadows against the back wall. Yet these shots are relatively brief and serve largely as punctuation within a much longer scene.

Mamoulian's shadow play in *Applause*, in contrast, uses *dynamic* shadows *during* directly recorded dialogue moments. The first key instance in *Applause*, discussed also in chapter 1, occurs during a nearly two-minute take featuring constant dialogue in which Hitch coerces Kitty into removing her daughter, April, from the convent. Within this take, Mamoulian stages his actors in three different places within the set, including a concluding position in which Kitty sits scrunched in the bottom of the frame as Hitch's cast shadow gesticulates menacingly (Figure 1.1). One might alternatively praise this expressive use of shadow play or decry it as "heavy-handed symbolism,"[36] but in the context of 1929, it may be most significant for injecting needed movement into a direct-dialogue sequence.

A second, albeit less salient, example of dynamic shadow play for a directly recorded conversation occurs later in the film when April breaks off her engagement with Tony at a restaurant. After beginning with a close-range framing of drumsticks striking a drum—a recurring rhythmic device for Mamoulian that I address later in the chapter—the camera dollies through a group of dancers before reaching the table where April and Tony sit. In the same shot, the duo begins a sync-sound conversation. Even before the camera rests on the duo, the segment is notable for its energy (the cymbal strike, a peppy rendition of "Give Your Baby Lots of Lovin' " played by the band, the roving camera), but Mamoulian manages to maintain some of that energy during the duo's lengthy, static verbal exchange by throwing the shadows of the dancers above April and Tony. As with the previous example, Mamoulian eventually shunts the duo to the bottom half of the frame, thereby allowing the shadows' movements to occupy more space. Such a device is multifunctional, as the revelers' shadows simultaneously remind the audience of the happiness that April and Tony will not have if they separate and help inject energy into a pivotal yet wordy scene.

Film Rhythm and Camera Movement

Because they are anchored in character movement, these examples of visual rhythm were—in certain respects—continuations of Mamoulian's stage methods. We should note, however, that Mamoulian's camera placement regularly augments movement: he puts the camera close to April's walking feet, and he frames his shots so that moving shadows occupy the majority of the image. Clearly, Mamoulian was interested in using devices of cinema to amplify tempo, and this leads us to the next two categories of movement, which he saw as specific to film alone. To Mamoulian, cinema was special because it included character movement while adding two unique arenas for pacing: camera movement and editing. It was for this reason that Mamoulian saw cinema as fundamentally rhythmic: in comparison to the stage, film *tripled* the visual ways in which a director could attain and control rhythm.[37]

As chapter 2 demonstrated, *Applause*'s camera movements were frequent, extensive, narratively expressive, and likely inspired partly by the fluidity of the late silent-era camera. What bears mentioning here is the degree to which Mamoulian felt such movements also helped create rhythm. In a 1932 lecture, Mamoulian outlined what he saw as six key functions of camera movement. Of these functions, only two—concentrating attention and signifying a character's optical point of view—were unrelated to rhythm. Three others—which Mamoulian saw as "closely intertwined"—were mood, rhythm, and tempo. The last function, for Mamoulian, was the "intensification of a design or a movement," by which he meant the doubling of a movement onscreen by camera movement.[38] In an article he wrote in the same year, Mamoulian elaborated further, arguing that rhythm was the single most important factor to consider when moving the camera, and that anyone moving the camera should be mindful of the "tempo" of the onscreen action. Camera movement, Mamoulian professed, must "follow out the same rhythm [as onscreen action], or, in some rare instances, increase it."[39] In a later interview, Mamoulian would point to the camera movement during Kitty's lullaby to April as an example. As chapter 2 demonstrated, the in-and-out movements during this five-minute shot convey intimacy while reminding audiences of the dangerous outside world. For Mamoulian, these slow, gliding dolly movements also constituted a rhythmic match with Kitty's soothing lullaby. Attaining and controlling film rhythm was a major reason that Mamoulian moved the camera so often in *Applause*.

Film Rhythm and Editing: Bad Entertainment

Picture editing was the other cinema-specific rhythmic tool that Mamoulian valued. Mamoulian disliked the word "cutting"—the standard industry term for editing at the time—because it suggested only the breaking apart of a film, not the more important act of construction. To Mamoulian, editing was about *assembling* a series of images, and the primary purpose for doing so was the enhancement of a film's rhythmic qualities.[40]

In *Applause*, Mamoulian's clearest example of editing grounded in rhythm occurs in what I call the "bad-entertainment" sequence, in which April witnesses her mother's degrading burlesque performance from a seat in the audience. The sequence, shot mostly silent, features extraordinarily rapid editing. The entire scene consists of forty-two shots, and even factoring in the first image—a twenty-six-second establishing shot—the average shot length (ASL) remains just under four seconds (Table 3.1). Though such an ASL would attract little attention in today's filmmaking, in the late 1920s and early 1930s the arrival of sound had extended ASLs to around eleven seconds, making the editing in this scene strikingly quick.[41]

Just as important as the scene's ASL is the distinct patterning and consistency of its shot lengths. Not including shots 1–3 and shot 42, which serve as lengthier long-range establishing shots, the scene divides clearly into two segments on the basis of shot scale, musical selection, and—most notably—shot duration. In the first segment, which spans shots 4–16 (in bold font in Table 3.1), Kitty—and then the other burlesque dancers—enter the stage, walk up and down the runway, and exit the stage. In this segment, which is accompanied on the soundtrack by a vocal and instrumental rendition of "Give Your Baby Lots of Lovin,'" Mamoulian generally places his camera at a medium distance from the subjects being filmed. The shots he provides are not just more rapid than the norm, but also unusually consistent in duration. This consistency becomes especially notable in shots 10–15, which depict the dancers taking the runway, shaking their breasts, and then exiting. Here, every shot occupies an extremely narrow range of 2.8 to 3.9 seconds. In the second segment (italicized in Table 3.1), which spans shots 17–41 and features a new instrumental number, the dancers take the stage again, and Mamoulian further escalates the scene's overall tempo. The music's pace is far faster, the shots are at closer range (thus enhancing the amount of movement within the frame), and the musicians are frequent subjects in these shots (a way of directing attention toward the increasing musical tempo). Most remarkably, the second segment's shot lengths are shorter and even more consistent. For twenty consecutive shots (shots 20–39, which is nearly the entirety of that segment), the shots all fall between 1.1 and 1.7 seconds.

The result is a scene oriented around two cinematic bursts of adrenaline that coincide with the gyrations of the chorus line. While in different hands these up-tempo moments might fuel a viewer's sense of excitement or titillation, Mamoulian's decision to push the camera uncomfortably close to his subjects instead ties this jolt of energy to invasiveness and grotesquerie (Figures 3.1 and 3.2). Mamoulian further condemns burlesque by bracketing

Table 3.1 A shot-by-shot breakdown of Mamoulian's rhythmic editing during the second burlesque number in *Applause*, which includes two series of rigorously consistent shot lengths timed with two different songs. The bold type denotes shots seen during the song "Give Your Baby Lots of Lovin'" and the italicized type indicates shots presented during the second, up-tempo number. These two rhythmic numbers are bracketed by establishing/reestablishing shots that begin and end the scene, which are in Roman (regular) type.

Shot #	Length (seconds)	Description
1	25.7	LS (long shot) as April and escort walk inside theater and toward their seats.
2	12.9	MS (medium shot) as they sit down and are yelled at by an audience member.
3	9.8	LS of dancer exiting the stage.
4	8.7	**(New song: "Give Your Baby Lots of Lovin'"). LS of Kitty entering the stage and beginning to sing.**
5	3.2	**CU (close up) on April's uncomprehending expression. She looks to the side.**
6	10.7	**MCU (medium close-up) camera tilts and pans to capture hecklers and then rests on April.**
7	7.7	**XLS (extreme long shot) of Kitty performing. More dancers appear on stage.**
8	5.1	Backs of seated customers; portion of dancers' legs visible on stage.
9	5.2	XLS as dancers walk onto the runway.
10	3.6	Top shot of walking dancers.
11	3.5	MS of Kitty shaking her breasts for the audience.
12	3.4	High-angle LS of the other dancers doing the same.
13	3.9	XLS of dancers walking on runway back in direction of the stage.
14	2.8	XLS of dancers walking on runway, with Kitty visible nearest the camera.
15	3.0	LS of Kitty as she hustles off stage.
16	1.8	LS of April hanging her head.
17	8.6	*(New up-tempo instrumental song): XLS of dancers' backs as they take the stage again.*
18	1.2	*MLS (medium long shot) of several male audience members.*
19	3.4	*CU tracking shot on backs of dancers' bare legs.*

Table 3.1 Continued

Shot #	Length (seconds)	Description
20	1.1	MS of audience members gesturing and pointing.
21	1.3	MCU of audience members.
22	1.2	Low-angle CU of a dancer's legs.
23	1.2	CU of audience member watching.
24	1.2	CU of dancer's face.
25	1.1	CU of audience member watching.
26	1.1	CU of dancer's face.
27	1.2	CU of audience member watching.
28	1.3	CU of dancer's face.
29	1.2	CU of audience member watching.
30	1.5	MS of swaying orchestra conductor.
31	1.3	CU of dancer's face.
32	1.3	CU of two dancers' hips.
33	1.1	CU of audience member watching.
34	1.1	CU of dancer's face.
35	1.5	CU of dancer's upper legs.
36	1.7	MS of bass player swinging his instrument.
37	1.2	CU of trombonist, his slide nearly hitting the camera lens.
38	1.6	XCU (extreme close up) of dancer's face.
39	1.7	XCU of audience member's face.
40	2.9	CU of Kitty's face. Dissolve to . . .
41	2.3	CU of April's face.
42	10.2	XLS, high-angle, of April and escort leaving their seats.

both burlesque numbers with shots of the dismayed April. One can easily interpret this scene as Mamoulian's personal commentary on burlesque, but such bracketing also encourages us to view everything in the sequence as April's subjective impressions of the show. Fueled by carefully chosen shot sequencing, music, camera proximity, and shot lengths, the scene's escalating pace gives us the sense that the vulgar, squalid burlesque world is overcooking in April's mind.

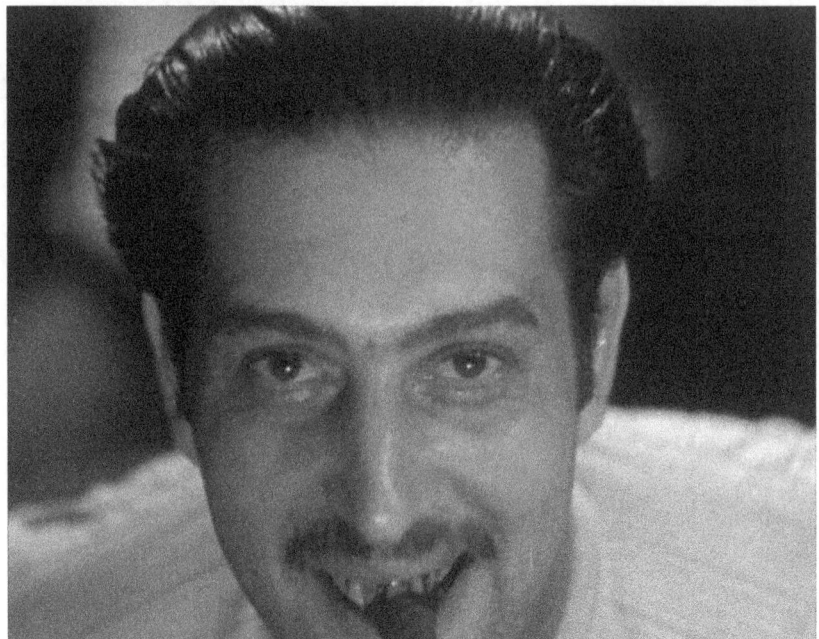

Figure 3.1. During the second burlesque number in *Applause*, as the editing pace escalates, Mamoulian discourages the movie audience from becoming enraptured by the performance by pushing the camera uncomfortably close to spectators . . .

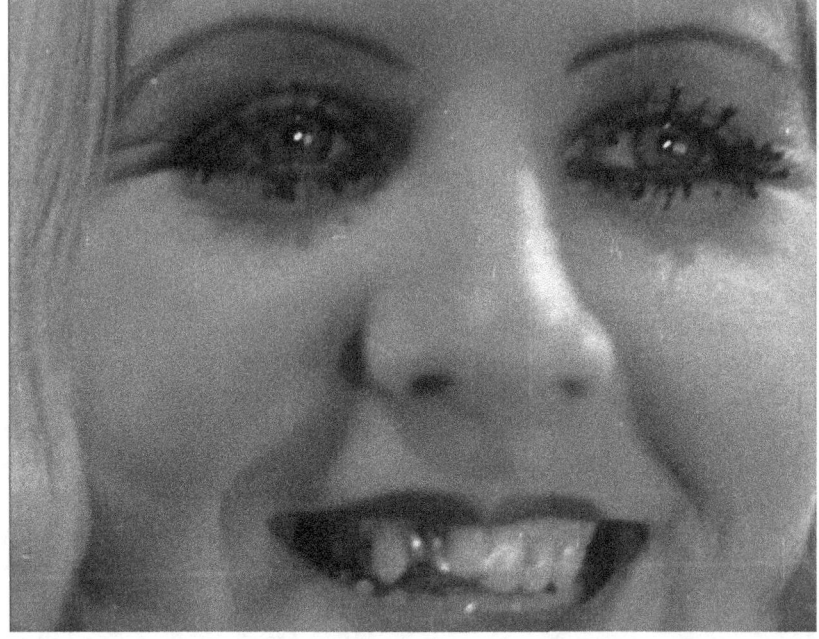

Figure 3.2 . . . and performers.

Applause's bad-entertainment scene stands as an early testament to the importance Mamoulian ascribed to sound-era rhythm, particularly where editing was concerned. As anyone familiar with Soviet montage editing knows, rapid editing was hardly new to cinema. It is difficult, however, to find a 100 percent talking film in the United States prior to *Applause* featuring a scene with such an overt experiment with rapid editing. Perhaps the closest pre-*Applause* example occurs in the shadow-play scene from *Hallelujah* mentioned above, which contains a crazed—and racially stereotyped—blend of religious frenzy and sexual desire at an all-black church revival meeting. At three different moments in this scene, Vidor uses a series of quickly edited facial close-ups: three shots when preacher Zeke (Daniel L. Haynes) first sees the woman he lusts after, Chick (Nina Mae McKinney), and his fiancée realizes what is likely to occur; two consecutive shots showing the disapproving looks of his mother and his fiancée; and five shots of Zeke and Chick locking glances while Zeke's father looks on expressionlessly. Vidor was—like Mamoulian—interested in rhythmic editing in early sound film, but the editing in this scene is not as lengthy, as consistently patterned, or as grounded in a single character's psychology as *Applause*. Only ten total shots in *Hallelujah* are similar in length to an adjoining one (compared to thirty-one in *Applause*), these rapid shots constitute a very small percentage of a much longer scene, and their shot lengths are not as consistent. For *Hallelujah*, rhythmic editing is a momentary stimulant; for *Applause*, it constitutes the organizing principle of an entire scene.

Film Rhythm and Sound

Mamoulian's image-based efforts to control and heighten rhythm were unusual in 1929, but all, in various ways, had lineages in silent-era filmmaking. What may be most notable about *Applause*'s rhythm is the way that the soundtrack itself creates a sense of energy. Sound, we saw earlier, was commonly cited as a reason for the slowdown of cinematic tempo at the time *Applause* was made, but *Applause*'s sound often does the opposite. For instance, the film's use of rapid-fire dialogue—especially during arguments between Kitty and Hitch—flies in the face of the slower, more enunciated deliveries common at the time.[42] *The Front Page*, released two years later, is often credited with showing the sound-film potentials of peppy dialogue. The argument scenes between Kitty and Hitch, however, deserve recognition not just for the rapidity of the dialogue, but for the way in which they set into clearer relief the relaxed exchanges between April and Tony, whose conversations generally feature a slower, more deliberate speaking style and comfortable pauses in the conversation. The scenes in *Applause* containing unusually dense, raucous background sounds described in chapter 2—the New York City streets, the jeering burlesque crowd, the burlesque music that seeps into every backstage space—also fuel the film's sense of energy.

Perhaps the most overtly sound-based rhythmic experiment in the film, however, is the noise symphony that Mamoulian wrote to accompany Kitty after she poisons herself. As noted in the previous chapter, Mamoulian created a contrapuntal, "life goes on" soundtrack during this moment, which included city noises generated by property men in an adjoining room. As we saw, these sounds become increasingly dense and loud. This, alone, conveys an escalating sense of tempo and urgency, but this "symphony" is distinctly rhythmic in two additional ways. First, Mamoulian included a ticking clock sound to keep all the noises—in his words—in "a rhythmic frame." Second, to make sure all sounds were produced at the pace he wanted, Mamoulian apparently grabbed a conductor's baton and literally conducted this "noise symphony."[43] The rhythmic ticking—and the symphony-like orchestration of city noises—clearly resembles Mamoulian's prior stage work in *Wings over Europe* and *Porgy*.

It is rare to find sound effects configured in rhythmic ways prior to *Applause* in US cinema. To my knowledge, the main precursor was Roland West's *Alibi* (April 1929), which repeatedly uses pronounced rhythms to mark the presence of the law. The film's opening contains more than a minute's worth of rhythmic jail sounds, including the sounds of a guard's nightstick and prisoners' marching feet, which thud roughly in double time with the nightstick's taps. Later examples include more sounds of tapping nightsticks and shrill police whistles when an officer calls for backup, and a suspect who confesses after a police officer's rhythmic vocal interrogation breaks him down. Still later, at a police headquarters phone-operator exchange, three operators speak in alternating bursts of short, rhythmic speech as they put out an arrest bulletin for a criminal. Along with *Alibi*, *Applause* was one of the few films from 1929 to self-consciously create a distinct beat and sense of rhythm via its non-musical sounds.

Thinking in parallel with a few other enterprising sound filmmakers, Mamoulian—at a time when the industry struggled with tempo—demonstrated how filmmakers could return to something resembling silent-era pacing methods, and how sound itself might be stylized in rhythmic ways. *Applause* deserves recognition for its early efforts to harness the tools of cinema to the control and escalation of cinematic tempo.

Experiments after *Applause*: Batons, Metronomes, Subjectivity, and Sound/Image Speed

By the time Mamoulian shot his next film, *City Streets*, in early 1931, cinematic rhythm in sound cinema seems to have been a greater industry concern, and like expressive sound (see chapter 2), one finds more films from this period using some of the pacing tools found in *Applause*. As discussed in chapter 2, boom mics enabled actors to move during dialogue scenes, and camera movement increased. Average shot lengths began to shorten as multiple-camera shooting was phased out, though they would not quite return to silent-film levels.[44] And while overtly rhythmic soundtracks remained rare, dialogue deliveries were beginning to quicken, and an incremental increase in re-recording gave filmmakers more control over sound-based pacing methods.[45] Films during this period were not necessarily imitating *Applause* directly, but Mamoulian had plainly hit upon values that the industry would embrace.

Mamoulian's ideas about rhythm remained fairly consistent in his later films, but one still periodically finds rhythmic experiments. Perhaps his most unorthodox approach was his on-set use of metronome and baton. Unfortunately, evidence on the extent to which he used these devices is slim. Speaking to a group of students in 1939, Mamoulian asserted, "I use a metronome quite frequently in pictures,—whenever precise and sustained timing is necessary for action or camera. You can use it on the set so that it is not picked up by the microphone."[46] On the stage, Mamoulian had rehearsed *Porgy*'s noise symphony with a baton,[47] and we saw that Mamoulian used a metronome to simulate a ticking clock in *Wings over Europe*. We also saw that Mamoulian wielded a conductor's baton to cue various noises after Kitty takes poison in *Applause*. Interviews indicate that he used a baton and/or metronome during the noise-symphony opening of *Love Me Tonight* and in many other parts of the film (see chapter 4), when Lily (Marlene Dietrich) sneaks out of her home to pose for a sculptor in *The Song of Songs*, and when the title character (played by Greta Garbo) from *Queen Christina* traverses her bedroom and touches objects to preserve them in her memory (see chapter 6). Production stills for *Dr. Jekyll and Mr. Hyde* and *Love Me Tonight* show Mamoulian wielding a conductor's baton. The actual extent of this usage, however, remains unknown.

More evident within the films themselves are two other atypical methods for rhythmic control: cinematic subjectivity and the literal speeding up and slowing down of image or sound. As discussed in chapter 2, Mamoulian was one of the earliest sound filmmakers to overtly explore subjective filmmaking, and these experiments are often accompanied by an increase in tempo. When April has a nightmare in *Applause*, when voice-over memories flood Nan's head in *City Streets*, or when Jekyll first transforms into Hyde in *Dr. Jekyll and Mr. Hyde*, Mamoulian enjoyed escalating the pace by using densely layered imagery and/or sound, thereby conveying a more dynamic and charged psychological experience.

Of these examples, Jekyll's transformation provides perhaps the oddest *and* clearest illustration of Mamoulian's belief that cinema was uniquely rhythmic and impactful. We saw in chapter 2 that Mamoulian used a re-recorded conglomeration of unfamiliar sounds during this moment. Doing so, to Mamoulian's mind, lent an added sense of what Mamoulian called "tension and urgency."[48] Two sounds during the transformation—Jekyll's panting and Mamoulian's own heartbeat—are decidedly rhythmic, and Mamoulian felt that the latter gave the sequence (like the ticking clock in *Applause*) its "rhythmic backbone."[49]

Further amplifying the pace are the two *visual* features that Mamoulian saw as unique to cinema: camera movement and editing. When Jekyll first takes the potion in a point-of-view shot, the camera begins panning in rapid circles. Though the room remains in focus for the first few moments, it quickly becomes blurred due to the speed of the pan. Mamoulian would later describe how the shot was attained:

> We had to completely loosen the camera, so it could freely revolve around its base, thereby subjecting all four walls of the set to photography.... In order to make it possible for the focus man to handle his duty efficiently, we placed him on the top of the camera box and tied him to it with a rope, so he handled the focus from up above. It was lucky for us that the assistant cameraman was of a diminutive stature.[50]

Mamoulian also employed editing via superimpositions. When the spinning camera begins to go out of focus, Mamoulian starts superimposing other blurred footage and faces from Jekyll's life. The whirling camera and superimpositions create an extraordinary degree of movement—especially for an early sound-era film—and this sense of speed is amplified further by the fact that the blurred superimposed footage moves in the opposite direction from the panning point-of-view camera. If rhythm and movement, as Mamoulian believed, held immense power, this moment offers one of his more persuasive pieces of evidence. The rapid pacing invokes the chaos and danger of Jekyll's transformation, as well as the freedom it affords him.

This rhythmic sensation of superimpositions combined with spinning camera movements was highly unusual—if not unique—in US cinema at this time. Occasional kinetic superimpositions *or* vertiginous camera movements can be found prior to *Dr. Jekyll and Mr. Hyde*, but they are not used in combination, and they are generally introductory flourishes rather than efforts to advance the narrative. *Broadway* (May 1929) opens with a thirty-second introduction to a New York City nightclub by superimposing exterior shots of the streets of Broadway with images of dancing and rowdy patrons. *Glorifying the American Girl* (December 1929) opens with three minutes of superimpositions that glamorize Broadway entertainment. *Little Caesar* (January 1931) does advance the narrative by using superimpositions to pump energy into a New

Year's Eve robbery and killing, but its superimpositions are not as kinetic as Mamoulian's. Rapid camera pans are rarer in early US sound cinema, and they are generally quite brief. In *Broadway*, the camera appears to swivel rapidly in 360-degree pans in two quick shots at the end of its splashy two-strip Technicolor finale. In *The Front Page*, Lewis Milestone's camera tilts rapidly up and down in rhythm with a song that a group of newspaper writers are singing. None of these rapid movements, however, occurs for more than a few seconds at a time, whereas Mamoulian's rapid panning lasts fifty-two unbroken seconds. Overtly subjective camera work had been embraced by the French Impressionists in the late silent era, but in the context of early sound production in Hollywood, *Dr. Jekyll and Mr. Hyde* clearly stood out for providing such sustained, abstract, and dynamic imagery.

Though *Dr. Jekyll and Mr. Hyde*'s distorted images and sounds are justified by a narrative moment that is psychological and supernatural, Mamoulian was also willing to warp *non*-subjective moments in rhythmic ways if he felt the situation warranted it. One of Mamoulian's more unorthodox ways for doing so was among his simplest: literally speeding up or slowing down images and sounds. As I will discuss in chapter 4, Mamoulian speeds up and slows down footage at various points in *Love Me Tonight*, including a comic moment when Maurice mounts and rides the rambunctious horse Solitude at preposterous speed. Five years later in *High, Wide and Handsome*, Mamoulian repeated this device by undercranking a shot of the eager Peter riding away on his horse to propose to Sally.

On at least one occasion, Mamoulian increased the tempo of a sound effect. In *High, Wide and Handsome*, the villainous Walt Brennon decides to use his railroad engine to transport men who will wreck the oil pipeline that Peter and his friends are constructing. The oil pipeline workers hear and see the arrival of the engine, but as the engine pulls to a stop, something unusual happens: the rhythmic chug of its wheels actually increases in tempo—the opposite of what would occur in reality. The result is a sonic mismatch on the level of realism, but a close correlation in terms of dramatic import. What mattered to Mamoulian was what the engine and its noise signaled to the workers toiling on the pipeline, and he used an increased sonic tempo to charge the moment with a sense of danger and adrenaline.[51] Whether internal or external to character psychology, Mamoulian always saw sound and image as fair game for rhythmic adjustments.

Musical Approaches to Non-Musicals

Implicit in everything examined so far is the belief that an artist's fundamental job is to set life to rhythm. This assumption drove Mamoulian's direction of

Rochester operas and Broadway drama. In cinema, it informed the pacing of his early sound films and his other unorthodox experiments. In the next chapter, we will analyze Mamoulian's work in musicals, the genre most clearly oriented around arranging life in such a manner. Before doing so, however, we need to examine one more topic: how Mamoulian used musical performances within his non-musicals to control pace and guide viewer response.

Examining Mamoulian's handling of diegetic musical performances reveals how strongly his sensibility was geared toward carefully choreographed—and rhythmically oriented—set pieces, no matter the genre. Mamoulian, himself, recognized this feature in his work. In an early 1970s interview, Mamoulian was asked to pick one of his non-musical film that still achieved an ideal blending of various types of rhythms. Mamoulian responded as follows:

> *Blood and Sand* is not a musical, obviously. But to me, right from the beginning, every action, every set, every [movement] of the camera was rhythmic and musical.... A true musical is when action becomes music, when imagery becomes music.... A design. Choreography. Rhythm. And I try to get that into every film I do. I think in *Blood and Sand* there are long, pictorial sequences where you have the music of movement and the music of the camera and the music of the montage.[52]

For Mamoulian, then, a "musical" number was not merely a matter of singing or performance, but rather involved a director's effort to rhythmically unify character action, camera movement, editing, and sound. Thus, to understand why Mamoulian played such a defining role in film musicals, it is useful to examine the ways in which Mamoulian managed to imbue even his non-musical films with elements commonly associated with the musical genre: musical performance, elaborate choreography, and—at times—a sense of lifting off from the prosaic physical world.

The sheer importance Mamoulian placed on the *rhythmic* nature of diegetic musical performances can be gleaned by noting several instances when Mamoulian opened a scene with a close-range shot of a musician's hands rhythmically beating on an instrument. Along with *City Streets* and *Blood and Sand* (see below), examples include a late scene in *Dr. Jekyll and Mr. Hyde* in which Muriel's hands rhythmically pound the piano keys in frustration, the restaurant breakup scene in *Applause* that begins with two close-range shots of a drum being rapidly struck, and a similar opening at a nightclub in *Rings on Her Fingers* that begins with a close-range shot of a drummer furiously banging on the drums (the name of the band is later revealed to be the "Rhythm Boys").

With the exception of *Applause*, which often features live music that plays at an independent rhythm while characters focus on more pressing matters,

Mamoulian generally selected diegetic music featuring tempos that were "in sync" with a character's mood or behavior. A simple example occurs during an early section of *Dr. Jekyll and Mr. Hyde*. The scene, set at the home of Muriel's father, shows Jekyll arriving late to the upscale gathering due to his charity work, only to be forgiven by fiancée Muriel. The sequence serves as the film's chief opportunity to convey the gloriousness of Jekyll's relationship with Muriel as well as his sexual desire for her, and Mamoulian expresses this by showing the couple dancing to two live waltzes. When Jekyll arrives, he begins to dance with Muriel to a moderately paced waltz, and the duo spins as they move across the dance floor. Because Mamoulian's roving camera keeps them closely framed, the sensation of rhythmic movement provided by the characters and camera remains strong. An erotic interlude in the garden, which I discuss in chapter 6, coincidences with a new waltz—Luigi Arditi's "Il Bacio"—played at a much faster tempo. Jekyll and Muriel then rejoin the party as "Il Bacio" continues to play, and the couple again spins in a tightly framed medium close-up, the camera still tracking continuously to follow their movements.

The rhythmic and movement-based foundation of this scene—along with the increasing musical tempo—provides a sense of romantic exhilaration and serves as an important means for indicating that Jekyll has become sexually charged by his proximity to Muriel. This tempo reaches its peak in the final shot, which features the five-piece orchestra playing "Il Bacio" at a continuously escalating pace. If the scene's rhythm reaches its height here, however, the next scene presents its antithesis. Mamoulian dissolves to an after-party image of the vacated chairs of the now-departed orchestra. This moment of visual and rhythmic emptiness sets the stage for what follows, as Muriel's father rejects Jekyll's pleas for a quick marriage to Muriel. The camera pans to the left to frame Muriel's father, who then walks over to Muriel and Jekyll, the camera panning right to follow his movements. The camera then slowly tracks forward to center on the ensuing conversation. When it becomes clear that Muriel's father will not relent, the camera grinds to a halt in medium shot, and for the next twenty-five seconds we experience nothing but a still camera trained on two men who stand rigidly in place and talk. Muriel's father has slowed down the couple's romance— and the film's rhythm—in its tracks.

Displaying the makers of music, and matching music's tempo to narrative situations, was important to Mamoulian. Also significant was Mamoulian's unusual tendency to use, and even showcase, what would have been seen as "ethnic" music from underrepresented or disadvantaged groups. This interest may have stemmed from Mamoulian's own minority status as an Armenian immigrant working in Hollywood, and it would directly inform his work in the folk musical. Mamoulian's first effort in this area comes during a brief yet telling moment in a nightclub scene in *City Streets*. In the film's initial typed screenplay, the scene was to have begun with a close-up of a canopy featuring the name of the nightclub, followed by a medium shot of the exterior of the club, and then a full shot of the club's interior, where people dance to music. In his copy of the screenplay, Mamoulian crossed out this sequencing and penciled in what appears in the finished film. The scene instead begins inside the nightclub with a close-range shot of a drummer's hand furiously striking a cymbal with a stick, and the camera then slowly tracks back to present a ten-person African American jazz band. Only after holding this shot of the band for several more seconds does Mamoulian finally dissolve to the shot of the dance floor that the script had designated.

Rhythmically, Mamoulian's change enables him to better characterize the nightclub as a space of exciting music and rapid rhythms. Yet the sheer decision to emphasize an all-black jazz band is also notable. Though African American jazz musicians had been featured in some short films—and Duke Ellington and his band had played an important role in RKO's Amos and Andy feature *Check and Double Check* (October 1930)—the foregrounding of African American bands in feature films was still relatively uncommon in early 1931.[53] A more typical handling of black jazz musicians can be found in another gangster film released in the same month as *City Streets*: William Wellman's *The Public Enemy*. In that film, a nightclub scene similarly opens with an all-black jazz band playing at a "black and tan" nightclub (a place with mixed black and white attendance). Yet unlike *City Streets*, *The Public Enemy* immediately obscures our view of the band by placing white dancers in the foreground. Then, within five seconds, the film entirely removes the jazz band from view by panning and tracking away from the band. This jazz band never reappears.

Mamoulian's unusual attentiveness to the African American jazz band in *City Streets* speaks to his lifelong love of the music making of various peoples, especially African Americans.[54] Throughout his career, Mamoulian regularly directed stage properties featuring nearly all-black casts (*Porgy*, *Porgy and Bess*, *St. Louis Woman* [1946], *Lost in the Stars* [1949]), though we should note that the music from these shows—outside of prominent black spirituals in *Porgy*—was not composed by African Americans. In cinema, Mamoulian worked within an industry less receptive to African American representation, which may account for the lack of black musicianship in his films aside from *City Streets*. Still, his subsequent movies would sometimes feature live musical performances designed to be specific to culturally marginalized groups. The rhythms of such music often serve as the organizing principle of the scene.

Two key examples occur in *We Live Again* (1934) and *Golden Boy* (1939). Adapted from Leo Tolstoy's novel *Resurrection* (1899), *We Live Again*'s opening scenes center on Prince Dmitri (Fredric March), a youthful idealist living in tsarist Russian who passionately believes in land and equality for all. As the film progresses, Dmitri loses his moral compass by descending into the casual cruelty and decadence found in the aristocratic military. Mamoulian portrays Dmitri's descent not through dialogue, but via a three-scene sequence dominated by two performances by a Romani band (referred to in the screenplay as a "gypsy" band[55]). Just prior to the sequence, a superior in the army had berated Dmitri for caring little for army/aristocratic behavior, which includes flirting with army wives. The superior disgustedly chucks a workers' rights tract Dmitri had been reading—titled *Land and Freedom*—into the fire, which Dmitri hurriedly rescues after the superior departs. The sequence that follows is nearly wordless and heavily grounded in musical rhythm. In the first scene, the Romani band—consisting of guitarists and singers—performs a slow-paced song for the aristocratic guests at a posh house party. One of the guests—apparently an army wife (toned down from a courtesan in Leonard Praskins's original screenplay[56])—encourages the reluctant Dmitri to drink more alcohol and kiss her. Following a very brief scene showing military training, the same band performs again, this time playing a tune that increases in tempo until it becomes a fast-paced dance, with a Romani man dancing to it. Accompanying this shift in musical rhythm, we find Dmitri a far less resistant man: he eagerly and easily smooches the reclining woman in his lap, callously slaps the face of a servant who accidentally spills a bit of alcohol, and lights a cigarette using a torn page from *Land and Freedom* as his match.

There is little doubt that the decision to emphasize music and rhythm in this sequence was Mamoulian's. In Praskins's original screenplay, only one shot had included the band in the frame. In the margin for this sequence, Mamoulian wrote "singer" and "guitarist,"[57] and in the finished film, the Romani band is a major sonic and visual presence. In the first segment, Mamoulian opens with a shot of only the band (Figure 3.3) before slowly panning and tracking away to show the partiers. The band then looms in the background of three additional shots, and their music is the only sound heard (Figure 3.4). In the third segment, the band largely dominates the soundtrack and is again prominent in the first shot. Mamoulian then cuts back to the band five more times.

Beyond its sheer presence, the Romani band's saliency and the rhythms of its music infuse the sequence with considerable meaning. In the sequence's opening shot, Mamoulian throws his signature elongated shadows of the musicians against the back wall (Figure 3.3). This visual emphasis helps remind viewers about the ideals Dmitri once held about aiding the poor. Thanks to the band's prominence, when Dmitri looks around nervously before kissing the army wife in the first segment, it is as if he is glancing at the band members themselves, perhaps as a tacit acknowledgment that he is turning away from his social-justice ideals and his love for commoner Katusha. By the second band-music segment,

Figure 3.3 In *We Live Again*, Mamoulian arranged for the Romani band and its music to play a central role during Dmitri's downfall scenes, opening with a shot of the band (with elongated shadows) . . .

Dmitri has plainly forgotten his ideals, but the saliency of the Romani performers still reminds the *viewer* of how far he has fallen. Moreover, the quickening of the music's pace in this scene—which culminates in a Romani dance at a frenetic clip—offers a simultaneously sincere and ironic musical accompaniment to the story. It is sincere in the sense that the quickening tempo (along with shorter shot lengths) reflects Dmitri's growing debauchery and his embrace of a wilder, more hedonistic lifestyle, a stereotyped association between "gypsy" music and "hot-blooded" behavior.[58] But because the film has framed this change as a descent for Dmitri, the music's celebratory tempo also emphasizes the bitter power dynamics of this society. Members of the lower classes, on this movie's terms, entertain the elites not because they are happy, but because those in power demand that they appear so. Their very presence underscores the wealth and power disparity that Dmitri once abhorred. Thus, when Dmitri slaps a waiter just as the music reaches its happy, fevered pitch, Mamoulian's use of rhythm helps cement the commoners' status as little more than paid servants who can be mistreated at will. The band's cheerful rhythm reflects the false narrative of a just society that the aristocrats cloak themselves within. This delusion is at the heart of what

Figure 3.4 ... and placing the performing band in the frame in many subsequent shots.

transpires in the remainder of the film, and Mamoulian makes the rhythms of indigenous musical performance central to this idea.

Unlike *We Live Again*, *Golden Boy*'s group-music performance is purely celebratory, but it is equally important culturally, rhythmically, and narratively. Midway through the film, aspiring boxing champion Joe Bonaparte takes love-interest Lorna (Barbara Stanwyck) to the flat of his Italian American family to have dinner. After dinner, the original screenplay had stipulated that the family—which includes Joe's immigrant father, his sister, his brother-in-law, and his Jewish neighbor Carp—hum a bit of an "Italian folk song." Mamoulian's handwritten screenplay annotations, which are extensive for this scene, indicate that he was responsible for eliminating the humming and instead having the entire group gather around the piano to sing an impromptu rendition of Luigi Denza and Peppino Turco's bouncy "Funiculì, Funiculà."[59] The moment is among the most joyous of Mamoulian's career, and though it lacks the biting irony of the peasant songs in *We Live Again*, it nevertheless features a song distinctive to a group of people performed by those far removed from wealth and privilege. *Golden Boy* is a story of a young man who seeks to use boxing to rise above the social and financial status of his working-class, immigrant family. Yet doing so, on *Golden Boy*'s terms, means selling out, doing harm to the world, and turning one's back on such values as nurture and beauty, qualities that—as chapter 1 discussed—are also conveyed via carefully framed Italian artwork in the Bonaparte flat. The peppy "Funiculì, Funiculà" thus not only injects a positive sense of energy and rhythm into a narratively appropriate space, but it also marks that space as inclusive (both the Jewish Carp and outsider Lorna are included in the number) rather than damaging. Moreover, it uses the rhythm of communal song to explain why Lorna might feel comfortable in that space, and why she begins looking out for Joe's best interests. Diegetic music performance, for Mamoulian, once again conveys narratively essential emotions and ideas through song selection and musical tempo.

Musical Performances and Darryl Zanuck

No discussion of Mamoulian's handling of diegetic musical performance and rhythm would be complete without examining two early 1940s films Mamoulian made for Darryl Zanuck at Fox starring Tyrone Power: *The Mark of Zorro* and *Blood and Sand*. Unlike *City Streets*, *We Live Again*, and *Golden Boy*, which arguably feature less-patterned bursts of rhythm, *The Mark of Zorro* and *Blood and Sand* appear to have been consistently organized around a particular set of rhythms across their running times. One reason for this difference may be that Zanuck, who worked closely with Mamoulian on both films,[60] was particularly attuned to film rhythm. In a 1941 memo to all of Fox's producers, Zanuck declared a film's "lack of tempo" as "public enemy #1," and he was known for favoring fast-paced cinema.[61] Live music is not wall-to-wall in either film, but when it is present, Mamoulian consistently ties it to other elements of film style, narrative ideas, emotional qualities, and broader rhythmic patterns.

The Mark of Zorro—a considerable hit—is the less overtly stylish of the two, yet it is a story driven by rhythmic contrasts. Early stretches of *The Mark of Zorro* paint a portrait of a nineteenth-century Southern Californian world that has run out of steam. We learn that Diego's father, the former alcalde Don Alejandro, has been forced from his position in favor of a corrupt ruler—Don Luis—who heaps onerous taxes on the impoverished peasantry. When Diego (Tyrone Power) is summoned by his father from Spain and arrives in California, the film presents a situation that appears stagnant and unchangeable: Diego's law-abiding father will not take back the alcalde title by subversive means, and the peasants lack the strength to resist.

To reflect this stasis, Mamoulian provides little in the way of overt rhythmic experiments in the early stretches of the California sequences. Early on, for instance, Diego walks into a California saloon to request passage to see his father.

Seated against the wall, a peasant guitarist—with a companion on either side—plays and sings a Spanish-language song. Mamoulian foregrounds the song sonically (it is the only sound heard as Diego enters the building) and visually (Mamoulian cuts twice to closely framed shots of the threesome). What appears to be the start of a diegetic performance, however, is halted in its tracks when Diego mentions he is the son of the alcalde. The song immediately stops, and the three peasants fearfully lower their heads so that we see only the tops of their sombreros.

Into this world of inertia and resignation rides Zorro, a character Diego creates by taking advantage of the superior swordsmanship and horseback riding he learned in Spain. Zorro's first appearance twenty-two minutes into the film epitomizes the rhythmic stylization that Mamoulian sought. Though the scene does not feature a musical performance, it remains notable for the tools Mamoulian uses to escalate the scene's tempo. In the original screenplay (written before Mamoulian entered the project), Zorro's entrance was to have totaled a mere four shots: a close-up of a taxation notice that a soldier puts up followed by Zorro's blade slashing it down, a longer shot of Zorro forcing the soldier to put up a new notice condemning the alcalde, a close up of this new notice, and a longer shot of Zorro tearing a "Z" into the tunic of the soldier and then galloping away.[62] Mamoulian expanded the number of shots to thirty-two and organized the scene around two distinct rhythms. In the slow-paced first half, which features the soldiers propping up the notice to a languid diegetic drumbeat, Mamoulian provides numerous shots of the peasants dejectedly sitting, their only motion the slow and simultaneous raising and lowering of their heads as they witness the posting of the new taxation notice. A shot of Zorro dashing into the plaza then introduces the fast-paced second half. As Alfred Newman's lively nondiegetic theme plays, Zorro rapidly tears down the notice, slashes the tunic, has a new message posted, and then gallops out of the plaza. The peasants, in turn, rise quickly and bustle excitedly, and the scene ends with a high-angle shot of their heads turning rapidly and excitedly as they read the new notice Zorro has posted. The shift in tempo is sudden and vital for the organizational structure of the film, as this escalation of tempo establishes Zorro as the needed spark that will change the peasants from a beaten-down people to an energized mass.

A central creative challenge, however, stems from the way in which Diego disguises his identity. To hide his true nature, Diego, in Mamoulian's version, adopts the same persona that Douglas Fairbanks had used back in the 1920 adaptation: a lethargic aesthete who finds even the shaking of hands to be fatiguing. The audience is made aware of this deception early on, but viewers must remain convinced that the real Diego is capable of Zorro's energy. Mamoulian handles this problem in two ways, and both are rhythmic. First, prior to Diego's arrival in California, Mamoulian was likely responsible for adding an opening scene that ties Diego's vigorous training in Spain to rhythmic noises. In the original screenplay, the film was to have begun by introducing a languishing Diego drinking and gambling, with no real hint of his physical abilities.[63] The finished film instead opens with a series of shots featuring Diego and his cohort practicing swordplay and competing at horseback riding.[64] To the swordplay shots, Mamoulian added the rhythmic clink of sword strikes. The first sword clinks we hear and see occur in three steady beats, followed by a one-beat pause (clink-clink-clink-pause; clink-clink-clink-pause). The next two sword-training shots then accelerate the tempo, moving from 120 beats per minute in the first shot to 150–160 beats in the second and third. In these latter two shots, we also hear more sword clinks between the pauses, thus furthering the sense of an escalating tempo.

Second, Mamoulian uses diegetic music during a dance scene midway through the film to remind viewers of Diego's potential to excite. In this scene, Diego arrives to dine at the home of love-interest Lolita (Linda Darnell) and her family. In the initial screenplay, following dinner, Diego and Lolita—who has been profoundly unimpressed by Diego's dullness—start dancing, and this enacts a change upon Lolita: "Gradually the pained expression leaves Lolita's face," explains the initial screenplay. "The beautiful dancing of Diego enraptures her. As the music ceases, she looks up into his face with a smile."[65]

In the finished film, Mamoulian adheres closely to this general description, but he seizes upon live music to offer a pronounced rhythmic moment. Mamoulian's marginal notes in the screenplay specify the song choice (the Hispanic folk song "El Sombrero Blanco") and feature a detailed breakdown of the spatial setup, camera positions, character movements, and shot selections on a blank page adjacent to the dance in the screenplay (Figure 3.5).[66] To introduce the patio where the dance will occur, Mamoulian once again trains his camera first on the musicians—here a seven-piece orchestra—before eventually panning toward the farther-away guests, a camera position he sketched beforehand in detail. After a section of dialogue the dance begins, with the orchestra providing the up-tempo music. Diego and Lolita begin turning separately in lackluster fashion, with the camera tracking slowly in and out (Figure 3.6). As Lolita is won over by Diego's dancing skill, however, Mamoulian increases the pace by moving the camera closer and cutting repeatedly to only Diego's feet as they tap to the escalating tempo of the music (Figures 3.7 and 3.8). The peppy song choice, the focus on rapidly pounding feet, and the gliding camera movements all enhance the tempo of a scene designed to suggest the spark that Diego generally keeps hidden. Once again, for Mamoulian, the rhythms of live performance serve as a means through which key plot points could be made.

Zanuck was pleased with the pacing of *The Mark of Zorro*. With *Blood and Sand*, however, he was not. "[*Blood and Sand*] is the worst edited film I have ever been associated with," a dismayed Zanuck (who had been involved with

MAMOULIAN AND RHYTHM 119

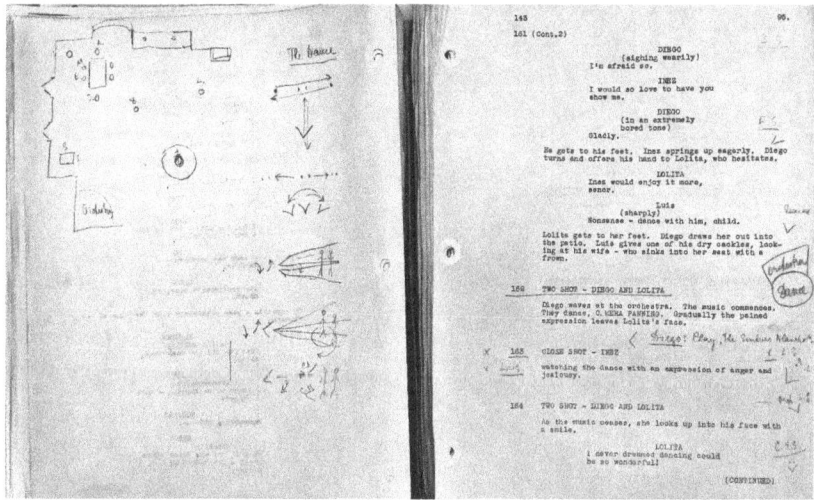

Figure 3.5 In his personal screenplay for *The Mark of Zorro*, Mamoulian penciled in the specific song ("El Sombrero Blanco") and included precise diagrams on the opposing page stipulating the layout of the scene and the ways in which the camera would capture the escalating musical tempo. This includes . . .

Figure 3.6 . . . a long shot for the start of the dance (see Mamoulian's second-from-the-top notation under "The Dance") . . .

Figure 3.7 ... and, as the tempo increases, closer-range shots of the couple's upper bodies...

filmmaking since 1922) informed Mamoulian in a confidential multi-page memo shortly after its release.

> We produced our picture in [a] lethargic style. The picture is long-winded and slow. The tempo is annoyingly dull. . . . I am more responsible than you because all along I knew in my heart that this picture did not have the correct mood or tempo. . . . Things like the dance in the first café, that I wanted them to cut down, should have been nothing more than a five-foot flash instead of a fifty-foot scene. Things like the big dance and song at the festival when [Juan] returns to Seville should have been boiled down to one brief scene. . . . We cut for pictorial and colorful effects rather than for story points and tempo."[67]

When he wrote these words, Zanuck was responding to the disappointing box-office returns of this expensive Technicolor production, and elsewhere in the letter, he pinpointed "unnecessary musical interludes" as a chief culprit.[68] It is likely true that for many viewers, the film feels slower-paced than *The Mark of Zorro*, and Zanuck's memo arguably points to a pitfall of showcasing musical performance so heavily. Mamoulian also—as chapter 5 will discuss—placed

Figure 3.8 ... and Diego's tapping feet (see Mamoulian's bottom notation under "The Dance").

considerable emphasis on the visual beauty of this film, which likely induced him to hold certain shots for lengths that Zanuck deemed too long. Still, the Spanish-set film does employ and embrace the rhythms of a wide range of Spanish music, including vaquero music, fiesta music, love music, music designed to be authentic to the bullring, and flamenco music at Spanish cafés.[69] Spanish opera singer and periodic actor Fortunio Bonanova served as a technical consultant on the film, and Zanuck himself pushed to have all the film's songs sung in Spanish.[70]

An analysis of music's rhythm-based functions in *Blood and Sand* could fill an entire chapter, but two key scenes in a Sevilla café—one at the film's beginning, one near the end—exemplify the importance Mamoulian placed on the rhythms of diegetic performance in the film. In the opening sequence, diegetic music—and its tempo and volume-level changes—is crucial for explaining why Juan, as a boy, wishes to become the greatest bullfighter in Spain. The film opens with Juan lying awake at night in his humble home and dreaming about fighting bulls (Color Plate 2). On the soundtrack, we hear only a lone guitar playing a song, which begins at a slow pace with dreamy harmonic notes (notes that are elevated in pitch because the guitarist only lightly touches the string). As Juan sneaks out of his home and hustles toward a bustling café where a party is being thrown for the great bullfighter Garabato (J. Carrol Naish), the film's pace quickens markedly: the music gets louder, its tempo increases, crowd noise is introduced, and we see—upon Juan's entry into the café—that this music comes from a small band accompanied by a flamenco dancer. Once the band is introduced, the film's rhythm increases still further: the room is packed with character movement, Mamoulian throws the sizable shadows of the band and flamenco dancer against the back wall to magnify their movements, and the now-furiously paced song culminates with the dancer hopping on top of Garabato's table to give him a special dance. Through musical tempo in this nearly wordless two-minute-and-fifteen-second opening, Mamoulian articulates the key dynamic that drives the film: Juan's desire to break away from the anonymity of poverty and seek the excitement and energy of public adoration.

Much later in the film, another diegetic performance in the same café emotionally conveys not what Juan desires, but what he has lost. A few scenes before the final bullfight that will take his life, Juan (Tyrone Power) brings his glamorous lover, Doña Sol (Rita Hayworth), to the café where his rival, Manolo (Anthony Quinn; now a more exciting bullfighter than Juan), is also dining. Juan remains captivated by Doña Sol's beauty, but Doña Sol—in a metaphor for the fickle, thrill-seeking bullfighting audience—wishes to move on to the next diverting matador. Manolo comes to the table, takes Doña Sol to the dance floor, and the duo performs a highly sexualized dance ("as sensuous as the Hays Office will allow," Zanuck instructed Hermes Pan, who choreographed it[71]). Juan is forced to sit still and watch, eventually shattering a glass in his hand in anger. What is striking about this scene is not just its sensuousness but also the time Mamoulian takes to showcase the musicians prior to the dance. Mamoulian opens the scene with a single take—lasting one minute and twenty-two seconds—showing nothing but the performance of a guitar song ("El Albaicin") that has no direct connection with the narrative. We begin with a shot of only the body of the guitar and a hand that alternatively plucks the notes and beats a slow rhythm against the guitar's body. The hand begins plucking at a much faster rate and then plays a tune that climbs in pitch and further increases in tempo. Matching this escalation in pace and intensity, Mamoulian begins a track back that eventually reveals the face of the guitarist. This is Vincente Gómez—who plays guitar music for much of the film and who composed "El Albaicin" and many other Spanish songs in the movie—in a cameo appearance. Mamoulian plainly wished to pay tribute to Gómez's musical contributions, but this introduction also cues the audience to attend closely to the music itself, which—by the time of the sensuous dance—"plays for" the bullfighter of the moment, which is no longer Juan. Fame, the music suggests, is transient, and Juan can ride its peak for only so long before giving way to the next temporary public sensation.

Conclusion

Possessing an ardent belief in the potentials of rhythm even before his entry into filmmaking, Mamoulian's work throughout his career reflected his theory that movement, pacing, and tempo were defining features of cinema. In *Applause*, Mamoulian's fidelity to these ideals enabled him to direct a film whose livelier pacing stood out from the early-sound norm. As Mamoulian's career progressed, the film industry—whether directly influenced by Mamoulian or not—more widely adopted these pacing aims, but Mamoulian remained focused on how to exploit cinema as a uniquely rhythm-based form. Focusing on character movement, camera movement, editing, and especially music, Mamoulian carefully planned and choreographed a wide array of scenes in which the rhythms of the film could directly evoke the ideas of the story.

It is this pronounced interest in choreographing the tools of cinema into a rhythmic, unified whole that makes many of his scenes feel like musical numbers. At their most energetic and triumphant—Jekyll and Muriel's dances, performances of "Funiculì, Funiculà" and "El Sombrero Blanco," the flamenco dance number in *Blood and Sand*—Mamoulian's segments did precisely what numbers in a musical often do: provide rhythmic, musical segments of wish-fulfillment designed to lift the spirits of characters and audience alike. We are now in a better position to understand why Mamoulian's work in the musical genre would prove to be his most enduring contribution to film history.

4

Mamoulian and the Musical

Applause, Love Me Tonight, The Gay Desperado, High, Wide and Handsome, Summer Holiday, Silk Stockings

Rouben Mamoulian directed six film musicals in his career: *Applause* (1929), *Love Me Tonight* (1932), *The Gay Desperado* (1936), *High, Wide and Handsome* (1937), *Summer Holiday* (1948), and *Silk Stockings* (1957). Despite this modest number, Mamoulian's contribution to the genre was extraordinary. He did pioneering work in each of the three subgenres that Rick Altman, in his foundational book *The American Film Musical*, has identified as the basic grammar of the American film musical across its history: the show musical (*Applause*), the fairy-tale musical (*Love Me Tonight*), and the folk musical (*High, Wide and Handsome* and *Summer Holiday*). His attempts to integrate music, dance, speech, and movement—and more generally to stylize the genre—displayed considerable foresight. In a mere six films, Mamoulian managed to lay early foundations for numerous elements of the genre while simultaneously offering some of the most audacious and experimental musicals made within the studio system.

Remarkably, Mamoulian's stage-musical legacy exceeds that of his film musicals. Mamoulian directed several of the most important stage musicals of the twentieth century, most notably *Porgy and Bess* (1935), *Oklahoma!* (1943), and *Carousel* (1945). Though Mamoulian would always remain conscious of medium specificity, his stage and screen musicals shared many goals, and he regularly brought the lessons he learned on the stage to his screen work, and vice versa. Thus, to understand how and why Mamoulian played such an important role in defining the potentials of the American film musical, one must pay close attention to his stage work as well. In doing so, we gain a clearer sense not just of Mamoulian's artistic mindset, but of the ways in which aesthetic approaches could be carried over and modified across media during the formative years of American film and theater musicals.

This chapter takes a chronological look at Mamoulian's adventures with the musical on stage and screen from the 1920s through the 1950s as he moved between these two modes. Some techniques would become integrated into the film musical's syntax and others would not, but for all three subgenres, Mamoulian's work pointed to key ideas. I begin with the first two film musicals Mamoulian directed: the show-musical *Applause* and fairy-tale musical *Love Me Tonight*.

In *Applause*, Mamoulian explored ways of making Hollywood's stage-bound musical numbers more cinematic, and he offered an unprecedently forceful examination of performer-spectator dynamics that would come to characterize show-musical syntax. In *Love Me Tonight*, Mamoulian provided a pathway for filmmakers who wished to infuse their musicals with extreme stylization. Mamoulian's stage production of George and Ira Gershwin's *Porgy and Bess* then signaled a shift toward folk- and land-based themes, which Mamoulian would immediately take up in his next two film musicals, *The Gay Desperado* and *High, Wide and Handsome*. For the latter film in particular, Mamoulian played a key role in grounding the musical in gritty land-based work, a concern that would typify folk musicals in later decades. Returning to the stage in 1943, Mamoulian's smash hit production of Richard Rodgers and Oscar Hammerstein's *Oklahoma!* displayed his interest in rhythm and land, along with a focus on tight narrative-number integration and the leads' relationship to the community. These features, which would come to define the folk musical on the screen, informed many of Mamoulian's own later stage musicals, most prominently *Carousel*. *Summer Holiday*, Mamoulian's late 1940s film musical, failed with critics and the public, but it nevertheless contained substantial and important folk-musical experiments, including efforts at integrating songs into the rhythms of daily life and overt re-creations of paintings. Mamoulian's career concluded with a skilled—if modest—integration of narrative and dance in *Silk Stockings*. Regardless of the type of musical in question, the history of the American film musical cannot be written without acknowledging Mamoulian as one of its central innovators.

Applause and the Show Musical

The show musical, according to Altman, structures its plot around the creation and production of a theatrical show. Such films allow the movie viewer a privileged peek behind the curtain, gratifying the viewer's curiosity about who and what goes into a stage production. Most closely associated with a series of landmark Busby Berkeley–choreographed Warner Bros. films from 1933—*42nd Street*, *Gold Diggers of 1933*, *Footlight Parade*—the show musical often implicitly links the spectators of these diegetic shows to a male audience, with women performing choreographed dances that de-emphasize them as individuals and configure them as visual patterns. Frequently, romance blossoms during rehearsals and, starting in 1933, the show musical often equated the show's success with the coupling of the leads, thereby fusing love, music, and artistic success.[1]

Mamoulian shot *Applause* in 1929, when many of these show-musical elements had yet to be established. Yet Mamoulian's film still managed to anticipate many key features. In his analysis of *Applause*'s second burlesque number ("Give Your Little Baby Lots of Lovin'")—where the dismayed April watches her mother's burlesque performance as male spectators leer and jeer—Altman points to ways in which Mamoulian forcefully presents a "veritable glossary of the show musical's eventual clichés." This includes the "opposition of the male orchestra to the female dancers," the movie audience's identification with the internal audience at the show, the "dark privacy" of "show-musical spectatorship," the turning of "women into pure pattern," and "the use of music-making as a sexual activity." "Rarely," Altman concludes, "has a director been as sensitive to the potential inherent in a new form as Rouben Mamoulian."[2]

How did Mamoulian manage to arrive at these ideas so early in the musical genre's history? The answer lies in two areas addressed in prior chapters: Mamoulian's preexisting devotion to stylization and medium specificity, and his particular attitude toward *Applause*'s subject matter. To grasp why these factors were important for the musical genre in 1929, we must first recognize the general state of affairs for musicals during that year. In terms of subject matter, *Applause*'s stage-oriented story would not have appeared unusual. Most early sound-era musicals prior to *Applause* centered on the lives of performers on and off stage, a topic that was also popular on Broadway in the 1920s.[3] Thanks to the commercial success of *The Jazz Singer* (October 1927) and, especially, *The Singing Fool* (September 1928) and *The Broadway Melody* (February 1929), studios in 1929 shot numerous musicals about show people, including *Broadway Babies* (June 1929), *Gold Diggers of Broadway* (August 1929), the burlesque-oriented *The Dance of Life* (August 1929), and *Glorifying the American Girl* (December 1929).[4] The numbers in these films, like in *Applause*, are generally performed on a stage for a diegetic audience.

Almost invariably, filmmakers—presumably reveling in their newfound ability to display top-tier stage performances on screens across America[5]—presented their numbers via a vantage point that simply emulated the ideal position of a spectator in the audience. In such a style, performance legibility ruled the roost, and there is little sense of any stylistic attitude being taken toward the numbers. Filmmakers commonly shot performances frontally, at eye level, and at a distance that was close enough to display the action clearly yet far away enough to reveal most—or all—of the action onstage. Sonically, filmmakers furthered the numbers' legibility by providing a clear, closely miked record of the singers and/or musicians, a microphone position that may not have matched the camera's distance but was in accordance with miking practices for phonograph and radio performances. Such approaches rested not on giving audiences a particularly cinematic experience, but on using cinema as a conduit for theatrical performance. One sees this approach as far back as the early Vitaphone shorts at Warner Bros., which began in 1926 and often featured stage-bound numbers. Virtually any feature-length film in 1928 and 1929—including the influential *Broadway Melody*—also favors this method. Certain performances in these films might include reaction shots from key characters, but the numbers routinely offer a clear record of the performance rather than a cinematic effort to heighten viewer response. Jean-Marie Lecomte has rightly called this a "deadpan" approach.[6]

At times, one does encounter camera positions that *lightly* accentuate the performance. In the May 1929 film *The Cocoanuts* (shot in the same Long Island studio with the same cinematographer as *Applause*), director Robert Florey filmed a group of female dancers using high angles—including an early instance of a top shot—that emphasize choreography, close-range low angles that accentuate the kicking legs of the dancers, and shots from the sides of chorus lines that offer dynamic framings. Another effort to accentuate performance in *The Cocoanuts* occurs during Harpo Marx's harp solo and Chico Marx's piano solo, where close-range shots of the performers' hands emphasize their skill and dexterity. One can admire the performers in both the "legible-yet-deadpan" and "light-performance-accentuation" styles, but in neither case does the camera or soundtrack appear to make a particularly strong statement about the number.

In contrast, Mamoulian, in *Applause*, manipulated film style to overtly dissect the relationship between stage performance and audience. Mamoulian's decision to examine the mechanics behind his numbers and take a stance on them stemmed not from prior show musicals, but from his belief that an artist should stylize to convey an attitude toward the material. As detailed in chapter 1, Mamoulian felt that true artists used the properties of their medium not to replicate reality, but to transform it. To Mamoulian, musicals, whether on stage or screen, held special power because the numbers themselves inherently called for an especially stylized treatment. Discussing stylization in a later oral history, Mamoulian argued that by definition,

> No musical should be done or can be done well by using the realistic method. If it is done naturalistically, it really cannot be good. Music itself proceeds on a much higher and less realistic level than words and the everyday prosaic action, so to speak. Therefore, the minute you have to do with music, you must uplift the whole scale and scheme of movement, of reeling, of thinking to a higher, more poetic level, so that your musical production does not walk in the dust of the earth but above it, in the air, if you will. It must float, like music floats, in the clouds, though its inner truths, its emotional roots come from the very soil of life.[7]

Thus, for Mamoulian, the musical's true potential lay in the numbers' encouragement of a stylized aesthetic that could enhance and elevate their emotions and ideas. Mamoulian also, however, believed that style should express a director's viewpoint, and therein lay the challenge of *Applause*. *Applause* features only burlesque numbers, yet as discussed in chapter 1, Mamoulian felt total disdain for what he saw as burlesque's poor performance standards and the lecherous emotions it instilled in the audience members. Here was a form that, for Mamoulian, did *not* proceed to a higher level, did not uplift, did not offer poetry, and *never* got above the "dust of the earth." In fact, Mamoulian would never even refer to *Applause* as a musical. This may be partly due to the fact that the stand-alone term "musical" in film was still a few years away when Mamoulian shot *Applause*,[8] but Mamoulian also probably did not see *Applause* as a true "musical" because he felt its burlesque numbers were unworthy of a style that would enhance their intended titillating qualities.

To resolve this clash between stylization and directorial viewpoint, Mamoulian's unorthodox solution was to first use film style to *de-emphasize*—rather than neutrally record or elevate—the numbers. Then, having detached the viewer from the appreciative internal audience of the burlesque show, Mamoulian stylizes so as to viscerally evoke what burlesque as a form does to those internal spectators. In doing so, Mamoulian put considerable focus on the spectators' response to the show, thereby demanding that the movie audience think far more carefully about spectator-performer dynamics than in prior sound musicals.

Mamoulian's stylistic decoupling of movie viewer and burlesque spectator begins immediately in the first onstage burlesque number—a rendition of Lucien Denni and Roger Lewis's 1911 ragtime hit "The Oceana Roll"—which takes place just after the ballyhoo scene that begins the film. Mamoulian opens the number by training his camera not on the onstage chorus line—which the burlesque patrons are presumably ogling—but on the orchestra pit. After first scanning the entire orchestra, the camera finally tilts up to the performers, but even here, our full view of the show is obstructed by Mamoulian's decision to pan across only the legs of the women, which kick listlessly. Thanks to Mamoulian's decision to shoot this first shot without directly recorded sound (see chapter 2), the women's leg kicks are out of synchronization with the music that was added later, but since Mamoulian aims to deride burlesque as a talentless affair, this actually aids the message.

Mamoulian's de-emphasis of the performance then becomes even more striking when Kitty—the star of the show—makes her grand entrance onstage. Within the logic of this stage performance, this is a star's entrance: she walks onstage after the chorus line has sung an introduction, enters in front of the chorus, receives applause, and wears an all-white, sparkling dress. At first, it appears that Mamoulian will stylistically honor this entrance: he marks Kitty's appearance by cutting to the "ideal," eye-level camera position so common during this period

Figure 4.1 In *Applause*, Kitty's "star" entrance briefly features the ideal-spectator vantage point typical of Hollywood's earliest musical numbers . . .

(Figure 4.1). Quickly, however, Mamoulian cuts to an oddly framed long-range shot that not only renders Kitty much smaller in the frame, but also features a pillar that nearly cuts off our entire view of her (Figure 4.2). More startling still, the camera then pans away from Kitty and toward the audience, until she is no longer visible in the frame at all.[9] A mere twelve seconds into Kitty's star entrance, the camera has announced its disinterest in the onstage show in favor of how that show affects its audience.

Augmenting the sense that the burlesque performance is not—in of itself— worthy of our attention is the sonic quality of the music. Based on what we hear, Kitty's microphone seems rather distant, resulting in lyrics that are garbled, indistinct, and nearly dwarfed by the volume level of the grinding orchestral accompaniment. Kitty's voice was almost surely recorded at a different time from the image in this shot, since she moves across the stage while singing. Yet even if her voice *was* recorded live, the challenges of nascent sound film technology would not explain Kitty's "bad" vocal recording. The film industry had, at this point, been shooting synchronized musical performances for three years, and the overwhelming majority had featured a sound balance favorable to the singer. Here, the poor sound seems designed to provoke movie audiences to

Figure 4.2 . . . but Mamoulian quickly undermines this presentation by cutting to a position in which our view of the stage is partially blocked by a pillar.

question why the burlesque audience is attending to this show in the first place. Astonishingly, the actress Mamoulian undermines via sound and image is none other than Helen Morgan, currently at the peak of her considerable stage career as a torch singer and a star in the massively successful 1927 musical *Show Boat*. The number stands as an extraordinary rejection of a stage performance in an era that treasured such performances.[10]

In the second number, which occurs when April returns from Wisconsin and watches her mother in horror from the audience, Mamoulian's stylistic choices similarly thwart any ability to share the internal audience's enjoyment of the show. The instrumentation for the song is cacophonous and grating, and when Kitty enters and begins singing, her voice is miked from a shockingly far distance, making it extremely quiet and highly reverberant. Consequently, Kitty's lyrics sound like unintelligible murmurs within a sea of orchestral noise. It is the *spectators* who are closely miked, their derisive comments quite audible and intelligible. This sound arrangement helps align the viewer further with the appalled April—we hear from *her* vantage point—and again emphasizes the surrounding apparatus of burlesque rather than the performers themselves. Mamoulian also uses camera framings during this portion of the scene that generally prevent us from becoming impressed by the performance.

One notable top shot of the dancers walking down the Y-shaped runway in symmetry may, in isolation, seem to emphasize performer coordination in a manner similar to *The Cocoanuts* (Figure 1.4). Yet the two shots that directly precede this top shot strongly undermine this sensation. In the first shot, Mamoulian frustrates any effort to see the performers by embedding the camera within the audience and training it on the backs of the audience members, resulting in only a small portion of the performers' legs being visible. In the second shot, Mamoulian seems to place his camera in an "ideal" position, except that he tilts down the camera just enough that the heads of the performers are chopped off from view. Both obstructed-view shots do strategically prevent us from seeing that the women on the runway have unfastened their shirts and are shaking their breasts at the audience, an action the censors—not to mention Mamoulian—frowned upon (see chapter 6). At the same time, such camera positions separate the cinema viewer from the experience of the burlesque spectators. Thanks to these choices, by the time Mamoulian's concluding rapid-fire montage articulates the effects of abrasive sexuality upon its amped-up male spectators (see chapter 3), the movie audience runs little risk of being similarly suckered in. Instead, Mamoulian's style encourages the viewer to step back and probe the mechanisms of burlesque entertainment and the distressing relationship it forms between performers and viewers.

Thus, Mamoulian—caught between his belief that musical numbers deserved a stylized treatment and his revulsion of burlesque—fashioned in *Applause* a cinematic approach that enabled him to *stylishly* lay bare what a stage show tries to accomplish. By the third and final number—in which April assumes the lead in the show to the crowd's roaring delight—Mamoulian has positioned his audience to sense (and be repulsed by) such soon-to-be-solidified aspects of the show musical as the ties between music making and sex, the objectification of women, and the dark identity of the audience. Though many later show musicals would be far less critical of these elements, the critique of them in *Applause* is what enables them to appear so saliently at such an early date. There was, to my knowledge, no precursor for such an overt interrogation of performer-spectator dynamics in US sound cinema.

In addition to hitting upon show-musical syntax, *Applause* more broadly offered an early demonstration of how a prominent cinematic style could control and heighten a spectator's response to musical numbers. Four years prior to *42nd Street*, *Applause* announced ways in which numbers might be presented not as neutral stage acts, but as cinematically enhanced experiences.

Love Me Tonight and the Fairy-Tale Musical

In *Applause*, Mamoulian was faced with musical numbers that—to his eyes—were unworthy of the earnest stylization that marked the musical as a great art form. Three years later, however, Mamoulian directed a very different type of film—the fairy-tale musical *Love Me Tonight*—in which he offered one of the most daring instances of cinematic stylization in his stage and screen career. If *Applause* trumpeted the *prospect* of cinematically stylizing musical numbers, *Love Me Tonight* served as an early demonstration of just *how* overtly a filmmaker could stylize number *and* narrative, especially when telling a story that seemed to exist in an otherworldly space.

Altman describes the fairy-tale musical as a subgenre that transports audiences to an insular, utopic, and nearly magical realm populated by storybook characters of great charm. With roots extending back to Ruritanian operetta, Viennese operetta, and the works of Gilbert and Sullivan, the fairy-tale musical spoke to American audience members' desires to be taken somewhere else.[11] Early sound-era fairy-tale musicals had included Warner Bros.' *The Desert Song* (1929), RKO's *Rio Rita* (1929), and—most relevant to *Love Me Tonight*—a series of musicals that Ernst Lubitsch had made at Paramount starring Maurice Chevalier, Jeanette MacDonald, or both: *The Love Parade* (1929), *Monte Carlo* (1930), *The Smiling Lieutenant* (1931), and *One Hour with You* (1932). These films by Lubitsch—particularly the first three—tell tales of royalty, mistaken identity, class difference, sexual desire, and champagne using a sophisticated style that playfully allows audiences to remember the artificiality of its fabricated world.

All four Lubitsch films had featured self-conscious touches, which likely emboldened Mamoulian to experiment with film style in *Love Me Tonight*. In *Monte Carlo*, a clock picks up various tunes sung in the film for its hourly chimes, and MacDonald's show-stopping number—Leo Robin and Richard A. Whiting's "Beyond the Blue Horizon"—emerges out of the rhythmic chugging of the train she rides in, with workers in nearby fields providing the backup chorus. *The Smiling Lieutenant* begins with a gag in which Chevalier's door remains closed for a male tailor but swings open immediately when a young woman shows up (the light outside his door then glows, giving the opening a mildly cartoonish feel). *One Hour with You* features periodic experiments with rhythmic, rhymed speech.[12] Such instances of stylization, many of them grounded in rhythm, help Lubitsch convey the sense of a slyly comedic and playfully constructed cinematic space.[13]

Along with these prior musicals, Mamoulian's decision to stylize *Love Me Tonight* was likely catalyzed by three other factors: the freedom Paramount granted him on this film, the story's especially pronounced fairy-tale quality, and his preexisting theories about rhythm and movement in art. In early 1932, Mamoulian—hot off the commercial success of *City Streets* (1931) and the Oscar-winning *Dr. Jekyll and Mr. Hyde* (1931)—was a star directorial talent at Paramount. Presumably for this reason, Paramount gave him the freedom to choose the property and direct the next Chevalier-MacDonald musical.[14]

Playwright Léopold Marchand—who had written the French-language translation of Lubitsch's *One Hour with You*[15]—encountered Mamoulian on the Paramount lot and alerted him to the synopsis of an obscure 1924 French play Marchand had written with Paul Armont, titled *Le tailleur au château* (*The Tailor in the Castle*). Changing the material freely to suit his interests, Mamoulian personally adapted the play into first a skeleton outline and then a fleshed-out treatment, which included his ideas for many of the numbers.[16] Only then did Mamoulian work with writers Samuel Hoffenstein, Waldemar Young, and George Marion Jr. to create the screenplay.

According to Mamoulian, the most appealing aspect of *The Tailor in the Castle* was its status as a modern-day fairy tale.[17] Upon reading the play synopsis, Mamoulian recalled a story his grandmother had told him about a princess who was making some embroidery when "a big wind snatched it away from her and carried it across many lands and many waters, landing it finally into the lap of a young and handsome prince." The prince fell in love with the embroidery and "travelled over the face of the earth until he found his princess."[18] This story would inspire the film's famous "Isn't It Romantic?" number.[19] It also, however, suggests that Mamoulian was keenly drawn to *Love Me Tonight*'s *literal* status as a fairy tale, a quality that could give him extra license for cinematic stylization. Moreover, the story reveals that Mamoulian enjoyed a personal and exuberant relationship with the material. This feeling had been absent from *Applause*, and it would encourage Mamoulian to elevate—rather than denigrate—*Love Me Tonight*'s numbers in what he saw as a manner befitting a true musical. Indeed, for Mamoulian, *Love Me Tonight* was his "first musical."[20]

To stylize *Love Me Tonight*, Mamoulian decided to orient nearly the entire film around the single organizing principle that had dominated much of his thinking for nearly ten years: rhythm.[21] As we saw in the previous chapter, Mamoulian, in his stage-directing days in Rochester and on Broadway, viewed rhythm as the lifeblood of a movement-based art form like theater. As far back as his experimental play *Sister Beatrice* (1926), Mamoulian had been drawn to the idea of using musical rhythm to unify such theatrical components as character movement, speaking, singing, and dancing. As chapter 3 detailed, Mamoulian felt that cinema's addition of camera and editing only underscored the importance of rhythm in the movies. Armed with a fairy-tale musical, Mamoulian saw his chance to use musical numbers as a springboard for a thorough stylization of all parts of the film, whether number *or* narrative.

Mamoulian's interest in rhythm was shared by Lubitsch, and this may be one reason that scholars frequently discuss these two directors together. Both men came from the stage, were heavily influenced by its musical traditions, and sought to bring them forward in film. Mamoulian directed operas and operettas in Rochester, while Lubitsch's influences ranged from Max Reinhardt's theater (which included experiments in pantomime set to music like *Sumurun* [1912] that Lubitsch acted in), cabaret performance, and operetta. Lubitsch had been experimenting with rhythm as far back as 1919 with the release of *The Oyster Princess*, which contains a series of strongly rhythmic set pieces via such devices as synchronized rhythmic footsteps, an exuberant orchestra conductor cueing the percussive beats of a foxtrot, and synchronized dancing that breaks out *en masse* across multiple spaces. Other silent German Lubitsch comedies like *I Don't Want to Be a Man* (1918), *The Doll* (1919), and *The Wildcat* (1921)—along with the drama *Sumurun* (1920)—feature sections of rhythmic filmmaking. It is unlikely that Mamoulian saw these films, since only Lubitsch's epics like *Carmen* (1918), *Madame DuBarry* (1919), *Anne Boleyn* (1920), and *The Loves of Pharoah* (1922) traveled widely outside of Germany. Still, Lubitsch and Mamoulian were kindred spirits in their interest in translating stage-rhythm principles into cinematic form.

Though Mamoulian was thinking in parallel with Lubitsch, his decision to stylize nearly the entirety of *Love Me Tonight* around rhythm remained ambitious and highly unusual. Lubitsch, Lea Jacobs argues, organized his early sound films subtly in terms of short rhythmic segments. Mamoulian's *Love Me Tonight*, in contrast, featured broader-scale and more salient rhythms, often centered on a distinct musical beat.[22] Few other extant US musicals prior to *Love Me Tonight* contained saliently stylized numbers at all. Beyond the United States, Mamoulian's most notable influence was likely René Clair's *Le Million* (released in the United States in May 1931), which similarly emphasizes musical rhythm for much of the film and offers methods found also in *Love Me Tonight*, including a question-and-answer song in the vein of "How Are You?" and the frequent synchronization of footsteps to music. Ultimately, however, *Love Me Tonight* offers a more rigorous, thoroughly stylized, and rhythmically organized film than even Clair provides in *Le Million*.

A close look at rhythm's role throughout *Love Me Tonight* reveals how frequently and overtly Mamoulian foregrounded it, and the ways in which he modulated it to express story ideas. *Love Me Tonight*'s opening number (which Mamoulian likely wrote independently from songwriters Richard Rodgers and Lorenz Hart, and Paramount staff member John Leipold, who assisted with some of the incidental music[23]) loudly proclaims rhythm's importance to the film. Over shots of Paris and then the city block where Maurice (Maurice Chevalier) lives, Mamoulian provides six slow chimes of a clock, followed by a worker breaking bricks with a sledgehammer. As Hannah Lewis has pointed out, doing so enables the film to begin exploring "the boundaries between music and noise."[24] Both sounds are steadily rhythmic by nature, but are they music? And are they stylized? We begin to get our answer only with the next noise: the snores of a man occurring precisely on the offbeat of the hammer strikes (or on beat 3, if we conceptualize the sledgehammer noises as operating in 4/4 time[25]). A woman then begins sweeping in double time to the hammer and snore (i.e., we hear the sweeps on beats 2 and 4 of a four-beat measure). Others subsequently join in, including a locksmith sawing and two cobblers fixing boots. Eventually, a woman turns on a gramophone, and its music (a joint composition by Rodgers and Leipold[26]) becomes the orchestral underscore for the scene and gradually morphs into the accompaniment for Maurice's first song, "The Song of Paree."

This rhythmic movement from urban sound effects to music may have been influenced by the beginning of *Le Million*, which begins with clock chimes that abruptly provide the orchestration to the first musical number. *Le Million*'s opening is less ambitious than Mamoulian's—Clair offers no "symphony" of noises—but both openings feature a number that emerges from an urban, seemingly non-musical world. Mamoulian's city symphony may also owe something to the beginning of *The Broadway Melody* (1929), where the songs performed by writers and musicians of Tin Pan Alley seem to materialize organically from the din of New York City. Yet the most proximate influence on *Love Me Tonight*'s opening was Mamoulian's own 1927 stage production of *Porgy*. Though *Porgy* was not a musical, Mamoulian—as we saw in chapter 3—had personally written a scene opening that featured a rhythmically constructed "symphony" of noises made by the working inhabitants of Catfish Row. As Mamoulian's early treatment for *Love Me Tonight* makes clear, Mamoulian saw *Love Me Tonight*'s opening as a "parallel" to that stage production.[27] Many of the sounds in *Love Me Tonight* are similar: both *Porgy* and *Love Me Tonight* contain the snores of a sleeper, a woman who sweeps a broom repeatedly in two short bursts, the sound of nails being hammered and shoemakers at work, and the noise of a rug being beaten with a stick. In the playscript for *Porgy*, we even find designated measure markings in Mamoulian's handwriting—4/4, then 2/4, and 6/8—that Mamoulian saw as the basis for *Love Me Tonight*'s noise symphony as well.[28] *Love Me Tonight*'s "sound symphony," Mamoulian wrote in the treatment, "will start in the rhythm of a slow 4/4 time going through 2/4, 6/8 and then becoming syncopated, very modern and very jazzy."[29]

In spite of *Porgy*'s clear influence, however, *Love Me Tonight*'s opening is no mere retread. Not only does it take advantage of recording sound prior to the image, as Jacobs points out,[30] but it functions in ways specific to *Love Me Tonight*'s overall project. As Mamoulian once explained in an interview, *Love Me Tonight*'s opening was critical because it established both the stylized world where the film takes place and the *rhythmic* patterning that drives much of the remaining film.[31] From this perspective, it matters not only that sonic rhythm is heavily emphasized at the outset, but that no other form of stylization threatens to compete with it. In particular, the visuals of this opening are decidedly ordinary. The first four shots show grainy stock-footage images of Paris, and even when Mamoulian shifts to a Fox Hills set to represent Maurice's city block in shot five, the visuals—aside from some unobtrusive rhythmic editing in a few sections—remain fairly non-stylized.[32] We see Parisians going about their daily routines, and the only lightly stylized visual moment within a shot occurs when two boys walk across the street with footsteps in unison. By downplaying visual stylization early on, the sonic rhythms become all the more prominent.

Only when "That's the Song of Paree" begins does Mamoulian allow the visuals to also become rhythmically stylized. We first meet Maurice as he wakes up and dresses for work while singing "That's the Song of Paree." When Maurice begins to sing, he starts moving rhythmically in ways that blur the boundaries between dance and regular movement. As Maurice sings about the various dances of other countries, he briefly pantomimes each one. When he stops his pantomime to put on his jacket, any hint of dancing has seemingly stopped, yet his actions remain synchronized to prominent words in the song: he pulls his right arm through the sleeve while singing, "cold or wet or *dry* [sleeve pull]," and pulls the fronts of the jacket together as he sings, "Paris starts to *cry* [jacket pull]." Is this dancing? Is it just normal dramatic action? Perhaps it is best thought of as rhythmic action or "dance-action," much like what Mamoulian had experimented with in *Sister Beatrice*.

Mamoulian's synchronization of sonic rhythm and visual movement becomes even more pronounced when Maurice walks outside and segues into Rodgers and Hart's next song, "How Are You?," while walking to his tailor shop. Here, the visual beat of Maurice's walk, which includes numerous stops and starts (often within the same shot), is timed precisely with the sonic beat of the song. Moreover, major actions like handshakes and the gestures of characters Maurice meets (sharp hand gestures in the air, hands on hips, finger pointing, etc.) are not just in tempo, but are routinely on the *downbeat* of the song. Such precision is notable in itself, yet these gestures simultaneously manage to look fairly natural, a testament to Mamoulian's oft-stated belief that the best stylization affects viewers without their fully noticing the device. Mamoulian would, in later interviews, claim that all the singing in the film was recorded on set, but it seems more likely that the image here was shot silent, with Chevalier lip-syncing to a playback recording.[33] Whatever the method, by the time Maurice arrives at his tailor shop, Mamoulian has announced *Love Me Tonight* as a film driven by rigorous attention to musical rhythm.

In *Love Me Tonight*'s first two numbers, Mamoulian uses rhythmic techniques found in *Sister Beatrice* and *Porgy*, albeit with modifications like playback. The film's third number, "Isn't It Romantic?," announces Mamoulian's intention to engage with rhythm on an overtly *cinematic* level as well, particularly via camera movement and editing. Early in the number, Maurice—sitting on a table in his tailor shop—turns to a three-part mirror as he sings. In a nod to Chevalier's musical-hall background and prior film roles—which had regularly featured direct addresses—Mamoulian trains the camera on the mirror, so that Maurice, via his reflection, looks directly at the viewer as he sings. Then, Mamoulian gives his camera movement a rhythmic role by panning to each portion of the three-part mirror each time Maurice completes a four-bar stanza.

Later in the same number, Mamoulian's play with rhythm becomes more audacious and experimental. After Maurice finishes his portion of the song and walks his customer, Emile (Bert Roach), to the door (both characters walk in synchronization to the underscore, another "dance-action"), Mamoulian famously allows the song to be passed from Emile to a taxi driver, to a musician, to marching soldiers, to a violinist, and finally to love-interest Jeanette (Jeanette MacDonald). As scholars have pointed out, this scene is significant for its recognition that a cinematic song can be organized on the level of a sequence rather than a single scene.[34] Equally important, Mamoulian modulates the song's tempo—as well as its orchestration—as it moves from one space to the next. As far back as his treatment, Mamoulian stipulated that the soldiers should sing in a march rhythm, and that Jeanette's rendition should be a "ballad or even a minuet in contrast to the jazzy fox trot of the song's inception with Maurice."[35] Not only do these rhythmic modulations occur, but when the violinist overhears it and dashes home to play it, the song morphs into a far slower and more virtuosic version, with small-scale *accelerandos* (speed-ups) and *ritardandos* (slowdowns)— another play with rhythmic alteration. This sets the stage for the conclusion of the song: the camera pans rightward to reveal Jeanette walking onto her balcony to sing the slowest-yet rendition of the song.[36]

If the city symphony that precedes "The Song of Paree"/"How Are You?" saliently announces the film's focus on rhythm, "Isn't It Romantic?" encapsulates what Mamoulian wishes to do with rhythm across the entire film, even during non-singing sections. For the remainder of the movie, Mamoulian seizes upon nearly every space and situation to overtly convey rhythm, yet like the "Isn't It Romantic?" number, Mamoulian's interest is in adjusting the beat in accordance with story needs. The difference in tempo between Maurice and Jeanette's versions of "Isn't It Romantic?," for instance, signals the differing tempos that Mamoulian will associate with the working-class gaiety of Paris versus the stodgy, stifling life of the castle-dwelling aristocracy. Shortly after Jeanette's introduction, Mamoulian ties many of the castle dwellers to a lethargic tempo, most strikingly in a comedic shot in which the castle's half-asleep house guests play a slow-motion game of bridge, with the servant's feet walking in tempo to a painfully sluggish instrumental rendition of Theodore Metz's 1896 hit "There'll Be a Hot Time in the Old Town Tonight." The pace of those at the castle who have just arrived from the city also helps establish a marked contrast between the rhythms of city and castle. This includes the fast-walking Vicomte (Charles

Ruggles, who is introduced *running* in the across-Paris race to the tune of a Rodgers-composed hurry motif) and later Maurice, who is given undercranked shots (shots featuring speeded-up motion) as he races up flights of castle stairs in synchronization to the music.[37] Later, during the stag hunt, Maurice will rapidly ride his horse in comically undercranked shots, while the stodgy nobility will return home from the hunt in slow motion.[38] Through overt changes in rhythm, Mamoulian marks clear divisions between the lifestyle of urban commoners and that of the nobility, thereby signaling that Maurice will offer exuberance, cheer, and—yes—romance to the castle. Joseph Horowitz has pointed to still other examples of rhythmic coordination between action and underscoring during narrative sections, including various characters' footsteps, the canter of Jeanette's horse, a bounding stag, and rushing dogs.[39] Mamoulian would later state that most of the film was shot with a metronome. "There was hardly a movement," he asserted, "that was not done strictly in rhythm with the music."[40] Because many of the "ordinary" activities found in these non-singing segments are rendered dance-like or musical, number/narrative divisions often seem less relevant, and the film as a whole—for some commentators—feels like one long musical number.[41] Consequently, the entire film arguably provides the sense of uplift more commonly reserved for only the numbers of a musical.

Mamoulian also manages to inject rhythm into the unlikeliest of places. Following a romantic scene between Maurice and princess Jeanette in a garden, Maurice lies in bed dreaming that the princess will continue to love him even after he reveals he is a mere commoner. Visually, Mamoulian provides nothing but the image of Maurice asleep in his bed and Jeanette asleep in hers, making the scene a seemingly poor candidate for a rhythmic approach. Yet Mamoulian still finds ways to stage it rhythmically. The scene begins with the camera tracking forward on Maurice asleep. Mamoulian then provides a voice-over featuring portions of the romantic garden conversation heard in the previous scene, before the conversation changes to what Maurice imagines in his sleep: when he tells her he is a tailor, Jeanette merely chuckles and responds, "isn't it romantic?" This voice-over harkens back to the voices Nan imagines in *City Streets* (see chapter 2), but Mamoulian doesn't stop there. If voice-overs can be spoken, Mamoulian seems to ask, why can't they be sung? The imagined conversation thus segues into a song performance of "Love Me Tonight," possibly the first musical number in a US sound film that takes place within a character's dream space.[42] Doing so imbues the scene with a sonic beat (like all musical numbers, "Love Me Tonight" contains a specific tempo), but Mamoulian also finds a way to organize the visuals around rhythm. During the first sixteen bars of the song—sung in voice-over by Jeanette—Maurice sleeps motionless on his left side (Figure 4.3). When it is time for Maurice's voice to join in for the next eight bars, Mamoulian marks his "entrance" by having Maurice roll over onto his back as he continues to sleep

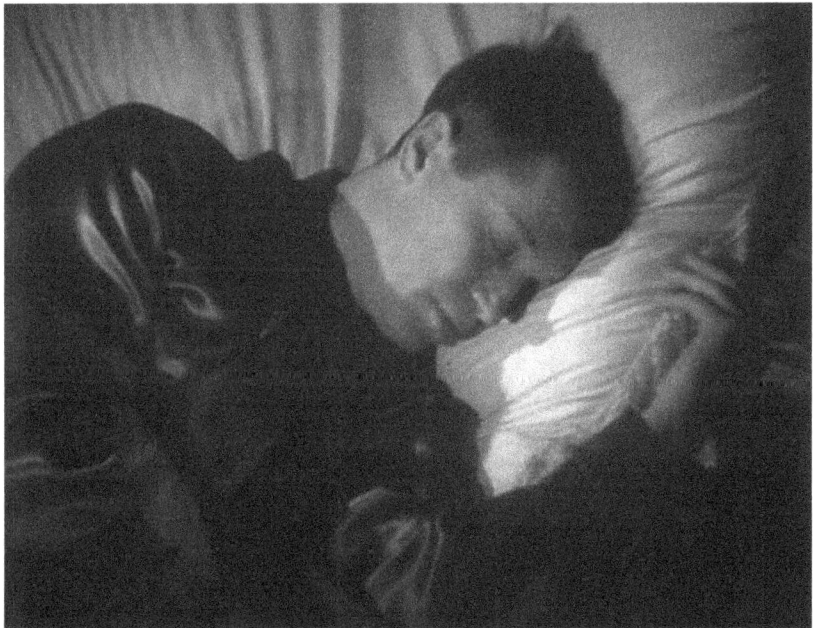

Figure 4.3 Rhythm even during sleep in *Love Me Tonight*. Maurice lays dreaming while lying on his side as Jeanette sings the first sixteen bars of "Love Me Tonight." . . .

(Figure 4.4). Following his eight bars, the duo sings the final eight bars in unison as Mamoulian moves to a split screen image of Maurice and Jeanette lying in their beds (Figure 4.5). The rhythm and structure of the song is thus matched by changes in character action and split screens, even though its two performers are nearly motionless.

Just as rhythm introduces the movie, so, too, does it "solve" the film's central plot problem in the final sequence. When Maurice reveals to the castle dwellers that he is a tailor, the Duke (C. Aubrey Smith) exclaims, "give him his money and throw him out," and Mamoulian launches into arguably the most rhythmically marked song in the film. That song is "The Son of a Gun Is Nothing but a Tailor," the title of which is eventually presented exclusively in a rhythmic whisper. To this chant, we see Maurice, now dressed as a tailor, exiting the castle (his footsteps synchronized to the chanted beat). Then, during a reprise of "Love Me Tonight," Jeanette does what only Maurice had done in the castle to this point: she dashes down the stairs and rides off on a horse at undercranked speed. As Jeanette chases down Maurice's departing train, Mamoulian provides a rhythmic montage that includes shots that alternate between pounding horse hooves and churning train wheels. Failing to convince Maurice that she could be happily married to him,

140 DEFINING CINEMA

Figure 4.4 Maurice rolls onto his back to "enter" the song for the next eight bars...

Figure 4.5 ... and a split screen marks the couple's duet for the final eight bars.

Jeanette rides across a field to a different part of the train track, with the camera again undercranked to speed up her movements. Jeanette proudly plants herself on the railroad track, forcing the train to grind to a stop and convincing Maurice that the duo should be married.

Narratively, such an ending does little to explain how the pampered Jeanette could thrive as a tailor's wife, or how Maurice will deal with a litany of in-laws who now appear to despise him for his deception. If the ending succeeds, it is because Mamoulian uses the driving force of the film—rhythm—to resolve the story. Jeanette engages in fast-paced movement commonly associated with Maurice, thus forcing Maurice—and the train he rides on—to adopt a stillness that had earlier been associated with Jeanette (Mamoulian's treatment notably stipulates that the train come to a "dead stop"[43]). Having reconciled the duo by allowing them to take on each other's rhythmic qualities, all that remains is for Mamoulian to remind us once more that theirs is a fairy-tale world, where stylistic saliency is welcome. Mystical steam from the stopped train envelopes the lovers, and Mamoulian dissolves to a final reference to the fairy tale that excited him in the first place: a completed tapestry of a prince wooing a princess, just as Mamoulian's grandmother told him.

Toward the Folk Musical: *Porgy and Bess*, *The Gay Desperado*, and *High, Wide and Handsome*

Love Me Tonight is often regarded as a pinnacle of the early sound-era musical, and this status may be due in part to how heavily Mamoulian stylized the film in an era when few filmmakers appeared interested in doing so.[44] Indeed, *Love Me Tonight* uses such extreme stylization that one might imagine Mamoulian had gone as far as he could with the musical genre. Mamoulian, however, had additional interests. As his career in musicals progressed, he increasingly turned to one of his major preoccupations: American culture and its music. This interest would lead him to direct foundational folk musicals.

Mamoulian's massive contribution to the American folk musical may seem odd considering his Armenian background, but Mamoulian's fascination with American culture was deep-seated and long-lasting. As a youngster living in Eastern and Western Europe, Mamoulian's favorite boyhood authors included Jack London, Walt Whitman, O. Henry, Edgar Allan Poe, and Bret Harte (see below).[45] Mamoulian's interest in American culture also likely played a role in his agreement to direct his Broadway breakthrough *Porgy* back in 1927. *Porgy* had been turned down by other theater directors who were apparently intimidated by a play set in an African American quarter of Charleston and featuring a nearly all-black cast.[46] Mamoulian, however, was excited by the opportunity to direct a show grounded in the culture of a distinct section of American society, even traveling to Charleston to gain a firsthand sense of the play's setting in Catfish Row. As discussed in chapter 3, Mamoulian was struck by what he felt was the near-constant singing of the Catfish Row community, and he consequently emphasized songs—especially spirituals—in his direction of *Porgy*. The noise symphony he composed for *Porgy*, moreover, was rooted in what he called the everyday "household and work noises" of Catfish Row.[47] Whether Mamoulian accurately captured this culture can certainly be questioned. Mamoulian spent only five days in Charleston,[48] and a firsthand account later surfaced that Mamoulian needed sizable instruction on black culture by his African American cast members.[49] Still, *Porgy* demonstrates Mamoulian was at least interested in *attempting* to ground his creative work within subsets of American culture, and the show's success would have only furthered his belief that this was a valuable endeavor.

Porgy, however, was no musical, and while Mamoulian remained proud of his "first" musical, *Love Me Tonight*, Mamoulian recognized that it remained closely connected to European operetta. Given Mamoulian's fondness for *Porgy*, his hunger for topics in American culture, and his interest in musicals, it is not surprising that when asked to return to Broadway after a five-year absence to direct the Gershwins' musical version of *Porgy*—titled *Porgy and Bess*—Mamoulian agreed.[50] Mamoulian was also a deep admirer of George Gershwin's music, and he likely saw in Gershwin a kindred spirit: a foreigner who embraced highbrow and lowbrow art forms and saw no reason to differentiate between the two.[51]

Today, *Porgy and Bess* is generally thought of predominantly as George Gershwin's accomplishment rather than Mamoulian's. Yet while Gershwin wrote the music and deserves credit for daring to bring an "opera" to the Broadway stage, Mamoulian—as Horowitz has pointed out—wielded considerable influence over the original production, both directly and indirectly. Gershwin adapted *Porgy and Bess* not from DuBose Heyward's novel *Porgy* (1925), which was the original source material, but from Mamoulian's 1927 stage version. The opera's scene-by-scene breakdown matches that of the play, many of the recitatives hew closely to the 1927 playscript, and the play's numerous set pieces largely recur in the 1935 version.[52] Gershwin also appropriated many of *Porgy*'s spirituals.[53] Thus, even if Mamoulian had not been tapped to direct, his impact would have been notable. But once he signed on, Mamoulian held tight control over the production. In 1935, Mamoulian was a prestigious and highly coveted director, having taken Broadway by storm with *Porgy* and directed a slew of respected Hollywood films. Gershwin, in contrast, was viewed by many critics as something of a pretender to high-class music. Mamoulian, during contract negotiations, indicated he would leave the production should creative differences arise, and Gershwin agreed to many of his changes.[54]

As Horowitz has documented, Mamoulian made significant alterations to Gershwin's work. Among them were moves that resonated with aspects of what Altman has called the folk musical. This form, which would not emerge as a full-blown subgenre in cinema until the 1940s, projected the audience into a mythical past, emphasized family groupings and the space of the home, centered on small-town and agricultural settings, and often featured musical numbers tied to work on the land and characters' fit within a larger community.[55] Though not all of these attributes are present in *Porgy and Bess*, Mamoulian's changes to the material reflect a similar determination to ground music within a particular subculture, an interest of Mamoulian's that we examined in chapter 3. In the original Gershwin score, the production was to have commenced with jazz pianist "Jasbo" Brown playing a song that—to Mamoulian's ears—evoked Harlem more than Charleston. Mamoulian removed it, thus enabling the more "Southern" sounding "Summertime" to open the production.[56] Mamoulian also took pains to not just retain—but expand—the symphony of noises heard in his 1927 play. In Gershwin's initial score, the symphony of noises was to have been merely pantomimed by the actors, with Gershwin's underscore providing the sound. Mamoulian, feeling that the noises were central for conveying the life of a community via the sounds of work, composed an "Occupational Humoresque" that closely resembled what he'd done in the 1927 play. Near the end of this composition, Mamoulian synchronized his noises with a portion of the chorus and orchestration that Gershwin had written, thereby enabling the noises to transition smoothly into the score.[57] As Altman points out, this enables Gershwin's music to appear to grow more organically from the daily tasks of a community.[58] Mamoulian also added a symphony of noises under what would become the most famous song in the production, "I Got Plenty of Nothing," including the sounds of "a dishrag, a shoe rag, a hammer, and two rugs."[59] In making these changes, Mamoulian was anticipating the folk musical, whose music would be tied closely to physical work and everyday life.

One additional Mamoulian influence bears mentioning, though it was not, precisely, a change to Gershwin's score. Back in the 1927 version of *Porgy*, the initial script had called for a closing scene in which Porgy, grimly and with "bowed head," rides his goat-pulled cart out of Catfish Row toward New York City and Bess, with little hope that he can make it there. Mamoulian—as Horowitz has demonstrated—had rewritten this ending so that Porgy rides off to a unison spiritual of "I'm On My Way," thus making his concluding action a triumphant one that is buoyed by the larger Catfish Row community.[60] Gershwin used this ending and made it famous in his composition for *Porgy and Bess*, but the idea was Mamoulian's. The chorus, Altman argues, would become a crucial folk-musical technique for binding individual to community.[61] Well before making his first folk musical in Hollywood, Mamoulian had used both *Porgy* and *Porgy and Bess* to experiment with connecting individuals to their broader folk community via the sounds of song and work.

Of course, Mamoulian was not African American, and while his interest in directing productions centered on black culture can be applauded, he was nevertheless attempting to portray a community he did not belong to. When *Porgy and Bess* opened, critical reception was mixed, including on the question of the extent to which Mamoulian and the Gershwins had truly captured black culture. While some critics—along with Todd Duncan, who played Porgy in the 1935 version— argued for the production's authenticity, others, including Duke Ellington, stated that the music was not distinct to black culture.[62] This, too, would anticipate later folk musicals, where music was typically the product of white composers who took inspiration from traditional or indigenous music yet offered their own interpretation of it. Mamoulian, always a staunch defender of Gershwin, would later praise Gershwin's score in ways that again demonstrate Mamoulian's artistic fit with the folk musical. Gershwin, Mamoulian argued—using the vernacular of the 1950s—didn't provide "Negro" music, but rather Gershwin's own musical expression of a particular culture.[63]

Whatever its benefits or drawbacks, *Porgy and Bess* was likely an essential turning point in Mamoulian's career. It gave him his first opportunity to use musical theater to evoke a particular stratum of American culture and move toward a goal that would increasingly obsess him: the creation of a distinctly American form of musical theater and film.

Following *Porgy and Bess*, Mamoulian apparently returned to Hollywood with a renewed determination to make musicals grounded within particular cultures and landscapes, because he immediately directed two movie musicals tied closely to these concerns. The first—*The Gay Desperado*—is set mostly in Mexico rather than the United States, yet Mamoulian's selection of the property reveals his fondness for the American Southwest landscape, as the exteriors were filmed outside Tucson, Arizona.[64] By his own account, Mamoulian chose to direct this unusual story when he and producer Jesse Lasky—who had signed Italian opera singer Nino Martini to a series of films[65]—agreed to take a ten-minute meeting with writer Leo Birinski, who pitched the basic premise of the film. Though much of the story sounded unpromising to both men, Mamoulian advocated for the project partly for the opportunity it gave him to shoot in a Western landscape.[66] From his youth onward, Mamoulian had been fascinated by the narrative tropes and imagery of the American Wild West. We saw that as a boy, Mamoulian counted Western writer Bret Harte among his favorite authors. During the period of his boyhood that he spent in Paris, Mamoulian discovered a French-language magazine about Buffalo Bill that caused him to fall in love with the Wild West.[67] By Mamoulian's account, he would buy photographic paper, wrap it up in a white paper, and draw on the white paper "Indians and cowboys and Buffalo Bill in ink. Then I'd put it out on the balcony in Paris and let the sun hit it. I'd take away the white paper and you'd have a negative there. But gradually it disappeared. It was like a flower. It lived for a few days, then got darker and darker and finally gone were the cowboys."[68]

As an adult, Mamoulian never lost interest in the American West. His first train journey to Hollywood in 1930 was marked by disappointment, as traveling companion (and Paramount executive) Adolph Zukor insisted that the shades be drawn all through the train's journey through the Southwest.[69] Once he settled in Beverly Hills, Mamoulian took regular desert vacations throughout his life to enjoy the landscape and collect and press flowers, and his sketches in his personal papers are filled with drawings of the desert.[70] In interviews, Mamoulian gushed about the Western movie genre whenever the subject was raised. In a 1953 oral history, for instance, Mamoulian called Western narratives the United States' most important and original artistic contribution and extolled the genre for being "our true folk-lore and our national folk-art," and for "forging the Great American Myth."[71] Mamoulian also adored the campfire music associated with Western lore, which he believed evoked the open country, suggested a more carefree lifestyle, and constituted—along with black spirituals—the basic folk music of America.[72] Though Mamoulian would never make a true Western, the genre holds commonalities with the folk musical, including the use of a mythicized past, the exploration of the individual versus the community, and a close relationship with the land. Mamoulian's love of the Western helps explain why the folk musical would become so important to his career.

The Gay Desperado is a rollicking South-of-the-Border farce that bounces between Latin American music (including songs by Mexican composers Juan José Espinosa, María Grever, and Manuel Ponce, and Guatemalan composer Miguel Sandoval) and European opera with wild abandon. It would not prove to be one of Mamoulian's more prescient or influential musicals, but it offered Mamoulian an early opportunity to experiment with stylizing musical numbers within an outdoor landscape. This effort is perhaps most notable during the film's songs that are set near a campfire located just outside a compound for Mexican bandits. During one song—Espinosa's "Las Alteñitas" ("A Gay Ranchero"), performed by Batista and his guitar trio known as the Trovadores Chicanos—Mamoulian experimented with how to frame his subjects with respect to their natural world. This includes a stylized shot in which banditos—wrapped in ponchos, hats pulled low, heads tilted downward—match the arrangement of cacti in the right of the frame (Figure 4.6), a configuration that appears repeatedly in Mamoulian's private sketch books as well (Figure 4.7).[73] During two later numbers, which feature opera singer Chivo (Nino Martini) singing with the group, Mamoulian uses the nearby campfire as a justification for casting and elongating the performers'

Figure 4.6 Mamoulian experiments with stylizing outdoor folk-oriented numbers in *The Gay Desperado* by framing motionless bandits in harmony with cacti...

shadows against the wall behind them, thereby augmenting the joy of campfire songs that Mamoulian associated with the American Southwest. At the end of the second number, everyone stands as the music swells, and in a manner reminiscent of the funeral scenes in *Porgy* and *Porgy and Bess*, the shadows grow even bigger (Figure 4.8). Through composition and shadow play, Mamoulian, in *The Gay Desperado*, began experimenting with how to stylize song performances within a distinctive rural environment.

If *The Gay Desperado* offered Mamoulian a modest yet important early opportunity to create a musical set within a particular landscape, his follow-up film, *High, Wide and Handsome*, constituted a considerable leap forward for the formation of the folk-musical subgenre. Set in nineteenth-century Pennsylvania, *High, Wide and Handsome* tells the story of Peter Cortlandt (Randolph Scott), a man living in the small town of Titusville whose obsessive efforts to be the first to use a derrick to extract oil—and then a pipeline to transport it—nearly wrecks his marriage to Sally (Irene Dunne), a free-spirited itinerant performer who meets and marries Peter early in the film.

At first blush, *High, Wide and Handsome* feels like another instance in which Mamoulian anticipated the direction where filmmakers would later go. *High,*

Figure 4.7 ... a composition that one finds frequently in Mamoulian's private sketches.

Wide and Handsome, Altman points out, is possibly the first musical "in which a folk syntax is openly and actively at work."[74] The film features countless elements that would become standard folk-musical traits. This includes the presentation of ritualistic activities (a jamboree and a wedding ceremony), an emphasis on working the land and tying the couple's fortunes to that work, the creation of a couple in which one (Peter) is rooted in the land and the other (Sally) injects energy into the community as a wanderer, and the presence of an outsider villain (business tycoon Walt Brennan) who tries to take power away from the land's local inhabitants.[75]

Figure 4.8 To stylize a later song in *The Gay Desperado*, Mamoulian throws the shadows of the performers against the exterior wall of the hideout.

Surprisingly, however, archival evidence suggests that Mamoulian was not primarily responsible for the presence of these features. Unlike many of his directorial efforts, Mamoulian joined *High, Wide and Handsome* relatively late in pre-production. Prior to Mamoulian's arrival, producer Arthur Hornblow had already secured a treatment and first full screenplay from Oscar Hammerstein and had signed Jerome Kern to provide the music. Hornblow hired Mamoulian in October 1936 when Mamoulian was in New York City attending the premiere of *The Gay Desperado*.[76] As a letter from Hornblow to Mamoulian makes clear, Mamoulian did not have the opportunity to read the first full screenplay until his arrival back in Hollywood in late October.[77] Mamoulian thus joined the project after many of the core elements of the story had been conceptualized and written. Hammerstein—who surely hoped to recapture the success he had enjoyed with Kern in *Show Boat* on stage and screen[78]—deserves considerable credit for many of the film's folk-oriented narrative elements.

In other respects, however, Mamoulian *was* a vital player on *High, Wide and Handsome*. Mamoulian's folk-musical contributions can be most powerfully felt, I would argue, in two key spheres: the film's avoidance of a picturesque approach to the story, and the cinematic methods used to, in the words of film historian

Plate 1 To reduce the color palette to nearly black and white following *Blood and Sand*'s first bullfight, Mamoulian sprayed the green leaves black on Doña Sol's dining-room table.

Plate 2 The impoverished Juan lies in bed fantasizing about bullfighting in *Blood and Sand*'s opening shot, an image directly inspired by . . .

Plate 3 . . . Bartolomé Murillo's *The Young Beggar*.

Plate 4 The first substantial instance of pure red in *Blood and Sand* coincides with Juan's new role as a professional bullfighter. Mamoulian opens the scene by providing images of Juan's *cuadrillo*, who wears faded colors. . . .

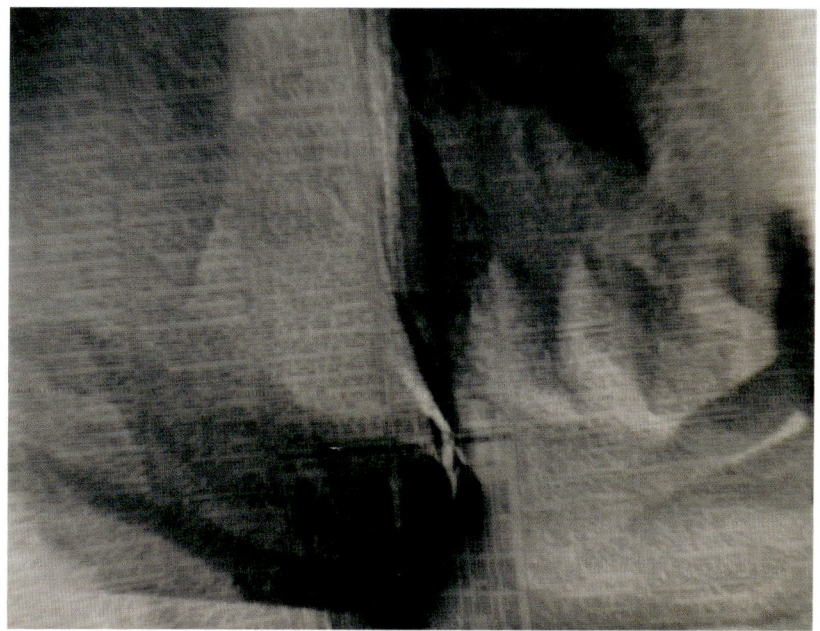

Plate 5 Mamoulian cuts to a newspaper ...

Plate 6 ... which is lowered quickly to reveal Juan, whose *mantilla* positioned behind his head offers a sudden burst of red.

Plate 7 During Juan's prayer before a bullfight in *Blood and Sand,* Mamoulian shines a green light on the faces of Juan's *cuadrillo* and personal assistant in an effort to imitate El Greco's color palette.

Plate 8 Mamoulian initially presents the drab backroom of the bar objectively in *Summer Holiday.* Belle wears a faded pink dress and there is minimal colored lighting against the wall.

Plate 9 Belle's first transformation—via Richard's subjectivity—in *Summer Holiday*. Belle sings in Richard's point-of-view shot....

Plate 10 Two shots later, Richard's out-of-focus point-of-view shot features saturated green lighting against the wall, a yellow-green light through the lattice, and a red light on Belle, though the shot's fuzziness makes these precise changes difficult to detect....

Plate 11 In the same shot, Belle comes into focus. Mamoulian has eliminated Belle's red spotlight, but her dress is redder, the wall remains a saturated green, and a yellow-green light still shines through the lattice....

Plate 12 In the shots following this transformation, Mamoulian keeps the viewer grounded in Richard's subjectivity by shining yellow, green, purple, and blue light against the back walls throughout the room (compare to Color Plate 8).

Plate 13 Belle's second transformation in *Summer Holiday*, again from Richard's point of view, concludes with Belle in her reddest dress (compare to Color Plates 9 and 11)....

Plate 14 A few moments later, Mamoulian shines a red light on Richard and Belle as they kiss, which connects red even more strongly to Richard's lust and his sense of glamour.

Plate 15 Color changes for Richard's disillusionment in *Summer Holiday*. Mamoulian shines a faint green light from frame right on Belle, and uses a fainter purple light to catch her cigarette smoke....

Plate 16 A bit later, after Richard rubs his eyes, the room returns to its prior color palette (same as Color Plate 8).

Jeanine Basinger, wed "an utterly realistic story based on historical fact to musical performance."[79]

High, Wide and Handsome's downplaying of a purely picturesque approach in favor of an emphasis on pragmatic work and its relationship to music would become standard in later folk musicals, but in 1937, it was highly unusual. As Altman discusses, King Vidor's early folk musical *Hallelujah* (1929) had featured a frank, non-beautified approach to landscape and had emphasized the cotton-picking profession of its black characters. The film was not immediately influential, however, as subsequent land or tradition-based musicals regularly stressed pictorial qualities. Two Frank Borzage–directed Dick Powell and Ruby Keeler films (*Flirtation Walk* [1934] and *Shipmates Forever* [1935]), for example, had focused on Powell's efforts to become an officer at West Point and the US Naval Academy, respectively, but in both cases, these institutions are shot largely as grand, beautiful spaces. By 1936, if a musical was set in, for instance, the mountains of Canada, that location was likely to serve not as an opportunity to explore land-based traditions, but merely as a beautified backdrop for romance, as it does in the Jeanette MacDonald–Nelson Eddy vehicle *Rose-Marie*.[80]

Such a picturesque approach was likely what producer Hornblow had in mind for *High, Wide and Handsome*. In an early letter to Mamoulian encouraging him to sign on as director, Hornblow explained:

> I see the production designed along lines of beauty and charm. Even the realities of the early oil fields can be given quaintness and visual interest. Our period and the mood of the story will serve as excellent blending elements between oil fields and pipe lines and Jerome Kern music.[81]

Such a letter indicates that Hornblow saw the "beauty," "charm," and "quaintness" of 1850s oil drilling as the way to allow oil work and musical numbers to coexist. Once Mamoulian came aboard, however, he appears to have been primarily responsible for moving the film *away* from these qualities. To prepare, Mamoulian made extensive use of Paramount's research department. A few of Mamoulian's research requests focused on ritualistic activities from the period—namely "sports and games suitable for jamborees of the period"—but the majority centered on gritty matters of oil-based work. Rather than request gorgeous paintings of the rolling Pennsylvania hills that would seem more in line with Hornblow's vision, Mamoulian asked for—and received—extensive pragmatic information: drawings and photographs of the original derricks by Edwin Drake, a Pennsylvania man who created the first commercial oil well in the United States; "details of oil-well boring: tools equipment, procedure, etc."; "details regarding dimensions of oil-rig equipment, and details of operation"; information on the day Drake discovered oil; notes on the "first gusher";

factual information on early pipelines; information on the first pipeline; information on early transportation (including of oil) and road conditions; and (once again) "derrick and drilling procedure."[82] As in *Porgy*, Mamoulian sought to ground his production in the authentic experiences of place and lived experience. In doing so, Mamoulian was again homing in on work and ritual, qualities essential to the later folk musical.

The finished version of *High, Wide and Handsome* indeed emphasizes labor to a very unusual degree for a musical of the period. An early drilling montage, for instance, includes numerous location shots of derricks being erected. The montage begins with an image of workers digging a hole with a shovel to manually operate a drill, followed by shots of increasingly complex drilling rigs. The montage concludes with shots of gushes from three different derricks. In a later, parallel montage depicting the labor of oil piping, we see workers dropping pipes off of horse carts, workers fastening them together via a wrench, and even a striking series of shots in which a horse cart gets stuck and a massive pile of gigantic pipes tumbles down the snowy hillside.

The sheer fact that such gritty images populate a movie with regular song-and-dance numbers makes *High, Wide and Handsome* an unorthodox musical in 1937. Equally notable, however, are the ways in which Mamoulian's directorial choices enable some of the *numbers*—though shot on indoor sets—to be tightly connected to land- and work-oriented aspects of the setting. Early in the film, for instance, Sally, having spent the night at the home of Peter and his grandmother, offers to help them by feeding their farm animals. Sally eagerly runs outside and begins her number ("To Fool a Simple Maiden") by singing to an actual pig while she feeds it. Serenading a pig is unusual by itself, but Mamoulian then makes an unexpected choice. In a number of prior films—including *Applause*, *City Streets*, and *Queen Christina*—Mamoulian had shown a fondness for a montage of human heads. In *High, Wide and Handsome*, Mamoulian modifies this technique (and shows his stripes as a lifelong animal lover[83]) by lavishing the Cortland farm animals with the same treatment. As Sally continues to sing, we begin with a close-up of a turkey, followed by brief close-ups of a rooster, a young bull, and a horse all listening attentively. Mamoulian then cuts to four horses, all lining up to listen, before cutting back to Sally still feeding the pig. Another round of animal close-ups shows them joining in the "singing" (and ultimately halting the song) with their own noises. As Altman points out, this "symphony of sounds" "manages to rhythmify the farm, to turn it into music, without romanticizing it."[84] Such sound and image choices stylize the musical number while simultaneously keeping it anchored in a work and land-oriented environment.

Mamoulian gives the animals another cameo to introduce the Titusville barn jamboree. The introductory shot opens with one of the longest of Mamoulian's

Figure 4.9 Tying musical performance to land and work in *High, Wide and Handsome*, Mamoulian introduces an 1850s jamboree by first showing livestock...

signature pull backs. Mamoulian begins by framing the horse (and its offspring) along with the turkey (Figure 4.9). The camera then tracks slowly backward to reveal first the square dance band and caller, and then the merry dancers themselves. He ends this nearly fifty-second take with a long-range high-angle shot of the musicians, dancers, and onlookers that anticipates the visual emphasis on community and ritual that John Ford would later lavish on his sound Westerns (Figure 4.10). Then, just as he did for the animal-feeding scene, Mamoulian gives the turkey, bull, colt, and owl reaction shots. The pull-back movement maintains our sense that the Titusville residents remain connected to land and labor even during their musical leisure time. Once again, musical performance is presented not as a mere diversion, but as a practice tied closely to a community's surroundings.

The resulting film was a very odd musical for 1937, as contemporary reviews attest. Upon its release, reviewers of *High, Wide and Handsome* immediately singled out the film's fusion of rugged realism and musical performance as its most innovative feature. *High, Wide and Handsome*, remarked the *New York Daily Mirror*, "departs refreshingly from the banal pretty-pretty tradition of films with music."[85] The *Herald-Express* (Los Angeles) remarked that it was "easily

Figure 4.10 ... before slowly pulling back to reveal the revelers dancing in the barn.

the most virile musical of the year."[86] Though some reviewers tied the film to other recent musicals like *Show Boat* (1936) and *San Francisco* (1936) that had captured colorful chapters of American history, many puzzled over what to even call a film like *High, Wide and Handsome*.[87] *High, Wide and Handsome* "is so completely a pioneering production," declared the *Hollywood Reporter*, "that there are no box-office standards by which to gauge it. In fact, a new word will have to be coined even to describe this operetta treatment of a dramatic episode from American history."[88] *High, Wide and Handsome* "defies ready classification," asserted *New York Times* reviewer Frank S. Nugent, who was nonetheless eager to try. In Nugent's estimation, the film was closer to "musical romance" than operetta, yet musical romance had "too tinkling a connotation to be applied to a rugged and virile historical saga."[89] For Philadelphia's *Evening Public Ledger*, the film was a "two-fisted operetta."[90] For the *Daily Variety* reviewer, *High, Wide and Handsome* was best classified as folksy, native operetta, and the film's most innovative element was the way in which it applied the operetta form to an "American scene."[91] Over the years, *High, Wide and Handsome* has receded in memory in favor of better-known 1940s and 1950s folk musicals, but in 1937, the efforts of Mamoulian and his collaborators to bind together work, land, community, and music were pioneering.

Narrative-number Integration and *Oklahoma!*

In the 1930s, Mamoulian explored his ideas for American musicals in bits and pieces. In *Love Me Tonight*, his interest in the potentials of rhythm took center stage, albeit in a fairy-tale world detached from reality. In *The Gay Desperado*, the American landscape became a space for musical performance, albeit in an absurd comedy set in Mexico. Both *Porgy and Bess* and *High, Wide and Handsome* were musical entertainments grounded in particular American locations. Both, however, lacked one element vital to Mamoulian: the full *integration* of narrative and number.

With the exception of color and stylization, Mamoulian probably wrote and spoke about narrative-number integration more frequently than any other topic. For clarity's sake, we can divide Mamoulian's interests in this arena into aesthetic and narrative integration. Aesthetically in the musical, rather than offering clear sonic and visual divisions between narrative and number, Mamoulian preferred to have his characters slide smoothly between talking and singing, and between ordinary actions and dancing. Such a goal—as chapter 3 demonstrated—was at the heart of his 1926 stage production of *Sister Beatrice*, which featured characters whose voices veered imperceptibly between speech and song, and whose bodies moved in "dance-actions" that resided somewhere between everyday motions and dance.[92] To Mamoulian, this blurring enabled a more powerful expression of the play's emotional ideas.[93] Narratively, Mamoulian sought numbers that expressed story ideas and/or advanced the narrative itself, rather than musicals whose stories ground to a halt to accommodate regular, narratively disconnected, song-and-dance performances.[94]

As chapter 1 noted, Mamoulian's interest in integrated musical theater may have been influenced by the brief time he spent at the Moscow Art Theatre in the mid-1910s. Mamoulian also, however, had a larger cultural motive in mind. Mamoulian, in a viewpoint likely informed by his status as a foreigner, admired what he saw as Americans' love of music and skill with rhythm, yet he felt they lacked a strong dramatic form that was uniquely American. Mamoulian enjoyed American productions of operas and operettas, but like his own *Love Me Tonight*, he felt that they would always remain rooted in European traditions.[95] Mamoulian believed that American vaudeville, burlesque, and musical comedy shows were less beholden to other countries, but he found these forms dramatically unsatisfying. Vaudeville and burlesque were disjunctive by design, and while musical comedy told a narrative of sorts, Mamoulian felt that at its core, it consisted of an "arbitrary conglomeration of songs," dances, and dialogue scenes.[96] Given Americans' interest in music, Mamoulian thought, why not combine these elements into something cohesive? As Mamoulian would later explain:

Why, in a country that is so sensitive and so genuinely in love with rhythm, music, dance, spoken word, words that are sung—why couldn't there be a new recipe for theatre that might have a legitimate claim to bring a new theatrical form? A recipe which would combine dialogue and dance and singing into one cohesive rhythmic design, wherein each element would be as effective and as potent, in propelling the plot and the theme, the mood and the character development, as words and action alone are in a dramatic play?[97]

Mamoulian believed deeply in this idea. Yet while he enjoyed presenting it as his own, we should note that such efforts at integration were unusual but not entirely new to musical theater *or* film. In musical theater, as historian Geoffrey Block points out, aspects of integration can be glimpsed as far back as the late 1800s in the work of such well-known Europeans as Gilbert and Sullivan, Johann Strauss, and Franz Lehár. In the United States, high-profile stage musicals like *Naughty Marietta* (1910), *Rose-Marie* (1924), *Show Boat* (1927), *Pal Joey* (1940), and *Lady in the Dark* (1941) contained elements of integration. Yet integration on the stage was the exception rather than the norm prior to 1943, when Mamoulian directed *Oklahoma!*, and musical numbers were indeed more commonly configured as attractions discrete from the storyline.[98]

Similarly, musical numbers in cinema often were not tightly integrated in the late 1920s through the mid-1940s, but plenty of attempts can be found in prominent films, including Mamoulian's own *Love Me Tonight*. Visually, as we saw, *Love Me Tonight* features "dance-actions." Sonically, a number like "How Are You?" puts rapid back-and-forth conversations into song and winds down into speech quite gradually. "The Son of a Gun Is Nothing but a Tailor" slides almost imperceptibly into singing, with rhythmic speech eventually giving way to a chant-like song. *Love Me Tonight*'s songs also show a concerted effort at narrative integration. Though the story does pause for the narratively irrelevant "Apache" song—clearly designed as a specialty number for Chevalier[99]—in general, *Love Me Tonight*'s numbers have a direct bearing on the existing narrative situation and its progress. Even the nonsensical "Mimi" is arguably incorporated into the story, as it reflects the ravings of a love-struck lunatic.[100] Prior to *Love Me Tonight*, the early Lubitsch musicals had featured a blending of speech and song in places, and the bulk of the numbers expressed character emotion. After *Love Me Tonight*, Berkeley's unintegrated numbers beginning with *42nd Street* were influential, but other prominent musicals—perhaps most notably the Fred Astaire/Ginger Rogers musicals beginning with *The Gay Divorcee* (1934)—frequently featured characters singing to express their emotions and shifting gradually between everyday motion and dance.

Aside from *Love Me Tonight*, Mamoulian's other musicals prior to *Oklahoma!* had not achieved especially close narrative-number integration. *Porgy and*

Bess—because it features constant music—could not, in Mamoulian's mind, be called an integrated musical.[101] *The Gay Desperado* and *High, Wide and Handsome* contain many songs whose lyrics are extensions of character thoughts and emotions, but both films feature clear divisions between narrative and musical passages. It would thus not be until *Oklahoma!* that Mamoulian's interests in rhythm, Americana, and integration would find their way into a single production. It was also a gigantic hit, running over three times longer than the record-holding stage musical at the time, sparking a massive interest in musicals with American subjects, popularizing the notion of integration, and ushering in an era of tighter integration between narrative and number.[102] Today, it stands as arguably one of the three or four most influential American stage musicals of the twentieth century.

Examples of *Oklahoma!*'s techniques for heightening aesthetic and narrative integration abound. Many song lyrics—written by Oscar Hammerstein—are often conversational and colloquial ("Kansas City," "I Cain't Say No," "People Will Say We're in Love," "All er Nuthin'," "Oklahoma!"). "The Surrey with a Fringe on Top" features back-and-forth song lines that are unusually close to conversation for the period, and in between choruses, characters speak their lines to instrumental underscoring. Dances—choreographed by Agnes de Mille—are extrapolations of narrative situations and fears, most famously Laurey's near-twenty-minute dream ballet that concludes the first act. More generally, *Oklahoma!*'s performers did not overtly play to the audience during their songs or dances like they often would in the specialty numbers of stage musicals at the time, thereby aiding the impression of a self-contained play that slides effortlessly into song and dances.[103]

Though *Oklahoma!*'s success and influence were enormous, and its methods were a close fit with Mamoulian's artistic ideals, his precise creative role remains contentious and unclear to this day. As many scholars have discussed, Mamoulian, Rodgers, Hammerstein, and de Mille did not get along during rehearsals. Once *Oklahoma!* became a hit, all fought bitterly to receive credit for the play's innovations.[104] In one sense, the project was likely a fortuitous merging of like-minded artists who valued similar principles, and thus the vexed question of who innovated what may not be essential. Still, existing evidence of Mamoulian's contributions can help us better understand his role in this formative musical and his creative choices in later folk musicals.

Like *High, Wide and Handsome*, the idea for *Oklahoma!* predated Mamoulian's arrival to the project. *Oklahoma!* was a Theatre Guild musical version of a commercially unsuccessful dramatic play by Lynn Riggs titled *Green Grow the Lilacs* (1930). Though the original play had apparently featured authentic folk music throughout the production, including cowboy laments, Rodgers and Hammerstein wanted a production that was inspired by folk songs and dances, yet contained entirely new numbers and elite dancers.[105] Mamoulian's entry into the project started inauspiciously. He was not the creators' first choice, and he apparently agreed to direct only because several planned film projects had fallen through.[106] Still, Mamoulian had a number of offers to direct plays at the time,[107] and his selection of *Green Grow the Lilacs* (as it was still called at this point) suggests that he recognized the property's potential when few did. Mamoulian's later stated reasons for selecting the property—the opportunity to integrate dance, song, action, and dialogue into a consistent whole, and the play's proximity to the Western genre and its Americana theme—seem consistent with his career interests to that point.[108]

Though Mamoulian would later claim that the initial script he received was sketchy and fragmented, Kurt Jensen has demonstrated that the script—which is housed at the Library of Congress—was considerably more complete. When Mamoulian first reviewed it, most of the songs were already in place, and the script had some integration present (along with specialty numbers, which were later removed).[109] Still, successful narrative-number integration required a director equally adept at handling dramatic and musical scenes, a characteristic Mamoulian had in spades by this point in his career. Firsthand accounts of rehearsals indicate just how seriously Mamoulian took the task of integrating song, speech, and dance sections, with Mamoulian directing all the songs (usually the task of the dance director) and devoting inordinate attention to rehearsals for "The Farmer and the Cowhand," a dance that is linked especially closely to the plot.[110]

Beyond the task of molding existing material, Mamoulian made key changes to the production. Most of his changes remained in place when the film opened in New York City, and a few did not, but taken together, they paint a picture of a director highly cognizant of the importance of integration, land, community, and rhythm. As Jensen points out, Mamoulian made cuts to spoken sections and songs in order to forge a tighter connection between story and song. *Oklahoma!*'s first three numbers—"Oh What a Beautiful Mornin'," "The Surrey with the Fringe on Top," and "Kansas City"—had appeared in the first play script, but Mamoulian pared down dialogue considerably so that these three songs seemed to, in Jensen's words, "tumble onto each other" in their advancement of the story. Mamoulian also cut the number "Boys and Girls Like You and Me" because he felt that it failed to advance the plot.[111]

More important from the perspective of the folk musical was Mamoulian's approach to the beginning and the end of the production. Altman has pointed to the lyrics of *Oklahoma!*'s opening number—"Beautiful Mornin' "—as an example of the subgenre's tendency to have music making be inspired by the sounds of nature ("all the sounds of the earth are like music," Curly sings).[112] Hammerstein—not Mamoulian—wrote these lyrics, but Mamoulian's experiments with staging the opening reveal the importance he placed on this emerging element of folk musicals. Originally, Mamoulian wanted a symphony of animal sounds to start the production and precede the opening song, a technique that resembles his symphony of noises in *Porgy* (and *Porgy and Bess*), as well as the animal symphony that chases away Sally at the end of "To Fool a Simple Maiden" in *High, Wide and Handsome*.[113] Though this idea would never be used, Mamoulian's copy of the play script does feature, in Mamoulian's handwriting, the sounds of dogs, turkeys, pigeons, a cow, and a horse in the play's earliest moments.[114] Mamoulian also arranged for a flock of white pigeons to fly across the stage as the curtain opened but was forced to abandon the idea after the first tryout in New Haven, when the uncooperative pigeons flew to the rafters, causing—in Mamoulian's words—"unexpected embarrassment to actors and no little white and fluffy damage to the scenery."[115] Still, these efforts demonstrate that Mamoulian was invested in the idea that the play's songs should feel as though they emerged organically from the natural world.

Though Mamoulian failed to emphasize nature to his liking at the beginning of the production, it seems likely that he was responsible for finding a way to connect music to land in the play's famous conclusion. We can tell, from archival evidence, that the show-stopping finale—a rousing choral rendition of the title song in which the leads' marriage is tied to a celebration of Oklahoma farming, landscape, and weather—was included only just before the play officially opened.[116] Other endings explored during rehearsals, according to Mamoulian, included an Agnes de Mille–choreographed dance.[117] Mamoulian, by his account, argued in rehearsal that a spirited, group-oriented choral number was needed, that Rodgers and Hammerstein quickly wrote it, and that Mamoulian staged it.[118] Credit for this finale has also—in other sources—been given to Guild producer Theresa Helburn and to de Mille.[119]

Archival evidence, unfortunately, does not provide a conclusive answer. In my view, however, there are two good reasons to suspect that Mamoulian's account has some validity. First, after the play's opening, Mamoulian gave interviews—and even hired a press agent—claiming credit for the play's innovations, including its quiet opening, the period of the costumes, the positioning of the first two songs, the casting of the leads, and the ending. Mamoulian's boasts prompted an angry cease-and-desist letter from both Rodgers and Hammerstein and the show's producers, who accused Mamoulian of fibbing about all of the above "contributions" *except* for the ending.[120] In his response letter, Mamoulian conceded no wrongdoing, but in later interviews he generally dropped these other "innovations" and focused only on the ending. De Mille did not take part in the cease-and-desist letter—which may account for why the letter did not mention the ending—but its absence in the Rodgers and Hammerstein note makes one suspect that this claim was legitimate.

Second, the staging of the number itself holds clear parallels to Mamoulian's prior work. By Mamoulian's account—affirmed by other sources[121]—Mamoulian had the chorus in the finale starting

> way up stage and gradually coming closer and closer to the footlights and then at the end almost stepping into the audience. Putting their feet on the footlights, leaning forward—which always brought the house down.[122]

While de Mille *may* have staged this herself, this method all but screams Mamoulian. As discussed in chapter 3, a group of mourners in one of *Porgy*'s signature scenes undergoes a similar movement, beginning closer to the back of the stage and approaching the footlights at the conclusion. Similarly, in Mamoulian's staging of the science fiction play *R.U.R.* (*Rossum's Universal Robots*) in 1930, the final act had concluded by having an "army of robots march to the edge of the stage toward the audience before the blackout."[123] It seems likely that Mamoulian pulled from his familiar bag of tricks to create one of the most famous moments in *Oklahoma!*

If this ending was, indeed, largely Mamoulian's vision, it shows him upping the ante in terms of the relationship between individuals, land, and community. Altman has pinpointed *Oklahoma!* as a key moment for the folk-musical syntax when the leads are absorbed into a collective community. The staging of the final scene fuels this sensation considerably, as it is the movement of the chorus/community itself—not Laurey and Curly in particular—that draws the audience's attention and "brings the house down."[124] Such an ending also enabled Mamoulian to mold a production whose broad logic included a rhythmic progression. As Mamoulian put it in a 1943 interview, "*Oklahoma!* might be called an organized progression of rhythms, which mount from a quiet beginning to the rousing ensemble at the end. . . . The whole performance has a rhythmic design."[125] Rhythm—the stuff of life in the fairy-tale musical *Love Me Tonight* and Mamoulian's lifelong passion as an artist—here became harnessed to a celebration of such folk-musical elements as nature, work, marriage, and community.

After *Oklahoma!*

After the extraordinary success of *Oklahoma!*, Mamoulian—an eclectic director by inclination—entered a rare period when he focused almost exclusively on a single kind of entertainment: the folk musical. With the exception of his 1948 theater production of *Leaf and Bough*—a failed non-musical that ran for only three performances—all his remaining 1940s works were continuations of the folk and integration elements found in *Oklahoma! Sadie Thompson*—Mamoulian's follow-up to *Oklahoma!*—was set in Pago Pago and thus can hardly be considered another piece of Americana, but it did feature another effort by Mamoulian to ground the musical in a sense of place via native singing and drumming.[126] Unfortunately, Mamoulian—perhaps on cloud nine in the wake of *Oklahoma!*— bogged down the production with elaborate and overproduced set pieces, and the play was a critical and commercial failure.[127]

Mamoulian, by his own admission, bore the mistakes of *Sadie Thompson* in mind on his next production: a re-teaming with Rodgers and Hammerstein, de Mille, and Theatre Guild producers Theresa Helburn and Lawrence Langner for the 1945 musical *Carousel*.[128] *Carousel* was a major hit, and while it would never do business comparable to the behemoth *Oklahoma!*, its popularity (it ran for 890 performances) further affirmed Mamoulian's belief that folk-based musicals attentive to rhythm and individuals' relationship to a larger community were worthwhile.

Carousel was based on the Ferenc Molnár play *Liliom* (1909), which had been set in Hungary. In a mark of Rodgers and Hammerstein's continued interest in American folk settings, the duo moved its location to coastal Maine, placed it in the past (the 1870s), and wrote songs grounded in the earth and seasons ("June Is Bustin' Out All Over"), work ("Blow High, Blow Low"), and ritual ("A Real Nice Clambake"). Like *Oklahoma!*, *Carousel* shows a clear interest in narrative-number integration. Several songs, including "If I Loved You" and "June Is Bustin' Out All Over," feature characters sliding easily between singing and speech. Elsewhere, an underscored conversation between Julie and Carrie transitions to a sung exchange ("You're a Queer One, Julie Jordan"), followed by another underscored conversation, and then Carrie's song, "Mister Snow."

As director of the show, Mamoulian's most important contributions likely included his staging of the play's rhythm-based opening and his methods for arranging the chorus onstage. In a highly unusual beginning, *Carousel* started with an "overture" of hurdy-gurdy music that eventually congeals into a waltz tune. Before the audience is ready (after all, no conventional overture has yet been presented), the curtain suddenly rises on the carousel and the fair.[129] According to the original play script, we see several lines of action, including a resistant child being taken off the carousel, carnival barker Billy flirting with a sailor's girlfriend, and Billy saving a carousel seat for the smitten Julie. What is most unusual about this opening, however, is that it is set not to singing or dancing, but rather entirely to pantomime (five and a half minutes of it, according to a 1945 Mamoulian interview).[130] An explanatory note in the play script puts it this way:

> This scene is set to the music of a waltz suite. The only sound will come from the orchestra pit. The pantomimic action will be synchronized to the music, but it will be in no sense a ballet treatment. The characters will move in rhythm with

the music. When they are supposed to be talking, they will move their mouths as if speaking in meter, but they will not be heard."[131]

A bit later in the pantomimic opening, Billy mouths the rhythmic words of a carnival barker, and the play script again specifies rhythm as the means through which characters respond. "Everyone on the stage," instructs the play script, "starts to sway unconsciously with the rhythm of his words . . . all but JULIE. JULIE just stands, looking at him over the heads of the others, her gaze steady, her body motionless. . . . BILLY becomes conscious of her."[132]

Hammerstein may have written these words, but they could have flowed just as easily from Mamoulian's pen. Like *Porgy*, *Love Me Tonight*, and *Porgy and Bess* before it, sound emerging from a community activity in *Carousel* "sets the world . . . into rhythmic motion," a crucial feature of the folk musical.[133] Once again, a Mamoulian production defined a community by its relationship to organic, ritualistic rhythms.

If the inclusion and staging of the chorus had been a means for emphasizing the folk community in *Oklahoma!*, *Carousel* offered Mamoulian further opportunities to arrange the chorus performers in a striking manner. In *Oklahoma!*, Mamoulian had conceptualized the chorus in the final number horizontally, with the group spread across the stage and moving toward the audience before the curtain dropped. For the "It Was a Real Nice Clambake" number in *Carousel*, Mamoulian apparently decided to do the opposite:

> I thought in *Carousel* I would use the chorus vertically, instead of horizontally. I had this set for the picnic scene. I had a couple of mounds there. Little hills with platforms behind them. I opened the scene with everyone lying flat on the floor. They just had food. "This Was a Real Nice Clambake." They start singing and they're all lying flat on the floor of the stage. Gradually, they start getting up. Then standing up and some of them get up on those mounds. Finally it gets up almost to the proscenium. The vertical treatment![134]

Once again, Mamoulian was interested in finding arresting ways to convey community-based ritual in the folk musical.

Hot off the successes of *Oklahoma!* and *Carousel*, Mamoulian agreed to direct a film-musical adaptation of Eugene O'Neill's dramatic play *Ah, Wilderness!* (eventually titled *Summer Holiday*) for Arthur Freed's unit at MGM. During preproduction, Mamoulian took a trip to the east coast to visit O'Neill, and Freed asked Mamoulian to check on a troubled theatrical production that Freed was producing on Broadway titled *St. Louis Woman*.[135] After reviewing the script and providing copious suggestions, Mamoulian eventually agreed to direct the production himself. The finished product—which Mamoulian substantially altered—became yet another 1940s Mamoulian stage musical that emphasized tight narrative-number integration, rhythm, and a dynamic staging of the chorus.

Mamoulian's changes to *St. Louis Woman* were so substantial that an analysis could easily fill its own chapter. The most striking, however, was Mamoulian's rewrite of the final scene. Featuring a black cast, *St. Louis Woman* tells the story of Augie, a successful St. Louis race-horse jockey who falls in love with a woman named Della. Augie suffers a series of bad races, and Della leaves him for a spell, but the couple is reunited at the conclusion. In the finale of the original play script, Della sits in a Saratoga (NY) bar with her new boyfriend, Rags. Augie then arrives with some new friends—his luck on the racetrack has returned. The play concludes with Augie whistling for Della, and they walk off together as the curtain falls.[136]

Dissatisfied with what he felt was an underwhelming conclusion, Mamoulian wrote a new scene centering on Augie's horse race against a rival, Barney, with the stakes magnified by having Della place a bet on Augie. In doing so, Mamoulian again embraced the opportunity to convey narrative progress through rhythm and song. Mamoulian dictated the following instructions to the play's songwriters, John Mercer and Harold Arlen:

> Through this scene, the music serves as a throbbing, rythmic [sic] undertone, over which we hear a jumble of excited ad libs which describe to us the events on the track: horses being led out, getting into formation and finally settling themselves at the starting line.
>
> Here, the usual awesome hush descends upon the people, the rythmic [sic] throbbing of the orchestra continues softly but uninterrupted.
>
> Then a violent outcry, "They're off!" releases a choral number which is the crowd watching the race. At first all the horses are running in a pretty uniform group. The singing is rythmic [sic], exciting, but on the soft side, the situation on the track being indecisive....
>
> Before I go any further, I would like to suggest that the crowd be divided musically, as well as story-wise, into two camps: Lil Augie's vs. Barney's.... I would also suggest that Augie's supporters be confined to tenors and sopranos, while Barney's are bases [sic] and contraltos....
>
> Augie is gaining the lead. This is the cue for an enthusiastic outburst in singing, combined perhaps, with occasional lines "shouted" over by Augie's partisans.... The section of the singing, after reaching a certain climax, begins to decrease, in view of the fact that now other horses are catching up with Lil Augie. The singing comes down to a softer, sustained rythmic [sic] level, which would denote that again there is no outstanding leader in the race.... Suddenly, Barney's horse noses out of the melee and, as Barney gains, his supporters burst

into a lively crescendo. The excitement and volume of singing grows in ratio with Barney gaining distance over the other horses.... There follows a short lap of sustained, terrific excitement which accompanies Barney and Augie running neck-to-neck. This calms down to a softer level in volume, denoting the suspense of this neck-to-neck situation.

After a spell . . . Barney starts emerging again and this time for keeps. The more distance he puts behind himself and Augie, the wilder the singing of the crowd.[137]

In the final play script, Augie wins the race rather than Barney, and at one point he finds himself neck and neck with an elite jockey named Danny Jenkins, but otherwise, the scene hews closely to what Mamoulian outlined. The eventual song, "Come on Lil' Augie," is decidedly rhythmic, in essence a chant, and the play script portrays it as a competition between the song/chants of Augie's versus Barney's supporters. At one point, the groups' chants are staggered:

ONE GROUP		
Here they come, here they come, in a cloud dust.		
Here they come, here they come,		OTHER GROUP
and it's win or bust.		They're all comin' in a cloud
If you can't hear the noise, then		of dust.
you're deaf and dumb.		They're all comin' and it's win
No two ways about it, here they		or bust.
Come		There ain't any doubt about it,
		Here they come!

Then, as Augie takes the lead, the rhythm escalates via alternations, as Danny and Augie now compete for the win:

COME ON, DANNY	(Alternating)	COME ON, AUGIE
COME ON, DANNY	—————	COME ON, AUGIE
DANNY	—————	AUGIE
DANNY	—————	AUGIE[138]

By *St. Louis Woman*, one can recognize such a scene as signature Mamoulian. Its climax centers on rhythmic, pace-based action, and musical corollaries like tempo and dynamics chart the race's progression. The boundaries between singing, shouting, and talking are blurred. And the integration of two characters into larger communities reflects Mamoulian's continued interest in folk-musical concerns.

Mamoulian's final 1940s stage musical, *Lost in the Stars*—an adaptation of the 1948 Alan Paton novel *Cry, the Beloved Country*—takes place in South Africa, but it again emphasizes land, family, and rhythm. Adapted by Maxwell Anderson—with music by Kurt Weill—*Lost in the Stars* (which again featured a predominantly black cast) opens with a song called "The Hills of Ixopo" that marks *Lost in the Stars* as a folk musical, with lyrics emphasizing such elements as grass, soil, earth, and cattle. This is followed by a song ("How Many Miles?") centered on family. Perhaps the most notable element in the play, however, is the inclusion of a nondiegetic chorus that regularly comments upon the action, at times generating a rhythmic thrust. At the end of the production's second scene, for instance, a black missionary, Stephen, decides to travel by train to Johannesburg to find his wayward son. As the chorus leader sings the song's lyrics ("White man go to Johannesburg / He come back / He come back"), the rest of the chorus repeats, in an imitation of the train noise, "Clink, clink, click." The chorus then continues this sound through the fade out at the end of the scene.[139]

In *Sadie Thompson, Carousel, St. Louis Woman*, and *Lost in the Stars*, Mamoulian honed and varied the approaches found in *Oklahoma!*: aesthetic and narrative integration, music emerging from the sounds of nature and community, an emphasis on the chorus, and the incorporation of the leads into a larger group. These techniques serve as valuable context, because in the midst of this series of plays, Mamoulian returned to cinema once more to direct *Summer Holiday*, his definitive take on the American folk film musical.

Summer Holiday

Summer Holiday occupies a curious place in the history of the Hollywood musical. Though a failure upon its release, *Summer Holiday* was quite innovative, in large part because Mamoulian was able to closely monitor nearly all aspects of production—his last opportunity to do so as a movie director. *Summer Holiday*'s use of color, alone, stood out (see chapter 5), but as a musical, it offered an array of methods for extraordinarily tight aesthetic and narrative integration. It also presented unusual ways of tying the cinematic stylization of its numbers to such folk elements as everyday rhythms, the mythicized American past, and community ritual, most notably by re-creating paintings and conveying painterly ideas. Though a major setback in Mamoulian's career, *Summer Holiday* nevertheless charted an ambitious pathway for subsequent musicals. The film thus deserves more attention than it has received, both for what it says about Mamoulian's values as a director of musicals and for its anticipation of techniques that would later be used in more successful films.

Mamoulian's determination to use close narrative-number integration, to stylize, and to focus on American folk traditions was a continuation of his personal interests, but it also stemmed from the way he conceptualized the adaptation of *Ah, Wilderness!* Because he was translating O'Neill's play from drama to musical, and from stage to screen, he viewed the film as a "double adaptation," as he put it in memos circulated to Irving Brecher (who adapted the material) and Harry Warren and Ralph Blane (who wrote the songs).[140] To perform this double adaptation, Mamoulian argued that one needed a firm grasp of what the musical genre could do that dramas could not, and what cinema could do that theater could not. Once this was established, the trick was to read through O'Neill's play to determine which sections could be enhanced by techniques specific to the musical genre, and to cinema.[141]

To shift from drama to musical, Mamoulian aimed for a method of substitution in which singing, dancing, and music would occur only when it "adequately replaces pages of the play's dialogue and consistently advances the story."[142] Doing so would—once again—require considerable narrative and aesthetic integration. Musical numbers not only needed to play a vital role in telling the story, but they needed to emerge as if from speech. "Singing," Mamoulian wrote, "must be interwoven and integrated with speech. Speech must range from everyday prose to rhythmic, cadenced sentences and to rhyming verse written to music."[143] Such an effort required, in Mamoulian's words, "a unified and rhythmic musical structure of story-telling where a song or a dance will tell the story just as much as spoken dialogue does."[144]

To shift from stage to screen, Mamoulian argued that plays were "better qualified to handle complicated ideas and thoughts, while the Screen is superbly equipped to deal with action, and visual imagery of both everyday life and imaginative make-believe."[145] An effective adaptation of *Ah, Wilderness!*, then, needed to condense the "intellectual texture of the play" while compensating for this loss through imagery that would enhance the material's emotional qualities.[146] Moreover, a worthwhile stage-to-screen adaptation would also require Mamoulian to cinematically stylize the material—particularly the numbers—in ways consistent with the Americana or folk quality of the play, which, to Mamoulian's mind, was a nostalgic journey to O'Neill's upbringing in turn-of-the-century Connecticut.[147]

Mamoulian's aims for *Summer Holiday* thus involved concepts and topics—integration, stylization, Americana—that he had been exploring for years. By the late 1940s, however, prominent folk-musical efforts in a similar vein had occurred before Mamoulian laid out his goals for *Summer Holiday*, most notably Vincente Minnelli's *Meet Me in St. Louis* (1944), which was released roughly a year before Mamoulian began work on *Summer Holiday*. Though not an adaptation of a play, *Meet Me in St. Louis* was also a nostalgic, family-focused Freed-unit folk musical that sought to integrate narrative and number. *Meet Me in St. Louis* looms large over *Summer Holiday*, and while Minnelli's film would exert more influence over later folk musicals, *Summer Holiday* remains an ambitious production.[148]

One can sense Mamoulian's level of ambition in *Summer Holiday*'s first number, "Our Home Town," which is a "passed-along song" between members of the Miller family.[149] "Our Home Town" bears a resemblance to the passed-along song that opens *Meet Me in St. Louis* (which in turn was likely influenced by the "How Are You?" number from *Love Me Tonight*[150]), but Mamoulian's degree of aesthetic and narrative integration exceeds that of *Meet Me in St. Louis* in many respects. *Summer Holiday*'s opening, which was originally to have begun with a rooster crowing in tempo[151] (yet another Mamoulian effort to connect nature to song in the folk musical), begins with Nat Miller (Walter Huston) singing as he leaves his newspaper office and walks down the Dannville, Connecticut, street where he resides with his family. Huston is no professional singer, a fact that likely strikes the viewer immediately, and by the time "Our Home Town" concludes, such unlikely actors as Frank Morgan and Agnes Moorehead have also sung. Doing so implicitly blurs the boundary between skilled performer and ordinary movie-audience member, an emerging folk-musical concept at the time.[152] Importantly for aesthetic integration, it also makes the singing feel a bit less "pure," and a bit more folksy or conversational.

The non-professional singers, however, are only the most salient means of aesthetic integration in this opening number. Far more complex is the way that the number weaves together singing, spoken verse, dialogue, and underscoring in a rhythmic manner that makes the act of distinguishing between narrative and number all but futile. Consequently, despite its status as a musical number, "Our Home Town" remains closely tied to the ordinary rhythms of the Miller family. During the first few stanzas of the song, which Nat provides while still in his office, it seems clear that he is singing, yet partway through Nat modulates his voice into speech as he interjects, "It's a nice town," in rhythm with the music. Then, when Mamoulian dissolves to Nat finishing his early portion of the song and approaching his house, it becomes impossible for a viewer to separate speech from song. As he walks, Nat delivers lines in rhymed verse, but one cannot boil down his utterances into singing or speech—he sometimes seems to be doing both at once. This feeling is enhanced by the orchestration, which matches his lines as if it were still accompanying a sung rendition of "Our Home Town." Thus, when Nat's son Tommy (Butch Jenkins) rushes out the door to encounter Nat, and Nat says (not sings), "hey, hey, what's the hurry?," we discover that we are listening to a conversation without realizing we had moved away from song.

The dynamic blurring of speech and song persists. Nat and Tommy continue talking, and though their sentences cease to rhyme, the background accompaniment's musical phrases remain synchronized with their lines. Then, as Nat steps into the house, we are introduced to his two older children—Arthur (Michael Kirby) and Mildred (Shirley Johns)—engaged in a friendly argument, and we witness a shift to a slightly different technique. The siblings walk down the stairs speaking in rhymed verse ("Where're you going today?" / "I won't say." "Bet I know just the same. / I can tell you her initials, I can tell you her name." "And you can mind your own business. Don't act like such a kid." / Well, you'd better not rush off till you say goodbye to Uncle Sid."). Here, however, the orchestration *separates* itself from their dialogue, providing a bouncy instrumentation of "Our Home Town" featuring its own distinct rhythm. Nat joins in the spoken conversation, mentioning "the train is always late," before finishing by singing the line, "in our home town." Here, his spoken lines bring him *back* in rhythm with the music, so that by the time he sings the "our home town" line, the background music accompanies him precisely.

So it goes for the remainder of the song. Family members continue to oscillate almost imperceptibly between singing and speaking. Sometimes they are in rhythm with the underscore, and other times they are not. In the next section of the song, for instance, we hear a conversation between the mother, Essie (Selena Royle), and Tommy. The conversation starts without rhymed verse, and with the background music no longer in rhythm with the characters' sentences. As the boy complains about restrictions, his gripes morph into brief singing in rhymed verse—with the background music matching the tune—before he leaves. The ensuing conversation between Essie and Nat is in spoken verse but with the underscoring out of the rhythm with their speech, except for one exchange ("And in his eyes I could almost see tears." / "He's said that a lot in the last 18 years."). A later exchange—between extended family members Lily (Moorehead) and Sid (Morgan)—again resides somewhere between speech and singing. Sid, who wants Lily to marry him, delivers more of his lines in something closer to song, while Lily—a skeptic—produces lines closer to speech, but not entirely so. Thus, in coordination with songwriters Warren and Blane, Mamoulian's opening functions as he envisioned it in his memos. From beginning to end, "Our Home Town" is a complicated, rhythmic, and ever-shifting dance of speech, singing, and musical accompaniment.

Efforts to merge these features were not entirely new, but I am aware of few prior films that contain the aesthetic complexity found in "Our Home Town." As we saw, *Love Me Tonight*'s "How Are You?" number is conversational, and it slides back to speech at the end, but its basic rhythmic elements—footsteps, gestures, and vocal utterances—remain strictly regimented within the singular rhythm of the song. Other, non-Mamoulian, examples of blending speech and song can also be found, especially in the early 1930s. *Hallelujah, I'm a Bum!* (1933) contains numbers that shift regularly between spoken verse and song, yet the underscoring, unlike "Our Home Town," remains tightly synced to vocal utterance. Lubitsch's *One Hour with You* (1932) and the little-known *Melody Cruise* (1933) do offer complex experiments in aesthetic integration that more closely resemble *Summer Holiday*. In *One Hour with You* (which features songs written by Oscar Straus, Leo Robin, and Richard Whiting), voices during the opening "Police Number" slip in and out of meter and rhyme. The buildup to "We Will Always Be Sweethearts" alternates rhythmically between the chatter of two best friends and their individual lines of dialogue, with the underscore only periodically synchronized with this rhythm. Characters slide smoothly into speech in "We Will Always Be Sweethearts" and "Three Times a Day," and in a later reprise of "We Will Always Be Sweethearts," the characters veer between rhymed verse and regular speech. The manic first five minutes of Mark Sandrich's extraordinarily experimental *Melody Cruise*—likely inspired by *Love Me Tonight*'s opening—feature footsteps, brooms, and shovels mickey moused to music, spoken verse, and a brief slippage into song. Later, in "He's Not the Marrying Kind" (written by Will Jason and Val Burton), an entire number consists of spoken verse synced to music as if it were a song, and a waiter's effort to avoid dropping his tray somehow manages to become a dance. Even the drama *You and Me* (1938) features a song ("Song of the Cash Register," by Kurt Weill and Sam Coslow) whose singer (Emery Darcy) oscillates between spoken verse and operatic singing, and an almost unclassifiable "Knocking Song" featuring mainly chanted verse. Such experiments were far from the norm, however, and none are tied to folk concerns. "Our Home Town" deserves credit for its rhythmic complexity and the extent to which its aesthetic integration is tied specifically to quotidian activities.

"Our Home Town" is also *narratively* integrated in several ways. As we saw, family members will be perfectly in sync with the music, before mild disagreements throw them slightly off the music's rhythm, only to be quickly recuperated within the larger background orchestration. Such a method portrays distinct individuals who are nevertheless defined by what they have in common, namely their hometown and their family—a key idea in *Summer Holiday*. Moreover, the song establishes important traits of the various family members. One gets a sense of Nat's level-headedness and love of his family and Tommy's antsy little-kid antics. When the song concludes with Nat's son, Richard (Mickey Rooney), and his girlfriend, Muriel (Gloria DeHaven), singing at the town's soda shop, the lyrics tie Muriel to her devotion to small-town New England life and Richard to spirited restlessness. The song also introduces narrative scenarios. We learn, for instance, that Sid is a longtime drinker in love with Lily, that Lily loves him yet remains dubious that he will reform, and that Sid is off to Waterbury to "make good." Narrative integration in film musicals was hardly new by this point, but *Summer Holiday*'s ability to pack considerable story information into a single song remains notable.

Seen from the perspective of aesthetic and narrative integration, "Our Home Town" differs considerably from the title song that opens *Meet Me in St. Louis*. In that justly famous number, we are—as in *Summer Holiday*—introduced to family members by witnessing many of them sing the same song. Doing so helps mark the Smiths, like the Millers, as a cohesive unit of mostly non-professional singers bound together by their provincial location. Tight aesthetic integration and a forward-moving narrative are not the goals for this song, however. In the dialogue buildup to the song, no one speaks in verse or rhythm, nor is earlier dialogue in sync with the underscore. Once the song begins—with daughter Agnes (Joan Carroll) singing it—we hear a sudden shift in sound quality, making the division between speech and song quite clear. Having moved to song, the film then stays there until the end—no one slips into anything that could be considered non-singing. During the song, characterization is minimal, and plot development nonexistent. The number offers little information about the Smith family members who sing it, and the incident that will set the story into motion (the revelation that Rose [Lucille Bremer] is expecting an important phone call during dinner) must wait until the song concludes. The number remains extremely effective for its joy and infectiousness, but a comparison to *Summer Holiday* helps demonstrate that Mamoulian was offering cutting-edge filmmaking even at this late date in his career.

What about Mamoulian's *second* stated aim: to find *cinematic* ways to enhance the emotional qualities of O'Neill's stage play? The folk musical's grounding in small-town America posed a challenge for a stylist like Mamoulian, who wished to convey a sense of authenticity while simultaneously stylizing space so as to augment the "lift" that he felt numbers should provide. Mamoulian's prior folk musical, *High, Wide and Handsome*, had partly sidestepped this issue by offering only occasional, light stylization. In *Summer Holiday*, however, Mamoulian found a more salient form of stylization appropriate to a folk musical: the incorporation of revered paintings depicting small-town and rural American life. As we saw in chapter 1, paintings were an important influence on Mamoulian, and he was especially captivated by the idea of rendering them lifelike. Both *Becky Sharp* (1935) and *High, Wide and Handsome* contain a dissolve from a painted portrait to a live-action shot of a character who holds the same pose and wears the same clothes, as if the painting had sprung to life. And as chapter 5 will demonstrate, *Blood and Sand* was a feature-length effort to emulate painting.

For *Summer Holiday*, Mamoulian intended much of the film to resemble the work of the American Regionalist painters Grant Wood, Thomas Hart Benton, and John Steuart Curry. In two of the film's numbers, Mamoulian takes this aim further by overtly imitating paintings. The first instance occurs during Richard's high school graduation scene, which features a performance of the school anthem, "Dan-Dan-Dannville High." "This song," Mamoulian wrote in a memo, should "combine two sections of different moods: one, rousing and boisterous, typical of the traditional school songs; the other, sentimental and touching, expressive in a way of the tenderly nostalgic feeling one usually has in connection with the memories of one's own school."[153] When viewing the finished film, Mamoulian's reasons become clear. When the song shifts to the "nostalgic" mood, Mamoulian initially stays within the real-world space of the school by depicting the high school singers and their parents. Then, however, in a series of shots that Mamoulian handwrote into the margins of his screenplay,[154] Mamoulian shift to shots that re-create classic paintings of Americana as if the characters within them were somehow witnessing the ceremony. Mamoulian begins by cutting from a shot of the diegetic spectators (Figure 4.11) to a live-action replication of Grant Wood's *Daughters of the American Revolution* (1932) (Figure 4.12, 4.13). He then re-creates other paintings, including Wood's *Woman with Plants* (1929) and *American Gothic* (1930, see this book's cover). Finally, Mamoulian brings us back to "reality"—and the end of the musical number—by cutting back to a long shot of the high school chorus.

In recreating these paintings, Mamoulian was exploiting a property specific to cinema (rather than theater) that resonated with folk-musical interests. Mamoulian had, in his 1946 stage production of *St. Louis Woman*, begun an early café sequence with a still image designed to look like a painting before setting the action into motion, but the scene did not—indeed, could not—precisely imitate a single painting.[155] Only by exploiting the singular vantage point of the camera—as well as the careful control of color that film stock afforded—could Mamoulian so closely replicate these paintings. Moreover, though Regionalist paintings were set in the present day, their association with reassuring, lightly romanticized images of small-town American life enabled Mamoulian to harness them to what he saw as the rose-colored memories found in O'Neill's play. Folk musicals, as Altman has argued, project the audience into a mythicized past, even sometimes featuring "sets based on the conventions of American painting."[156] By directly referencing painterly influences, Mamoulian displayed this folk-musical technique at a moment when it was only just becoming popular.

Again, one finds apparent similarities to *Meet Me in St. Louis*. During pre-production on that film, Minnelli had aimed to evoke—though not directly imitate—the paintings of Thomas Eakins.[157] In addition, Minnelli structures his film around four seasons, and for each season, he begins with a sepia photograph of the Smith family's Victorian mansion before dissolving into a colorized version of the same shot set in motion. Though Mamoulian may have been inspired by this technique, his use of still art sprung to life in *Summer Holiday* is different. For Minnelli, the sepia photographs serve as scene-setting *introductions* to the colorized, live-action world he will then portray. For Mamoulian, such overt

170 DEFINING CINEMA

Figure 4.11 Inserting Regionalist paintings into a turn-of-the-century high school graduation number in *Summer Holiday*. Mamoulian cuts from characters within the story listening to the students perform a song . . .

Figure 4.12 . . . to a live-action replication of Grant Wood's famous painting, *Daughters of Revolution*, as if the women in the painting were witnessing the ceremony.

Figure 4.13 Grant Wood's *Daughters of Revolution* (1932).

references to American art are instead inserted into the musical numbers themselves, thereby offering the stylistic lift that Mamoulian sought.

A few scenes later, Mamoulian follows up the graduation sequence with a celebratory Independence Day picnic number whose overriding graphic element is painting. Within the number, Mamoulian daringly uses the *tableau vivant* to suggest the binding together of the community as they engage in different festivities. The number begins with an unremarkable shot: a man, in close-up, plays a trumpet. However, the image then cuts to a longer shot and tracks back to reveal that townspeople are freezing in place to recreate Archibald MacNeal Willard's famous 1875 painting, *The Spirit of '76*. The re-enactors subsequently bow to the applauding audience, indicating that this *tableau vivant* occurred *within* the film. Later, however, Mamoulian includes a *tableau vivant* with no diegetic justification. The first shot of the women's section of the party begins as another *tableau vivant*, this one seeming to evoke a Winslow Homer painting. A group of women—frozen in place—play croquet, with one woman's mallet raised to strike the ball (Figure 4.14). The figures then go into motion ("like an etching come to life," as Mamoulian would put it in a later interview[158]), but we see no audience and hear no applause—there is no indication that they were performing a tableau for anyone at the picnic.

Like the re-creations of paintings during the Dannville High number—which no character remarks upon—it is as if we, the audience, have traveled inside a painting during this Fourth of July number. Augmenting this sensation is the quality of the images themselves, which, Altman argues, evoke the sense of being perfect paintings rather than real life (the food at the picnic, for instance, remains uneaten).[159] Mamoulian even uses a series of whip pans that move us between various images of men drinking together during the "Independence Day" number as a

Figure 4.14 A *tableau vivant* with no story justification in *Summer Holiday*. The shot begins with women frozen in position before springing into motion.

way to suggest a painter's bold brush stroke.[160] Mamoulian thus links together the citizens of Dannville not just via community activities, but by cinematic choices that place the whole community within painterly images during certain musical numbers. Theirs is a shared, nostalgic, and utopic community, united by painterly recreations, *tableaux vivants*, and whip-pan "brush strokes."[161]

How well all these innovations work within the larger film is an open question. Mamoulian, writing well before the movie was released, laid out his integration goals for *Summer Holiday* in an article before writing, "Whether the results will be successful or not, I am profoundly convinced that in this method lies the future of the musical theatre in America. . . . If [*Summer Holiday*] fails, it will be an individual failure, and I will still believe in the principle which has guided its filmic structure."[162] Given the film's poor reception, Mamoulian's words proved more prescient than he may have liked. Though the film today has its admirers, few would place it alongside such canonical integrated Freed-unit musicals as *Meet Me in St. Louis*, *The Pirate* (1948), *On the Town* (1949), *An American in Paris* (1951), or *Singin' in the Rain* (1952). In addition to Rooney's performance—which was widely panned by contemporary critics[163]—the film arguably struggles to reconcile its darker moments (Sid's alcoholism, Richard's barroom adventure with a prostitute) with the warm, nostalgic Technicolor glow of small-town America.

Still, as I have argued, we should not ignore the audacity and magnitude of the film's innovations. In addition to the film's complex use of integration and its stylized incorporation of paintings, Mamoulian presented one number—"Weary Blues"/"Sweetest Kid I Ever Met"—through Richard's subjective and distorted viewpoint, a topic I address in the following chapter. MGM's *The Pirate*, *On the Town*, and *An American in Paris* contain celebrated examples of psychologically based numbers, but Mamoulian shot this scene a full year before any of these films entered production. One such number—Gene Kelly's famous fantasy ballet that concludes *An American in Paris*—was inspired by painters active in France including Raoul Dufy, Pierre-Auguste Renoir, Maurice Utrillo, Henri Rousseau, and Vincent van Gogh, and even features a direct recreation of Toulouse-Lautrec's *Chocolat Dansant* that starts as a *tableau vivant* before springing to life.[164] The sequence has been deservedly celebrated for its own merits, but *Summer Holiday* had already signaled the potential of merging musical number and painting. Whatever its faults, *Summer Holiday* reveals a director still innovating and pointing in promising new directions.

Coda: *Silk Stockings* and Dance Integration

Despite directing pioneering stage and screen productions in the 1940s, Mamoulian found himself unemployed for most of the 1950s. *Summer Holiday* had been a pricey Technicolor film, making its poor showing at the box office alarming to studio executives. On the stage, Mamoulian alienated himself by abandoning rehearsals on *Arms and the Girl* (1950)—a musical he felt indifferently toward—for eight weeks to direct *Lost in the Stars*, a move that proved quite costly to the Theatre Guild, which produced it.[165] Outside of *Arms and the Girl*, the only new 1950s production that Mamoulian would complete in either medium would be *Silk Stockings*, an adaptation of the eponymous recent Broadway play (with music by Cole Porter) that was, itself, an adaptation of Ernst Lubitsch's film *Ninotchka* (1939).

In the movie version of *Silk Stockings*, the male protagonist is Steve Canfield (Fred Astaire), a Paris-based movie producer who woos and wins over dedicated Russian communist Ninotchka (Cyd Charisse), only for the couple to be separated when duty calls Ninotchka back to Russia. Though the sheer opportunity to direct again no doubt appealed to Mamoulian, what apparently excited him most about *Silk Stockings* was the opportunity to focus on dance as an integrative element. *Silk Stockings* starred two top-tier dancers in Astaire and Charisse, and Mamoulian was eager to use dance as a primary way of telling the story and expressing character thoughts and feelings.[166]

Mamoulian, in interviews, always voiced satisfaction with the film's integration of the dance numbers. In particular, Mamoulian was fond of a pre-production anecdote where he played a starring—and heroic—role. After watching Astaire and Hermes Pan's choreography for "All of You," a romantic number between Astaire and Charisse, Mamoulian told Astaire that the dance was insufficiently integrated. The story then follows the familiar Mamoulian formula (see the Introduction): though Astaire initially objected, even the legendary dancer eventually recognized Mamoulian's superior judgment.[167]

Based on this anecdote, one might imagine that *Silk Stockings* was yet another Mamoulian-dominated musical that demonstrated the triumph of total integration. Archival evidence, however, paints a different picture. If one compares Mamoulian's numerous and lengthy pre-production memos for *Silk Stockings* to the finished product, we see a director still intent upon innovating yet possessing little of the clout he had enjoyed in his earlier years. Mamoulian's memos are filled with intriguing dance-integration ideas that never saw the light of day. For Ninotchka's "Without Love" number, for instance—sung after she gets drunk on champagne—Mamoulian, perhaps inspired by "Binge Dance" from *It's Always Fair Weather* (1955), wanted a "tipsy ballet" in which Ninotchka "performs a series of lovely ballet steps, doing it all with grace and beauty. But being somewhat tipsy, she now and then loses control of herself, starts falling down or begins to fade, etc. etc. Every time this happens, Steve comes to her rescue and carries her over the hurdle; then steps aside again until the next emergency."[168] In the finished film, Ninotchka sings while merely sitting at Steve's feet. When Ninotchka returns to Russia, Mamoulian wanted to insert a number prior to "Red Blues" that would have brought back the split-screen device from his earliest films. Called "the scene of nostalgia," Ninotchka was to have begun thinking about Steve, which would motivate a wipe that stopped in the middle of the frame to reveal Steve trying, unsuccessfully, to get a visa to Russia. Steve was then to sing a reprise of "Paris Loves Lovers," and on opposite sides of the split screen, each character was to dance in perfect unison with the other, each imagining the other's presence.[169] Nothing like it appears in the film. For the "Red Blues" number itself, Mamoulian wanted Steve to be seated in a French café and watching a singer, only to have the number shift into Steve's fantasy as the singer turns into Ninotchka.[170] Then, in an idea that feels suspiciously derivative of Oscar Levant's fantasy piano concert in *An American in Paris*, Mamoulian wanted to have the real Ninotchka listening to a record and imagining the performers. "Gradually [they] all become Canfields; every instrument is played by Canfield and Canfield is dancing to a band composed of himself, as it were. . . . Porter may feel like writing something new for this."[171] Porter did not, apparently, feel like it, and the visuals that accompany the song in the film take place entirely outside Ninotchka's fantasy space.

The result is a film whose dancing is far less integrated than Mamoulian would later acknowledge. Mamoulian seems to have had some success integrating the dancing found in the first number, "Too Bad," a song where Steve uses women and food to convince the Russian commissars to stay in Paris. Some of Steve's actions—including setting the dance in motion and spontaneously tapping items on the table—resemble Mamoulian's description in a pre-production memo and reflect Steve's role as a devious instigator.[172] Mamoulian also appears to have succeeded at making Ninotchka's "Silk Stockings" dance "gradually become more and more rhythmic, and then blossom into a full dance."[173] Yet "Fated to Be Mated," which Mamoulian thought should be a pantomimed marriage proposal, is an exuberant—even goofy—dance that arguably captures the thrill of romance but doesn't express Ninotchka's feelings of torn loyalty. "Red Blues," a song about depressing life in the Soviet Union, features one of the liveliest dances of the film. The choreography clearly intends to evoke memories of gay Paris, but it hardly fits the despondent mood of the larger scene. And the concluding number—"Ritz Rock and Roll"—is an Astaire specialty number whose choreography has little bearing on the story.[174]

In spite of these setbacks, one number—"All of You"—*did* provide Mamoulian with one final realization of his goals. The number advances the plot: it marks the point at which Ninotchka begins falling in love with Steve. Equally important, Astaire and Pan's choreography precisely reflects this dynamic. Ever the pursuer, Steve sings the first chorus of "All of You" while partly circling the couch upon which Ninotchka sits motionless and emotionally unmoved. Steve then turns to dance. At first, Steve engages in spontaneous dance movements, a reflection of his efforts to get Ninotchka to be less calculating and more freewheeling. Finally, he pulls Ninotchka off the couch, and her graceful leg flair as she stands suggests her potential to be swayed. From then on, the dance is choreographed around Steve's eagerness and Ninotchka's interest yet reluctance. Steve spins Ninotchka, who begins wandering off before Steve grabs her and pulls her close. Steve dances while holding the passive Ninotchka, arms slack at her sides. Steve spins Ninotchka again and claps for her to stop, which she unwittingly does, a signal that he is winning her over. Ninotchka then becomes a full participant in the dance, matching Steve's steps and movements, often while touching. Still, the dance never loses sight of the situation: when the couple is not touching, Steve—the pursuer—generally faces Ninotchka who, as the reluctant one, keeps her back to him. Integrated dance was far from new in 1957—Astaire had been doing it as far back as his 1930s "challenge dances" with Ginger Rogers—but for one last time, Mamoulian managed to elicit a sequence that met his ideals for narrative integration and the stylized, emotional lift that musical numbers could provide.[175]

That Mamoulian should end his film career with a more modest production after playing such a foundational role in musicals is ironic, yet reflective of his diminished status. *Silk Stockings* was a critical and commercial success, however, and likely as a result, Mamoulian was hired as director of the film adaptation of *Porgy and Bess* (1959). Yet Mamoulian was ultimately fired from the project and replaced by Otto Preminger (see the Introduction). He never completed another movie, musical or otherwise.

The 1950s is often called the "Golden Age" of the American film musical, yet during this decade, Mamoulian increasingly became an outsider to the very form he'd been so instrumental in developing. When one examines Mamoulian's entire career, however, it becomes clear that his contributions to the musical genre were enormous. Mamoulian's earliest musical (*Applause*) displayed future show-musical syntax and announced, at a key moment, ways in which cinema style could more forcefully shape a viewer's experience with musical numbers. *Love Me Tonight* pointed to ways in which a musical might be conceptualized as a supreme work of stylized fantasy, and charted an early course for aesthetic integration. Mamoulian's subsequent musicals—deeply informed by his stage experiences—advanced new potentials for the folk musical in its formative stage (*High, Wide and Handsome*) and just prior to its heyday in the 1950s (*Summer Holiday*). It is thus no surprise that numbers from heralded 1950s musicals routinely owe something to Mamoulian's work. In *It's Always Fair Weather* alone, for instance, the "Blue Danube" mental trio recalls the mental duet from *Love Me Tonight*, while the rhythmic "Situation-Wise" number evokes the equally rhythmic "The Son of a Gun Is Nothing but a Tailor" *Love Me Tonight* number. Only through a careful examination of his stage and screen work—and the ideas and aspirations they harbored about stylization, rhythm, Americana, community, and integration—can we fully recognize Mamoulian's vital place in the development of one of the most beloved genres in American film history.

5
Mamoulian and Color

Becky Sharp, Blood and Sand, Summer Holiday, Silk Stockings

We are really painters, painting a story on the screen.[1]

As long as I can remember, I have been consciously moved by color almost as much as by music.[2]

—Rouben Mamoulian

Color occupies a unique place within Mamoulian's filmmaking career. For film sound, film rhythm, and the musical genre, Mamoulian first observed existing efforts by filmmakers before charting distinct stylistic pathways in his own films. For three-strip Technicolor, however, Mamoulian was literally *the* first filmmaker to complete a feature-length movie (*Becky Sharp* [1935]) in this form. Once Mamoulian got a taste of color filmmaking, the topic would obsess him for the remainder of his career. From 1935 through the 1950s, Mamoulian wrote more articles on color than on any other subject, and he took extensive steps to understand it, including investigating scientific research and diving into a thorough study of the medium of painting.

Directing *Becky Sharp* is significant in and of itself, but Mamoulian's later color films would continue to innovate. Following *Becky Sharp*, Mamoulian directed three more Technicolor movies: *Blood and Sand* (1941), which won the Oscar for Best Color Cinematography; *Summer Holiday* (1948); and *Silk Stockings* (1957). Although the last takes a more conventional approach, the others featured rigorously planned color schemes that enabled color to assume an unusually large and intricate storytelling role. Both films also contained highly unorthodox experiments, including conceptualizing color filmmaking as a series of moving paintings in *Blood and Sand* and *Summer Holiday* and the use of subjective color in *Summer Holiday*. Whether helming the industry's first three-strip Technicolor feature or returning to color filmmaking in later work, Mamoulian's approaches remained groundbreaking, influential, and widely praised.

Color is so commonplace in films today that it is often implicitly thought of as an automatic and unexpressive feature. When Mamoulian directed *Becky Sharp*,

Blood and Sand, and *Summer Holiday*, however, color was by far a minority practice, a status that encouraged filmmakers to think about showcasing it and making it integral to the viewer experience. Even within this context, Mamoulian's level of attention to color was exceptional. Regardless of production circumstances or preparation time, Mamoulian used color with a rigor and saliency that provoked basic questions. What should a full color film look like? What were the optimal methods for color control? In what ways—and through what methodological frameworks—might color be made to suit narrative, thematic, or emotional elements of a film? What, ultimately, were the advantages of lavishly colored film images, and did such attention to aestheticism come with any drawbacks?

This chapter moves chronologically through Mamoulian's four Technicolor films, examining his conceptions of—and experiments with—color. Though Mamoulian was called upon suddenly to direct *Becky Sharp*, he still managed to establish and carry out a set of carefully conceptualized ideas about color that fit his larger theories of stylization and signaled key possibilities. If *Becky Sharp* served as a preliminary experiment, *Blood and Sand* and *Summer Holiday* stood as more fully realized statements about color's potential.

Becky Sharp and Color Theory

When Mamoulian directed *Becky Sharp* in 1935, color itself was nothing new. Almost from cinema's inception, filmmakers made use of some form of color. In the earliest years, frame-by-frame hand coloring—followed shortly by mechanized stencil coloring, tinting, and toning—came into use.[3] By the early 1920s, some sort of color process—most commonly tinting and toning—could be found in somewhere between 50 and 80 percent of films.[4] The 1920s also saw the development of various two-strip Technicolor systems, and when sound arrived in the late 1920s, many prominent films featured a reel of two-strip Technicolor footage within an otherwise black and white film.

Technicolor filmmaking fell out of favor in the early 1930s, however, and by 1932, nearly every film was shot exclusively in black and white.[5] In this same year, the Technicolor company completed a new, *three*-strip process that finally allowed filmmakers to use a full array of color options. Three-strip Technicolor would eventually become widely used, but initially, the major studios were hesitant to invest in this costly technology. The earliest three-strip films thus came not from the major studios but from Walt Disney, who signed a two-year contract to produce his "Silly Symphony" series of short, animated films in Technicolor, with RKO merely distributing rather than footing the production bill.[6] Seeking to "blaze new trails in the entertainment industry," as historian Richard Jewell has put it, millionaire Jock Whitney and his cousin Cornelius

Vanderbilt Whitney—at the encouragement of former RKO head Merian C. Cooper—formed Pioneer Pictures in 1933 with the expressed purpose of making three-color films.[7] After producing an experimental live-action short titled *La Cucaracha* in 1934, Pioneer Pictures produced the feature-length *Becky Sharp* the following year.[8]

In hindsight, it seems logical that Pioneer Pictures would tap a prominent innovator like Mamoulian for three-strip Technicolor's feature-length debut, but this was not Pioneer Pictures' original plan for *Becky Sharp*. Producer Kenneth Macgowan initially signed Lowell Sherman as director, but shortly into production, Sherman contracted pneumonia and died suddenly on December 28. Only after Sherman's death was Mamoulian—who appears to have had no prior relationship with the project—approached to direct. This circumstance is important, because it meant that Mamoulian joined a project whose development had occurred without his input, and whose raison d'être was a stylistic element that Mamoulian—a consummate planner—had little time to consider. Mamoulian signed a contract on January 2, 1935, to direct *Becky Sharp*, and while he would later claim to have had "four or five weeks" to plan the film,[9] diary entries indicate that he began shooting on January 7, a mere five days after inking the contract. Shooting ceased on January 17 when Miriam Hopkins—who played the title character—was also stricken with pneumonia, and production did not resume until January 28, which would have given Mamoulian a bit more time to plan.[10] Still, Mamoulian was thrust into a situation where he had little opportunity to acquire knowledge about Technicolor filmmaking or prepare for the shoot.[11]

Mamoulian would thus come to see *Becky Sharp* more as a catalyst for his subsequent interest in color than as a full exploration of color film's potential. In spite of these limitations, however, Mamoulian was able to discard all of Sherman's footage and have portions of the screenplay rewritten to his liking. Mamoulian's experience with *Becky Sharp* also allowed him to develop the contours of a lasting theory of color, because after the film was completed, he wrote several articles explaining his ideas about color and their application to *Becky Sharp*.

Mamoulian's 1935 writings on color constitute an opening volley from a pioneering director newly excited by color's expressive possibilities. These writings help illuminate the underlying theories behind the color methods found in *Becky Sharp* and Mamoulian's subsequent Technicolor work. They also demonstrate how firmly Mamoulian grounded his color theory in his broader conceptions of artistry that we have explored in previous chapters. For starters, Mamoulian's writing makes it clear that he was intrigued by color because—like the concept of rhythm—he viewed it as an especially impactful device. Since every object in the real world has form and color, Mamoulian wrote in 1935, the careful use of color could double the image's affective power.[12] Like his approach to such cinematic tools as rhythm and narrative-number integration, Mamoulian advocated an approach in which strict realism was jettisoned in favor of stylized moves that would enable a filmmaker to enhance the dramatic import of a scene. And in a manner that resonated with Mamoulian's prior cinematic interests in artwork and rendering objects expressive, Mamoulian asserted that a director of Technicolor films was now operating in the realm of motion *paintings*, not just motion pictures.[13]

A bit more unusual from the perspective of Mamoulian's theories of artistry was his firm belief that Technicolor design should adhere to preexisting color associations. White, Mamoulian repeatedly stated, was suggestive of purity, black of sorrow, red of passion, green of hope, and yellow of madness. Such rigidity is not commonly found elsewhere in his writing, but Mamoulian did—in accordance with his broader beliefs about art and storytelling—feel that directors should harness these associations to the emotional beats of the narrative. Filmmakers, Mamoulian argued, should "take advantage of the mental and emotional implications of color and use them upon the screen to increase the power and effectiveness of a scene, situation, or character."[14]

Though many of these principles derived from Mamoulian's general artistic notions, his ideas were also likely influenced by two other prominent figures involved with *Becky Sharp*: color designer Robert Edmond Jones and the film's Technicolor consultant, Natalie Kalmus. Mamoulian would later claim full credit for *Becky Sharp*'s color plan, asserting that Jones acquiesced to his demands and that Mamoulian removed Kalmus from the set early in production.[15] Both figures, however, had been considering color for a longer period than Mamoulian, and both advanced positions in their writing that matched Mamoulian's in certain respects. Jones, like Mamoulian, argued that color should be stylized and tied closely to the drama and to viewer emotion. Kalmus, like Mamoulian, stressed that color needed to remain in service to the mood or tone of the story. While Kalmus was more flexible on the topic of color coding than Jones or Mamoulian, all three argued that colors carried innate associations that needed to be harnessed and exploited.[16] Presumably, all three were also mutually affected by the commercial imperative to promote three-strip Technicolor, but it also seems likely that some of Mamoulian's early color ideas were inspired by those of his collaborators.

How did Mamoulian's emerging color theories play out in *Becky Sharp*? We are fortunate to have a detailed assessment of the film in Scott Higgins's *Harnessing the Technicolor Rainbow: Color Design in the 1930s*. Higgins, in a chapter-long analysis, argues that *Becky Sharp* belongs primarily to the "demonstration mode" of early three-strip Technicolor filmmaking, which involved overtly testing and drawing attention to color. By Higgins's count, sixteen of *Becky Sharp*'s twenty-one scenes foreground color, often by withholding it before revealing it. Another assertive color strategy, Higgins demonstrates, involved placing characters in front of a neutral (often gray) set, so that the colors of their costumes stand out. Higgins's analysis focuses especially on the famed Richmond Ball sequence, which features—among other color devices—the repeated pulsing of warm colors, deliberately jarring cuts to contrasting colors, and strong hues highlighted in the shadows of low-key lit shots. The result, in Higgins's estimation, is a film that regularly demonstrates color's potential as a meaningful element, yet whose conspicuous use of color prevents it from being an entirely viable model for later story-driven Hollywood filmmaking.[17]

Thanks to Higgins's clear articulation of many of *Becky Sharp*'s color methods, we can narrow our focus to how Mamoulian's specific ideas about artistry contributed to *Becky Sharp*'s color design, which aspects of the film Mamoulian was most responsible for, and how *Becky Sharp* laid out color ideas that Mamoulian would pursue more rigorously in subsequent films. Among the best resources for considering Mamoulian's contributions is the *Becky Sharp* shooting script that Sherman used prior to his death, which is included in Mamoulian's papers at the Library of Congress. Looking at differences between Sherman's screenplay (written by Francis Edwards Faragoh) and Mamoulian's finished film is not a foolproof determination of Mamoulian's influence, since others might have been responsible for some of the changes. Still, by comparing the two—especially in conjunction with Mamoulian's statements about the film—we can pinpoint three vital elements of *Becky Sharp*'s color design that very likely stemmed from Mamoulian: the effort to ease into color in the early going; the attempted buildup to warmer colors throughout the film's first half; and specific methods of color choreography during the film's color centerpiece, the Richmond Ball.

Oozing into Color

By Mamoulian's account, when he first reviewed the footage that Sherman had shot prior to his death, one of his chief complaints was the ample presence of red in the film's opening scene. Mamoulian, as we shall see, had a particular fascination with red throughout his career because he found it uniquely arresting and forceful. "It is no accident," Mamoulian was fond of saying, "that the traffic lights all over the world are red for 'stop.'"[18] Mamoulian would ultimately attempt to build *Becky Sharp*'s color design around the suppression and striking revelation of red, but even before this film, archival evidence indicates that he had explored red's expressive potential on the stage. Early in his Theatre Guild production of *Congai* (1928), the half-Vietnamese, half-French woman Thi-Linh is forced to watch her Vietnamese lover, Kim Khouan, be married to another woman because Kim's family will not permit Kim to marry a "half caste." In the typed playscript, Thi-Linh stands with her mother, dismayed, as the Temple door opens and Kim's large marital party marches past. Thi-Linh, according to the play script, was to have collapsed in grief in the center of a "steel blue light" before the scene blacked out. In the margin of his play script, Mamoulian denoted that a red spot, instead, be turned up to accentuate this moment of intense emotion, and the stage diagram and final light plot for the scene affirm that this change was used.[19]

In the following act, Mamoulian again modified the color plan to enable red to play a pronounced emotional role. Kim pays a surprise visit to Thi-Linh—who now lives with a soldier named Paul—and announces that he is free to be with Thi-Linh but must first leave for battle. During this conversation, Paul discovers the duo and slaps Kim, who then leaves for war. As Thi-Linh and Paul denounce each other, the glow of the setting sun projects the silhouettes of the departing soldiers against the left wall of the set. Originally, the red of the setting sun was to have appeared only when the soldiers began marching, but Mamoulian—in a marginal note—changed the emergence of red to come earlier: at the precise moment when Paul discovers the duo and advances toward them threateningly.[20]

Given Mamoulian's prior interest in red as a climactic color, it is not surprising that when Mamoulian viewed Sherman's rushes for *Becky Sharp*'s opening, he was displeased. According to the screenplay, Sherman's version of *Becky Sharp* began in the living room of Miss Crawley's house, and the film opens not just with the color red, but with a wide array of sparkling colors. The first shot, the screenplay informs us, is a "LARGE CLOSE UP of a bejeweled hand. Diamond, ruby, emerald dart quick flashes of color as the hand presses against a yawning mouth. Swiftly the CAMERA PULLS BACK, widening the angle to a—CLOSE UP of Miss Crawley on the chaise longue."[21] Assuming this description matches the footage that Mamoulian viewed, Sherman's version of *Becky Sharp* opened by bombarding viewers with a maximum of saturated colors—including a red ruby—before pulling back to allow viewers to take in the larger scene.

For Mamoulian, such an opening use of color was not just dramatically illogical but also an inappropriate way to introduce three-strip color to audiences accustomed to black and white. As he explained in a 1935 article, "How was I to introduce color to audiences unused to it and bound to be a little shocked by it? Should I thrust it on them with a bang? That, definitely, I was sure was wrong. So [the film] began with the palest of tints, only building up later, as the drama of the story itself climbed to the stronger brighter colors."[22] As he put it in a later interview, "I wanted to start with black, white, grey; then ooze into colour."[23]

The finished version bears this out. As Higgins notes, Mamoulian's opening scene begins in an essentially black and white mode before providing splashes of color against a neutral palette. We begin not with sparkling jewels, but with a shot of a closed gray curtain, which enables the beginning to simulate a black and white film. Color then emerges slowly. First, a woman's head pokes through the curtain, the warm hue of her skin—and pale-yellow hair bow and collar—providing the film's first, albeit mild, splash of color. Then, in a move that may have been influenced by hit film *Rio Rita*'s (1929) introduction of two-strip color midway through the movie, the curtain is thrust back, revealing nine of Amelia's classmates wearing an array of diversely colored outfits.[24]

Mamoulian further oozes into color in this shot by tracking backward as the girls rush in a line toward Amelia (Frances Dee), enabling their colored outfits to catch the eye by de-grouping and moving rapidly. Mamoulian's version thus, like Sherman's, begins with a track back, but Mamoulian conceptualizes this movement for an opposite effect: to withhold and *then* reveal color. Even these colors, moreover, are not as vivid as what was proposed in the screenplay Sherman shot from. Amelia's satin hat, bow, and shawl, for instance, are brownish red, a more subdued color than ruby red.[25] As Mamoulian's scene progresses, colors are vivid thanks largely to the decision to shoot the characters against a largely gray background. This technique, too, may have had a stage influence: Mamoulian's own direction of an opera scene from *The Barber of Seville* back in 1924. In a contemporaneous newspaper article penned about his *The Barber of Seville* production, Mamoulian described his use of silvery-gray curtains that he arranged in a semicircle around the stage, thereby allowing the set's blue, orange, red, and yellow colors to enjoy greater prominence.[26] In *Becky Sharp*, gray curtains similarly provide a neutral background against which more vibrant colors can be displayed.

Red and the Richmond Ball

By easing into color, Mamoulian was likely striking a compromise between Pioneer Pictures' desire to show off color—the driving logic behind Sherman's opening—and Mamoulian's belief that the strongest colors should appear only as the drama escalates. This belief that color saliency should match the emotional tone of the story—which would persist in Mamoulian's later Technicolor work—drove Mamoulian toward a second color goal for *Becky Sharp*. For the film's first half, Mamoulian wished to build only gradually to warm colors—particularly reds—so that they would become most prominent at the dramatic Richmond Ball sequence that occurs halfway through the film, in which a fancy gathering is interrupted by Napoleon's cannon fire and attack on Waterloo.[27]

Here, Mamoulian was only partially successful. As Mamoulian would later acknowledge, Becky spends so much time in the early going flirting with soldiers—who wear the mandatory red British uniform—that a fully consistent movement toward pure red was not possible.[28] Mamoulian would later chalk this up as a problem with the story he was given, but as Higgins points out, Mamoulian's frequent reliance upon dramatic colors against neutral backgrounds also lessens the buildup toward explosive color at the ball. Still, even in the finished film one can see evidence of Mamoulian's efforts to move slowly toward red in the film's first half. Early on, Mamoulian tends to avoid pure reds aside from the soldiers' uniforms, and because Becky flirts with more soldiers as the narrative progresses, their red uniforms appear in greater numbers as the film approaches the Richmond Ball sequence. A gambling-room scene that immediately precedes the ball features eight soldiers—all dressed in scarlet red—grouped around a table and discussing Becky's charms.

Red and the Richmond Ball

If Mamoulian was not entirely successful building to red, he does appear to have been the driving creative force behind the colors found in the Richmond Ball sequence. Even here, however, we must differentiate between the *ideas* about color design for this scene and the *methods* by which those aims are achieved. In articles and interviews, Mamoulian took great pride in the scene's increasing warm colors once Napoleon's booming cannons break up the ball. What Mamoulian omitted in these accounts is that the screenplay that predated his arrival already contained this general idea. In the Sherman script, the film was to have cut repeatedly to the night sky as the sounds of cannon fire increased, beginning with a "single ball of fire" and then cutting back later to "racing, flaming spheres" in the night sky.[29] In subsequent cut backs, the sky was to have taken on a "faint pink glow, which slowly becomes brighter" until eventually, "the sky is now alight with racing meteors of fire."[30] Eventually, according to the screenplay, "the sky is ablaze," and by the time Amelia and her husband, Osborne (G. P. Huntley), share their final embrace (a scene not present in the finished film), "the sky is red."[31] The fleeing guests, too, were to have built toward red. As the guests run from the ball, the screenplay called for "a fighting, panicky group at one of the exits. A mass of reds in the half-light . . . then more and more . . . a flaming crushing mob . . . the reds grow in intensity until the entire screen seems to glow."[32]

Still, while the idea of building toward red occurred before Mamoulian was associated with the project, the precise methods for attaining this effect appear to have been Mamoulian's doing, and they reveal a director who was homing in on the color elements most under his control. Among the most important changes from the Sherman script is the almost total avoidance of the red sky once Napoleon's cannons begin firing. Instead, Mamoulian centers his color control on elements that would drive his later Technicolor films: costume, character movement, and editing. In the Sherman script, the initial cannon fire was to have been depicted via shots showing Amelia watching first a "single ball of fire" rising in the sky, followed by "another single flare" and the "low, ominous rumble" of cannons.³³ Mamoulian, instead, cuts back to the mansion's interior *before* the cannons are fired and initially provides four different reaction shots to the blasts from inside the mansion: first a group of four soldiers, then the Duke of Wellington, then soldiers gambling at tables, and then ladies at the party sitting and resting.

Since the first and third shots feature numerous soldiers clad in scarlet, Mamoulian retains the strong red that images of the night sky would have provided while centering this moment more squarely on the guests' *reactions* to war, rather than the battle itself. This may have been done because red-sky effects would have been challenging thanks to the newness of the Technicolor process, but it also enables red to become more closely aligned with the emotions of the guests. Moreover, because Mamoulian avoids focusing on the night sky, he gains more creative control over his orchestration of warm colors. The night sky—according to the logic of the scene—can move in only direction: from small to large amounts of red. Party guests, in contrast, can be cut to at will, and Mamoulian can set in motion any party guest he chooses. Thus, by orchestrating the scene around shots of the guests, Mamoulian can use any number of color progressions as the scene develops.

Mamoulian would later claim that when his guests flee the mansion, he grouped them by color from cold to warm, thereby allowing a unified movement toward red.³⁴ As Higgins notes, however, Mamoulian's color arrangement is actually more complex, as it moves through *multiple* waves of color progressions. Thanks to color grouping, character movement, and careful editing, the fleeing guests create a color palette that moves from monochrome, to cool, to warm, before returning to monochrome once more and repeating the pattern. Often this effect is achieved by having color-grouped characters race across the screen in a single shot, while at other times editing produces this cool-to-warm pattern. Once the non-military guests have departed, the soldiers who run through the mansion are handled similarly: we see several shots of soldiers in blue capes dashing through the mansion hall, followed by multiple shots of soldiers in red capes. Later, a high-angle exterior shot of more running soldiers uses a colored red light to further bathe the screen in red before Mamoulian once more reverts to a shot of a blue-caped procession of soldiers as they ride away on horseback, followed by red-caped soldiers.³⁵ The effect is thus, to quote Higgins, a series of "pulses,"³⁶ and while it differs somewhat from Mamoulian's later descriptions, this result is possible only through Mamoulian's decision to use the partygoers—and their costumes and movements—as his central means of color control.

By conceptualizing color in this manner, Mamoulian was pulling from three ideas central to his broader artistic approach: choosing expressivity over realism, matching device to emotional tone, and prioritizing rhythmic experiences.

Mamoulian, in articles and interviews, enjoyed pointing out that because the British officers hear the news of Napoleon's impending arrival first, they would—according to strict realism—logically leave first. Doing so, however, would mean beginning with a salient dose of the most arresting color in the palette. For Mamoulian, moving from cool to warm was dramatically and emotionally "correct," which mattered more than realism. Moreover, by configuring the guests' exit in terms of color *pulses*, the Richmond Ball sequence shows Mamoulian advancing rhythmic ways of conceptualizing color design. Not coincidentally, as the guests and soldiers flee in color-pulsating groups, their elongated shadows appear against the back wall of the mansion. As we saw in chapter 3, shadow play was a favored Mamoulian device to inject tempo and energy into a scene, largely because it enabled a filmmaker to amplify movement. Here, shadow play allows both the figures themselves and their shadows to move rapidly across the frame, their different rates of movement enhancing the sense of dynamism all the more. Color scoring *and* shadow play combine to give the Richmond Ball sequence considerable thrust and energy.

Becky Sharp stands as an important early experiment with matching three-strip Technicolor to dramatic mood, the broad-scale building toward particular colors and palettes, and the use of costume, character movement, and editing to exert exacting control over an audience's moment-by-moment color experience. Still, *Becky Sharp*'s immediate influence on subsequent filmmaking proved to be a mixed bag. The film was not a commercial success, and as Higgins has demonstrated, the next Technicolor film—*The Trail of the Lonesome Pine* (1936)—would avoid many of *Becky Sharp*'s strident color techniques in favor of a more restrained approach. The film fared better at the box office than *Becky Sharp*.[37] Later Technicolor features—beginning with *The Adventures of Robin Hood* (1938)—would incorporate a good dose of *Becky Sharp*'s assertive style. Even these more assertive films, however, typically aimed for a balance between restrained and salient color and avoided the color-blocks-against-a-neutral-background technique in *Becky Sharp* in favor of greater intricacy between costume and background.

Still, assertive color schemes remained an important tool over the ensuing decades, and *Becky Sharp* set the initial standard for this mode of filmmaking. One should also remember that as much as Mamoulian wished to use assertive color sparingly, he was also tasked with selling a new product: three-strip Technicolor itself. The goals surrounding *Becky Sharp* were thus somewhat different from later Technicolor fare. Ultimately, the film served as a vital demonstration of what three-strip Technicolor could accomplish, and it presented a box of tools for all others to draw upon.

For Mamoulian, *Becky Sharp* served mainly as a creative spark, an opportunity to wet his beak in color theory and its cinematic applications. By 1940, when Mamoulian was offered his second shot at Technicolor filmmaking, he had studied color extensively and was ready to put his developed color theories into action.

Preparing for *Blood and Sand*

Blood and Sand stands as Mamoulian's definitive take on three-strip Technicolor. Archival evidence indicates that, unlike *Becky Sharp*, Mamoulian was in near-complete control of the film's color design and that it was his central concern through all phases of production. *Blood and Sand* adopts a number of color techniques found in *Becky Sharp*—including a gradual build toward warmth via carefully placed fabrics, choreographed character and camera movement, and editing—but realizes these aims with a newfound rigor, consistency, and subtlety. The film also takes a concept only touched upon in Mamoulian's writings prior to *Blood and Sand*—color cinema's connections to painting—and pushes this idea to unprecedented extremes in 1941. Mamoulian thus uses *Blood and Sand* to ask fundamental questions about—and offer innovative answers to—broad-scale color design, Technicolor's relationship to painting, and cinematic methods for enhancing color's impact. The result is a film that reveals with unusual clarity both the advantages and potential drawbacks of aesthetic beauty in Technicolor films.

In a sense, *Blood and Sand* was six years in the making for Mamoulian. Excited by color yet frustrated by his lack of knowledge, Mamoulian—upon completing *Becky Sharp*—began studying color from "every angle" he could think of, including history, psychology, artistry in painting, and science. This included consulting scientific research on the "muscular activity" that resulted when viewers experienced different colors, research that appeared to confirm to Mamoulian what he had already suspected: that warmer colors—especially red—provoked the most intense reactions.[38] The most important aspect of Mamoulian's color study, however, was a European vacation Mamoulian undertook to study paintings in various galleries across the continent. Mamoulian spent August through November 1937 in Paris, London, and Italy, and diary entries feature extensive notes on the paintings he viewed each day.[39]

Thus, when Twentieth Century–Fox studio head Darryl Zanuck offered Mamoulian the chance to direct another Technicolor film, Mamoulian was eager to show off what a well-informed, deeply theorized, and painstakingly detailed approach to color filmmaking might look like. The first step, for Mamoulian, was to develop a "color plan" or "color script" for *Blood and Sand*. This involved, in Mamoulian's words, working out color in as much "detail as the dialogue, including every piece of furniture, every prop, every costume."[40] In truth, this notion of detailed color planning was not as original as Mamoulian would later imply. Kalmus had urged filmmakers to plan for color in this manner back in 1935, and the Technicolor advisory service would have provided a color script as a matter of course.[41] Using his own color script did, however, mean that Mamoulian (unlike in *Becky Sharp*) could get ahead of this service, making it easier for him to serve as the guiding figure in color planning from pre-production through post-production.[42]

In a few respects, the resulting product was fairly traditional. *Blood and Sand*—by Mamoulian's own account—contains some basic color coding, with the steady-minded and faithful Carmen (Linda Darnell) dressed largely in blues and whites, and the tempestuous Doña Sol (Rita Hayworth) more commonly providing flashes—and sometimes full onslaughts—of warm colors like orange and red.[43] Juan (Tyrone Power) is often dressed in browns—which to Mamoulian suggested that he remained a "beggar at heart"—and his disapproving mother (Alla Nazimova) frequently wears "funereal black," as if mourning for her dead husband *and* preparing for the inevitability of her son's death.[44]

In many other respects, however, *Blood and Sand*'s color design was more original. This was particularly the case for the film's overt evocations of the work of famous painters and the rigorous use of various color palettes to track the precise rise-and-fall arc of its central character.

Cinema as Painting

Based on the 1908 novel by Vicente Blasco Ibáñez, *Blood and Sand* tells a cautionary tale of Juan Gallardo, who rises from poverty to become the best bullfighter in Spain, only to decline due to the sexual temptations of a dangerous woman named Doña Sol and the mercurial bullfighting crowd's love of cruelty and barbarism. To mark the various stages of Juan's rise-and-fall story, Mamoulian took the unprecedented approach of dividing his film into sections whose color palette would be inspired by one or more renowned painters, most of them Spanish. For most of the film's early scenes, which show the impoverished Juan in his hometown of Sevilla yearning to become a bullfighter, Mamoulian drew upon the "bronze-browns and blacks" of Bartolomé Murillo, particularly his realist portrayals of the poor. For two short scenes on the Sevilla streets when Juan is still a boy, Mamoulian took inspiration from Joaquín Sorolla and his striking evocations of sunlight. Later, for a scene in Juan's dressing room with his admirers after he becomes Spain's top bullfighter, Mamoulian turned to Italian painters Titian and Paolo Veronese for their "luxury of color and strong suggestions of bustling movement."[45] For a scene just prior to the film's first bullfight, when Juan and his cuadrilla pray in a chapel near the ring, Mamoulian modeled his color palette after the gray-greens and blues of El Greco. For the ensuing bullfight itself, which marks Juan at the peak of his professional life, Mamoulian drew upon Francisco Goya, "with his dramatic and vivid colorings." Finally, when Juan is invited to socialite Doña Sol's home for dinner, Mamoulian sought images that evoked Diego Velázquez, "the great master of light and shadow."[46]

Mamoulian's desire to explicitly emulate painters throughout much of *Blood and Sand* stemmed in part from long-held beliefs about an artist's proper relationship to authenticity, stylization, and beauty. Mamoulian, as we saw in prior chapters, sought to vividly evoke particular environments and ways of life as far back as his smash-hit stage production of *Porgy* (1927), and he continued such efforts in his 1930s and 1940s folk musicals. To Mamoulian, painting was a logical influence for such endeavors because he felt that painters were uniquely equipped to graphically capture the color, mood, and landscape of a country.[47] At least as important, however, was the idea that painting enabled a director to enhance authenticity through *stylization*. The painters Mamoulian most admired did not aim for strict realism, but rather used particular color palettes to elevate certain qualities of the subjects they were painting. Mamoulian, as a film artist, shared this aim. Mamoulian also saw, in painting, an opportunity to increase the elegance of his cinematic images, which fit with his larger belief that an artist should try to bring more beauty into the world.

Most broadly, by emulating paintings in *Blood and Sand*, Mamoulian aimed to make a statement about nothing less than the definition of color cinema itself. As we saw, back in 1935 Mamoulian had suggested in his writings that color films were best conceptualized as "motion paintings," not "motion pictures." It was not until *Blood and Sand*, however, that Mamoulian offered a full-blown demonstration of what this might mean. For *Blood and Sand*, Mamoulian quite literally wished to create the images as if he were a painter who happened to be working with moving images instead of paint and canvas. Color filmmakers, Mamoulian wrote in a 1941 *American Cinematographer* article, "are essentially making a series of paintings. What does it matter if we are not painting our picture with watercolor or oil paint, but with colored light projected on a white screen?"[48]

Mamoulian's on-set behavior during *Blood and Sand* demonstrates just how seriously he took the comparison between film and painting. Mamoulian placed by his director's chair what he referred to as the "Mamoulian palette," which consisted of two types of items. The first was "a chest of shawls, drapes, and other pieces in every color of the spectrum" that would enable Mamoulian to "paint" by adorning the set and actors with what he saw as the most suitable colors.[49] The second—and more audacious—item was a spray gun and a wide array of paints. If one studies "a painting in minute detail," Mamoulian wrote when explaining his method, "you will see that the painter . . . used almost every imaginable color" to create his or her "highlight-and-shadow effects."⁵⁰ To replicate this technique, Mamoulian turned his spray gun upon sets, props, and actors' clothing. This constituted a marked change from the one-note backgrounds he had worked with in *Becky Sharp*. Spray-paint jobs included—by Mamoulian's account—the chapel scenes and the interior of Doña Sol's mansion. For the latter, Mamoulian claimed that he sprayed the entire set black and white, which included spraying the green leaves black on Doña Sol's dining-room table (Color Plate 1).⁵¹ And like a lone painter toiling away at one's work, Mamoulian would later assert that he personally and single-handed sprayed the set, often to the dismay of his collaborators. "I had to do it myself," he once told an interviewer, "because you didn't want somebody else blamed for messing up the scene. If I mess it up, it's my fault. I don't like to put the blame on other people."⁵²

As unlikely as such an account may sound, archival evidence offers ample support. Partway through shooting, an irate Zanuck—after seeing the rushes for the Doña Sol banquet scene—sent the following memo to Mamoulian:

> If I ever saw a table as scantily arranged in my own home I would throw the butler through the window. [Production manager William] Koenig tells me that you had the finest set of silver in California on the set and that you personally stripped the table. If you would stop making last minute changes such as painting chairs and spraying ferns which all take time and energy and would rely upon our competent department heads the same as the other directors do on this lot, including John Forde [sic], Henry King and others, I am sure that the final result will not offend you or anyone.... I cannot sit by and see obvious mistakes made as well as any directorial over-shooting or operating outside of his directorial activities. [Set decorator] Tommy Little is the highest paid man in the motion picture business, in his job, and incidentally recognized as the most competent. This is true of everyone on this lot from [art director] Dick Day to [composer] Al Newman, and I cannot understand why you have to spray ferns and paint chairs when none of the other directors have any cause for complaints.⁵³

Clearly, Mamoulian was exhibiting highly unusual behavior. Prior Technicolor directors did not walk around spraying sets. Moreover, while earlier Technicolor films like *The Adventures of Tom Sawyer* (1938) and *The Wizard of Oz* (1939) may have taken inspiration from the cover art of the original novels, the filmmakers did not—to my knowledge—conceptualize huge portions of their films as extensions of paintings. Mamoulian's focus on colored shawls and drapes likely stemmed from his experience with using costume as a means of color control during *Becky Sharp*'s Richmond Ball sequence, but in 1941, there were no clear precursors for his emulation of paintings or his on-set sprayings. Only a decade later would Mamoulian's approach prove prescient, with such celebrated color films as *An American in Paris* (1951), *Moulin Rouge* (1952), and *Lust for Life* (1956) also attempting to imitate painting.

Painting and Color Control

Beyond stylization and the prospect of emotional authenticity, what, in 1941, did Mamoulian gain by grounding his color palette in paintings? First and foremost, Mamoulian found a more sustained framework for color control than in *Becky Sharp*. One of Mamoulian's principal goals for *Blood and Sand* was to connect the color red—along with warm colors in general—to the two dangers that befall Juan: bullfighting and the lure of the beautiful-yet-fickle Doña Sol (in bullfighting critic Curro's words, "death in the afternoon" and "death in the evening"). In a goal that echoed his prior attempts in *Becky Sharp*, Mamoulian wanted to withhold *all* strong flashes of pure red during Juan's boyhood scenes, with red emerging only when the audience first meets the adult Juan, who is now a professional bullfighter. Then, Mamoulian wished to build gradually to increasingly warm colors until reaching a climax in the bullring midway through the film, when Juan solidifies his title as Spain's greatest bullfighter and sees Doña Sol for the first time. With no warmer place to go after this bullfight, Mamoulian sought to pare back his color palette to black and white during Doña Sol's dinner party before again building toward warmer colors as Juan becomes increasingly entangled with Doña Sol, a relationship that proves ruinous for Juan's marriage and career.[54]

Because Mamoulian thought of painterly styles as featuring specific—and different—color palettes, he could select painters whose color schemes matched his broader plans for the ebb and flow of warm colors across the film. Adhering to Murillo's palette for Juan's boyhood scenes, for instance, results in an almost total exclusion of saturated warm colors. Indeed, the film's resonance with Murillo's realist paintings is particularly strong, perhaps in part because for certain shots, Mamoulian had a specific Murillo painting in mind. Mamoulian's marginal annotations in his screenplay reveal that he composed *Blood and Sand*'s opening shot (Color Plate 2), and a later shot in which Juan (still a boy) speaks to his mother as she scrubs the floor, with Murillo's 1640s painting *The Young Beggar* in mind (Color Plate 3). For *Blood and Sand*'s first shot, Mamoulian penciled into his screenplay margin, "Brown & Black (Murillo's beggar)," a likely reference to the black shadows and subdued brown-gray palette one finds in the painting. In the screenplay margin for the floor-scrubbing shot, Mamoulian again noted the Murillo painting and also wrote "Sun and shadow" in the margin, an apparent reference to the sunlight in Murillo's painting that streams into the frame from a nearby window and casts a dynamic rectangle of light. Such lighting, which appears in both of the *Young Beggar*–inspired shots, helps justify the subdued colors in the painting's shadows. Many other shots from *Blood and Sand*'s early sections—such as Juan's nighttime run down a Sevilla street toward the café or his nighttime effort to woo the young Carmen at her window—do not appear to have been inspired by a specific Murillo painting, but they feature hard pools of bronze-gold light within a darkened frame that echoes *The Young Beggar* and other Murillo realist paintings. The Murillo section additionally features considerable matte work, meaning that viewers are often literally looking at paintings.

Even on rare occasions in these opening scenes when the color red appears—the handle of Juan's bullfighting sword in the opening shot, for instance—they serve as mere teases, constituting brief flashes in small portions of the frame. As a result, the film's first major blast of saturated red is extraordinarily vivid. We first meet the adult Juan—now officially a bullfighter—riding on a train with his cuadrilla. In the scene's first three shots—which show the faces of the cuadrilla but not of Juan, whose face is obstructed by a newspaper he holds—color remains subdued, and pure red is nowhere to be found. Manolo (Anthony Quinn) wears a faded pink undershirt, El Nacional (John Carradine) wears black as usual, and his other two companions wear faded red and dirty white shirts (Color Plate 4). The fourth shot thus comes as a visual jolt: Mamoulian cuts closer to Juan, who pulls down his newspaper to reveal his face and the flaming-red *muleta* that is draped behind his head (Color Plates 5 and 6). This sudden reveal of color has parallels to the neutral gray curtain that opens to display color at the start of *Becky Sharp*, but because Mamoulian has spent *Blood and Sand*'s first twenty minutes largely in Murillo's restrained color mode, this revelation of assertive color is more striking. The scene also serves as our first introduction to Power, currently the biggest star in Hollywood, which additionally motivates this boldness.

Mamoulian's use of the palettes of El Greco and Velázquez similarly enables his subsequent waves of color warmth to be more impactful. Though Mamoulian would claim that he progressively built to warm colors up through the film's first bullfight—which occurs at the one-hour mark—his strategy is better described as a series of alternations between vivid and subdued color schemes, a sort of broad-scale use of the pulsating colors found in the Richmond Ball sequence. An early dressing-room scene, for instance, in which Juan meets with the press and prepares for a bullfight that afternoon, features the Titian and Veronese-influenced royal blues and scarlet reds that underscore his reputation as Spain's top bullfighter. Rather than moving immediately to the bullfight, however, Mamoulian provides a gray-green palette for the El Greco–inspired chapel scene. Mamoulian, by his own account, sprayed the set—which includes a back wall and giant statue of the crucified Christ—"green like the patina of old bronze," along with subdued grays and blues.[55] To further restrict color to grays and greens,

Mamoulian took the extraordinary step of shining a pale-green light on the faces of Juan's cuadrilla to eliminate the pinks of their skin tone (Color Plate 7).[56] Colored light was not unheard of: it had appeared prominently in *La Cucaracha* and *Becky Sharp*, and the innovative *Gone with the Wind* (1939) had featured some form of it in nearly a third of its segments. By the late 1930s, however, colored light tended to be reserved for transitions, and when filmmakers used it in a major scene, they nearly always provided diegetic sources (such as flame or moonlight) to justify its presence.[57] Illuminating actors with a diegetically unmotivated green light was thus extremely unusual, and it demonstrates Mamoulian's strong commitment to a painterly aesthetic featuring a narrow range of colors. Later in the film, Mamoulian's use of Velázquez's black and white palette indeed drains virtually all color from the image, which sets the stage for flashes of color warmth that Doña Sol's attire provides in film's second half.

Cinema and Its Limitations

Though emulating painting suited Mamoulian's mentality as a stylist, it had the potential to clash with his avowed preference for medium specificity. Mamoulian, himself, was aware of this problem. None of us, Mamoulian assured readers in his *American Cinematographer* article about *Blood and Sand*, "made a slavish attempt to imitate" painting. "That would have been fatal. We were working in a different medium."[58] Indeed, both archival and filmic evidence makes it clear that in spite of painting's influence, Mamoulian made such cinematic devices as character movement, camera framing, camera movement, and editing central to the audience's color experience. In Juan's first dressing-room scene, for instance, Mamoulian introduces the Titian- and Veronese-influenced scene not via a stationary extreme long shot of the room—the painterly approach—but by first tracking past various onlookers, who wear black, gray, brown, white, and muted blue clothing. Only then does Mamoulian pull back to reveal Juan's royal-blue section of the room, thereby enabling camera movement to more strikingly display color. Later in the scene, Mamoulian—in accordance with detailed annotations in his screenplay—introduces warmth by arranging to have Juan's assistant, Garabato (J. Carrol Naish), and bullfighting critic Curro (Laird Cregar) manipulate warm-colored fabrics in conjunction with closer-range shots.[59] Later in the film, the reintroduction of red colors on Doña Sol's patio is achieved by editing between a series of camera positions and movements that only gradually emphasize the scarlet-red colors of Doña Sol's nails, carnations, and chess pieces. Among the devices here is a fountain on the patio that—through various camera positionings—is made to first repress, and later reveal, the color red.[60]

Mamoulian, in short, remained mindful of cinema and how it could enhance his ideas for color. Even so, archival materials help illuminate several problems particular to cinema that Mamoulian could not entirely overcome. First, to convincingly portray the two bullfights featured in the film, Mamoulian and his crew shot footage of actual bullfights in Mexico City, which they edited together with studio work featuring the film's principal actors.[61] As we saw, Mamoulian had wanted the bullfights to feature climaxes of red. His efforts are evident in studio work, where he could easily organize close-range shots of the grandstands or characters in costumes so that red colors are prominent. Mamoulian had limited color control in his location work, however, which contains far more washed-out reds. Second, the sheer expense of commercial filmmaking also interfered with Mamoulian's aims. A painter can toil slowly at potentially negligible financial cost, but Mamoulian was working in an expensive medium with a multitude of paid collaborators, and his labor-intensive approach to color contributed to the film running substantially over budget, much to Zanuck's dismay.[62] Third, Mamoulian disliked the look of the finished print, finding certain images in the Murillo section too blue or too red.[63] This complaint, internal memos reveal, was a symptom of the fact that color printing decisions and variabilities in projection-bulb brightness could alter the look Mamoulian had attained through his on-set "painting."[64]

Perhaps the most broad-reaching drawback to Mamoulian's approach, however, stemmed not from painting-cinema incompatibilities, but from Mamoulian's own decision to shape his images in the mold of the aesthetes he had studied so carefully on his trip to Europe. The result is an exceptionally beautiful film, but the approach clashes with a different Mamoulian principle: that stylization should communicate the artist's viewpoint on the material. Mamoulian felt somewhat ambivalent toward bullfighting, but in general, he disliked the sport. Though he saw beauty in the movements of the matador and bull, he was horrified by the suffering of animals. At heart, Mamoulian would later acknowledge in an interview, "I hate the damned thing; I don't think beauty compensates for the other side."[65]

Such an attitude is difficult to detect with any consistency in *Blood and Sand*. A smattering of anti-bullfighting messages can be found—including by El Nacional, Juan's mother, and Garabato—but they are infrequent. Mamoulian was also handicapped by censorship restrictions, which prevented him from directly showing spikes (known as banderillas) or sword thrusts into the bull, or showing close-range shots of the bull suffering.[66] But probably the central diluting force was Mamoulian's own decision to emulate classically beautiful paintings, which threatens to obliterate any stark critique of bullfighting. *American Cinematographer*, at any rate, seemed to think so. "We're no judge of bull-fighting form," wrote the *American Cinematographer* film reviewer upon

Blood and Sand's release, "but this picture, we believe, is the first to capture in any way the grace, daring and pageantry which have made bull-fighting the favorite sport of Spain and the Spanish-American nations, and do it in a way even a Nordic can appreciate."[67] *Blood and Sand* stands as a work of incomparable Technicolor innovation and beauty, even if it remains diluted as a piece of critique.

Summer Holiday: One Night in a Barroom

Mamoulian's final movie to feature innovative Technicolor was *Summer Holiday*. As discussed in chapter 4, Mamoulian's central interest in *Summer Holiday* was how to faithfully translate the source material—Eugene O'Neill's non-musical play *Ah, Wilderness* (1933)—from stage to screen, and from drama to musical. Still, *Summer Holiday* stands as an important Technicolor work, both for its continued emphasis on painterly color palettes and—especially—for its unusual foray into color-driven subjectivity.

Like *Blood and Sand*, part of *Summer Holiday*'s color palette sprung from specific painters that Mamoulian saw as thematically relevant. In chapter 4, we saw that the film's high school graduation musical number features direct imitations of paintings by Grant Wood. Wood, along with fellow Regionalist painters Thomas Hart Benton and John Steuart Curry, also served as the main inspirations for the film's *general* color design. In a pre-production memo about color, Mamoulian informed his collaborators that *Summer Holiday* "should be treated as a long, continuous series of paintings,"[68] and he later stated that for *Summer Holiday*, the Regionalists taught him the "marvelous things you can do just by using different shades of the same colour."[69] The choice of the Regionalists as inspiration might seem odd since they were known for focusing on contemporary Midwest farmland while *Ah, Wilderness!* had been set in turn-of-the-century Connecticut. Mamoulian, however, likely felt that the Regionalists' reassuring images of rural and small-town life fit with what he saw as the play's tender portrayal of small-town America.[70] Mamoulian also probably saw parallels between O'Neill's play and qualities that were widely associated with the Regionalists by the 1940s: an escape from modern urban space, a distinct sense of place and rootedness, tinges of romanticism fueled by charmingly picturesque and decorative imagery, and the sense of a locale where base instincts could be repressed and evil could be avoided.[71]

The most significant color experiment in the film, however, is the use of color in a pivotal barroom scene to convey naïve teenager Richard's (Mickey Rooney) subjective experiences as he drifts from infatuation to drunkenness to disillusionment with a twenty-something prostitute named Belle (Marilyn

Maxwell). Salient efforts to tie color to character subjectivity are difficult to find prior to 1946, when Mamoulian shot *Summer Holiday*. In one sense, of course, *any* subjective shot in a Technicolor film—even a mere point-of-view shot—provides subjective color, since the audience is visually positioned within a character's headspace. What is unusual about the barroom scene in *Summer Holiday* is the *overt* shift in color to accompany a character's subjective experience, and—especially—the elaborate blow-by-blow *sequencing* of increasingly subjective color. Prior to *Summer Holiday*, *The Wizard of Oz* (1939) had justified its sudden move from black and white to color via Dorothy's dream, and within Technicolor-only films, a few had tied color changes to character subjectivity. The Paramount musical *Lady in the Dark* (1944) features numbers that are explicitly configured as the dreams, hallucinations, and memories of central character Liza (Ginger Rogers). Those numbers contain far more vibrant colors than during story sections—including an early number centered on the color blue—thus marking them as particular to Liza's subjectivity. Fantasy numbers in *Up in Arms* (1944), *Ziegfeld Follies* (1945) ("The Limehouse Blues"), and *Yolanda and the Thief* (1945) feature a shift toward more saturated colors for musical numbers that exist within a character's headspace. A brief non-musical (and non-American) example of striking subjective color appears in the British film *Black Narcissus* (1947), which was shot at the same time as *Summer Holiday* but released a year earlier. Late in *Black Narcissus*, Michael Powell and Emeric Pressburger place a red filter over the camera during a point-of-view shot to denote the anger and insanity of lapsed nun Ruth (Kathleen Byron). Such examples are rare, however, and I am unaware of any prior color film that offers the intricate progression of subjective color changes found in *Summer Holiday*. Thus, for the final time in his career, Mamoulian blazed an innovative color pathway for future filmmakers to explore.

Characteristic of Mamoulian, the barroom scene increasingly builds toward the color red. The impact of this color design is heightened by the fact that the film's prior hour of running time—set exclusively within the wholesome Dannville community—almost entirely avoids that color. *Summer Holiday*'s opening centers on the happy Miller home, which features primarily greens, grays, beiges, browns, and whites. The next segment, a romantic scene between Richard and girl-next-door Muriel (Gloria DeHaven), takes place mostly in the Dannville town park, which enables Mamoulian to emphasize lush greens. The following scene—Richard's high-school graduation—favors a black and white palette. Only during the film's dynamic Fourth of July town celebration does the color red seep more prominently into the frame, but even these scenes do not approach the saliency of the warm colors in the barroom scene. Mamoulian thus sets up the barroom scene's explosion of warmth by erecting a binary approach to color, in which pure red is reserved almost exclusively for nefarious entertainment that lays beyond the boundaries of small-town acceptability.

Though a viewer could easily miss it, the first hint that Mamoulian will tie eye-popping colors at the bar to Richard's mindset occurs a few scenes earlier, when Richard and his older brother's friend, Wint (Hal Hackett), walk from Richard's home toward a dance hall. This walk had been Mamoulian's personal addition: "I should like to pick up the two boys before they enter the café," Mamoulian explained in a pre-production memo:

> We show them walking away from the placidly respectful streets of their home town into a shadier and more mysterious neighborhood. We see the street where the little café is located. First, as it actually is: a tawdry little lane with occasional dull passers-by and a few blinking lights over the marquee of the café, desperately trying to be glamorous. Then we see the same street as Richard sees it: Now it becomes a mysterious thoroughway, with romantic shadowy figures lurking in the corners, under the lamp posts, some even wearing black capes, turned up collars, lowered brims of hats—an atmosphere fraught with smoldering adventure and danger; and then the bright lights of the café as mischievous and alluring as the proverbial Moulin Rouge in Paris.[72]

Though the finished film does not match Mamoulian's description in every respect, it does adhere to this general trajectory. In the first two shots, Richard and Wint walk down a dimly lit trash-strewn alley featuring low-saturation colors. At the end of the second shot, Richard comments that the street is "very romantic," and Mamoulian cuts to the duo walking out of an archway, the camera panning right to follow them as they approach the dance hall. This shot features more color saturation than before: a woman in a deep-red dress stands to the left of the dance hall, while another woman to the right—clearly coded as a prostitute—wears saturated purple. The yellow lights from the music hall also cast a warm glow on the street. This color-based shift toward subjectivity is subtle, but it sets the stage for the barroom scene that follows.

The barroom scene itself was taken directly from O'Neill's play, which features Richard attempting to impress a prostitute named Belle in a dingy back room. Richard, unfamiliar with alcohol, becomes increasingly intoxicated and enamored with Belle in equal measure before attempting—unsuccessfully—to reform her. The scene is vital to both play and film because it marks a turning point and resolution to Richard's central conflict. Richard, up to this moment, has been presented as a precocious teen: he is talented as a student, but directs his intellectualism toward a rejection of his town and assertions that he knows far more about the world than he does. The barroom scene is the point where Richard recognizes his naivete: he ultimately finds himself unsure of what to do and becomes disgusted by the encounter, which causes him to return home and embrace the values of his small-town family and community.

Archival records demonstrate that Mamoulian was obsessed with this scene from an early date. What excited him most was the opportunity to use color-based subjectivity to enable audiences to experience—rather than merely understand—Richard's feelings. O'Neill, Mamoulian wrote in a pre-production memo, could use only the words Richard speaks to help the audience to grasp Richard's point of view and shifting mindset throughout the scene. As a result, the theater audience remained "detached" and "objective," was always "conscious of the sordidness which permeates the entire episode," and thus could not fully feel this formative experience from Richard's perspective. As we saw in chapters 2 and 3, Mamoulian had been fascinated by cinema's potential to illuminate character subjectivity for as long as he had been making films. For *Summer Holiday*, Mamoulian saw color as the central means through which this could be accomplished.[73]

From the earliest pre-production memos, Mamoulian planned for this lengthy sequence to be an extended musical number that would move frequently between singing and speech (eventually becoming the two-part "Weary Blues"/"The Sweetest Kid I Ever Met" song in the film). Doing so was consistent with the musical adaptation goals Mamoulian had in mind for the project (see chapter 4), but it also helped justify an enhanced level of color stylization. The most prominent way that Mamoulian expresses Richard's shifting subjective impressions through color is the use of three different costumes for Belle. Belle's faded pink dress, which she wears at the start of the scene, is an objective rendering of her attire. As Richard becomes drunker and increasingly romanticizes Belle, her subsequent two dresses become redder. Scholars have noted a variety of other changes, including her increased hat size, her increasingly plunging neckline, and her bigger and brighter jewelry.[74] More subtly, Mamoulian employs colored-lighting shifts to mimic Richard's changing mental state. Such colored lighting not only enhances the scene's reds, but it allows an *array* of saturated colors to pop forward to match Richard's romanticized viewpoint. Colored lighting, found sporadically in Mamoulian's prior Technicolor films, thus emerges in tandem with his more familiar costume-based control of color in this scene.

The most detailed rundown of Mamoulian's color changes can be found in a production memo that Mamoulian wrote. The descriptions in this memo largely match the finished film, and they are especially valuable for pinpointing the role that colored lights play in the sequence's trajectory. Mamoulian begins by lighting the scene in standard fashion. An opening establishing shot pans and dollies past double doors that separate the rest of the bar from the back room before resting upon Belle and Richard, who sit at a table in the center of the room (Color Plate 8). To convey the barroom's ordinariness, Mamoulian lit this shot—and the ones leading up to Belle's first transformation—using traditional white lights (with the exception of a yellow light at the bar behind the swinging door). The background of the opening shot contains a curtained area, but at this point, the area is almost completely dark. Belle wears the faded pink dress, with ample red rouge on her cheeks and crowned eyebrows, which was designed to signal her identity as a cheap prostitute.[75]

The scene's first shift to Richard's subjectivity features an array of color changes that range from salient to inconspicuous. The most obvious change comes when Belle appears in a new, darker pink dress, with significantly less rouge on her cheeks. Augmenting this change is a less-evident shift to colored lighting. As stated earlier, colored lighting was fairly rare in Hollywood at this point, and when it occurred, it habitually contained a physical diegetic source. The use of colored lighting for *subjective* purposes was thus highly unusual. We first enter Richard's subjectivity when Belle leaves the table and walks to the sideboard. In medium long shot, we see Belle from Richard's optical point of view looking directly at the camera and singing "Weary Blues" (Color Plate 9). Mamoulian cuts to Richard drinking and pantomiming its effects before cutting again to Richard's point-of-view shot.

During this second point-of-view shot, a deviation from Mamoulian's production-memo instructions—likely made in post-production—occurs that makes the colored lighting change less obvious. Originally, to facilitate Richard's subjective transformation of Belle into a more glamorous woman, four lights were to have been brought up simultaneously on a "slow count from one to four": a "green light on the wall and palm," a "yellow-green [light] through lattice of sideboard," a "red [light] on Belle," and "white pin spot on Belle's face (to counteract the red)." Following this lighting change, the image was to have gone out of focus, to be matched by a shot of Belle in her new, dark-pink outfit.[76] In the finished version, the shot begins when the point-of-view shot is *already* out of focus, meaning that these lighting changes have already occurred (Color Plate 10). It is unclear who made this excision, but it results in greater subtlety. A viewer might sense, at the beginning of this blurred shot, that the area around Belle is greener than before—and that Belle herself appears particularly red—but the blurred image makes these colored-lighting changes harder to pinpoint. Belle's new dress is Mamoulian's most salient announcement of his shift to subjective color; it is through colored lighting that we are encouraged to drift less conspicuously into Richard's subjectivity.

Thanks to Mamoulian's understated approach to colored lighting shifts, only an eagle-eyed spectator is likely to note that the scene now contains numerous colored lights illuminating the entire set. Though Mamoulian eliminates the red light as Belle comes into focus, the saturated green light on the wall—and the yellow-green on the sideboard—that Mamoulian brought up during Belle's transformation remain (Color Plate 11). As the scene progresses and we see the rest of the bar, *all* the walls are lit by the same saturated green color. Moreover, when Belle sits back down at the table with Richard, the curtains in the background now feature yellow backlighting, and the recess behind the curtains, though still quite dark, contains faint purple-blues (Color Plate 12).[77]

When Belle undergoes her second transformation and appears in a scarlet-red dress, Mamoulian finds additional ways to use red lighting to emphasize this color. Richard drinks his heavily laced "gin fizz," and once again—in Richard's point-of-view shot—the image of Belle begins to blur. As with the prior transformation, Mamoulian—on the set—had preceded this blurring by slowly turning up a red light on Belle (and a white pinpoint on Belle's face). This time, however, the transformation point-of-view shot begins with Belle partly in focus as the red light illuminates her, allowing her to appear even redder during this second transformation. Mamoulian again kills the red light when the camera regains its focus to reveal Belle in her scarlet dress (Color Plate 13), but a few moments later, when Richard kisses Belle in close-up, Mamoulian escalates red further by shining a red light on the duo (Color Plate 14).[78] In Mamoulian's subjective color language, Richard's kiss features him at the height of his passion.[79]

If Mamoulian's colored lighting enables the viewer to experience Richard's romanticization of the scene, so too does it subsequently articulate his disillusionment. Belle provides Richard with what she calls a "real kiss." This proves to be too forward for Richard, who suggests that Belle leads the "wrong kind of life" and ought to "be a wife." As he sings these lines, Mamoulian shines a faint green light on Belle's face and a faint purple light on her hat and dress. The effect is unobtrusive, but it can be detected by the faint highlights of green on Belle's hair, necklace, arm, and chest, and the purple light that catches Belle's cigarette smoke (Color Plate 15). Thanks especially to the green light—which does not produce a conventionally attractive skin tone—Belle appears less glamorous and seductive. Then, when Belle responds to Richard's efforts to reform her by saying, "Shut up, you bore me," the deep green lights that illuminate the walls and the yellow backlights on the curtains recede, thereby reverting the room to its original "harsh and sordid aspect" (Color Plate 16).[80] All that remains is for Richard to take one more look at Belle, who now wears her original faded pink dress and heavy rouge.

As I have suggested, overtly subjective color was quite rare at the time, and the detailed sequencing of it was possibly unprecedented. Later, higher-profile Technicolor efforts from Powell and Pressburger—*The Red Shoes* (1948), *The Tales of Hoffmann* (1951)—would famously contain color-driven subjectivity, but one should remember that Mamoulian did it earlier. *The Red Shoes* features a splashy Technicolor ballet midway through the film that evokes dancer Victoria's (Moira Shearer) subjectivity as she performs. The feature-length Technicolor film ballet *The Tales of Hoffmann* contains several overt moments of subjectivity, including a sequence from the vignette "The Tale of Antonia" in which Antonia (Ann Ayars) is tricked by the evil Dr. Miracle (Robert Helpmann) into seeing her mother. The illusion is presented subjectively, and like *Summer Holiday*, the scene features a reality-fantasy-reality progression that moves toward increasingly warm, saturated colors during the illusion, only to reassert the shabbiness of the real locale at the end. The technique yields impressive effects, yet Mamoulian's efforts in a similar vein preceded it by several years.

The barroom scene itself is stunning, but the extent to which it is effective within the larger film can be debated. Richard's subjective impressions in this scene are certainly vital to the story, but his color-saturated viewpoint is *so* vibrant and visually captivating that it threatens to steal attention from the "correct" viewpoint on the scene—that the nurturing experiences of home and community are ultimately more appealing than bars and sex workers. As with *Blood and Sand*, the potential pitfall stems from Mamoulian's desire to beautify the image via Technicolor, even when portraying problematic or "immoral" entertainment. Whether it is bullfighting in *Blood and Sand* or slumming it at the local bar in *Summer Holiday*, when eye-popping colors are reserved for the "wrong" attraction, those colors can render glamorous and desirable that which the film seeks to condemn. Ironically, perhaps Mamoulian's gift *and* his Achilles' heel was his ability to mount extraordinarily beautiful, innovative, and stimulating Technicolor scenes.

Silk Stockings and Color Restraint

Mamoulian's final Technicolor film, *Silk Stockings*, does not feature the innovative color strategies found in his prior three films. The movie was a significant commercial success, however, and it demonstrates that if need be, even a stylist like Mamoulian could embrace a restrained mode of color filmmaking.

Subdued color, archival records indicate, was Mamoulian's stated preference for *Silk Stockings*. The film was shot in the widescreen CinemaScope process, which had debuted four years earlier with *The Robe* (1953). Mamoulian found CinemaScope productions overstuffed with colors, and he sought, in the words of a pre-production memo, to "go to theother [sic] extreme of sparse, yet eloquent and expressive color treatment."[81] In the finished film, the restrained mode unsurprisingly includes scenes set in the Soviet Union, a crusher of pleasure and individuality according to the film's narrative. More surprisingly, this restrained mode also encompasses Paris, a contrasting space of romance and decadence. In a later interview, Mamoulian claimed that he wanted Paris's color palette to evoke silk stockings themselves—a capitalist commodity that the Russian Ninotchka

(Cyd Charisse) finds "alluring and exciting"—and thus wanted the setting's principal colors to be "nude, golden beige, warm honey, and flesh pink."[82] The finished film largely bears out this plan. The hotel lobby where the three Russian commissars stay is predominantly off-white, and while their royal suite includes lavender chairs and royal-blue curtains, its dominant colors remain off white, beige, and brown. The flat owned by Paris-based movie producer Canfield (Fred Astaire), in accordance with a pre-production Mamoulian memo, is even more "subdued in color,"[83] consisting largely of tan, beige, and gray furnishings, and a brown wood floor. The two leads—Canfield and Ninotchka—also generally fit this restrained palette, often dressing in conservative grays or dark blues with mere flashes of color (such as Canfield's pink socks, or the muted greens and pinks that emerge on Ninotchka's clothing as she falls in love).

Only in the wardrobe of American movie star Peggy Dayton (Janice Paige) and during the film's final number can anything resembling Mamoulian's early experiments with assertive color be found. Peggy, on the movie's terms, is a brainless consumer liked by neither Steve nor Ninotchka, and her loud clothes—and loud character—expresses what Ninotchka abhors and fears about Western culture. For a press conference that reveals her ignorance of famous novels and novelists, Peggy wears a heavily saturated green dress that contrasts with her bright red hair. She dons a highly saturated cyan dress in her next scene and later wears two outfits—scarlet red and then bright pink—in an effort to woo composer Peter Boroff (Wim Sonneveld). Steve, and the Parisian world he inhabits, look restrained and tasteful by comparison, which helps persuade the viewer that the dedicated communist Ninotchka might find Steve—and Western culture—classy, romantic, and appealing.

Intriguingly, *Silk Stockings* concludes with an Astaire specialty number—Cole Porter's "Ritz Rock and Roll"—whose color design bears a strong resemblance to the opening scene from Mamoulian's very first Technicolor film. Ninotchka, lured back to Paris, sits down in a restaurant to watch a musical number featuring Canfield. The lights dim, and Mamoulian cuts to a closed gray curtain. The curtain then raises to reveal a stage whose dim lighting results in a virtually black and white image. The lights come on, revealing flashes of costume-based color (pink and green dresses; Astaire's red sash) against a gray background. Like *Becky Sharp*, then, a segment begins with a closed gray curtain that is pushed away to present splashes of assertive colors in an otherwise black and white shot. Astaire enjoyed tight creative control over his dances, and the archive remains unclear on Mamoulian's level of input for this scene. Yet if nothing else, *Silk Stockings*' concluding number testifies to the enduring influence of basic Technicolor approaches pioneered by Mamoulian, including a withhold-then-reveal pattern for color and the use of strong color blasts against a neutral background. Mamoulian's final scene of his career brings three-strip Technicolor color right back to where he began it.

Conclusion

For color filmmaking, Mamoulian remains best known for having directed the first three-strip Technicolor movie. Yet as I have argued, *Becky Sharp* was merely the starting point for a director who pursued a series of innovative color ideas in an even more rigorous and consistent manner in his later work. As with the topics discussed in prior chapters, Mamoulian's approach to color was an extension of carefully theorized and lucidly articulated ideas about artistry, cinema, and film's relationship to other media. This included stylizing color to convey authenticity and emotional truth, molding the cinematic image as if it were a painting, planning broad-scale color patterns and shifts, emphasizing aesthetic beauty, and grounding all efforts within such story-based concerns as dramatic tone, character trajectory, and character subjectivity. In their day, Mamoulian's color approaches were pathbreaking, especially his early color control methods, his emulations of painting, and his use of color subjectivity.

Mamoulian's engagement with color also helps clarify ways in which he incorporated lessons from other art forms while remaining mindful of the specific capabilities of cinema. Theater was always an important touchstone for Mamoulian because it helped him determine what he did *and* did not wish to do with cinema. As we saw in prior chapters, Mamoulian was never interested in merely reproducing theater on film, but he *was* willing to draw upon certain theatrical techniques to solve cinematic problems, such as film rhythm and narrative-number integration. For color filmmaking, Mamoulian used ideas from painting and theatrical lighting, yet he applied them in distinctly cinematic ways. Rather than simply emulate painting in *Blood and Sand*, Mamoulian used camera movement, character movement, and editing to enhance the painterly qualities he sought. Rather than merely adopt a theatrical lighting method for *Summer Holiday*'s barroom scene, Mamoulian harnessed colored lighting to a subjective experience that only cinema could provide. Far from a theatrical interloper who dazzled and then faded, Mamoulian's understanding of a variety of art forms enabled him to ask and answer fundamental questions about cinema's unique identity *and* its relationship to other forms.

6

Mamoulian and Filmmaking under Censorship

Applause, Dr. Jekyll and Mr. Hyde, The Song of Songs, Queen Christina

When they put a fence in front of you, you either retreat or you jump over it. Sometimes these obstacles help.[1]

When you want something, don't put it in the script.[2]

Art is made through its limitations.[3]

—Rouben Mamoulian

In many respects, Mamoulian forged early pathways for sound films that would prove to be long-lasting. Yet even as he was fashioning innovations in expressive sound, film rhythm, and the show, fairy-tale, and folk musical, Mamoulian was experimenting in another area that the film industry would instead curtail: sexually risqué filmmaking. Though Mamoulian is seldom discussed from this perspective, his harnessing of film stylization to sexuality was striking and highly unusual in the early sound era.

The industry, at the time, took notice. With the possible exception of Cecil B. DeMille, no filmmaker during this period appears to have experienced more censorship conflicts than Mamoulian. Mamoulian's adventures with censorship ran the gamut, from the period when the Production Code had not been written (*Applause* in 1929) to the Studio Relations Committee's (SRC) regulation of *City Streets* (1931), *Dr. Jekyll and Mr. Hyde* (1931), *Love Me Tonight* (1932), and *The Song of Songs* (1933), to newcomer Joseph Breen's near torpedoing of *Queen Christina* in early 1934, when a more stringent enforcement of the Production Code was imminent. Though Mamoulian's risqué filmmaking was short-lived and ultimately could not closely anticipate mainstream Hollywood practices in the late 1930s and 1940s when censorship was more rigorous, his censor-bending techniques show a filmmaker intent upon defining sound cinema as an adult-oriented medium that could overtly use the tools of cinema to render the sexual dimensions of its stories more palpable. The sexual potential of cinema remains a vital topic today, and Mamoulian's work allows us to see some of the earliest efforts to stylize sound film for this purpose. Mamoulian's experiments under censorship also help clarify the constraints that existed from 1929 to 1934 and shed new light on the censorship questions and methods of evasion explored by the industry during these years.

This chapter centers on four films—*Applause, Dr. Jekyll and Mr. Hyde, The Song of Songs*, and *Queen Christina*—whose sexual content pushed against censorship boundaries. The first three center on the familiar trope of men looking at the female form; the fourth, instead, adopts a more cerebral approach to sexuality grounded in female psychology. All four use stylization to convey distinct viewpoints on sex, with *Applause* decrying the crude objectification of women and the other three instead encouraging the audience to see sexuality as beautiful, healthy, and stimulating. Other contemporaneous directors were also exploring sex: Ernst Lubitsch thrived on indirection and omission to portray a world of sophisticated sex, while DeMille and Josef von Sternberg—in different ways—loaded up the mise-en-scène in sexually provocative ways. Mamoulian's contribution was to show how a salient sound-era style could address sex frankly, convey a particular stance toward it, and render it subjective and exciting—all while generally avoiding the display of censorable images. In his early films, Mamoulian illuminated powerful methods through which a sound filmmaker might present sexual content more arrestingly under censorship.

Censorship and Mamoulian

Censorship concerns predated Mamoulian's arrival to filmmaking by at least two decades. As far back as the late aughts, when state and local censor boards were formed to regulate what could and could not be shown in particular areas, US filmmakers had been forced to pay attention to content and approach. Thanks to a landmark 1915 Supreme Court ruling, film until the 1950s was legally defined as a business rather than an art form and thus was not constitutionally protected free speech.[4] Mindful of this ruling, and fearful that the federal government would intercede if public opinion turned against the industry, Hollywood had already taken steps toward self-censorship prior to the arrival of sound. These steps included the 1924 publication of "The Formula," which advised studios on which properties were appropriate for filmic adaptation, and a 1927 list known as the "Don't and Be Carefuls," which enumerated topics that external censorship boards and reform groups cut from Hollywood films.[5]

Given these factors, Hollywood might well have adopted a formalized mechanism for censorship anyway, but the arrival of synchronized sound in the late 1920s hastened this move. One of the industry's concerns—reflected in the

Production Code document and expressed frequently in publications of the time—was that sound inherently brought viewers closer to reality, which could cause "immoral" onscreen behavior to appear more vivid and appealing.[6] The film industry was also worried that by committing to 100 percent talking films, which all the major studios did in 1929, movies were moving closer to Broadway theater, an entertainment that could include swearing and topless women.[7] More pragmatically, the industry feared that cutting moments from scenes at the demand of external censors would create a far more disjointed film than was the case in the silent era, thus upping the need to steer filmmakers away from problem content *before* a movie was completed.[8]

With these concerns in mind, Hollywood's trade association—the Motion Picture Producers and Distributors Association (MPPDA)—began drafting an official Production Code document in late 1929, and the SRC served as the mechanism through which the Code was enforced beginning in March 1930.[9] As Lea Jacobs points out, by 1931, SRC head Jason Joy considered it "mandatory" for studios to submit their pre-production screenplays to the SRC, and the organization monitored each finished film as well.[10] The reign of the SRC—from 1930 to 1934—is often called the "Pre-Code" era, but this is a misnomer: there *was* a code during this period and it *was* enforced. However, many films from 1930 to 1934 were distinctly different from later studio fare because the SRC adopted a more lenient interpretation of the code than its successor (the Production Code Administration [PCA]), and also because the SRC failed to fully appreciate how certain approaches—particularly tacked-on endings and film style's ability to affect meaning—would impact viewers.[11] Still, although SRC's focus and level of enforcement would differ from the PCA's, both organizations shared the same goal: to help studios make commercially successful films that external censorship boards would pass without eliminations. The SRC and PCA's function as an *aid* to filmmakers can be difficult to remember given the clashes that could and did occur between these organizations and the studios, but the industry never envisioned the SRC and PCA as entirely inflexible enforcers of the Production Code. Both groups existed to work *with* filmmakers, and every screenplay and finished film submitted could be the subject of negotiation and compromise.[12]

Mamoulian, who entered filmmaking just as the industry was gearing up for mandatory self-censorship, harbored complex viewpoints on the subject. On the one hand, Mamoulian felt that great art—which for him included cinema—was by definition beautiful and uplifting. People, Mamoulian believed, were born debtors, living as they were in a world filled with the magnificence of art and nature, and artists owed it to society to contribute in a way that would make the world a better place.[13] Such aspirations resonated with the Production Code, which argued that films should elevate the moral standards of the people who view it.[14] Mamoulian also felt that censorship was valuable for ensuring that a filmmaker remained within the boundaries of good taste rather than succumbing to the temptation to make money via "vulgar or obscene material."[15] More abstractly, Mamoulian did not find censorship terribly bothersome because he viewed art as being defined by its limitations. Art, for Mamoulian, was never about completely free expression, but rather about paring down an object by imposing artistic control on the finished work. For Mamoulian, "the great artists have a built-in self-censorship, self-discipline, because art is subject to stringent control by the critical mind of the creator."[16] Though Mamoulian acknowledged that film censorship could be irritating at times,[17] he believed that to censor was, on a basic level, part of the process by which all art is created.

This philosophy made Mamoulian receptive to the possibility that censorship could even function as a boon to creativity and livelier filmmaking. Often, Mamoulian argued, when a censor said, "'You can't do this,' you found a better way."[18] As an example, Mamoulian liked to point to a late scene from his film *Summer Holiday* (1948) in which a father (Walter Huston) is forced to give a sex talk to his son. Though the father speaks fumblingly in the play upon which the film is based, he still says lines that could not be approved by the Code.[19] The filmmakers were thus forced to provide an even more halting speech in the film, so that the father cuts off his sentences before arriving at the forbidden words. To help convey the father's increased nervousness in the film, Huston nervously grabs an Abraham Lincoln clay bust his son had molded and unconsciously reduces it to a nondescript blob. The scene was a favorite of Mamoulian's, and it came about only because censorship had limited his creative options.[20] In such instances, censorship, for Mamoulian, had prevented an artist from doing what Mamoulian most abhorred: using the most obvious method to achieve a result.[21] As Mamoulian once put it after his film career had concluded, Code-era censorship "frequently brought about higher artistic inventiveness, a more subtle and eloquent way of achieving one's points—indirection in the arts is more effective than the proverbial straight line between two points."[22]

Even as Mamoulian praised the *general* ideals of censorship, however, his belief that cinema was a serious art form—and not, in the words of the Supreme Court, a "business, pure and simple"—regularly put him at odds with the Production Code and its enforcers. To Mamoulian, the introduction of the spoken word to cinema necessarily signaled the arrival of more mature subject matter onscreen.[23] Mamoulian also believed that art should never be merely frivolous entertainment, and that even as it uplifted, it should not hide from view the reality of the world one lived in. To Mamoulian, films that resided only in the trivial or the superficial were tantamount to feeding people nothing but lollypops or chocolate bars, a junk-food diet that "dulls our conscience and lulls it into stupor."[24] Mamoulian wanted to make beautiful, uplifting films, but he sought to achieve this aim via the exploration of subject matter that made censorship bodies uneasy.

When Mamoulian's standards of appropriate cinematic entertainment did clash with censorship groups, sex was the inevitable reason. Two anecdotes about sex that Mamoulian enjoyed telling can help us understand what he tried to achieve in his early sound work. The first, a lengthy joke, involves a Kansas City salesman who always dreamed of visiting Paris. Eventually, he saves up enough money to go there. Upon his arrival back in Kansas City, his friend (referred to here as "the little guy") asks him to talk about the trip:

"Well," he said, "I tell you the evening I spent there, I went to a café at night and I sat at a table with a brandy, inside the orchestra was playing a Strauss waltz, the moon was high in the sky, beautiful chestnut trees, people going by, the most exotic dresses, selling some things. Fantastic. Nothing like Kansas City. Just a dream." Then he said, "Over there sat at a table a beautiful woman with a veil over her face, with a drink, beautifully dressed, the moon was up there, the waltz was playing, I looked at her, she smiled at me. Only in Paris, nothing like it in Kansas City." So he said, "You know I got enough courage, I took my brandy, I joined her, I said, 'may I sit with you?' I sat there, the waltz was playing, she was smiling at me, we were drinking this brandy, there is just nothing like it in Kansas City. We finished and she said, 'Can I give you a ride to your hotel?' I said that would be wonderful. And this limousine drove up with a chauffeur, beautiful car, and she said, 'This is my car.' I get in and she said, 'Would you like to have a nightcap with me before you go to your hotel?' And I said I would love it. We got through with this limousine, the moon and everything. Nothing like this in Kansas City. We drive to this beautiful house, we go in there into the drawing room, Louis the XIV chairs and champagne and ice, and she says, 'Would you excuse me a minute?' And she walked away and I sat there with this champagne and everything and dreamed—nothing like Kansas City. She came back and she said, 'I made myself more comfortable.' And she had this magnificent negligee on, looking like a vision of beauty." And he said, "This is just incredible. And she took me by the hand and said, 'Would you come with me?' and she took me out of the room and into her bedroom. Such a beautiful bed. There I was." He said, "Should I stop?" This little guy says, "Well, come on, tell everything." "Well," he says, "after that it was just like Kansas City."[25]

Mamoulian was also, in his later years, fond of saying that had he ever been given the opportunity to direct a revue on Broadway, he would have included a striptease in reverse. A naked woman would have walked onstage to the boredom of the audience. As she began to dress, however, the performance would become increasingly more interesting.[26]

Both anecdotes reveal Mamoulian's preference for a frank yet *indirect* presentation of sexuality, often centered on looking at the female body. As a creative artist, actual sex and nudity did not especially interest him, but he cared deeply about the apparatus that surrounded it—the tease, the excitement, the anticipation—and the ways in which he could stylistically mold an audience's response to these elements. *Applause*, *Dr. Jekyll and Mr. Hyde*, *The Song of Songs*, and *Queen Christina* all, in different ways, show the extent to which he used film style to push the envelope in terms of daringness and saliency, all the while avoiding censorable imagery that was "just like Kansas City."

"The Picture Is Strong and Thoughtful"

When Mamoulian shot *Applause* in the summer of 1929, the Production Code did not exist—drafts of the document did not commence until the fall of 1929, and the Code would not be formally adopted until early 1930.[27] Practically speaking, the main censorship hurdle for *Applause* was simply to be passed by local, state, and international censorship boards. At the same time, however, filmmakers knew that industry-regulated self-censorship was afoot. *Applause* was thus shot and released at a time when the industry was in the early stages of exploring and defining the parameters of censored sound filmmaking.

Unfortunately, archival censorship records for *Applause* do not begin until the film entered post-production. At that point, a paper trail appears of the MPPDA's advice to Paramount and the verdict from external censorship boards. Even this partial record, however, makes it clear that many censorship bodies were both unnerved by, and impressed with, *Applause*. When the SRC reviewed the finished film in September and October 1929, they expressed concern over individual lines of dialogue. Jason Joy, who would be tasked with enforcing the Production Code the following year, worried that dialogue indicated that Kitty and Hitch were not initially married.[28] James Fisher, who also worked at the SRC, pointed out that phrases like "dirty doublecrossin' broads," "everybody in the whole damn house," "too damn high hat," and "some God forsaken farm," contained words that violated the "Don'ts" on the "Don'ts and Be Carefuls" list. Fisher also singled out a line from Kitty (Helen Morgan) about the burlesque performers—"why there's a couple dames in this show that's as good Catholics as anybody"—as cause for concern.[29]

What alarmed the SRC more than anything, however, was that the film was set in the burlesque world, a form of entertainment that by the late 1920s centered on women stripping to full or partial nudity.[30] Although *Applause* showed no actual nudity, Fisher voiced concerns about the brief costumes worn by the burlesque dancers, particularly the one worn by April in the film's final scene.[31] Joy, in a letter to *Applause*'s producer Walter Wanger, was more explicit, suggesting that Paramount eliminate the moments "in which the anatomy of Helen Morgan and/or the show girls are [sic] the most intimately revealed."[32] Yet even as the SRC expressed these concerns, the organization clearly saw *Applause* as a positive artistic moment for sound cinema. Joy, in his letter to Wanger, prefaced his suggested eliminations by writing, "The direction, photography, and general production value seem to us to be examples of a new forward step in picture-building which, I am sure, will greatly please the regular motion picture patrons and which should attract to the theatre new and more critical patrons who are not in the habit of patronizing the usual motion pictures."[33] Letters circulated within the MPPDA also display admiration for the film. A censorship letter likely from MPPDA head Will Hays to Jason Joy, for instance, read, "Incidentally, the direction and photography are quite unusual and, in our opinion, the picture will cause considerable commendable discussion."[34] Fisher perhaps summarized the MPPDA's contradictory feelings best when he wrote, "The picture is strong and thoughtful, portraying with brutal realism and fidelity a certain stratum of human life—that of the burlesque Theatre. As such, it will probably be condemned in its entirety by the supersensitive and puritanical while the more tolerant will find it excellent entertainment."[35]

The MPPDA's assessments of *Applause* would come to epitomize the censorship situation Mamoulian found himself in during the early 1930s. Mamoulian's unapologetic interest in the dynamics of sexual desire made censorship groups uncomfortable. The question *Applause* and subsequent Mamoulian films raised was this: to what extent could evident artistry justify the inclusion of sordid or sexually pronounced subject matter? How far could one go where sex in sound cinema was concerned?

In the case of *Applause*, Paramount banked on the film's artistry. Almost none of the MPPDA's recommended changes appear in the finished film. For Kitty's line about Catholics in the burlesque chorus, Paramount did blot out the word "Catholic" on sound-on-film versions and instructed exhibitors to turn down the fader when the word was spoken in sound-on-disc versions,[36] but their other stated concerns were not addressed. Paramount likely gained confidence from the fact that Mamoulian—who shot *Applause* in Paramount's Astoria studio on Long Island—worked closely with the New York state censor board during production to ensure the film would pass without eliminations.[37] This took care of an important market and suggested to the industry that Mamoulian's film would adequately placate censorship bodies.

Paramount also likely stuck with Mamoulian's version of *Applause* because the film, as we saw in earlier chapters, takes unmistakable steps to condemn burlesque's cheap commodification of female sexuality rather than showcase the female form. This is likely what Fisher had in mind in his summary letter assessing *Applause*'s censorship situation when he praised the film for its "strong and thoughtful" approach to the subject matter's "brutal realism." As we saw,

Mamoulian's approach was heavily influenced by his personal abhorrence of burlesque, which he would describe using such words as "sordid," "dreadful," "shameful," and "degrading."[38]

Mamoulian's disgust for burlesque strip shows may seem hypocritical for a director who, in two upcoming films, would stylistically *emphasize* the act of female undressing. What likely differentiated burlesque from Mamoulian's own later depictions of disrobing, in Mamoulian's mind, was burlesque's visual cheapness and—perhaps—its particularly pointed and unadorned form of female display. As Richard Allen has demonstrated, Florenz Ziegfeld and his imitators in the 1920s were putting on more culturally respectable topless shows on Broadway. These shows featured elegant costumes and sets (along with more passive sexual displays), which granted them a cultural status akin to the "cosmopolitan worldliness of Paris."[39] Burlesque, a working-class entertainment that lacked Broadway's resources, was a fading business by the late 1920s that had little to sell except increasingly blunt displays of nudity. Mamoulian, who prided himself on being cultured, likely bought into this dichotomy. Moreover, as we have seen, he viewed stylization, elegance and creativity as the true qualities of artistic expression. Mamoulian found none of these in burlesque.

Admittedly, some of the film's condemnations of burlesque had been baked into the story prior to Mamoulian's arrival, such as Kitty's exploitation at the hands of the unscrupulous Hitch, the quasi-incestuous sexual harassment from Hitch that April experiences when being trained for burlesque, April's angry denunciations of burlesque, and Kitty's suicide when the business unceremoniously dumps her. But Mamoulian plainly wished to go further, and it is his stylization of the film's three burlesque performances where Mamoulian arguably offers his most visceral condemnations of burlesque. As we saw in chapter 4, Mamoulian aimed to *show* a business that profited by sexually exciting its customers without creating scenes that would sexually excite *viewers* of *Applause*. As earlier chapters demonstrated, Mamoulian found a range of stylistic methods in the first two numbers that distanced the viewer from the experience one might have as a typical burlesque patron, including obstructed stage views, distant mikings of singers, a camera that wanders away from the dull stage show, and a rapid montage of uncomfortably close male faces leering at the display of female flesh. Assisting the film's anti-burlesque message in the final number—when April takes the burlesque stage as the lead performer—is the use of clear visual parallels to a prior number that April, as an audience member, witnessed and abhorred.[40] The first shot of April's performance in the final number begins with a superimposition of the face of Kitty (who has just killed herself) and April onstage performing. This stylistic move suggests that April's decision to be a burlesque performer is tantamount to suicide, but it also echoes a moment in the second number when a similarly slow dissolve occurs from Kitty's face as she

Figure 6.1 In *Applause*'s final number April's framing and actions . . .

dances onstage to April's stricken face in the audience. Then, as April continues to perform in the final number, one of the more dynamic and expressive shots frames April in a head-on medium close-up as she gyrates and shakes her breasts for the burlesque audience. The shot scale, framing, and action are nearly identical to how Kitty had been shot in the earlier burlesque performance that April watched (and later in April's unpleasant dream about burlesque). These visual similarities mark April as essentially performing in her own nightmare (Figures 6.1 and 6.2).

By making sexual exploitation his primary subject and stylizing the topic in highly critical ways, Mamoulian provoked basic questions about the kind of entertainment sound cinema might provide. Hollywood had no tiered ratings system—every film produced was ostensibly suitable for every kind of viewer—yet *Applause*'s forceful takedown of sexual commodification was arguably appropriate only for older audience members, not for children. This, at any rate, was the conclusion reached by the New York censorship board. Though the board passed *Applause* without eliminations, the group stipulated that the film was not suitable for family audiences, children, and young people.[41] Other censorship boards, however, were less comfortable defining a mainstream sound film as adult-only entertainment. Some

MAMOULIAN AND FILMMAKING UNDER CENSORSHIP 213

Figure 6.2 ... echo Kitty's during an earlier number that April abhorred, thereby marking April as essentially performing in her own nightmare.

boards—such as Ohio and British Columbia—rejected the film entirely, and others like Pennsylvania and Chicago demanded many eliminations in an effort to make the film more appropriate for all viewers. In the reel featuring the rapid-fire montage alone, for instance, the Chicago board (at times reducing shots of women walking backstage to "breast shaking") required the elimination of:

> [The] second dance scene on stage where woman moves body and shakes breasts as chorus girls come on stage and standing [sic] with girls. Close scene of woman on runway shaking breasts. Woman on stage shaking rear (back view). All scenes of girls' bare legs alone and in groups. Scenes of semi-nude girl exercising back of stage, standing and bending over, man bumping into her and scene of girl after she straightens up.... Same [semi-]nude chorus girl (in white) at left of picture walking back of scenes and scene as camera shifts of [sic] semi-nude girls at right of picture. Kitty in dressing room walking across room with daughter to man, shaking her breasts. Kitty sitting in chair putting on hat where she shakes her breasts and Kitty gettin [sic] up, standing shaking breasts, up to the time she turns and goes from room.[42]

It is unclear what, precisely, Paramount executives concluded from their experience with *Applause*. Although Paramount believed in *Applause*'s artistic importance, the film struggled with external boards and, as we have seen, would later suffer at the box office.[43] Mamoulian would not be invited by Paramount to direct another film for a year. Nevertheless, at a time when the industry was just beginning to grapple with what an appropriately censored sound film should look and sound like, *Applause* announced itself as a sexually frank, adult-oriented, moralistic, and stylized sound-cinema option.

"CAMERA-JEKYLL"

By the time Mamoulian began shooting his second film, *City Streets*, for Paramount in January 1931,[44] a formalized Production Code document had been written that—at least on paper—answered many of the questions that *Applause* implicitly raises. In language that would have likely sunk *Applause*, the Production Code cautioned against scenes of undressing, forbade "undue exposure," and warned against silhouettes, asserting that they could often be "more suggestive than actual exposure."[45] The Code also warned against "stimulat[ing] the lower or baser element,"[46] a stipulation that *Applause* was probably more successful at following. Most problematic for Mamoulian's interest in cinema, however, was the Production Code's skepticism that sound films could be appropriate for only adults. Film, the Production Code authors asserted, inherently appeals to "every class" of person, whether "mature, immature, developed, undeveloped, law abiding [or] criminal." For this reason, the authors argued, and because films could so easily be duplicated and circulated, it would be quite difficult to confine a film to only "certain selected groups."[47]

The Production Code looked daunting on paper. Yet from 1930 to 1934, the SRC remained relatively lenient in their interpretation of the code. This leniency enabled Mamoulian to frequently test and expand the parameters of censorship where sex was concerned. *City Streets*, a gangster film, contains little sexual content, and it would prove relatively uneventful for Mamoulian. The film breezed through the SRC and was singled out for concern only after its release when reform groups began complaining about gangster films.[48] Mamoulian's next film—*Dr. Jekyll and Mr. Hyde*—however, returned Mamoulian to the topics of male desire and the female body, and gave Mamoulian his first real opportunity to discover how far he could push his stylization of such topics under the Production Code.

Unlike *Applause*, which focuses primarily on a mother-daughter bond, *Dr. Jekyll and Mr. Hyde* centers unabashedly on its central character's sex drive. We should note that Mamoulian was hardly the first to find sexual desire interesting under the Production Code. By the time Paramount released *Dr. Jekyll and Mr. Hyde* in December 1931, the industry had been making films featuring relatively explicit moments of sexual desire for two years. Many of the more salient examples occur in characters who—like Jekyll—reside in the upper classes. *Untamed* (November 1929) centers on wealthy heiress Bingo (Joan Crawford) who—having spent her childhood in the jungle with her oil-investor father—goes into the "civilized" world unaware of social norms and repeatedly ogles love-interest Andy (Robert Montgomery) in a sexual manner. In *The Divorcée* (April 1930)—a film widely credited for establishing a franker treatment of sex in the early 1930s—the first shot of the central couple shows them embracing and kissing for a full seven seconds (and implicitly much longer, since we first view them via a slow pan that only gradually brings them into the frame). "My head's going around like a pinwheel," Jerry (Norma Shearer) exclaims when the kiss finishes, and the couple then agrees that they must marry very soon, plainly to act on their sexual desire. DeMille's *Madam Satan* (September 1930) features an hour-long masquerade party that showcases revealing costumes and offers such provocative lines as, "if you go to hell with me, you may find it heaven." In *The Easiest Way* (February 1931), advertising executive Brockton (Adolphe Menjou) eyes his employee—lingerie model Laura (Constance Bennett)—in her underwear and proceeds to buy her furs, a car, and jewelry. And in *Strangers May Kiss* (April 1931), Lizbeth (Shearer again) disrobes to her lingerie as love-interest Alan (Neil Hamilton) watches before Alan walks closer and the duo embrace and kiss.

Yet while depictions of pronounced sexual desire were not unusual by the end of 1931, what does appear to have been quite rare is Mamoulian's emphasis on *subjectively* articulating a character's desire, thereby encouraging audiences to more fully align with—and share the mindset of—a sexually aroused character. In the films mentioned above, sexual desire is regularly told from an objective viewpoint or—in the case of the bizarre *Madam Satan*—displaced onto outlandish costumes. Bingo's sexual desire in *Untamed*, for instance, is conveyed via external shot–reverse shot editing and—a bit later—long shots of her eyeing Andy in his undershirt. The couple in *The Divorcée* kisses in extreme long shot and then full shot, and their excitement is articulated mainly via ensuing dialogue. *Strangers May Kiss* depicts Lizbeth's disrobing and the couple's kiss in a single medium shot. The viewer knows that Alan is looking at Lizbeth by seeing his reflection in the mirror, not via a point-of-view shot. *The Easiest Way* does contain a point-of-view shot from Laura's perspective as Brockton looks at Laura sexually from head to toe, but the ensuing cut to Laura is positioned well *away* from the optical viewpoint of the aroused Brockton. In all these examples, the camera remains always external to the aroused character's headspace. The viewer is thus implicitly asked to mainly observe—rather than fully participate in— erotic desire.

Mamoulian's decision to plunge viewers into the sexually charged mind of the title character in *Dr. Jekyll and Mr. Hyde* stemmed partly from his interpretation of that character. Unlike in earlier versions of the story, Mamoulian wanted Jekyll and Hyde to embody the values of spiritual versus animal impulses rather than good versus evil. To Mamoulian, "animalistic" sexual desire was a healthy and universal aspect of the human psyche, not something to be automatically condemned. Mamoulian wanted audiences to understand that Jekyll is psychologically forced to create Hyde not because he wishes to enact his evil impulses without paying a societal penalty—as was the case in the novel—but because his healthy sexual desire for fiancée Muriel was being repressed.[49] As one scholar has remarked, Mamoulian's version of the story is "alone in openly tracing the cause of Jekyll's troubles to the frustration by society of his own perfectly natural . . . desires."[50]

It is unclear whether Mamoulian or the writers of the film's treatment (Percy Heath and Samuel Hoffenstein) first thought of the idea that Hyde emerges as the outgrowth of Jekyll's repressed sex drive.[51] What *is* clear, however, is that Mamoulian was responsible for deciding to *subjectively* portray his sexual desires. From the earliest moments in the film, Mamoulian announces *Dr. Jekyll and Mr. Hyde* as an experiment in cinematic subjectivity. In a widely commented-upon opening, Mamoulian—and his cinematographer Karl Struss—begin with a three-and-a-half-minute series of nothing but point-of-view shots from Jekyll's perspective as he plays the organ, converses with his butler, looks in the mirror, walks out the door of his home, rides in a carriage, and enters the lecture hall where he is to speak. This shooting strategy was first spelled out not in early screenplay drafts, but in a document titled "Shooting Continuity as Dictated by Rouben Mamoulian." In this document, Mamoulian repeatedly refers to this technique as "CAMERA-JEKYLL" and explains that for the first two scenes "the part of Jekyll is taken and acted by the CAMERA, so each of the two scenes are [sic] photographed in one continuous shot."[52] Though the completed film features several cuts rather than a single long take, the effect remains striking, partly due to the length of time devoted to nothing but point-of-view shots, and partly because the technique necessitates that numerous people—including the butler, the coachman, a doorman, and several students—look directly at "camera-Jekyll" and address it.

This was not, despite Mamoulian's later claims to the contrary, the first instance of sustained point-of-view filmmaking in the sound era. In *Inspiration* (January 1931)—released several months before Mamoulian began work on *Dr. Jekyll and Mr. Hyde*—director Clarence Brown and his cinematographer, William Daniels, had provided a fifty-five-second point-of-view shot from the perspective of a man named Vignaud (Oscar Apfel) who is searching for his wife, Yvonne (Greta Garbo). During this tour-de-force shot, the camera travels through three doorways and includes a woman looking at—and speaking to—the camera/Vignaud. Brown's shot, however, is a one-off moment, whereas Mamoulian's point-of-view camerawork introduces a strategy that will recur throughout the film. Moreover, this opening point-of-view shot announces the principal means through which Mamoulian will later explore and vividly render sexual desire. The opening shots do not themselves suggest this desire, but their presence underlines two basic elements that will drive it: the *act* of looking and the way in which one *processes* and *responds* to one's environment.

A few scenes later, Mamoulian first equates point-of-view shots with sexual desire during a romantic scene between Jekyll (Fredric March) and fiancée Muriel (Rose Hobart) in a garden. The scene begins traditionally but moves toward closer-range and subjective framings as the conversation becomes increasingly sexually charged. When Jekyll expresses his desire to "marry" (i.e., have sex with) Muriel immediately, Mamoulian places the couple in a typical two-shot at a medium-shot distance. As the mood intensifies and Jekyll continues to talk about his urge to marry now ("I can't wait any longer"), Mamoulian moves to a closer-range but still-objective two-shot. When Jekyll states that he is frightened of his level of love (i.e., sexual desire) and tells Muriel that "the unknown" (i.e., sexual experience) "wears your face," Mamoulian shifts to the scene's first point-of-view shot, a close-up of Muriel staring directly at the camera (Figure 6.3). After a brief head-on close-up of Jekyll, Mamoulian provides an extreme close-up of only Muriel's eyes, followed (again briefly) by Jekyll's. Mamoulian once described close ups as a "gigantic tete-a-tete" that creates "an almost terrifying intimacy between you and the screen."[53] Here, Mamoulian's point-of-view close-ups mark not just the intensity of sexual desire, but also its uncomfortable, confrontational urgency.

The rose garden scene is merely a prelude, however, to the film's most explicit depiction of subjective sexual excitement: the scene in which the working-class saloon-girl Ivy (Miriam Hopkins), who has just met Jekyll and sees him as a means of potentially bettering her situation, performs a striptease for him in her flat. This would prove to be the film's most transgressive scene in the eyes of the SRC, and it remains one of the most stylistically striking depictions of sexual desire in the entire SRC era. Mamoulian's handling of the scene—and its rollercoaster ride with the SRC—is thus worth examining closely.

The film's unusually vivid approach to sexual desire occurred partly because Mamoulian did not play straight with the SRC. When the SRC reviewed the screenplay for this scene prior to shooting, they expressed no concern. When the group viewed the finished film, however, they would ultimately force Mamoulian to cut a portion of the striptease. The SRC's shift was not due to an error on their part but rather occurred because Mamoulian opted to substantially alter the sequence *after* the SRC had approved the screenplay. In the typed

Figure 6.3 When Jekyll becomes sexually excited during his conversation with Muriel in *Dr. Jekyll and Mr. Hyde*, Mamoulian switches to head-on, close-range shots, including shots from Jekyll's optical point of view.

screenplay reviewed by the SRC, no on-camera striptease even occurs. Ivy tells Jekyll to avert his eyes so she can undress, and the image cuts to an exterior courtyard, where Jekyll's friend Lanyon (Holmes Herbert) speaks to a constable. The image then cuts to Ivy, now in bed and "drawing the covers up over her." Jekyll enters the shot, Ivy kisses Jekyll, and Lanyon then enters to fetch Jekyll from the room.[54] Unbeknownst to the SRC, however, Mamoulian's personal screenplay—now housed among his papers at the Library of Congress—looked considerably different. In the margin, Mamoulian handwrote a shot sequence in which the camera *never* cuts to the courtyard and instead stays in the apartment to show Ivy undressing.[55]

This added sequence was likely indebted to the opening of *Congai*, a play Mamoulian had directed back in 1928. *Congai* begins with a passionate love scene between Thi-Linh (Helen Menken) and Kim Khouan (Theodore Hecht), which involves Thi-Linh standing, unfastening her *sinh* (tube skirt), and holding it as a screen as she "slips into the shallows of the pool."[56] At the end of the scene, the lights dim, Thi-Linh rises to her feet ("a dim nude figure," according to the play script[57]), and the couple embraces. In *Dr. Jekyll and Mr. Hyde*, Mamoulian sought to similarly toy with—and titillate via—female nudity, only here, he wished to channel this action through Jekyll's subjectivity. Such a goal may seem contradictory given his prior condemnation of stripping in *Applause*, but Mamoulian likely saw a big difference between burlesque's blunt display of female flesh and his efforts to use indirection and the devices of cinema to elegantly suggest—but not depict—the nude female form.

In the finished film, Jekyll and Ivy's interactions in the flat initially remain outside Jekyll's subjectivity via long and medium shots and a close-up of Ivy forwardly taking Jekyll's hand and placing it on her leg (an action that Mamoulian also handwrote into the script[58]). When Ivy decides to take her clothes off, however, the style changes. "You turn your eyes away now," instructs Ivy in a two-shot. Jekyll walks out of the frame and Ivy sits on the side of the bed facing Jekyll. Instead of cutting to the courtyard as stipulated in the script, Mamoulian cuts to a shot of Ivy (Figure 6.4), sitting in the same position on the bed and facing the camera head-on in a manner not dissimilar from Muriel in the rose garden (Figure 6.3). Then, in an action spelled out in Mamoulian's marginal notes, Ivy smiles at the camera, slowly leans down as the camera tilts down to follow her movements, lifts her skirt up to her waist, kicks off her shoes in the direction of the camera, and takes off her garter and throws it at the camera.

To a certain extent, this cut to Ivy's actions as Jekyll walks away injects a level of ambiguity into the scene that would prove helpful for censorship bodies uncomfortable with the idea of a man watching a woman undress. Because Jekyll has walked in the opposite direction from Ivy, and because Mamoulian does not provide reaction shots of Jekyll looking at her, there is a bit of room to conclude that he is not watching her performance. Even though Ivy seems to be performing for *someone*, and later shots of Jekyll's feet show his toes pointed toward the off-screen Ivy, this small level of ambiguity may have been the reason that Mamoulian was able to salvage this portion of the scene. What followed, however, proved to be too much for the SRC. Following another head-on shot (presumably from Jekyll's point of view) of Ivy removing a stocking and garter and throwing the latter toward the camera, the release version shows a brief shot of Jekyll's cane flicking the garter back at Ivy. Abruptly, the image cuts to Ivy, covered by a bedspread, finishing a climb into bed. A viewer can tell here that an ellipsis has occurred because as Ivy arranges the bedspread over top of her, a brief side view—as well as a shot of their embrace a few moments later—indicates that she is naked (or nearly so) beneath the bedspread (Figure 6.5).

The reason for this ellipsis is that Mamoulian's original cut had featured an extraordinarily lengthy and titillating series of shots. Ivy was to have caught the garter that Jekyll flicked back, "mischievously"[59] put it back on her bare leg, and taken off the other stocking. Mamoulian's shooting notes then stipulated that the following occurred:

Figure 6.4 A post-production excision to *Dr. Jekyll and Mr. Hyde* mandated by the SRC. Ivy looks directly at the camera/Jekyll and begins to undress in this and subsequent shots. . . .

Figure 6.5 Abruptly, the image cuts to a shot of Ivy, now apparently nude, arranging her bedspread.

[Ivy] gets off the bed and stands up.

CAMERA PANS UP
to Ivy's smiling face. She takes her jacket off, disclosing the bodice and drops it on the floor. Then, still looking at Jekyll, she starts unfastening her skirt.

CAMERA PANS DOWN
as the skirt falls on the floor in an embroidered circle of lace and ruffles. Ivy steps out of it.

CAMERA PANS UP
Smiling with sly shyness, Ivy slowly turns her back to Jekyll (Camera) and takes her bodice off throwing it back into the Camera. Then she turns her face over her shoulder smiling at Jekyll.

After a quick cut to Jekyll's feet, the "toes still facing in the direction of Ivy," the following occurred in Mamoulian's original version:

FULL FIGURE SHOT
of Ivy standing by the bed with her back to Jekyll. Her right arm reaches for the thin bed-cover. She pulls it up toward herself, turns around and faces Jekyll, using the cover as a screen. With her other hand she releases her petticoat and lets it fall to her feet.[60]

Then, in the same shot, Mamoulian's original version made use of a favorite device: the cast shadow. According to his shooting continuity, the lamp on Ivy's "night-table behind the bed projects the silhouette of her slim figure on the cover."[61] Ivy then gets into the bed, and the excised part ends.

The parallels to *Congai*'s opening—the use of a screen to obscure the nude body and a naked concluding embrace—are clear. Broadway was a far more permissive venue than Hollywood, however, and when the SRC viewed Mamoulian's cut of this scene, they strenuously objected. Though the organization never cited a specific passage from the Code, they likely felt that point-of-view editing would, in the words of the Production Code, "stimulate the lower or baser element." The striptease also flies in the face of the Production Code's caution against scenes of undressing, its ban on "undue exposure," and its warning that silhouettes could often be "more suggestive than actual exposure." The SRC may have further worried that Jekyll's "sin" of lusting after Ivy seemed more acceptable because the film presents it as an understandable outgrowth of his stifled desire for Muriel.[62] With these concerns likely in mind, the SRC sent a letter to Paramount that leveled four objections at this scene. First, the SRC argued that the entire undressing segment was simply too long. Second, the SRC expressed concern over what they called a "note of anticipation" from Jekyll as he watches Ivy disrobe. Third, the SRC stipulated that Jekyll should not be watching the undressing. Fourth, the SRC stressed that, under no circumstances, should the audience know that Ivy has taken off all her clothes. Ultimately, the SRC conceded the need, for story purposes, to indicate Jekyll's attraction to Ivy, but felt that the scene's length and sexually charged nature could lead viewers to conclude that the goal was pure titillation.[63]

Aside from curtailing the sheer length of the segment, it would be difficult to argue that the censored release version adequately addressed the SRC's concerns. Assuming the audience concludes that Ivy is undressing in point-of-view shots, Jekyll's act of looking and his note of anticipation remain clear. Moreover, excising the latter part of the striptease not only fails to hide the fact that Ivy is nude, but it also permits audiences to write in an even more explicit scenario than what Mamoulian had shot. In Mamoulian's original cut, we know that Ivy avoids showing Jekyll her breasts or genitalia. In the release version, however, the film jumps from the beginnings of a striptease (mostly in Jekyll point-of-view shots) to its naked conclusion (still from a Jekyll point-of-view shot). Thus, one could easily surmise that Ivy had performed a striptease to complete nudity for Jekyll *before* reaching for the bedcover.

Ultimately, Mamoulian's unsanctioned decision to use subjective filmmaking to convey sexual desire seems to have caught the SRC in an irresolvable bind. The SRC recognized that *Jekyll* needed to be interested, but the code forbade filmmakers from overtly stimulating the *audience's* sexual interest. For Mamoulian, however, the very impetus for subjective camerawork had been to get the audience to feel what Jekyll feels throughout the film, whether in terms of his strong sex drive or the liberating effect of his transformation into Hyde.[64] Mamoulian had stylistically conjoined Jekyll and the audience in this scene, and the two could not be separated back out without sacrificing coherency.

When Jekyll begins leaving the room after kissing Ivy in bed, Mamoulian handwrote one final change in the margin of his personal screenplay that further fuses cinematic subjectivity and arousal. In the typed script, after Lanyon enters to discover the kiss and the two start to leave, Ivy merely says, "Come back soon, won't you?" Jekyll says that he cannot, and the image dissolves to Jekyll and Lanyon walking down the street and conversing about Jekyll's behavior. In a marginal note, however, Mamoulian added content and filming techniques that appear nearly verbatim in the finished film.[65] As Jekyll leaves the room with Lanyon, Ivy arranges herself so that her bare leg, with garter attached, is visible hanging off the bed. A few shots later, Ivy delivers the "Come back soon, won't you?" line as specified in the screenplay. Then, in a highly unorthodox move, both the sound of Ivy's voice and her bare leg persist as Jekyll and Lanyon walk away from Ivy's flat. We hear whispered variations of "come back" and "soon," and Mamoulian superimposes Ivy's swinging leg over Jekyll and Lanyon for a full thirty seconds. The clear implication is that Ivy's sexuality has left a lingering impression on Jekyll, much as an earlier lingering dissolve of Muriel had appeared onscreen over another shot of Jekyll and Lanyon after the sexually frustrated Jekyll had failed to push forward the wedding date. Though the SRC never objected to the leg-swinging superimposition, such deeply subjective imagery and sounds might well have excited some of its viewers.

Clear evidence that even the SRC's toned-down version of the striptease was risqué for its time comes from the responses of the external censor boards. Many boards cut parts of the striptease that Mamoulian had managed to save during SRC negotiations. Ohio, Saskatchewan, Manitoba, Chicago, England, Japan, and New Zealand cut shots of Ivy undressing. Ohio and Alberta cut shots of Ivy in bed (the Ohio board specifically objected to the shot of Ivy's bare back as she pulls the bedspread over her front, presumably because the shot indicated nudity so overtly). Japan cut the shot of Jekyll kissing the naked Ivy in bed. Ohio, Alberta, and Chicago cut shots of Ivy's swinging leg, while Ohio and Chicago removed Ivy's line of dialogue, "Come back soon." The Saskatchewan and Manitoba boards also apparently disliked the sexual playfulness of the scene, cutting the sound of Ivy laughing.[66]

Ultimately—and unlike many prior films from the "Pre-Code" era that had been content to explore sexual desire from an objective distance—*Dr. Jekyll and Mr. Hyde* found ways to use attention-grabbing devices to submerge the audience in the mind of a sexually aroused man and keep it there for a considerable period. Such an approach helps explain Jekyll's psyche, but we should note that it also more problematically sets up the horrific sexual sadism—depicted with a startling level of explicitness for the period—that Hyde will later enact upon Ivy. When Hyde and Ivy first meet in the dance hall, for instance, Mamoulian provides head-on shots that are similar to the rose garden scene in which Jekyll professes his desire for Muriel: first a point-of-view close up from Hyde's perspective of Ivy looking trapped and terrified (Figure 6.6), and later a concluding shot—signaling the impending rape of Ivy—in which Hyde, from Ivy's point of view, moves toward the camera until only his eyes are in the frame. These two shots may have been partly inspired by the rape scene from the smash-hit silent film *The Son of the Sheik* (1926), which similarly marks the rapist's advance by providing a close-range shot of a character looking directly at the camera and later an extreme close-up of only a character's eyes. Yet because Mamoulian has visually connected such head-on shots to prior shots from Jekyll's perspective, the implication emerges that no matter how healthy a sexual drive may be, it can erupt into something abhorrent.

Figure 6.6 In *Dr. Jekyll and Mr. Hyde*, sexual desire, presented as natural and healthy in prior Jekyll point-of-view shots (see Figures 6.3 and 6.4) is reconfigured as sadistic and crushing in Hyde's point-of-view shot of Ivy.

Like in *Applause*, Mamoulian was engaging with the question of how far was too far when sex was in play, and what it meant to produce a sound film under the auspices of heightened censorship. "The story point—Jekyl's [sic] attraction to Ivy—must be saved," the SRC had acknowledged to Mamoulian in post-production negotiations, but "no one should be permitted to conclude that [the undressing scene] is dragged in to simply titillate the audience."[67] Yet Mamoulian had a different film in mind: one that *required* subjective titillation and arousal to explain its characters' behavior. Whether exciting, arousing, exploitive, or hypocritical, Mamoulian's work in *Dr. Jekyll and Mr. Hyde* once again forged a cinematic pathway for accentuating the erotic and adult-oriented possibilities of sound film.

"Our Next Big Problem"

Mamoulian followed *Dr. Jekyll and Mr. Hyde* with *Love Me Tonight*, another distinctly "Pre-Code" product. Though the film's dialogue and song lyrics are worthy of a censorship analysis, the archive is murky on Mamoulian's precise contributions to these areas, and film style in *Love Me Tonight* does not carry the same sexual impact. Mamoulian's next movie, *The Song of Songs*, however, returned him squarely to the role he had occupied in *Applause* and *Dr. Jekyll and Mr. Hyde*: a filmmaker intent upon using innovative stylization to explore the relationship between the male look and the female form. Here, however, Mamoulian upped the ante in two respects: more overt and repeated references to nudity in particular; and the linking of sexually risqué content to *literal* artworks, thereby audaciously suggesting that nudity, sexual desire, true love, beauty, and artistry could be one and the same. *The Song of Songs* is not well known today, but in its time, the film was a massive headache for the SRC, and it remains one of the most transgressive films of the entire "Pre-Code" era. Thanks especially to the existence of the pre-production screenplay and copious post-production communication between Mamoulian, Paramount, and censorship groups, *The Song of Songs* offers a clear view of Mamoulian's aims and methods and the extent to which his personal sensibilities clashed with conventional expectations.

The Song of Songs was an adaptation of the eponymous 1908 novel by Hermann Sudermann and the 1914 play by Edward Brewster Sheldon. Mamoulian's 1933 version centers on Lily (Marlene Dietrich), a repressed yet passionate country girl who agrees to pose nude for a young male sculptor named Waldow (Brian Aherne) to help create what both believe will be a masterpiece: a statue about a woman yearning for ideal love. What begins as a professional relationship shifts one night when Waldow—following a flirtation initiated by Lily—embraces and kisses the naked Lily while she is posing, and the couple embarks on a happy (and plainly sex-filled) love affair. Concerned that he cannot support Lily as a poor artist, Waldow makes the mistake of agreeing to let the wealthy Baron von Merzbach (Lionel Atwill) woo Lily, and the baron successfully coaxes Lily into marriage after lying about the reasons behind Waldow's departure. The film then becomes a study in contrasts: where Waldow's sculpture serves as a testament to his love for Lily, the baron sees Lily's body in a different way—as an opportunity to "mold" Lily into a great lady by controlling and possessing her. Lily's experiences with the baron nearly ruin her before a meeting with Waldow and a look at the finished statue at the end of the film rekindle hope for a happier future together.

Before examining a few key scenes, a brief description of the film's journey through its production phases is in order. When Mamoulian was asked to direct this property, he was—by his later account—initially reluctant, as he found the story old-fashioned and didn't wish to break up the von Sternberg–Dietrich partnership that had yielded five films to date. He eventually agreed to direct it largely out of contractual obligation, and he does not appear to have played a major role in shaping the screenplay, which was approved by the SRC during pre-production without major incident.[68] Once on board, however, Mamoulian embraced the opportunity to use various tools at his disposal—especially camera movement, framing, editing, and actor performance—to more tightly fuse together some of the story's key topics: artistry, aesthetic beauty, great love, sexual desire, and nudity. This involved, in particular, using film style to make nude female statues in Waldow's studio function as correlates for Lily's bare flesh when she disrobes to model for him, including during the scene when the duo falls in love. These stylistic moves had not appeared in the SRC-approved screenplay, and they were the primary reason that the SRC did an about-face and flatly rejected Mamoulian's finished film unless substantial cuts were made.

Rather than acquiesce to the SRC, Paramount and Mamoulian decided to fight back, causing SRC head James Wingate to privately notify Hays that the film would be "our next big problem."[69] In a violation of industry policy, Paramount submitted Mamoulian's cut to the New York censor board for review *before* it had been granted a seal by the SRC. As part of the case submitted to both the New York board and the SRC, Mamoulian took the unusual step of sending a three-page letter explaining his viewpoint on art, cinema, and its relationship to *The Song of Songs*' sexually risqué material. His letter—along with communication from the SRC—crystallized the fundamental issues that he and the SRC were facing, which extended well beyond the matter of merely trimming or removing shots. In the eyes of the SRC, stylistically tying nude statues to Lily as she models served merely as pointed, exploitative, and unwelcome reminders of Lily's offscreen nudity. Yet in his response letter to the SRC, Mamoulian argued that such shots emphasized not nudity, but rather the creation of art and the glories of a "great love" that was emerging between Lily and Waldow.[70] To bolster his case, Mamoulian enclosed a list of the nude statues found in Waldow's studio and the prestigious awards those statues had won.[71] In the letter itself, Mamoulian argued the following:

> I believe that scenes dealing with the love story of the SONG OF SONGS and taking place in the background of the studio with its sculpture, are of such a nature as to invoke only the best and not the worst in human nature. I have tried very honestly and very hard to avoid anything that might look like sensationalism or exploitation of "nudity" as box-office attraction because even the slightest suspicion of that would really make me permanently unhappy. I have already sent you a full list of all the statues used in the film and in it you will discover that every single statue without exception, is an individual piece of art created by sculptors of international and distinguished reputation. They are the kind of statues that you see in art galleries, public museums, city halls and public schools. Most of the actual statues used in the film have been exhibited in museums and galleries and many of them have won high prizes.

The main statue in the SONG OF SONGS, as you probably know from newspapers, is on its way to the Chicago World's Fair, to be exhibited to millions of visitors who will be there from all parts of the world. I have tried not to be either obvious or unduly suggestive in any scene in the picture dealing with the love in its different phases between the sculptor and the girl, and I think that in every shot that includes statues, it is not "nudity" that stands out, but beauty symbolized through the human form. It is not for nothing that through the many centuries of development, the human race, in its search for beauty and its desire to express it in a concrete visual form, has always chosen for its medium, the form of a human body.[72]

There is good reason to think that Mamoulian's argument was earnest. As we saw in earlier chapters, Mamoulian enjoyed animating artworks or rendering them expressive throughout his career. Mamoulian's defense was ultimately unsuccessful, however, as the New York censor board sided mainly with the SRC. This strengthened the SRC's hand, and Mamoulian was compelled to remove certain shots. Still, in mounting his case, Mamoulian forced the SRC to come to terms not just with the topic of nudity, but also with the broad-scale assumptions about sound cinema that undergirded the Production Code document itself. What constituted "nudity" in sound cinema, and how palpably were filmmakers permitted to render sexual desire in scenes involving the naked female body? Could representations of nudity be acceptable if positive values—true love, artistic creation, beauty—were associated with them? Were the female body and eroticism even appropriate subjects for a mainstream sound film in the first place? Were such efforts sinful? Exploitative? Artistic? More broadly, what was the sexual potential—and cultural status—of mainstream sound cinema?

We can best glimpse Mamoulian's engagement with these questions—and the SRC's response to them—by examining two sequences in Waldow's studio. The first depicts Lily's initial decision to disrobe and pose for Waldow, while the second portrays the emergence of the couple's love affair during a nude modeling session. As we shall see, Mamoulian did not entirely get his way, but both scenes remain striking for the period, and they illuminate the hotly contested issues that arose between Mamoulian and the SRC.

The first scene, when Lily first poses nude, had generated little concern when the SRC reviewed the screenplay before filming began. The SRC did eliminate a few dialogue references to Lily's nudity, and they suggested shooting a replacement shot in case external boards rejected an image of Lily's shawl dropping to the floor, but there is little evidence that the SRC felt the scene would be especially troublesome.[73] The scene's post-production problems stemmed from Mamoulian's decision to alter the screenplay during shooting by using expressive framings, camera movements, and editing to accentuate Lily's act of undressing.

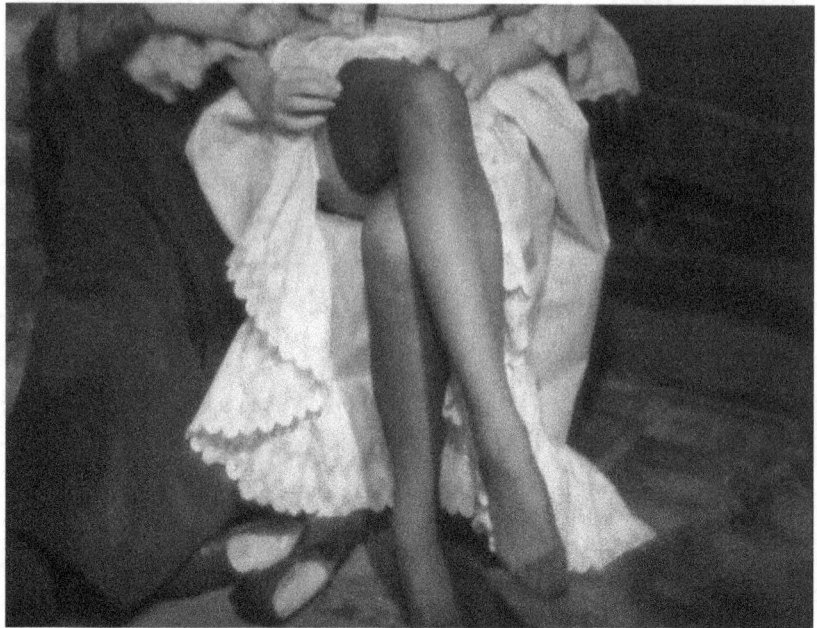

Figure 6.7 Depending on one's perspective, Mamoulian emphasizes disrobing and/or the initiation of great art in *The Song of Songs*. As Lily takes off her stockings …

In the original screenplay, Lily was to have walked behind a curtain, removed her clothing, and put on a smock, with the film merely cutting from a shot of Waldow preparing to sculpt to a single shot of Lily undressing.[74] Though the same actions occur in Mamoulian's version, the cinematic techniques differ substantially. When Lily crosses her legs, lifts her skirt, and begins to take off her stocking, Mamoulian whip-pans left before stopping on the crossed legs of a nude statue in shadow (Figures 6.7 and 6.8). An off-screen light then illuminates the legs starting at the top and ending at the bottom, a clear metaphor for disrobing. Two shots later, the camera shows Lily in medium shot taking off her undergarment before whip-panning to a statue draped in cloth. Mamoulian then suggests the process of unveiling by having Waldow's arm reach into the frame and remove the cloth, revealing a statue of a naked woman in medium long shot.

On the surface, such shots can easily be read as redundant and titillating reminders of disrobing and nudity. This, at any rate, was Wingate's interpretation when he reviewed the finished film. As he explained his post-production letter, the shots of nude statues violated the Production Code and needed to be removed because they repeated the story information that Lily was disrobing, thereby serving merely to "concentrate the minds of the audience on the fact

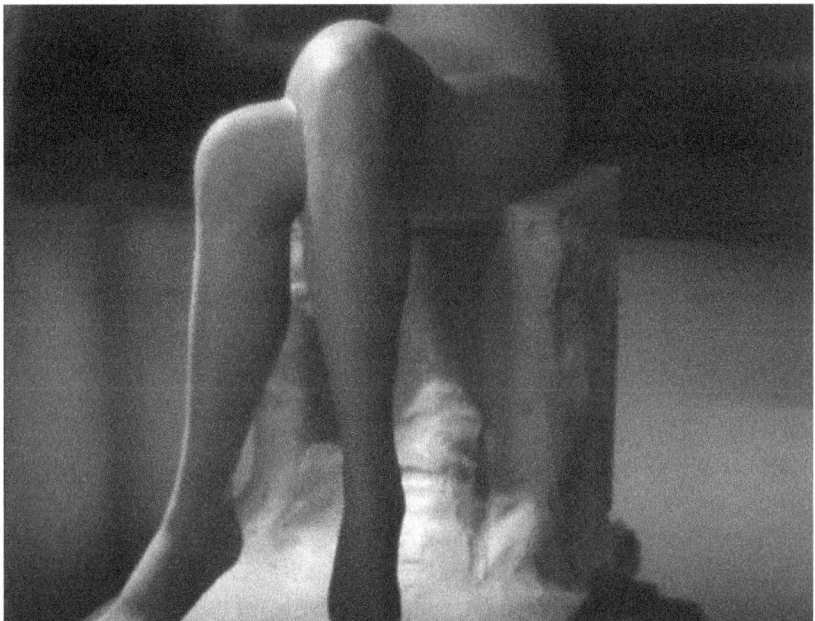

Figure 6.8 ... Mamoulian whip-pans to an identically framed shot of a sculpture's bare legs, and those legs are then illuminated starting at the top and ending at the bottom.

that . . . the girl is nude."[75] Yet contextually, one could argue—as Mamoulian did in his letter—that Lily's act of undressing deserved stylistic emphasis not for titillation, but because Lily's action reflects her fervent desire to help create a beautiful artwork depicting great love. Lily's decision to undress, the screenplay makes clear, is driven by the fact that she sees in the planned Song of Songs statue an embodiment of the biblical verses about perfect love she passionately reads to herself every night. And Waldow, according to the dialogue, sees the statue—which requires a nude model—as a way to shake himself out of a creative rut. From this perspective, the unveiling emphasized by Mamoulian's whip-pans to the statues articulates the potential to create great art, not the act of disrobing per se. Fueling this argument is the fact that Pyotr Tchaikovsky's "Pathétique" Symphony—widely considered a "great work"—plays when Lily drops her smock to pose nude. The filmmakers explicitly chose this song to further the sense that Lily aims to help generate a superb work of art.[76]

The SRC, however, remained skeptical of this argument. Though the organization never responded directly to the points raised in Mamoulian's letter, they surely recognized that Mamoulian had a movie to defend, and that he may well have had artistry *and* titillation in mind (which Mamoulian did not see as necessarily separate). Ultimately, the two nude-statue shots survived in the release version because Mamoulian agreed to alter the moment a bit later in the scene when Lily drops her smock in front of Waldow to pose for the statue. In his initial cut, Mamoulian had edited from Lily removing her smock to a shot of a stone plaque of a naked woman, a plaque that can be seen in other shots that survive in the finished version (Figure 6.9). In post-production negotiations, the SRC eventually decided that if this most overt reference to female nudity were eliminated, the other statue shots could be safely included.[77]

The *second* scene that got Mamoulian into hot water with the SRC again equates nudity with art and beauty, but it daringly uses film style to link these elements to Waldow's sexual desire in particular, and to the act of sex itself. In this scene, Lily arrives, flirts with Waldow, and then begins to pose nude. Waldow, overcome with sexual desire as he molds the statue and looks at Lily, walks toward her and embraces her. The duo kiss and the scene fades to black, a clear indication that sex is about to occur.

The SRC's post-production concerns about this scene stemmed partly from Mamoulian's decision to film it differently from what was indicated in the original screenplay, an issue the SRC had contended with in the earlier scene as

Figure 6.9 In Mamoulian's original cut of *The Song of Songs*, the stone plaque seen in this shot was to have been correlated more closely with Lily's later state of undress, an association the SRC found too explicit.

well. Here, however, the SRC also appears to have been guilty of inconsistency. In their pre-production review, the SRC complained about small-scale details, but the organization made no objection to the premise of the scene. By the time the SRC viewed this scene in post-production, however, their critique had shifted to include the scene's basic premise: that it focused on a man's growing arousal at the thought and sight of a naked woman. The scene, Wingate informed Paramount in the SRC's post-production letter, violated the "clause of the Code which includes under the heading of nudity 'any lecherous or licentious notice thereof by other characters in the picture.'" Wingate also asserted that Waldow's "snatching up of the presumably nude girl" was "altogether too explicit from a Code standpoint."[78]

Wingate's shift was likely driven partly by the fact that while *The Song of Songs* was in production, the SRC faced increased pressure from Hays to tighten Code enforcement.[79] The SRC's change of heart was also, however, sparked by the ways in which Mamoulian used subjective filmmaking—along with silhouettes and actor performance—to convey Waldow's growing interest. To see how he did this—and grasp what particularly bothered the SRC—we can divide the sequence into three sections: Waldow's preparations to mold the statue while Lily disrobes behind a curtain, the duo's more distant interactions when Lily emerges to pose, and the kiss and embrace that conclude the sequence.

For the first segment, the typed screenplay that the SRC reviewed indicated that the camera would remain objective, cutting between two shots of Waldow working on his sculpture and one shot of the screen behind which Lily disrobes, with only a dress thrown across it to visually suggest her act of undressing.[80] When reviewing this section of the screenplay, the SRC had simply stipulated "that undue prominence be not given to [Waldow's] handling of the [statue's] breasts." To film the scene, however, Mamoulian opted to throw Lily's silhouette against the wall as she takes off her stockings in one shot and her dress in another shot, thereby more pointedly emphasizing disrobing. Equally important, he presents these shots from Waldow's optical point of view, which suggests his increasing arousal. In the image preceding the first silhouette shot, Waldow looks toward the curtain. Mamoulian cuts to Lily's silhouette via Waldow's point-of-view shot (Figure 6.10) and then cuts back to Waldow's reaction: he walks to the Song of Songs statue, caresses its shoulders in a decidedly non-sculptor-like way, and looks longingly in Lily's direction (Figure 6.11). Mamoulian then cuts back to the second silhouette shot—again from Waldow's point of view—of Lily removing her dress before cutting back again to Waldow, who continues to caress the statue as if it were Lily's body and not his artwork. Waldow's hands avoid touching the statue's breasts (per the SRC's instructions), but Mamoulian compensates for this "loss" by using Lily's silhouette to pointedly reference Lily's actions and Waldow's interest.

Figure 6.10 Arousal and intimacy during a nude modeling session in *The Song of Songs*. In Waldow's point-of-view shot, Mamoulian throws Lily's shadow against the wall as she disrobes behind a screen. . . .

Technically, the Production Code prohibited such sexualized use of shadow play, and the SRC could not have been happy that Mamoulian had included it without prior approval. In post-production negotiations, Mamoulian managed to keep the two silhouette shots described above by agreeing to remove a third silhouette of Lily that appeared in this same sequence of shots. It seems unlikely that this excision significantly diluted the sexualized message of this segment, however. The two remaining silhouettes are plainly tied to Waldow's gaze, thereby enabling Waldow's touching of the statue to convey his arousal.

The second segment features Waldow continuing to caress the statue as if it were Lily's body even after Lily emerges from behind the curtain and drops her shawl. When viewing the finished film, this moment deeply troubled the SRC because it blatantly portrayed a sexually aroused man. Yet here, Mamoulian had not exactly pulled a fast one. Waldow's use of the clay statue as a correlate for Lily's body had actually appeared in the screenplay the SRC reviewed. In that screenplay, both characters recognize that Waldow is touching Lily's skin by proxy:

Figure 6.11 Mamoulian cuts to Waldow, whose touching of the statue becomes sensual rather than professional. . . .

CLAY STATUE—CLOSEUP—
The breasts and shoulders are dominant in this angle with Waldow's deft hands shaping them, smoothing them.

DOUBLE CUT:

LILY—CLOSEUP
Her head and as much of her shoulders as Mr. Hays will allow.

Lily reacts delicately to Waldow's hands. It is as if he were touching, not the clay but her own living flesh.

Her eyes half close as in surrender.[81]

After reading this scene, the SRC—in their official pre-production letter and a story conference with the filmmakers—had cautioned against using camera angles that emphasized the breasts and again stipulated that "Waldow's shaping of the clay breast should be impersonal and casual."[82] In their post-production review of the film, the SRC seems to have been satisfied with the camera angles, but they remained deeply concerned that Waldow's handling of the statue was a disingenuous violation of the code. In a revealing internal SRC memo, Alice Ames Winter—tasked with representing the "interests of women" for the SRC[83]—argued strenuously that Mamoulian had breached the spirit of the code by filming the statue exactly as if it were the naked body of Lily that audiences were not permitted to see. As Winter described it, "you get flashes of [Lily's] head and shoulders, not showing her body, then you go back to him feeling of [sic] the plaster body under his hands exactly as if it were real flesh—this with sensuous motions and with an emphasis on the breasts—which is extremely suggestive."[84] Fueling this assumption, the reviewer argued, was the statue's face, which "of course bears a reproduction of Dietrich's face."[85] "In other words," Winter concluded, "the use of the statue again and again seems to be nothing but a means of getting around the Code by using the plaster image exactly as if it were a living thing."[86]

Of course, having Waldow caress the statue as a substitute for Lily's naked body was precisely what the screenplay the SRC approved had called for. Perhaps for this reason, Wingate did not stress Winter's criticism in his rejection letter, instead pointing more generally to the problem of overtly indicating a character's arousal. The archive is somewhat unclear on what, precisely, Mamoulian was eventually forced to remove from this segment, but he appears to have excised mainly the moments when Waldow strokes the breasts of the statue.

As Winter's letter indicates, the level of eroticism in this segment was shocking by 1933 standards, an opinion shared by more recent commentators (Mamoulian scholar Tom Milne calls the final version of this scene "extraordinarily erotic"[87]). For starters, even though Waldow spends little time touching the statue's breasts in the final cut, his hands periodically move toward them before quickly shooting back up to the shoulders, as if struggling to contain his arousal. Perhaps more important, Lily's reaction shots—which the SRC never modified—fuel the erotic buildup to the kiss. As Waldow caresses the statue, we see several shots of Lily framed from the shoulders up. Initially, she looks upward in the statue pose she is supposed to assume. As she increasingly realizes what Waldow's caressing of the statue means, however, she lowers her head, looks directly downward (Figure 6.12) and then suspiciously back at Waldow. One could interpret this downward look as one of modesty, as she looks for the smock to cover herself. It is also plausible, however, that Dietrich was responding to the scene as originally conceptualized: she is responding to the touches that Waldow gives her by proxy. In spite of the SRC's cuts, the finished film leaves little doubt about the sexual undercurrents of the moment.

The scene then concludes with the third segment, which features a directorial flourish indicating sex after the fade-out that Mamoulian was ultimately forced to eliminate. In the screenplay approved by the SRC, the scene was to have ended

Figure 6.12 A bit later, Lily glances downward as she poses and then upward at Waldow, as if feeling his touch via the statue.

with a shot of Waldow kissing Lily, followed by a close-up of the head and torso of the statue.[88] Mamoulian's initial cut instead concluded with Waldow carrying the naked Lily toward another room before the camera slowly panned away to show first the curtains and then the flowers that Lily had brought for Waldow before finally resting on the full nude statue against the rock wall (the same statue seen in Figure 6.9). Presumably concerned by such a pointed reference to off-screen nudity and sex, the SRC suggested that Mamoulian fade out immediately after the duo begins embracing and kissing.[89] Mamoulian strongly resisted this change but was forced to remove it so that the film could be granted a seal.[90]

As with the first scene, Mamoulian's stylized use of statues during moments of undress provoked questions about whether—and to what purpose—a filmmaker could emphasize the proximate presence of a nude body. The second scene, in addition, implicitly asked whether sexual desire and nonmarital sex could be portrayed as idealistic and glorious under self-censorship. If—like Mamoulian—one felt that nudity, sexual desire, great art, romance, and sex could healthily co-exist, then the nude statue that Waldow and Lily create might plausibly serve as a symbol of their beautiful sexual relationship. The Production Code document, however, viewed any presentation of the nude or partially nude female body as a potentially "immoral" effort designed to "put a 'punch' into a picture," and it looked upon nonmarital sex as sinful.[91] Mamoulian's creative decisions in these scenes were no doubt driven also by his identity as a heterosexual male, and the film's one-sided nudity and uneven power dynamics between the couple—a cultured male painter and a naïve woman from the country—should not be ignored. Yet in the context of 1933 censorship, *The Song of Songs* may be most notable as a limit case, where a filmmaker intent upon allowing sex to be a sublime subject of popular cinema explored how far he could go within a Production Code that saw nudity as exploitive and sexual desire as lecherous.

The result is a film that, even in its surviving form, conveys nudity and sexual desire with a forcefulness and persistence that is virtually unparalleled in the "Pre-Code" era. Prominent movies like *Red-Headed Woman* (1932), *Call Her Savage* (1932), and *She Done Him Wrong* (1933) had contained pointed reminders of female undressing just out of view, whether via shoulders-up framing, framing only bare legs, or undressing behind a screen. Naked female bathing can be found in *The Love Parade* (1929), *The Sign of the Cross* (1932), *Red Dust* (1932), and *The Barbarian* (1933). Nude statues are present—though often on the periphery—in such films as *Untamed*, *The Easiest Way*, *Strangers May Kiss*, *Red-Headed Woman*, *Trouble in Paradise* (1932), *She Done Him Wrong*, and Mamoulian's own portrayal of Ivy's flat in *Dr. Jekyll and Mr. Hyde*. These examples, however, tend to be either de-emphasized within the mise-en-scène or merely one-off moments in the film. Among these examples, Mamoulian's *The Song of Songs* is alone in suggesting that a censored sound film might consistently and stylishly use suggested nudity throughout a film to articulate key ideas within the story, including sexual desire, beauty, and uplift. Such efforts, depending on one's perspective, arguably make Mamoulian inconsistent and exploitive (given his strong anti-objectification messaging in *Applause*), a champion of free expression in commercial sound cinema, or even both at once. At the very least, *The Song of Songs* showed Mamoulian still intent upon exploring methods by which sexual content could be rendered more palpable under censorship.

When it was finally released in August 1933, *The Song of Songs* continued to provoke questions about whether the scenes in Waldow's studio constituted a sincere merging of artistry, great love, and sex, or whether they served as an underhanded means for injecting sex and nudity into the film. For some reviewers, the film's use of the Song-of-Songs statue earnestly reflected beauty and love. Mamoulian, gushed a British reviewer for *Cinema*, "makes [Lily's] nude statue the symbol of the beauty of the soul and body so passionately desired and so wantonly destroyed by the fleeting love of man and it is this statue that stands, spiritually, between the two whom her life is chiefly entangled."[92] For a critic from Kansas City, the film was to be admired for breaking boundaries on eroticism: "Mr. Mamoulian," argued the reviewer, "by an ingenious use of his camera, has been able to create a more arrestingly physical sensation in his love scenes than DeMille ever has been able to accomplish with Hadrian's villa filled with squirming, undraped extras."[93] For Louisville (KY) critic Dan Thompson, the film's big accomplishment had more to do with naked female flesh: "At last," extolled Thompson, "the movies have found a way to show a beautiful actress completely nude on the screen without arousing the wrath of the censors."[94] As with *Applause* and *Dr. Jekyll and Mr. Hyde*, Mamoulian's stylistic assertiveness and embrace of sexual subject matter sparked fundamental questions about what a censored sound film could be.

"The Rhyme and Cadence of Poetry"

Though Mamoulian made daring use of style in *Applause, Dr. Jekyll and Mr. Hyde*, and *The Song of Songs*, the films' fundamental topics remained fairly traditional for the period: male desire, the male gaze, and its impact on the female body. While Mamoulian was directing these movies, certain other early 1930s films were examining sexual desire and power from a more female-oriented perspective. In *The Divorcée*, Norma Shearer plays a career woman who sleeps with a man to even the account with her philandering husband. Movies like *She Done Him Wrong*, *Red-Headed Woman*, and *Baby Face* (1933) explore how a woman might instrumentally—and successfully—use sex to gain wealth. *Female* (1933) centers on a woman who attains the conventional power of men, serving as president of an automobile manufacturing factory and enjoying casual sex with numerous male employees. Just when Mamoulian seemed stuck in a conventional, male-focused approach to sex, however, he directed *Queen Christina*, a film that *did* make female power and sexuality a central topic.

Viewed today, *Queen Christina* remains one of the most forward-looking films of the "Pre-Code" era. Scholars have pointed to the film's liberal attitudes toward gender and sexuality, particularly its hints about Christina's lesbian relationship with her maid-in-waiting, Ebba. The presence of sex in *Queen Christina* is also unusually pronounced. Midway through the film, Don Antonio (John Gilbert)—who has the bed curtains drawn—asks his manservant, who is unaware that Don Antonio is sharing his bed with Christina (Greta Garbo), to fetch "two chocolates," a clear indication that Don Antonio is spending all his time in bed with Christina (the two are not married). Though risqué, both elements can be found in screenplay drafts prior to May 1933, when Mamoulian left Paramount and officially began work for *Queen Christina* at MGM, thus making it unlikely that he thought of these ideas.[95]

Archival records *do* make it clear, however, that Mamoulian conceptualized and executed a different censor-bending moment in the film: the now-famous scene in which Christina walks around the hotel room she has shared during three days of sex with Don Antonio, touching each object so as to forever remember it.[96] This segment, and the inn scenes preceding it, nearly sank *Queen Christina* when the SRC reviewed it in post-production, and Mamoulian's ability to push it past the censors would be his last victory before the more stringent years of the PCA's reign began. Equally important, the scene was Mamoulian's final effort during the SRC years to use stylization to fuse beauty, love, and sex, this time by orienting a sex-laden scene around the inner life of a female character.

Even prior to Mamoulian's arrival, MGM knew that the inn sequences would be vital to the picture. Though officially an original screenplay, *Queen Christina* was based upon the life of Christina as presented by the August Strindberg play *Kristina* (1903) and Faith Compton Mackenzie's novel *The Sibyl of the North* (1931). Because Garbo was playing the lead, and because Christina was famous for abdicating the throne, MGM concluded early in pre-production that only a glorious love affair—which Garbo was well known for in her films by 1933—would adequately explain Christina's abdication and maintain audience sympathy for her decision.[97] Screenwriters Salka Viertel and Margaret Le Vino thus created for Garbo a character of considerable power and intelligence who longed for intellectual and physical freedom beyond the constraints of her castle. Doing so helped mark Christina's three-day love affair with Don Antonio at the inn as a unique and special experience in her life, yet initial screenplay drafts show the screenwriters struggling to find a scene that would convey the affair's level of importance to Christina. In early drafts, one finds efforts to mark the inn as special by making it a locale of sexual frankness so as to contrast it with formal, antiseptic castle life, which features efforts at an arranged marriage, a lack of free time, and constant public scrutiny. Only after Mamoulian's arrival, however, does the room-touching scene appear, a scene that instead uses low-key stylization to convey the liberating effects of the love affair upon Christina's psyche.

Mamoulian's room-touching scene features no undressing or overtly sexualized movements, and it likely seems tame to modern eyes. To the eyes of the censors in 1933, however, the scene's context made it quite dangerous. When the SRC read the final draft of the pre-production screenplay, which included the room-touching scene, they expressed concern that the scene occurred after Christina and Don Antonio had roomed together for three days. Rather than indicate a sexual relationship, the SRC suggested, the filmmakers might convey "merely the beginning of real romantic love. Alluding to the fact that Christina initially dresses as a male at the inn to avoid being recognized as the queen, the SRC wrote, "perhaps it would be possible to change the sequence in such a way as to show that Antonio leaves the room after discovering that his companion is a girl."[98] Walter Wanger, *Queen Christina*'s producer, placated the SRC by agreeing to shoot the inn scenes in multiple ways to provide flexibility during the film's post-production SRC review. Although the SRC, as we shall see, nearly succeeded in eliminating a portion of the room-touching scene, Mamoulian's original vision ultimately remained intact in the release version.[99]

Regular moviegoers in 1933 would have recognized, in the room-touching scene, familiar features of Garbo's prior love scenes in her US silent and sound films, including inclement weather, flame, and an emphasis on touch and tactility. What viewers had not seen before, and what arguably gives the scene much of its power, is the *rhythmic* stylization of Garbo's movements. Rhythm, as we saw in chapters 3 and 4, was one of Mamoulian's most cherished artistic principles. To the beat of an offscreen metronome (not heard on the soundtrack of the finished film), Mamoulian arranged for Garbo to walk around the room touching objects for nearly three and a half wordless minutes. A detailed description of these minutes can help us grasp the scene's precision, its relationship to rhythm, and the ways in which Garbo's movements are configured to convey the beauty and freedom of sexual experience.

The rhythmic movements begin when Christina rises from a reclined position near Don Antonio and—in a long-range master shot—walks across the room to touch the top of a dresser, a candlestick, and a case before moving left to gaze into a nearby mirror. Mamoulian cuts to a medium close-up of Christina peering into the mirror, cuts to the object of her gaze (the seated Don Antonio), and then cuts back to the medium close-up of Christina, who rubs a canister with both hands before turning to walk out of frame. Mamoulian cuts again to the master shot, where Christina touches the wall before sitting at a spinning wheel and giving it a turn with her hand. After a brief Don Antonio reaction shot, Mamoulian cuts to a medium close-up of Christina spinning the wheel once more. She gets up, and Mamoulian cuts back to the master shot, where Christina strokes some wool, walks to the bed, and slowly lies down on it. In medium close-up, Christina rests her head on the pillow, embraces it, and kisses it. After cutting to Don Antonio's somewhat puzzled expression, Mamoulian offers an extreme close-up of Christina's face, from hairline to chin, as she gazes in Don Antonio's direction and then happily closes her eyes. Mamoulian returns to the master shot, where Christina gets up and touches a tapestry. A close-up shows her gazing at the tapestry before Mamoulian cuts again to the master shot, where Christina walks to the bedpost and gives it a lengthy embrace with her eyes closed. This wordless stretch ends when Christina explains to Don Antonio, "I've been memorizing this room. In the future, in my memory, I shall live a great deal in this room."

It is impossible to say with certainty which shots in this segment made use of the on-set metronome, but many of Christina's movements in the scene's master shot appear to be on a consistent beat. Mamoulian first cuts to the master shot when Christina rises from the floor and takes six steps to the room's dresser at approximately 50 beats per minute (bmp). Christina's subsequent touching of first a candle and then a case on the dresser occurs a bit more slowly (around 35–40 bmp), but the 50-bmp tempo resumes in other places during this master shot. After Christina sees the spinning wheel, for instance, she takes two steps and then sits on a chair by the wheel, with all three motions occurring at roughly 50 bpm. Her subsequent walk toward the bed is at a somewhat brisker pace, but when she begins to lie down on it, first by placing her right knee on the bed, then by leaning over and resting her hands on the pillow, both motions resume the 50-bmp pace. Christina holds this pose (Figure 6.13) before finishing her downward motion, resulting in one of the most dance-like motions in the scene. On the soundtrack, a nondiegetic song—which Mamoulian would later call a "Spanish symphony"[100]—plays, and few of Christina's movements are in direct synchronization with this music, which was presumably added in post-production. Yet Christina's movements still maintain a distinct—if unobtrusive—rhythm.

"My ambition as a director," Mamoulian said in 1934 when explaining his use of the on-set metronome in this scene, "is to convey the rhyme and cadence of poetry in pictorial images."[101] The scene is a continuation of Mamoulian's interest in

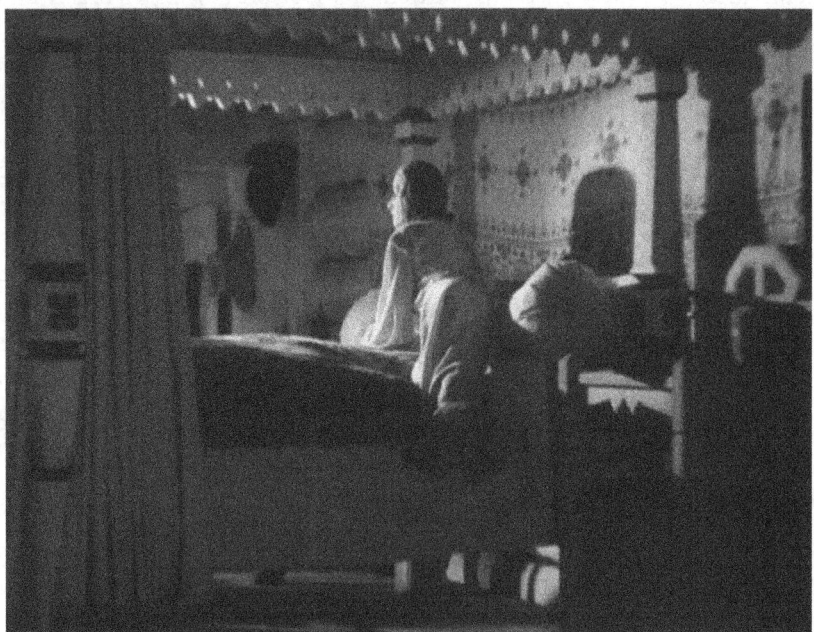

Figure 6.13 Likely to the beat of Mamoulian's on-set metronome, Garbo in *Queen Christina* gracefully pauses while lowering herself onto the bed.

stylizing moments surrounding love and sex, yet here, the main stylistic method is rhythmic control. Thanks in part to the duration and rhythms of Christina's actions, one can more vividly sense elements vital to Christina and to Garbo's persona: the importance she places on the love affair and the extent to which she flings herself into—and clings to—love. Christina's actions and their rhythms also call attention to the tactile qualities of a room that has been the venue of three days of sex. Her rhythmic movements as she contemplates and remembers her sex-filled adventure tie the love affair to a sense of poise and grace. Great love and great sex are thus rendered beautiful in a stylized manner that solved the film's major story problem and suited Mamoulian's artistic sensibilities.

As we have seen, however, the SRC did not share Mamoulian's belief in the beauty of nonmarital sex, and *Queen Christina*'s subsequent censorship path would again demonstrate that Mamoulian was toeing the edges of what the SRC would accept. Initially, victory for the studio seemed at hand. When the SRC viewed the final cut of *Queen Christina* on December 20, 1933, they remained extremely concerned with what they called "the bedroom scene."[102] The organization agreed, however, to withhold judgment until the New York censorship board examined the film, in spite of the fact that doing so once again violated industry policy. Unlike *The Song of Songs*, the New York censorship board agreed with the studio, approving the inn sequences without a change except for the elimination of Garbo's voice in bed in the chocolate scene (to remove the sense of her "material presence," according to an internal Paramount memo).[103]

Assuming that the SRC would concur with the New York censor's verdict, Paramount began playing *Queen Christina* in New York City.[104] Unfortunately, MGM appears not to have anticipated the impact that Joseph Breen—who would run the industry's self-censorship branch for the next two decades—would have on final negotiations with the SRC. Breen—tasked by Hays with enforcing the Production Code more strictly—became the official head of the SRC on January 1, 1934, just in time to lay down the gauntlet on *Queen Christina*. In a far harsher and more definitive letter than anything MGM had encountered on the project to date, Breen zeroed in on Mamoulian's handling of the bedroom scenes. Quoting the Production Code itself, Breen stated that these scenes made "sexual immorality . . . attractive and beautiful" and therefore constituted a "definite Code violation." Breen suggested that MGM eliminate everything from the maid unloosening Christina's boots two scenes earlier through early shots of the room-touching scene. Breen further decreed that in the room-touching segment, Garbo be kept entirely away from the bed, and especially not be shown "lying across the bed and fondling the pillow."[105]

Had Breen gotten his way, such alterations surely would have done major damage to the film on both an emotional and narrative-coherence level. The sequence was saved only when MGM appealed the case to the Hollywood Jury (which consisted of Hollywood producers Benjamin Kahane, Jesse Lasky, and Carl Laemmle Jr.), who sided with MGM over Breen.[106] Six months later, the Hollywood Jury would be abolished and Breen's reign as the head of the more stringent PCA would begin. Mamoulian won the battle on *Queen Christina*, but he would not win the war.

For the SRC, *Queen Christina* likely amounted to little more than another headache caused by a director intent upon ignoring instructions. Within Mamoulian's oeuvre, however, the film is significant for continuing to merge artistry, beauty, and sex while simultaneously offering a new formulation of sexual desire. Not only does the scene employ an unusual rhythmic approach to convey the beauties of love and sex, but Mamoulian's method also enables him to convey sexuality from a more cerebral—rather than flesh-based—perspective. Intrinsic to Christina's room touching is the act of processing and contemplating one's environment and experiences, an idea driven home especially by the fifteen-second extreme close-up of Christina's face as lays on the pillow and gazes at Don Antonio (Figure 6.14). This shot resonates with other close-ups in the film that denote Christina's strength of mind and inner life, including during a scene in which she verbally outmaneuvers an angry mob that has stormed her castle. The shot's most significant parallel, however, is with the famous image that concludes

Figure 6.14 Mamoulian's extreme close-up of the title character in *Queen Christina* during the room-touching scene marks her as a person with a rich inner life, an image and idea that resonate . . .

Figure 6.15 ... with the film's famous final shot.

Queen Christina. In a forty-five-second shot, the camera begins on Christina's full body as she sets sail for unknown waters before slowly tracking forward to ultimately frame Christina from just below her mouth to her forehead (Figure 6.15). Thanks to Garbo's blank expression—apparently Mamoulian's idea[107]—Christina's feelings remain somewhat ambiguous, but because of similar extreme close-ups at other points in the film, we are encouraged to read this final shot as a testament to Christina's intelligence, resilience, and self-sufficiency. Rather than focus on female undress or the male gaze, Mamoulian's stylized room-touching scene ties beauty, sexual desire, and longing to the mindset of a strong and powerful female character who leads a rich intellectual life.

Conclusion

After *Queen Christina*, Mamoulian's films would never again portray sexual desire or experience in such a stylistically vivid manner. *We Live Again* (1934) features a "seduction" scene, but the film was actually praised by the PCA as "a model for the proper treatment of illicit sex in pictures."[108] *Becky Sharp*'s (1935) pointed sex references had been tempered by Breen prior to Mamoulian's arrival to the project, and there is little evidence that Mamoulian tried to bring them forward again. The PCA raised a bit of concern over *The Gay Desperado* (1936), but only for its suggestions that gangster movies encouraged a life of crime. *Golden Boy* (1939) worried the PCA because of its indications that Lorna was Moody's "kept woman," but this was easily addressed before shooting began by having the duo reduce their amount of physical contact. The major censorship concern in *Blood and Sand* (1941) involved the level of graphic detail for the bullfight (see chapter 5), while *Rings on Her Fingers* (1942) contained only small issues pertaining to dialogue and wardrobe—matters that Mamoulian appears not to have been involved with. *High, Wide, and Handsome* (1937), *The Mark of Zorro* (1940), and *Silk Stockings* (1957) faced no significant problems.[109]

Only during the barroom scene in Mamoulian's penultimate film, *Summer Holiday* (1948), did Mamoulian return to the subject matter and cinematic flourishes that resembled his "Pre-Code" days. As discussed in chapter 5, the scene centers on inexperienced, college-bound Richard (Mickey Rooney), who spends time drinking in a dive bar with a "chorus girl" named Belle (Marilyn Maxwell). In a manner reminiscent of Ivy's striptease, Mamoulian films a good portion of the scene from Richard's optical point of view. Yet unlike in the "Pre-Code" era, Mamoulian followed Breen's instructions for handling this scene to the letter. Breen, in addition to having the filmmakers remove suggestions that Belle was a prostitute, closely monitored the actions and physical contact in this scene, insisting that "care" be taken when Belle removes a cigarette from her stocking, that Belle not sit in Richard's lap, and that no "passionate, prolonged, or open-mouthed kissing" occur.[110] In accordance with these instructions, the camera stays in long shot when Belle bares her leg to get a cigarette, presents kisses lasting no more than a few seconds, and never shows Belle sitting in Richard's lap. Mamoulian's days of shooting segments without the approval of the censors and winning them over in post-production were over.

Perhaps surprisingly, it was mainly on the stage where Mamoulian was able to continue his explorations of subjectively rendered sexual desire. *Oklahoma!* (1943) contains a famed ballet dream sequence that explores Laurey's complex sexual desires, but the sequence was arranged and choreographed by Agnes de Mille, not Mamoulian. Mamoulian's follow-up play, *Sadie Thompson* (1944), however, pulled directly from his early sound-era interests. Adapted from Somerset Maugham's 1921 short story "Rain," Mamoulian, who co-wrote the book for *Sadie Thompson* with Howard Dietz, crafted a subjective and sexualized dream number from the perspective of upright missionary Davidson to mark the crucial moment when he succumbs to his sexual desire for Sadie. During this moment in Mamoulian's March 1944 copy of the script, Mamoulian penciled in a "temptation" ballet (later titled "The Mountains of Nebraska") that appears in a later version of the play script.[111] In a description that closely resembles Mamoulian's writing style, the play script indicates that Davidson's sexual desire in the number is first signaled by Davidson stopping near the string curtain that serves as the door to Sadie's room. These strings, according to the play script, "sway a little, and parting them in the middle a long woman's leg appears. It is a stylization of Sadie's leg with the red laces of her shoe holding it from ankle to thigh in fiery circles." A bit later, an apparent instance of nudity is included, as the audience discovers, "with Davidson that, instead of the South Seas panorama [in the background], it is the breast-like hills of Nebraska that are seen through the veranda. Over the edge of the window sill, two arms appear, followed by the torso of a woman with her head bent down, her hair covers her face so that only arms and breasts glisten in the dark."[112] Even when lacking a camera that could force audiences into the optical viewpoint of a character, Mamoulian still found ways on the stage to insert audiences into the aroused headspace of a central character.

Though Mamoulian's adult-oriented brand of "Pre-Code" filmmaking would prove impossible for filmmakers to imitate during the next few decades, there is evidence that other early 1930s filmmakers initially followed in Mamoulian's footsteps. Mamoulian's influence seems clearest in the stylistic approach taken by Stephen Roberts's *The Story of Temple Drake* (1933), which remains one of the most audacious films made within the Hollywood studio system.[113] Based on William Faulkner's controversial 1931 novel *Sanctuary*, *The Story of Temple Drake* most closely echoes Mamoulian's work in its articulation of sexual desire via subjective camerawork and head-on shots. Fifteen minutes into the film, Temple Drake (Miriam Hopkins again) and her escort lie on the ground dazed after their car crashes in the remote woods. In a point-of-view shot from the perspective of a man we learn is a gangster/bootlegger named Trigger (Jack La Rue), we see the bloodied escort and then Drake illuminated by Trigger's flashlight. The camera then tilts down to take in Drake's legs in a manner similar to Mamoulian's handling of Ivy's striptease. Here, however, the moment is configured as disturbing rather than playful because Drake is not a willing participant—at first, she is not even aware of being looked at. The point-of-view shot thus characterizes Trigger as an invasive creep and signals that Drake is now in constant sexual danger.

During two later scenes in which Drake lives with Trigger in what is implied to be a brothel, Roberts conveys sexual desire—and possibly Drake's increasing entrapment—through strikingly close-range, head-on, subjective shots that echo how Mamoulian had shot a similar scene with Ivy and Hyde. The closest-range shot is reserved for the moment when Trigger is at his most forceful and menacing, telling Drake, "You're going to stay. You'll like it here." As with *Dr. Jekyll and Mr. Hyde*, such shots ask the audience to vividly participate in an uncomfortable engagement with male force and sexual desire.

Ultimately, Mamoulian's early 1930s films occupy an odd place in the history of censorship and sex in the cinema. Their risqué techniques do not directly anticipate more heavily censored filmmaking in the next few decades, but they also do not anticipate the situation in the late 1960s and early 1970s, when the arrival of a tiered ratings system catalyzed a rapid shift toward direct representations of nudity and simulated sex. Indeed, the depictions of sex and nudity during these years would bother Mamoulian far more than Breen's PCA enforcement ever did, perhaps because they reminded him of the direct sexual displays of burlesque that he abhorred. A lack of stringent censorship, Mamoulian complained in the early 1970s, has resulted in boring sex scenes that amount to "watching naked people engaging in gymnastics." "I object to them," Mamoulian maintained, "not because of their so-called immorality . . . [but] because they are so obvious and bloody dull."[114] In his early 1930s work, Mamoulian modeled a form of cinema that was indirect yet pointed, that teased rather than showed, and that employed devices distinct to cinema to alternatively condemn crass sexual exploitation, maximize eroticism, or vividly render the glories of sexual experience.

Conclusion

Mamoulian's Legacy

After failing to complete two straight films—*Porgy and Bess* (1959) and *Cleopatra* (1963)—Mamoulian would never again direct a movie. In interviews he granted in the 1960s and 1970s, Mamoulian always presented himself as an active director, regularly considering and developing projects. In truth, however, Mamoulian's role within the film world had transitioned from filmmaker to interviewee. This role proved important, however. With auteur-based criticism on the rise, the 1960s and 1970s served as an opportunity for studio-era Hollywood directors to define their importance to cinema and mold their legacies in the history books. Alfred Hitchcock's interviews with François Truffaut, which resulted in the landmark publication *Hitchcock/Truffaut* (1966), were exemplary of how a director might shape one's stature by speaking extensively about themes and techniques. Mamoulian had already trumpeted his filmmaking approaches in interviews and articles from the 1930s onward, but in the 1960s, 1970s, and 1980s, he increasingly fixated on technical innovations and supposed "firsts": the first to move the camera in the sound era, the first to use two microphones, the first to re-record soundtracks, the first to use voice-overs as memories, the first to use synthetic sound. Implicitly, he also presented his ideas about narrative-number integration, color scripting, painting-based color, and color-based subjectivity as though they had no precursor.

The end result has surely not been what Mamoulian intended. As discussed in the Introduction, though early film historians reproduced many of Mamoulian's claims, over time Mamoulian's fixations on technical innovations rebounded on him, with scholars reducing him to *only* his experiments and casting him as a director of novel techniques who otherwise failed to leave a lasting or sophisticated mark on cinema.

This book has attempted to bring forward a more nuanced perspective. By focusing closely on Mamoulian's theories, his films, archival materials, and the filmmaking contexts within which he worked, I have tried to better clarify the level of innovation he brought to the American film industry and reassess the historical significance of his work. In many cases, Mamoulian's contributions have proved more complex than either his interviews or subsequent film histories have acknowledged. Mamoulian's innovations and methods are often best understood not in terms of "firsts," but rather as prescient and conceptually rigorous explorations of film's potential as an art form. Mamoulian was not the first to move the camera in the sound era, but the frequency of those movements during direct-dialogue scenes, their duration, their level of expressivity, and their patterning across a film were highly unusual and announced the camera's expressive potential at a time when cinema seemed beholden to theater. Mamoulian was not the first to utilize two microphones or re-recording, but his use of these technologies showed a prioritization of film sound as a constructed product that would prove to be long-lasting. Mamoulian *was* likely among the very first to use a voice-over memory in an American film, but the device is arguably just as important as a demonstration of the value of overtly constructed, subjective sound. It is difficult to find an instance prior to *Dr. Jekyll and Mr. Hyde* of the post-production mixing of sounds that do not occur in one's external environment, but the device is perhaps most notable as a conceptual prototype of world making found in later cinema. Mamoulian was hardly the only person working in theater or film who sought tighter narrative-number integration, but his methods for doing so were creative and intricate. Mamoulian was not the first to utilize color scripting, but his use of color filmmaking to emulate painting and construct subjective experiences was quite unusual. Through these methods, he offered key models for color control and pointed to color cinema's ability to incorporate other art forms *and* offer uniquely cinematic experiences.

This book has also explored a variety of concerns and methods that have less commonly been tied to Mamoulian's work yet still anticipated subsequent filmmaking in important ways. In the musical genre, Mamoulian was among the earliest filmmakers to present a musical number that resided exclusively in the headspace of a character in *Love Me Tonight*, and his interest in subjective numbers would persist in *High, Wide and Handsome* and—especially—the barroom sequence in *Summer Holiday*. Mamoulian was also notable for laying bare the performer-viewer dynamics that would come to characterize the popular show-musical subgenre, and he directed pioneering work on both stage and screen that anticipated the heyday of the folk musical in the late 1940s and 1950s. Additionally, Mamoulian was a key figure in the creation of sexually risqué filmmaking under censorship. Other concerns—such as making statues "talk" and his intensive focus on rhythmic stylization in a film like *Love Me Tonight*—are hardly part of standard practice today. They were notable at the time, however, and they offered models for filmmakers interested in expanding a director's arsenal of tools during a formative period of film history.

This study of Mamoulian has also stressed the intellectual coherency and consistency *behind* Mamoulian's work, a topic that has received little attention. Mamoulian directed in many genres, and his innovations occurred in a wide range of domains, but Mamoulian—in writing and in practice—was consistently driven by a singular desire to aggressively define cinema's potential as a great art form. Entering filmmaking during a transitional moment, Mamoulian regularly engaged in the fundamental process of *locating* what he saw as the essential tools of sound cinema and determining *how* those tools could be used to most palpably impact the spectator. All of Mamoulian's striking stylistic choices—including his reassertion of visual techniques like camera movement and rapid editing; his expressive soundtrack construction; his experiments with pacing and rhythm; his explorations of the potentials of show, fairy-tale, and folk musicals; his formulation of various color designs; and his use of cinematic techniques to explore sex and excite audiences—stemmed from an effort to identify vital cinematic tools and press hard on their expressive potential. These aims—and their frequent flashiness—enabled Mamoulian to erect a foundation upon which many later filmmakers, including auteurs who are better known than Mamoulian today, could build.

As I have indicated throughout the book, Mamoulian's precise level of influence on later film style and technique remains difficult to pinpoint. Mamoulian was not the only filmmaker whose work anticipated later practices, and I have noted preceding or parallel examples throughout the book that may have been equally or more influential. Still, the resonances between Mamoulian's efforts and later cinema remain striking. Many 1950s musicals, as we have seen, featured experiments with cinematic form that echoed Mamoulian's prior work, with filmmakers like Vincente Minnelli and Gene Kelly overtly acknowledging this debt. In modern cinema, the frequency of camera movement has only increased, multitrack sound recording and post-production re-recording remain standard practice, voice-overs—including those tied to memories—are common, and sound technicians now delight in mixing together unusual or altered sounds to build new science-fiction and fantasy worlds. Though musicals are no longer the bread-and-butter Hollywood genre they once were, the most recent musical Best Picture winner—*Chicago* (2002)—grounded its numbers in subjectively rendered fantasies. This is not to say that Mamoulian remains a direct influence on these films and practices. It does, however, mean that Mamoulian helped lay down a set of sound-cinema ideas and techniques that continue to be harnessed to a wide array of popular American films today.

In the end, it is the conceptual *ideas* behind Mamoulian's innovations—and their ramifications for cinema as an art form—that probably matter the most. At the end of a 1972 conversation at the Center for Advanced Film Studies at the American Film Institute, Mamoulian offered the following advice to aspiring filmmakers in the audience:

> Don't ever imitate. . . . What makes a filmmaker is . . . individuality [and] uniqueness. You don't want to be like anyone else. You can learn nothing from

me or from any other director. What you can profit by are some basic artistic principles. If something I believe in hits a responsive chord in you—let's say rhythm—use it. But use it your own way. When you get an "insane" idea, if you can theoretically justify it, do it. Don't back out. Do it, because it's going to be the best thing in the picture.[1]

Perhaps more than any other recorded statement, Mamoulian's advice encapsulates his importance to film history. Mamoulian's specific innovations *were* unusual, and thus warrant close attention. Yet his most significant achievement was the salient advancement—in both theory and practice—of a promising, flexible, and enduring set of principles that spoke to cinema's potential as a uniquely impactful art form. By understanding Mamoulian's theories, his films, and the context within which he worked, we gain nothing less than a clearer picture of the stylistic history of American sound cinema.

APPENDIX 1

Completed Films Directed by Mamoulian

Applause (Paramount, 1929)
City Streets (Paramount, 1931)
Dr. Jekyll and Mr. Hyde (Paramount, 1931)
Love Me Tonight (Paramount, 1932)
The Song of Songs (Paramount, 1933)
Queen Christina (MGM, 1933)
We Live Again (Samuel Goldwyn/United Artists, 1934)
Becky Sharp (RKO, 1935)
The Gay Desperado (Pickford-Lasky/United Artists, 1936)
High, Wide and Handsome (Paramount, 1937)
Golden Boy (Columbia, 1939)
The Mark of Zorro (Fox, 1940)
Blood and Sand (Fox, 1941)
Rings on Her Fingers (Fox, 1942)
Summer Holiday (MGM, 1948)
Silk Stockings (MGM, 1957)

APPENDIX 2

Plays Directed by Mamoulian

* This list does not include plays that failed to move beyond try-out performances, or later revivals that he also directed. Source: Mark Spergel, *Reinventing Reality: The Art and Life of Rouben Mamoulian* (Metuchen, NJ: Scarecrow Press, 1993).

London
The Beating at the Door (1922)

Rochester, NY
Rigoletto – Act III (1923)
Faust – Prison Scene (1923)
The Barber of Seville – Act II (1924)
Volga Boatmen's Song – Movie Prologue (1924)
Tannhäuser – Act III (1924)
Romeo and Juliet – Act I (1924)
The Queen of Spades – Scenes (1924)
Shanewis (1924)
H.M.S. Pinafore – Act I (1924)
The Queen of Hearts – Movie Prologue (1925)
Faust – Act III (1925)
A Bit of Erin – Movie Prologue (1925)
Carmen (1925)
The Prince Goes Hunting – Movie Prologue (1925)
Aida – Scenes (1925)
Romeo and Juliet – Scenes (1925)
The Pirates of Penzance (1925)
Prologue to the Iron Horse – Movie Prologue (1925)
A Pompeian Afternoon – Movie Prologue (1925)
The Boastful Braggart – Movie Prologue (1925)
The Spectre in Bed – Movie Prologue (1925)
A Serenade in Porcelain – Movie Prologue (1925)
Gems from the Merry Widow – Movie Prologue (1926)
Sister Beatrice (1926)
Pictures in Melody – Movie Prologue (1926)
Carmen – Scenes (1926)
A Night at the Inn – Movie Prologue (1926)
Maytime in Kew – Movie Prologue (1926)
The Game of Love – Movie Prologue (1926)
The Count of Luxembourg (1926)
The Flute of Krishna – Movie Prologue (1926)
Then and Now – Movie Prologue (1926)
A Corner in Spain – Movie Prologue (1926)

A Dream in a Wax Museum – Movie Prologue (1926)
A Forest Episode – Movie Prologue (1926)
The Phonograph of Tomorrow – Movie Prologue (1926)

Theatre Guild School – Scarborough, New York, and New York City
Enter Madame (1926)
Clarence (1926)
He Who Gets Slapped (1926)
Seven Keys to Baldpate (1926)

New York City
Porgy (1927)
Marco Millions (1928)
These Modern Women (1928)
Congai (1928)
Wings over Europe (1928)
The Game of Love and Death (1929)
R.U.R. (Rossum's Universal Robots) (1930)
A Month in the Country (1930)
Die glückliche Hand (The Hand of Fate) (1930)
A Farewell to Arms (1930)
Solid South (1930)
Porgy and Bess (1935)
Oklahoma! (1943)
Sadie Thompson (1944)
Carousel (1945)
St. Louis Woman (1946)
Leaf and Bough (1949)
Lost in the Stars (1949)
Arms and the Girl (1950)

APPENDIX 3

Additional Films Consulted

1918
Carmen
Eyes of the Mummy, The
I Don't Want to Be a Man

1919
Doll, The
Oyster Princess, The
Madame DuBarry (aka *Passion*)

1920
Anna Boleyn (aka *Deception*)
Dr. Jekyll and Mr. Hyde
Sumurun

1921
Wildcat, The

1922
Blood and Sand
Loves of Pharoah, The

1924
Last Laugh, The
Marriage Circle, The

1926
Flesh and the Devil
So This Is Paris
Son of the Sheik, The
Temptress, The
Torrent

1927
Jazz Singer, The
Love
7th Heaven
Sunrise
Student Prince in Old Heidelberg, The

1928
Four Sons
Hangman's House
Lights of New York, The
Mysterious Lady, The

Sally
Singing Fool, The
Street Angel
Wild Orchids
Woman of Affairs, A

1929
Alibi
Berth Marks
Blackmail
Broadway
Broadway Babies
Broadway Melody, The
Bulldog Drummond
Canary Murder Case, The
Cocoanuts, The
Coquette
Dance of Life, The
Disraeli
Eternal Love
Flying Fool
Glorifying the American Girl
Hallelujah!
Hell's Heroes
Hoose-Gow, The
In Old Arizona
Kiss, The
Last of Mrs. Cheyney, The
Letter, The
Love Parade, The
Madame X
Marianne
Men o' War
Perfect Day
Rio Rita
Romance
Sally
Saturday Night Kid, The
Single Standard, The
Shakedown, The
Sunny Side Up
Taming of the Shrew, The
They Go Boom!
Trespasser, The
Unaccustomed as We Are
Untamed
Vagabond Lover, The
Virginian, The
Weary River
Wild Party, The

APPENDIX 3   257

1930
All Quiet on the Western Front
Animal Crackers
Anna Christie
Big Boy
Big House, The
Big Trail, The
Billy the Kid
Bishop Murder Case, The
Blue Angel, The
Check and Double Check
Cuckoos, The
Danger Lights
Dawn Patrol, The
Divorcee, The
Dixiana
Doughboys
Free and Easy
Golden Dawn
Hell's Angels
Madam Satan
Mammy
Min and Bill
Moby Dick
Monte Carlo
Morocco
Redemption
Romance
Show Girl in Hollywood
Under a Texas Moon
Under the Roofs of Paris
Unholy Three, The
Way for a Sailor
Whoopee!

1931
Cimarron
Dishonored
Dracula
Easiest Way, The
For Us, Liberty!
Frankenstein
Front Page, The
Inspiration
Le Million
Little Caesar
Mata Hari
Possessed
Public Enemy, The
Sin of Madelon Claudet, The

Smiling Lieutenant, The
Squaw Man, The
Strangers May Kiss
Susan Lenox: Her Fall and Rise

1932
As You Desire Me
Blonde Venus
Call Her Savage
Grand Hotel
Greeks Had a Word for Them, The
One Hour with You
Red Dust
Red-Headed Woman
Scarface
Shanghai Express
Sign of the Cross, The
Strange Interlude
Trouble in Paradise

1933
Another Language
Baby Face
Bed of Roses
Blood Money
Christopher Strong
Female
Hallelujah, I'm a Bum!
I'm No Angel
Ladies They Talk About
Melody Cruise
She Done Him Wrong
Story of Temple Drake, The

1934
Flirtation Walk
Gay Divorcee, The

1935
Ah, Wilderness!
Little Colonel, The
Mississippi
Shipmates Forever
Top Hat

1936
Captain January
Garden of Allah, The
Lloyds of London
Pigskin Parade
Ramona

Rose Marie
San Francisco
Show Boat
Swing Time
Trail of the Lonesome Pine, The

1937
Nothing Sacred
Snow White and the Seven Dwarfs
Star Is Born, A

1938
Adventures of Robin Hood, The
Adventures of Tom Sawyer, The
Alexander's Ragtime Band
Goldwyn Follies, The
In Old Chicago
Kentucky
Marie Antoinette
Sweethearts
You and Me

1939
Dodge City
Drums along the Mohawk
Gone with the Wind
Gulliver's Travels
Jesse James
Little Princess, The
Ninotchka
Private Lives of Elizabeth and Essex, The
Swanee River
Wizard of Oz, The

1940
Irene
Maryland
Northwest Passage
Return of Frank James, The
Thief of Bagdad, The

1941
That Night in Rio
Western Union

1944
Cover Girl
Lady in the Dark
Meet Me in St. Louis
Rains Came, The
Up in Arms

1945
Where Do We Go from Here?
Yolanda and the Thief
Ziegfeld Follies, The

1946
Duel in the Sun
Harvey Girls, The

1947
Black Narcissus

1948
Pirate, The
Red Shoes, The

1949
On the Town

1951
American in Paris, An
Tales of Hoffmann, The

1952
Singin' in the Rain

1953
Band Wagon, The

1955
It's Always Fair Weather

Notes

Introduction

1. William Stull, "Amateur Movie Making," *American Cinematographer*, August 1932, 44.
2. Mark Spergel, *Reinventing Reality: The Art and Life of Rouben Mamoulian* (Metuchen, NJ: Scarecrow Press, 1993), 171–72.
3. Anon, "Through the Editor's Finder," *American Cinematographer*, June 1941, 271.
4. Arthur Knight, *The Liveliest Art: A Panoramic History of the Movies* (New York: New English Library, 1957), 159.
5. The auteur theory never congealed as an entirely unified concept, but those who ascribed to it generally fixated on thematic and stylistic patterns. For further discussion, see Andrew Sarris, "Notes on the Auteur Theory in 1962," in *Film Theory and Criticism*, 7th ed., ed. Leo Braudy and Marshall Cohen (New York: Oxford University Press, 2009), 451–54; and Peter Wollen, "The Auteur Theory," in ibid., 455–70.
6. Andrew Sarris, *The American Cinema: Directors and Directions, 1929–1968* (New York: Octagon Books, 1982), 160.
7. For Mamoulian biographies, see Spergel, *Reinventing Reality*, and David Luhrssen, *Mamoulian: Life on Stage and Screen* (Lexington: University Press of Kentucky, 2013). The only book-length study of Mamoulian's films is Tom Milne, *Mamoulian* (London: Thames & Hudson, 1969). For a book-length consideration of Mamoulian's contributions to *Porgy and Bess*, see Joseph Horowitz, *"On My Way": The Untold Story of Rouben Mamoulian, George Gershwin, and "Porgy and Bess"* (New York: W. W. Norton, 2013).
8. For an assessment of "Great Man" historiographies and their place in film history, see Robert C. Allen and Douglas Gomery, *Film History: Theory and Practice* (New York: Alfred A. Knopf, 1985), 110–13.
9. Based on Spergel's careful research, it is likely that Mamoulian traveled with his mother and sister so that his mother could perform in her theatre troupe in Paris. The likely duration was two years (*Reinventing Reality*, 25).
10. Spergel, *Reinventing Reality*, 35.
11. Rouben Mamoulian, "Mamoulian First Used Camera at Eastman School, He Recalls," *Democrat and Chronicle* (Rochester, NY), February 11, 1934.
12. Much of the information from this paragraph draws from Spergel, *Reinventing Reality*, 9–36.
13. For a discussion of the controversy in the 1950s, see Spergel, *Reinventing Reality*, 225.
14. Paramount Pictures contract, February 27, 1928, Subject File, Paramount Pictures, Box 190, RMP.

15. Rouben Mamoulian, interview by Steven Greenberg, T2/P43.
16. Spergel, *Reinventing Reality*, 171–72.
17. Ibid., 145.
18. Ibid., 151–52.
19. Ibid., 155.
20. Ibid., 167.
21. The one-year, two-film contract was signed on October 28, 1940, and can be found in Subject File, Twentieth Century–Fox Film Corp., Box 200, RMP.
22. These directorial offers by Zanuck to Mamoulian can be found in Subject File, Twentieth Century–Fox Film Corp., Box 200, RMP. Zanuck vents his frustration at Mamoulian's refusal in Zanuck to Mamoulian, July 5, 1941, and Zanuck to Mamoulian, October 20, 1941. Both letters appear in Subject File, Twentieth Century–Fox Film Corp., Box 200, RMP.
23. W. M. Goetz to Mamoulian, August 25, 1941, Subject File, Twentieth Century–Fox Film Corp., Box 200, RMP.
24. Daryl Zanuck to Lew Schreiber, May 1, 1944, Subject File, Twentieth Century–Fox Film Corp., Box 200, RMP.
25. Though Mamoulian had clashed with Rodgers and Hammerstein on *Oklahoma!* in particular, he was friends with both men throughout the 1950s (see General Correspondence, Oscar Hammerstein, Box 41, RMP and General Correspondence, Richard Rodgers, Box 48, RMP). It seems unlikely they blocked him from directing the films.
26. The *Porgy and Bess* saga was widely reported on by the trade press. A synoptic account can be found in Spergel, *Reinventing Reality*, 220–28.
27. "Viv" (Mamoulian's personal secretary) to Rouben and Azadia Mamoulian, January 20, 1961, Employees, Box 7, RMP.
28. Lasky to Mamoulian, October 24, 1942. Lasky to Mamoulian, November 13, 1942. Lasky to Mamoulian, November 19, 1942. Lasky to Mamoulian, February 2, 1943. All four letters are in General Correspondence, Jesse Lasky, Box 44, RMP.

Chapter 1

1. Jack Stinnett, "New Yorker at Large," *Enquirer* (Cincinnati, OH), August 11, 1937, 1.
2. Rouben Mamoulian, interview by Steven Greenberg, T3/P121.
3. Ibid. Rouben Mamoulian, Columbia University oral history, 44.
4. Rouben Mamoulian, "Bernhardt versus Duse," *Ararat*, September 1957.
5. One first sees this tendency in 1939 when Mamoulian was invited to attend a course titled "History of the Motion Picture" at Columbia University and talk specifically about his own films. Though he expressed reluctance at first, the moments he discussed were those that would become staples of his later interviews: his "invention" of two-track sound recording in *Applause*, the voice-over in *City Street*, synthetic sound in *Dr. Jekyll and Mr. Hyde*, and the slow track in using multiple diffusions for the final shot in *Queen Christina* (Mamoulian, "The Art of Films," lecture, December 6, 1939).

By the mid-1960s, when Mamoulian's historical legacy was at stake, he talked far more frequently about his innovations and no longer professed any reluctance to do so—indeed, he would often introduce them in interviews without being asked.

6. Mark Spergel, *Reinventing Reality: The Art and Life of Rouben Mamoulian* (Metuchen, NJ: Scarecrow Press, 1993), 12.
7. Ibid., 9–36.
8. Ibid., 10.
9. Ibid., 10.
10. Rouben Mamoulian, interview by William Becvar, Tape 1, p. 6.
11. Joseph Horowitz, *"On My Way": The Untold Story of Rouben Mamoulian, George Gershwin, and "Porgy and Bess"* (New York: W. W. Norton, 2013), 10–13.
12. Vahktangov, for instance, was amazed by what Stanislavski did with *Twelve Night*, a 1917 First Studio production that broke the fourth wall. I am indebted to Sharon Carnicke for this information.
13. For considerations of Mamoulian's possible intellectual debt to Vakhtangov and Stanislavski, see Spergel, *Reinventing Reality*, 33–41, and Horowitz, *"On My Way,"* 10–12, 81. For discussions of Stanislavski's non-realist efforts, see Sharon Marie Carnicke, "Rethinking 'Stanislavskian' Directing," in *The Great European Stage Directors, Volume 1: Antoine, Stanislavski, Saint Denis*, ed. Peta Tait (London: Methuen Drama, 2019), 91–111; and Sharon Marie Carnicke and David Rosen, "A Singer Prepares: Stanislavski and Opera," in *The Routledge Companion to Stanislavsky*, ed. R. Andrew White (London: Routledge, 2014), 120–38. More generally, I am indebted to Carnicke for helping me think through Mamoulian's Russian influences.
14. Horowitz, *"On My Way,"* 11.
15. Rouben Mamoulian, "The Essence of Theatrical Art," lecture, 1923–1924. For another analysis of Mamoulian's theater writings during his Rochester years, see Horowitz, *"On My Way,"* 79.
16. For a useful summation of the components of the medium-specificity argument and critiques that can be leveled against it, see Noël Carroll, "The Specificity of Media in the Arts," *Journal of Aesthetic Education* 19.4 (1985): 5–20.
17. Rouben Mamoulian, "Mamoulian First Used Camera at Eastman School, He Recalls," *Democrat and Chronicle* (Rochester, NY), February 11, 1934.
18. For instance, Arnheim—an anti-realist who favored expression over representation—first published his *Film as Art* book in 1932 (Arnheim, *Film as Art*), while Balázs, who argued that film should capitalize on its uniqueness, was active as a theorist in the 1920s (see Balázs, *Early Film Theory*, which contains two of his books: *Visible Man* ([1924] and *Spirit of Film* [1930]). Both writers, however, were at this time publishing in German. My thanks to Daniel Wiegand for his thoughts on Balázs.
19. Rouben Mamoulian, "The Use and Abuse of Perambulation," lecture, July 19, 1932.
20. For one of many examples, see Rouben Mamoulian, "The World's Latest Fine Art," *Cinema Arts* 1 (1936): 22.
21. Mamoulian, "The Art of Films," 9.
22. Rouben Mamoulian, "Common Sense and Camera Angles," *American Cinematographer* 12.10 (February 1932): 9.
23. Rouben Mamoulian, *Dialogue on Film* (1972), 19.

24. Rouben Mamoulian, "Visual Anti-Realism" (July 1938).
25. Mamoulian, "The Art of Films," 8.
26. Mamoulian, "Common Sense and Camera Angles," 9.
27. Mamoulian, *Dialogue on Film*, 30.
28. David Bordwell, Janet Staiger, and Kristin Thompson, *The Classical Hollywood Cinema: Film Style and Mode of Production to 1960* (New York: Columbia University Press, 1985), 25–27.
29. Rouben Mamoulian, "Time for Audiences to Do Their Part," August 3, 1965, 4.
30. Stephen Prince, *Classical Film Violence: Designing and Regulating Brutality in Hollywood, 1930–1968* (New Brunswick, NJ: Rutgers University Press, 2003), 109.
31. Mamoulian, "*Dr. Jekyll and Mr. Hyde*," 41.
32. Burns Mantle, *Porgy* review, *New York Daily News*, October 11, 1927, *Porgy* file, RMP.
33. J. Brooks Atkinson, "Negro Lithography," *New York Times*, October 11, 1927, *Porgy* file, RMP.
34. Alexander Woollcott, "The Guild's Curtain Rises," *New York World*, October 11, 1927, *Porgy* file, RMP.
35. Alan Dale, "Play of Negro Life Rare and Colorful Gem," *New York American*, October 11, 1927, *Porgy* file, RMP.
36. Mamoulian, *Dialogue on Film*, 18–19.
37. Annotation in the October 10, 1927, *Porgy* playscript, *Porgy* file, RMP.
38. J. Brooks Atkinson, review of *Marco Millions*, *New York Times*, January 10, 1928, *Marco Millions* file, RMP.
39. Rouben Mamoulian, interview by Bennet T. Oberstein, August 1973, 82. The light plot called for a spot that would shine so that the marching soldiers' shadows "show clearly and distinctly on the Left wall of the set" (Light Plot for *Congai*, *Congai* file, RMP).
40. Mamoulian was fond of saying that theater impresario Max Reinhardt saw the device, used it in a subsequent production, and gave Mamoulian credit for it. An entire article tying Mamoulian to the device can be found in a press clipping from the Lake Wales, Florida, *Daily* (*Porgy* file, RMP). Given Reinhardt's influence on the shadow-laden films of German Expressionism, however, it seems more plausible that Reinhardt influenced Mamoulian.
41. Mamoulian, "*Dr. Jekyll and Mr. Hyde*," 41.
42. Mamoulian, "The Art of Films," 57. Lucy Fischer points to this attribute of shadows in "*Applause*: The Visual and Acoustic Landscape," in *Film Sound: Theory and Practice*, ed. Elisabeth Weis and John Belton (New York: Columbia University Press, 1985), 235–36.
43. Mamoulian, *Dialogue on Film*, 8
44. Annotation in January 9, 1931, *City Streets* screenplay, *City Streets* file, RMP.
45. In the final planned script prior to initial director Lowell Sherman's death, the threat of war is indicated merely by an exterior shot of a small group of Napoleon's soldiers on a battlefield at sundown. Mamoulian crossed out this scene in his copy of the script and wrote the word "Napoleon" in its place—an indication of Mamoulian's intention to use shadow play to represent this military leader. Annotation in December 10, 1934, *Becky Sharp* screenplay, *Becky Sharp* file, RMP.

46. Rouben Mamoulian, interview with Anthony Slide, Anthony Slide collection, MHL.
47. Rouben Mamoulian, "Stage and Screen," unpublished article, 8.
48. For further discussion of Mamoulian's use of camera angles in *Applause*, see Fischer, "*Applause*," 185.
49. Mamoulian, interview by Greenberg, T1/P18.
50. Mamoulian, "The World's Latest Fine Art," 21.
51. Mamoulian, "Stage and Screen," 6.
52. Mamoulian, interview by Oberstein, 4.
53. Overtly asserting a directorial viewpoint, especially mid-scene, runs counter to the relatively low level of self-consciousness that Bordwell has argued typically occurs during such moments (Bordwell et al., *The Classical Hollywood Cinema*, 25–27).
54. Mamoulian, "The Use and Abuse of Perambulation," 6.
55. Mamoulian alludes to this function, albeit in a discussion of editing, in *Dialogue on Film*, 28.
56. Mamoulian, interview by Greenberg, T3/P137.
57. Mamoulian's markings also indicate that he contemplated an additional split screen in the film when Kitty calls burlesque manager Gus Finebaum and learns that her star is fading in burlesque. According to the marking, a horizontal wipe was to have been used to juxtapose Kitty and Gus. This annotation appears in the October 8, 1929, *Applause* screenplay, *Applause* file, RMP. The date is presumably inaccurate, since it coincides with the film's debut. This date appears on the first piece of paper in the archive folder, but the folder later contains a separate—and undated—cover for the screenplay. Simply for reference purposes, I will use the October 8 date throughout the book.
58. Mamoulian, "The Art of Films," 37.
59. Mamoulian was so invested in holding the split screen midway through that he originally wanted it to last far longer: whereas in the finished film the split screen lasts for only a few seconds, Mamoulian's notes indicate that he had at one point planned for it to extend until Hitch walks down the hall and approaches Kitty's room (October 8, 1929, *Applause* screenplay, *Applause* file, RMP).
60. Barry Salt, *Film Style and Technology: History and Analysis* (London: Starword, 1983), 155.
61. Ibid., 195.
62. Mamoulian, "The Art of Films," 54–55. Unsurprisingly, a Mamoulian annotation indicates that the filmmakers protected themselves by also shooting the transition via the dissolve that is written in the screenplay (annotation in October 8, 1929, *Applause* screenplay, *Applause* file, RMP).
63. Mamoulian, "The Arts of Films," 55.
64. Mamoulian once described this split screen as articulating a "dramatic confrontation" between Muriel and Ivy (Mamoulian, interview by Greenberg, T2/P65), and the confrontational aspect of this image is arguably fueled by the images' incompatibility.
65. Mamoulian, interview by Greenberg, T2/P60.
66. Mamoulian, "The World's Latest Fine Art," 21.
67. Bordwell et al., *The Classical Hollywood Cinema*, 4.

68. In a marginal note detailing a scene breakdown, Mamoulian wrote, "Dissolve from April's glass to Kitty's" (annotation in October 8, 1929 *Applause* screenplay, *Applause* file, RMP).
69. Annotation in undated *City Streets* script [Box 57, Folder 3], *City Streets* file, RMP.

Chapter 2

1. Rouben Mamoulian, *Dialogue on Film* (Interview with the American Film Institute, 1972), 33.
2. Richard Koszarski, "The Greatest Film Paramount Ever Made," *Film History* 15.4 (2003): 436.
3. Rouben Mamoulian, interview by John A. Gallagher and Marino A. Amoruco, 16.
4. Ibid.
5. Rouben Mamoulian, 1929 diary, RMP.
6. For details on microphones in the period, see Barry Salt, *Film Style and Technology: History and Analysis* (London: Starword, 1983), 229; and Rick Altman, "The Technology of the Voice, Part 1," *Iris* 3.1 (1985): 3–20. As a Western Electric licensee, Paramount would have presumably been using Western Electric's condenser microphone.
7. According to John Belton, the two major camera types—the Bell & Howard and the Mitchell—were silenced by so-called blimps in 1929 ("Awkward Transitions: Hitchcock's 'Blackmail' and the Dynamics of Early Film Sound," *Musical Quarterly* 83.2 [Summer 1999]: 229). However, not only do Mamoulian's descriptions of moving the camera for *Applause* indicate that the blimp was not yet in use at Astoria, but his cinematographer, George Folsey, is credited with developing a blimp six months after completing work on *Applause* (Koszarski, "The Greatest Film Paramount Ever Made," 439).
8. Crafton discusses the soundproof booth in *The Talkies: American Cinema's Transition to Sound, 1926–1931* (Berkeley: University of California Press, 1997), 230–31.
9. Belton, "Awkward Transitions," 231.
10. Michael Slowik, "Experiments in Early Sound Film Music: Strategies and Rerecording, 1928–1930," *American Music* 31.4 (2013): 450–74.
11. Lea Jacobs, "The Innovation of Re-Recording in the Hollywood Studios," *Film History: An International Journal* 24.1 (2012): 8.
12. For discussions of multiple-camera shooting, see David Bordwell, Janet Staiger, and Kristin Thompson, *The Classical Hollywood Cinema: Film Style and Mode of Production to 1960* (New York: Columbia University Press, 1985), 304–8; Belton, "Awkward Transitions," 230–31; and Crafton, *The Talkies*, 244–48.
13. Belton, "Awkward Transitions," 231.
14. Salt, *Film Style and Technology*, 229.
15. Crafton, *The Talkies*, 240–41; Salt, *Film Style and Technology*, 230.
16. Bordwell, Staiger, and Thompson, *The Classical Hollywood Cinema*, 302.

17. Rick Altman, "Afterword: A Baker's Dozen Terms for Sound Analysis," in *Sound Theory/Sound Practice*, ed. Altman (New York: Routledge, 1992), 251. Michel Chion discusses sync points in *Audio-Vision: Sound on Screen* (New York: Columbia University Press: 1994), 59.
18. Lea Jacobs, *Film Rhythm after Sound: Technology, Music, and Performance* (Berkeley: University of California Press, 2014), 110–11.
19. For a fuller discussion of how Hollywood saw the stage as an early model for its product, see Crafton, *The Talkies*, 69–70.
20. Ibid., 73–76.
21. Koszarski, "The Greatest Film Paramount Ever Made," 436–37.
22. Mamoulian, Columbia University oral history, 78.
23. Crafton, *The Talkies*, 74.
24. Ibid., 405.
25. Richard Koszarski, *Hollywood on the Hudson: Film and Television in New York from Griffith to Sarnoff* (New Brunswick, NJ: Rutgers University Press, 2008), 193.
26. Mamoulian discussed his dislike of multiple-camera shooting in Mamoulian, "The Art of Films" (lecture, December 6, 1939), 24–25.
27. The Paramount pressbook trumpeted *Applause*'s camera movements, asserting, "approximately eighty-five percent of the scenes in the picture are photographed in motion (Al Wilkie, "Highlights of Applause," *Applause* MPPDA PCA records, MHL). A *New York Times* article from September 1929 centered on Mamoulian's use of the moving camera ("Mamoulian's Camera," *New York Times*, September 22, 1929, 201). Recent scholars who have commented upon *Applause*'s camera movements include Lucy Fischer, "*Applause*: The Visual and Acoustic Landscape," in *Film Sound: Theory and Practice*, ed. Elisabeth Weis and John Belton (New York: Columbia University Press, 1985), 232–46; and Patrick Keating, *The Dynamic Frame: Camera Movement in Classical Hollywood* (New York: Columbia University Press, 2019), 69–70.
28. Keating, *The Dynamic Frame*, 15–54. This trend is also discussed in Bordwell, Staiger, and Thompson, *The Classical Hollywood Cinema*, 307.
29. Keating, *The Dynamic Frame*, 42, 59–61.
30. Theresa L. Geller, "Dorothy Arzner," *Senses of Cinema* 26 (May 2003).
31. *Broadway*, which gained considerable attention for its use of the crane in a sound film, features far more camera movement than the norm, but these movements appear to have occurred when direct sound was not in use.
32. Mamoulian stated that Folsey declared that the lullaby scene featured "the first trucking shot" (Mamoulian, *Dialogue on Film*, 13). In the early 1980s, Mamoulian began claiming credit for personally mounting wheels on the camera booth (Mamoulian, *The American Film Institute Seminar* [1981], 1TA/P6; Mamoulian, interview by Hargrave, 265; Mamoulian, interview by Gallagher and Amoruco, 16). Back when Mamoulian was still active in filmmaking, he offered more nuanced—and historically accurate—accounts (see Mamoulian, "The Art of Films," 24).
33. David Bordwell, "Camera Movement, the Coming of Sound, and the Classical Hollywood Style," in *Film: Historical-Theoretical Speculations*, ed. Ben Lawton and Janet Staiger (Pleasantville, NY: Redgrave Publishing, 1977), 29. Belton, "Awkward

Transitions," 228–29. Even the massive Warner Bros. "icebox" was mounted on wheels that could, in theory, be moved (with "cables dragging," as Crafton has pointed out [*The Talkies*, 230–31]).
34. Belton, "Awkward Transitions," 229.
35. Keating, *The Dynamic Frame*, 42.
36. Paramount released a pressbook for *Applause* calling the film an "entirely new type of screen entertainment," thanks largely to Mamoulian's "constant movement of the photographic recording instrument" (Al Wilkie, "Highlights of *Applause*," Paramount Pictures press sheets, MHL).
37. For an exception, see "Sound Perspective Used in 'Applause,'" *The Film Daily*, September 15, 1929, 10.
38. Rouben Mamoulian, "Visual Anti-Realism: The First in a Series of Papers Challenging the Realistic Conception of Art," July 1938, RMP.
39. Rouben Mamoulian, "The Psychology of Sound: The Second in a Series of Papers Challenging the Realistic Conception of Art," July 1938, RMP, 2.
40. Ibid., 3–4.
41. Ibid., 4. The underlining is in the original source.
42. Ibid., 11.
43. Ibid., 11.
44. For a thorough account of popular song's dominant role in the early sound era, see Katherine Spring, *Saying It with Songs: Popular Music and the Coming of Sound to Hollywood Cinema* (New York: Oxford University Press, 2013).
45. Crafton, *The Talkies*, 271.
46. Examples of the movement toward constructed—rather than directly recorded—sound after *Applause* include the increased use of the boom mic instead of microphone placement based on camera position (Altman, "Sound Space," in *Sound Theory/Sound Practice*, ed. Altman [New York: Routledge, 1992], 52–53) and the increased use of re-recording throughout the 1930s (Jacobs, "The Innovation of Re-Recording").
47. Annotation in October 8, 1929, *Applause* screenplay, *Applause* file, RMP.
48. Rouben Mamoulian, interview by William Hare, 127. In earlier interviews, Mamoulian did not specify when he recorded Kitty's track (Mamoulian, "The Art of Films," 26–27; Mamoulian, Columbia University oral history, 79–81).
49. Mamoulian offers a particularly detailed description of the recording method for the lullaby scene in Mamoulian, Columbia University oral history, 79–80.
50. I am grateful to Lea Jacobs and Martin Barnier for helping me work through the technical logistics of this scene.
51. Mamoulian, Columbia University oral history, 80.
52. To name just a few examples, in a single shot in *In Old Arizona* (January 1929), Tonia and Mickey speak and then kiss in the foreground before Tonia's cook appears a considerable distance in the background and scolds them. The sounds of all three voices are direct and intelligible, meaning that multiple microphones would have been hung. In *Alibi* (April 1929) police officers, speaking into three different telephone speakers, put out a description for a wanted murderer. Each voice sounds closely

miked, making it highly likely that recording microphones are located in all three telephone receivers.
53. Mamoulian would later claim that his use of re-recording was unprecedented. See, for instance, Mamoulian, Columbia University oral history, 82.
54. Jacobs, "The Innovation of Re-Recording in the Hollywood Studios," 12.
55. Ibid., 10–11.
56. Koszarski points to this alternative recording method in "The Greatest Film Paramount Ever Made," 439.
57. Jacobs, "The Innovation of Re-Recording in the Hollywood Studios," 12.
58. Mamoulian discusses the medium-specific nature of his sound approach to the lullaby scene in Mamoulian, "The Art of Films" 25–27.
59. Jacobs, "The Innovation of Re-Recording in the Hollywood Studios," 6.
60. Rick Altman, with McGraw Jones and Sonia Tatroe, "Inventing the Cinema Soundtrack: Hollywood's Multiplane Sound System," in *Music and Cinema*, ed. James Buhler, Caryl Flinn, and David Neumeyer (Hanover, NH: University Press of New England, 2000), 351–52; Altman, "Establishing Sound," *Cinémas* 24.1 (2013): 28.
61. Fischer, "*Applause*," 244–45. A 1929 account stated that "sound perspective" was attained in "an important story sequence" by hanging microphones in two different parts of the theater, recording them on separate tracks, and adjusting volume levels via post-production re-recording ("Sound Perspective Used in 'Applause,'" 10).
62. See especially the annotations in the October 8, 1929, *Applause* screenplay, *Applause* file, RMP.
63. As Fischer puts it, "sounds from other locations aggressively pursue" the film's central characters ("*Applause*," 239).
64. Direct-sound location shooting was not unheard of prior to *Applause*. Key examples include the American Southwest in *In Old Arizona*, an airfield in *The Flying Fool* (June 1929), and Astoria's own *Glorifying the American Girl* (released after *Applause* but shot before it), which featured a lengthy direct-sound scene on the shore of Lake Success in Manhasset (Koszarski, *Hollywood on the Hudson*, 192). My viewing of extant films indicates that direct-sound shooting in *urban* space—the predominant location work in *Applause*—was quite rare, however.
65. Mamoulian penciled "Ave Maria" into the margin of his screenplay (October 8, 1929, *Applause* screenplay, *Applause* file, RMP).
66. Annotation in October 8, 1929, *Applause* screenplay, *Applause* file, RMP.
67. My thanks to Martin Barnier for reminding me of this precursor.
68. Mamoulian, "The Art of Films," 45–46.
69. Mamoulian, "The Psychology of Sound," 8–9.
70. Koszarski, *Hollywood on the Hudson*, 198.
71. Belton, "Awkward Transitions," 244.
72. Mamoulian, "The Art of Films," 33.
73. Ibid., 34.
74. *City Streets* production files, MHL.
75. For details on the increasing directionality of microphone technology, see Altman, "The Technology of the Voice, Part I," and Crafton, *The Talkies*, 238.

76. The Mole-Richardson boom mic was manufactured in 1930, and during that year, the boom mic was used at all the major studios (Bordwell, Staiger, and Thompson, *The Classical Hollywood Cinema*, 299, 302). One can see the boom mic in use in *Free and Easy* (March 1930), a fiction film about Hollywood filmmaking.
77. Jacobs's careful research indicates that sound-on-film re-recording was less of an experimental practice by 1931, a shift likely catalyzed by improvements to signal-to-noise recording that were nearly concurrent with the commencement of *City Streets'* shooting. Still, she points out that at Paramount (as well as Warner Bros. and RKO), directly recorded sound was typically favored over re-recording (Jacobs, "The Innovation of Re-Recording in the Hollywood Studios," 10–19). Paramount production records show two days devoted to re-recording for *City Streets* (*City Streets* production files, MHL).
78. Altman, "The Technology of the Voice, Part I," 10; Crafton, *The Talkies*, 238.
79. Mamoulian's personal screenplay for *City Streets* leaves little doubt that these shot choices were his. The talking statue idea appears only in his handwriting in the margins, and he spells out in precise detail the exact shot selections and timings that appear in the finished film (annotations in undated *City Streets* script [Box 57, Folder 3], *City Streets* file, RMP).
80. Mamoulian, interview by Gallagher and Amoruco, 18.
81. Sarah Kozloff, *Invisible Storytellers: Voice-over Narration in American Fiction Film* (Berkeley: University of California Press, 1988), 28–29.
82. The first screenplay for *City Streets* that is housed in Mamoulian's papers at the Library of Congress features Mamoulian's extensive handwritten annotations surrounding the voice-over scene. The voice-over itself, however, already appears in the typed portion of the screenplay. "Below the sound of [Nan's cellmate's] snores," the screenplay instructs, "like an undertone can be heard the voices of The Kid and Nan, talking as they did in the visitors' room" (annotation in January 7, 1931, screenplay, *City Streets* file, Paramount Pictures scripts, MHL; and undated *City Streets* script [Box 57, Folder 3], *City Streets* file, RMP). Whether Mamoulian had a hand in this typed screenplay instruction remains unclear. Though the heavy annotations might suggest this was Mamoulian's first look at the screenplay, Mamoulian appears to have been involved with the project *before* this screenplay was written. By Mamoulian's account, Paramount contacted him about directing another film "exactly a year" after *Applause* debuted at the Criterion Theatre, and Mamoulian eventually asked Dashiell Hammett to provide a synopsis for *City Streets* after Mamoulian struggled to find material he wished to direct (Charles Higham, *The Celluloid Muse: Hollywood Directors Speak* (London: Angus & Robertson, 1969], 133). Though one cannot simply take Mamoulian at his word, the timing does fit: Mamoulian would have been approached by Paramount in early October 1930, and Hammett's story—then titled *After School*—was written in early November 1930 (*City Streets* file, Paramount Pictures scripts, MHL). It is also worth noting that the story outline Hammett wrote in November 1930 does not make reference to a voice-over, meaning that this innovation was not Hammett's. This information suggests that the screenplay was molded under Mamoulian's guidance, but it is possible that credit for the initial flashback voice-over idea rests instead with credited screenplay writers Oliver H. P. Garrett and

Max Marcin. Unfortunately, no author is listed for the January 7, 1931, script where the voice-over first appears (*City Streets*, Paramount Pictures scripts, MHL).
83. Mamoulian, Columbia University oral history, 90.
84. Annotation in undated *City Streets* script (Box 57, Folder 3), *City Streets* file, RMP.
85. Mamoulian touched upon these goals in many different contexts and interviews. For an early conversation about these aims, see Mamoulian, "The Art of Films," 39–42. When discussing the John Barrymore 1920 adaptation, Mamoulian pointed out that a mere dissolve was used to show the change. To Mamoulian's mind, by 1931 more effort was needed to ensure that audiences would accept the change (Mamoulian, Columbia University oral history, 93).
86. Mamoulian, Columbia University oral history, 95.
87. Mamoulian, "The Art of Films," 41.
88. For Mamoulian's discussions of this composite soundtrack, see Mamoulian, "The Art of Films," 41–42; Mamoulian, "The Psychology of Sound," 8; Mamoulian, Columbia University oral history, 95–96; George Stevens Jr., *Conversations with the Great Moviemakers of Hollywood's Golden Age* (New York: Alfred A. Knopf, 2006), 176; and Mamoulian, interview by Thomas R. Atkins, 42–44.
89. In the physical world, a candle only emits the kind of sound heard in *Dr. Jekyll and Mr. Hyde* when recorded by sound technology, gongs are always heard in real time, and the recorded sound of a heartbeat was apparently not commonly heard in 1931.
90. For a detailed description and analysis of this "stew," see Neil Lerner, "The Strange Case of Rouben Mamoulian's Sound Stew: The Uncanny Soundtrack in *Dr. Jekyll and Mr. Hyde* (1931)," in *Music in the Horror Film: Listening to Fear*, ed. Lerner (New York: Routledge, 2010), 55–79.
91. Mamoulian, "The Psychology of Sound," 8.
92. Rick Altman has discussed aspects of sound mediation at length in "The Material Heterogeneity of Recorded Sound," in *Sound Theory/Sound Practice*, edited by Altman (New York: Routledge, 1992), 15–31 and "The Technology of the Voice," Part 1 and 2.
93. Lerner, "The Strange Case of Rouben Mamoulian's Sound Stew," 68.
94. William Whittington, *Sound Design and Science Fiction* (Austin: University of Texas Press, 2007), 101–5. Whittington also points to such films as *2001: A Space Odyssey* (1968) and *THX 1138* (1971) as examples of the industry's new interest in sound montage.
95. Lerner, "The Strange Case of Rouben Mamoulian's Sound Stew," 71.
96. Mamoulian, "The Psychology of Sound," 7.
97. Mamoulian, interview by Steven Greenberg, T4/P173. The name for the piece appears in Vicente Gómez, "Musical Index for 'Blood and Sand,'" *Blood and Sand* file, RMP.
98. To Mamoulian, the vase crash in *Love Me Tonight* occupied mental, not physical, space (Mamoulian, Columbia University oral history, 97–98). Mamoulian discusses the pen-scratching sound in Mamoulian, "The Psychology of Sound," 5. Mamoulian worked hard on the typewriter noise in post-production, at one point complaining in a memo, "the dubbing of Ninotchka typing is too conservative. Her typing should sound almost like a fast, dry, machine gun firing and the typewriter bell should be short and precise (not diffused)" (Memo from Mamoulian to Lela Simone, André Previn, and Conrad Salinger, February 5, 1957, *Silk Stockings* file, RMP, p. 2).

99. In Mamoulian, "The Psychology of Sound," 9, Mamoulian makes it clear that he intended to portray the walls themselves as talking.
100. Andrew Sarris, *The American Cinema: Directors and Directions, 1929–1968* (New York: Octagon Books, 1982), 160.
101. Mamoulian was also friends with O'Neill, and had directed O'Neill's *Marco Millions* at the Guild in 1928.

Chapter 3

1. Rouben Mamoulian, Columbia University oral history, 23.
2. Rouben Mamoulian, "The Art of Films" (lecture, December 6, 1939), 27.
3. Lea Jacobs, *Film Rhythm after Sound: Technology, Music, and Performance* (Berkeley: University of California Press, 2014), 20. For her conception of film rhythm, see especially 1–57.
4. Mark Spergel, *Reinventing Reality: The Art and Life of Rouben Mamoulian* (Metuchen, NJ: Scarecrow Press, 1993), 27–28.
5. Charles Higham, *The Celluloid Muse: Hollywood Directors Speak* (London: Angus & Robertson, 1969), 129.
6. Rouben Mamoulian, *Dialogue on Film* (Interview with the American Film Institute), 1972, RMP, 10.
7. "Mephistopheles of Operatic Tradition Abandoned in New Eastman School Production," *Rochester Democrat and Chronicle*, December 17, 1923, *Faust* file, RMP.
8. "Opera Company to Repeat 'Faust,'" January 1925, *Faust* file, RMP. Spergel, *Reinventing Reality*, 40–45.
9. Mamoulian, Columbia University oral history, 23.
10. Ibid.
11. Rouben Mamoulian, "Mamoulian First Used Camera at Eastman School, He Recalls," *Democrat and Chronicle*, Rochester (NY), February 11, 1934, RMP, 1.
12. Mamoulian, Columbia University oral history, 19–23.
13. Sharon Marie Carnicke and David Rosen, "A Singer Prepares: Stanislavski and Opera," in *The Routledge Companion to Stanislavsky*, ed. R. Andrew White (London: Routledge, 2014), 120–24; Sharon Marie Carnicke, "Rethinking 'Stanislavskian' Acting," in *The Great European Stage Directors*, Vol. 1: *Antoine, Stanislavski, Saint Denis*, ed. Peta Tait (London: Methuen Drama, 2019), 92, 100–2.
14. "Rhythmic Motion, with Music and Words Allied, Revealed in 'Sister Beatrice' Performance, *Rochester Democrat and Chronicle*, January 16, 1926. William P. Costello, "Dance School's Stage Debut Success," January 26, 1926. Amy H. Croughton, "Many Enjoy Maeterlinck Production," January 26, 1926. All reviews appear as clippings in the *Sister Beatrice* file, RMP. The "genuine impression of sincerity" praise can be found in the "Rhythmic Motion" review.
15. Mamoulian, Columbia University oral history, 22–23.
16. Spergel, *Reinventing Reality*, 53.

17. Mamoulian, Columbia University oral history, 54.
18. Ibid., 54–55.
19. *Porgy* playscript, October 10, 1927, *Porgy* file, RMP.
20. Annotation in *Porgy* playscript, October 10, 1927, *Porgy* file, RMP.
21. Ibid.
22. Ibid.
23. Ibid.
24. Ibid.
25. Mamoulian, *Dialogue on Film*, 18–19.
26. Mamoulian, Columbia University oral history, 71.
27. For the three-minute claim, see ibid., 72, and Mamoulian, *Dialogue on Film*, 21. For five minutes, see Mamoulian, interview by Bennet T. Oberstein, 23.
28. Mamoulian's gasping claim can be found in Mamoulian, *Dialogue on Film*, 21.
29. Rouben Mamoulian, interview by Steven Greenberg, T3/P100–101.
30. Jacobs, *Film Rhythm after Sound*, 2–5.
31. Ibid., 2–3.
32. Bordwell discusses these tendencies in David Bordwell, Janet Staiger, and Kristin Thompson, *The Classical Hollywood Cinema: Film Style and Mode of Production to 1960* (New York: Columbia University Press, 1985), 304.
33. Jacobs discusses these issues in *Film Rhythm after Sound*, 1–20.
34. Rouben Mamoulian, interview by Harry A. Hargrave, 258.
35. Ibid.
36. Patrick Keating, *The Dynamic Frame: Camera Movement in Classical Hollywood* (New York: Columbia University Press, 2019), 70.
37. Mamoulian, *Dialogue on Film*, 20.
38. Rouben Mamoulian, "The Use and Abuse of Perambulation" (lecture, July 19, 1932), 6.
39. Rouben Mamoulian, "Common Sense and Camera Angles," *The American Cinematographer* 12.10 (February 1932): 26.
40. Mamoulian, "The Art of Films," 27–28.
41. Bordwell, Staiger, and Thompson, *The Classical Hollywood Cinema*, 304.
42. Donald Crafton, *The Talkies: American Cinema's Transition to Sound, 1926–1931* (Berkeley: University of California Press, 1997), 447–56.
43. Mamoulian, "The Art of Films," 33–34.
44. Bordwell, Staiger, and Thompson, *The Classical Hollywood Cinema*, 304–6.
45. Jacobs, *Film Rhythm after Sound*, 166–216; Jacobs, "The Innovation of Re-Recording in the Hollywood Studios," *Film History: An International Journal* 24.1 (2012): 5–34.
46. Mamoulian, "The Art of Films," 47.
47. Mamoulian, Columbia University oral history, 55.
48. Ibid., 95.
49. Mamoulian, "The Art of Films," 42.
50. Ibid., 40–41.
51. Mamoulian, "The Psychology of Sound."
52. Rouben Mamoulian, interview by William Becvar, Tape 5, p. 11.

53. For an analysis of early sound-era jazz shorts, see Jennifer Fleeger, *Sounding American: Hollywood, Opera, and Jazz* (New York: Oxford University Press, 2014), 91–121. See Krin Gabbard, *Jammin' at the Margins: Jazz and the American Cinema* (Chicago: University of Chicago Press, 1996) for an assessment of Duke Ellington's film career (especially 160–68). As Richard Koszarski points out in *Hollywood on the Hudson: Film and Television in New York from Griffith to Sarnoff* (New Brunswick, NJ: Rutgers University Press, 2008), Paramount's Astoria studios did not seriously commit to black musicians in its short films until 1932 (205).
54. Mamoulian, interview by Becvar, Tape 2, p. 6.
55. *Resurrection*, adapted by Leonard Praskins, June 5, 1934, *We Live Again* file, RMP.
56. Ibid.
57. Annotations in *Resurrection* screenplay, June 5, 1934, *We Live Again* file, RMP. Though it is a bit less clear, Mamoulian's markings also seem to denote the escalation of tempo found in the second scene. Prior to Praskins, Preston Sturges wrote an adaptation of the property that bears little resemblance to Praskins's screenplay. Sturges's version is housed in the CYRL.
58. Anna A. Berman, "Scripting Katyusha on the Way to an Operatic Adaptation of *Resurrection*," *Slavic and East European Journal* 55.3 (Fall 2011): 409.
59. Annotations in *Golden Boy* screenplay, February 7, 1939, 88–90, *Golden Boy* file, RMP.
60. Mamoulian cared little about their third film, *Rings on Her Fingers*, which he directed merely to fulfill his contract (Mamoulian, interview by Greenberg, T2/P45–46).
61. Jacobs, *Film Rhythm after Sound*, 1.
62. John Taintor Foote, *The Mark of Zorro* screenplay, November 9, 1939, *The Mark of Zorro* file, RMP. The archive is unclear on precisely when Mamoulian began work on *The Mark of Zorro*, but he spent all of November 1939 on the east coast, and no record of his involvement on *The Mark of Zorro* appears up to that point (Mamoulian, 1939 diary, RMP).
63. Ibid.
64. It is highly likely that Mamoulian personally inserted this training scene. It resonates with a moment of training found in *We Live Again*, which itself was inspired by a summer Mamoulian spent as a boy near a military barracks in the Caucasus. Mamoulian mentions watching members of the cavalry galloping up to clay figures of people and cutting their heads off, which we see as part of the training footage at the start of *The Mark of Zorro* (Mamoulian, interview by Becvar, Tape 5, p. 11).
65. Foote, *The Mark of Zorro* screenplay, November 9, 1939, *The Mark of Zorro* file, RMP.
66. Annotations in *The Mark of Zorro* screenplay, July 2, 1940, *The Mark of Zorro* file, RMP.
67. Memo from Darryl Zanuck to Rouben Mamoulian, June 4, 1941, *Blood and Sand* file, RMP.
68. Memo from Zanuck to Mamoulian, June 4, 1941, *Blood and Sand* file, RMP.
69. For a long list of songs that the filmmakers tried to secure prior to filming, see the letter from Gustav Mohme to Robert T. Kane, "Fox Film de Mexico, S.A.," December 6, 1940, *Blood and Sand* file, RMP.

70. Memo from Fortunio Bonanova to Rouben Mamoulian, March 26, 1941, *Blood and Sand* file, RMP. Though Bonanova served as a consultant, he would later become angry with the film's musical inaccuracies. Among Bonanova's list of grievances was the fact that the filmmakers recorded the soundtracks to the film's bullfights in Mexico rather than Spain, thereby resulting in a popular Mexican song—"Diana"—being heard in the background (Letter from Bonanova to Mamoulian, August 2, 1941, *Blood and Sand* file, RMP).
71. Story conference with Darryl Zanuck on Final Script of January 24, 1941, p. 11, *Blood and Sand* file, RMP.

Chapter 4

1. Altman, *The American Film Musical* (Bloomington: Indiana University Press, 1987), 200–12.
2. Ibid., 218.
3. Ibid., 205–6.
4. For a detailed discussion of these musicals, see Barrios, *A Song in the Dark: The Birth of the Musical Film* (New York: Oxford University Press, 1995), 189–221.
5. As Crafton has demonstrated, both Lee DeForest and Warner Bros.' pioneering work on synchronized sound in the 1920s involved the assumption that sound film would primarily serve as a means for providing top-tier musical entertainment to small towns across the country (*The Talkies: American Cinema's Transition to Sound, 1926–1931* [Berkeley: University of California Press, 1997], 63–88).
6. Jean-Marie Lecomte, "Rouben Mamoulian's *Applause* and the Birth of the Disenchanted Musical," *Studies in Musical Theatre* 2.2 (2008): 157.
7. Rouben Mamoulian, Columbia University oral history, 68.
8. Rick Altman, *Film/Genre* (London: BFI, 1999), 31–34.
9. Lecomte points to some of these visual techniques for de-emphasizing the number—including the obstructive pillar and wandering camera—in "Rouben Mamoulian's *Applause* and the Birth of the Disenchanted Musical," 157–58.
10. Perhaps the closest corollary in the period is Josef von Sternberg's German film *The Blue Angel*, which was shot a year after *Applause*. Von Sternberg similarly dissects the commodification of sex via such distancing devices as an obstructive pillar.
11. Altman, *The American Film Musical*, 129–58.
12. Lea Jacobs, *Film Rhythm after Sound: Technology, Music, and Performance* (Berkeley: University of California Press, 2014), 143–47.
13. For more on referentiality in Lubitsch's early musicals, see Altman, *The American Film Musical*, 146–49.
14. Rouben Mamoulian, interview by Steven Greenberg, T2/P39–40.
15. Edward Baron Turk, *Hollywood Diva: A Biography of Jeanette MacDonald* (Berkeley: University of California Press, 1998), 360.

16. Both Mamoulian's skeleton outline and his treatment are housed within the *Love Me Tonight* files at the RMP. Though the situation isn't entirely clear, based on the language found in the treatment to describe the numbers, it appears that Mamoulian conceptualized the numbers and their handling in the treatment before giving them to Rodgers and Hart to write. Mamoulian's description of the numbers "The Song of Paree," "How Are You?," "Isn't it Romantic?," and "The Son of a Gun Is Nothing but a Tailor," in particular, are a close match with the finished film.
17. Mamoulian, interview by Greenberg, T1/P24.
18. Rouben Mamoulian, "The Art of Films" (lecture, December 6, 1939), 51.
19. Mamoulian, interview by Greenberg, T1/P24–25.
20. Mamoulian, Columbia University oral history, 96.
21. Mamoulian, "The Art of Films," 55–56.
22. Jacobs, *Film Rhythm after Sound*, 109–65.
23. Housed in the Paramount Pictures music department is a complete original score for *Love Me Tonight*. The collection includes all the songs and incidental arrangements, with the conspicuous absence of the noise symphony. Because of its absence, as well as the fact that Mamoulian wrote *Porgy*'s noise symphony, it seems highly likely that he wrote the *Love Me Tonight* noise symphony himself.
24. Hannah Lewis, "*Love Me Tonight* (1932) and the Development of the Integrated Film Musical," *Musical Quarterly* 100.1 (2017): 12.
25. For a fine-grained musical breakdown and analysis of this noise symphony, which includes a 4/4 measure analysis, see Jacobs, *Film Rhythm after Sound*, 113–122.
26. This musical credit—and every additional one in this section—derives from the original score for the film, housed in the music department at Paramount Pictures.
27. Mamoulian, treatment for *Love Me Tonight*, p. 27, *Love Me Tonight* file, RMP.
28. Annotations in *Porgy* playscript, October 10, 1927, *Porgy* file, RMP.
29. Mamoulian, treatment for *Love Me Tonight*, p. 2, *Love Me Tonight* file, RMP.
30. Jacobs, *Film Rhythm after Sound*, 113.
31. Rouben Mamoulian, interview by John A. Gallagher and Marino A. Amoruco, 19.
32. *Love Me Tonight* production records, MHL.
33. Mamoulian's claim that all singing was recorded on set appears in Mamoulian, interview by Greenberg, T4/P148–149. Jacobs, however, points out that Chevalier can at one point be detected rushing to the next spot to hit a cue timed with the playback (*Film Rhythm after Sound*, 147). It is also plausible that Mamoulian used a metronome here to help Chevalier keep his movements on the beat.
34. Altman, *The American Film Musical*, 152–53.
35. Mamoulian, treatment for *Love Me Tonight*, p. 8, *Love Me Tonight* files, RMP.
36. For another analysis of rhythmic modulation during "Isn't It Romantic," see Joseph Horowitz, *"On My Way": The Untold Story of Rouben Mamoulian, George Gershwin, and "Porgy and Bess"* (New York: W. W. Norton, 2013), 94.
37. As Jacobs points out, Maurice's musically synchronized movements progressively increase in tempo, with Mamoulian eventually undercranking a shot identical to the previous one of Mamoulian racing up a staircase (*Film Rhythm after Sound*, 125).
38. For Jacobs's analysis of the film's contrary modes of pacing, see ibid., 124–26.
39. Horowitz, *"On My Way,"* 94–98.

40. Mamoulian, "The Art of Films," 55.
41. Jeanine Basinger points out this tendency in criticism in *The Movie Musical!* (New York: Alfred A. Knopf, 2019, 67.
42. The only possible exception I am aware of is a fantasy two-strip Technicolor number titled "Dancing the Devil Away" from *The Cuckoos* (April 1930). In a black and white extreme long shot, Anita (Dorothy Lee) is instructed to resist the temptation of the devil, which prompts smoke to appear in the foreground that transitions us into a Technicolor number. The extreme long shot makes it difficult to interpret the number as occurring from a particular character's perspective, however, and the number instead appears to be a musical picturization of a concept.
43. Mamoulian, treatment for *Love Me Tonight*, p. 27, *Love Me Tonight* files, RMP.
44. See, e.g., Barrios, *A Song in the Dark: The Birth of the Musical Film* (New York: Oxford University Press, 1995), 357–62.
45. Rouben Mamoulian, interview by William Becvar, Tape 2, p. 5.
46. Mark Spergel, *Reinventing Reality: The Art and Life of Rouben Mamoulian* (Metuchen, NJ: Scarecrow Press, 1993), 57.
47. Mamoulian, Columbia University oral history, 54.
48. Mamoulian, interview by Becvar, Tape 2, p. 6.
49. Spergel, *Reinventing Reality*, 65–67.
50. Those are the three reasons Mamoulian gave for directing *Porgy and Bess* in Mamoulian, Columbia University oral history, 103.
51. Horowitz, *"On My Way,"* 8–9.
52. Ibid., 111, 115–16.
53. Ibid., 119.
54. Ibid., 114; Spergel, *Reinventing Reality*, 160.
55. Altman, *The American Film Musical*, 272–327.
56. Mamoulian describes this opening-song change in Mamoulian, interview by Bennet T. Oberstein, 44, and it is affirmed in Horowitz, *"On My Way,"* 134–35.
57. Mamoulian, interview by Oberstein, 45. Horowitz, *"On My Way,"* 117–18.
58. Altman, *The American Film Musical*, 299.
59. Horowitz, *"On My Way,"* 130.
60. Ibid., 1–17.
61. Altman, *The American Film Musical*, 309.
62. Horowitz, *"On My Way,"* 128–45.
63. Mamoulian, Columbia University oral history, 111–12.
64. Mamoulian, "The Art of Films," 55.
65. Charles Higham, *The Celluloid Muse: Hollywood Directors Speak* (London: Angus & Robertson, 1969), 139–40.
66. Mamoulian, interview by Greenberg, T4/P175–178.
67. Mamoulian would later state that he chose to direct *The Mark of Zorro* partly because its setting was similar to where Harte set his stories (Higham, *The Celluloid Muse*, 140).
68. Mamoulian, interview by Becvar, Tape 2, 5–6.
69. Spergel, *Reinventing Reality*, 112.

70. Drawings and sketches by Mamoulian, Miscellany, Box 207, RMP.
71. Mamoulian, Columbia University oral history, 115–16.
72. Rouben Mamoulian, interview by Russell Birdwell. See especially 88.
73. Drawings and sketches by Mamoulian, Miscellany, Box 207, RMP.
74. Altman, *The American Film Musical*, 300.
75. Ibid., 298–305.
76. Mamoulian, 1938 diary, RMP.
77. Arthur Hornblow to Rouben Mamoulian, October 5, 1936, *High, Wide and Handsome* file, RMP. Mamoulian's diaries indicate that he arrived back in Hollywood on October 19 (RMP).
78. There is good reason to think that Hammerstein himself had *Show Boat* on the brain when he wrote the synopsis. The parts of Sally and Molly were originally written for Irene Dunne and Helen Morgan, respectively, both of whom starred in *Show Boat* on stage and screen. Molly Fuller's character as a down-and-out saloon singer echoes Julie from *Show Boat*, and the character trajectories of Sally and Peter in the initial synopsis resonate with Magnolia and Ravenal: Sally was to have become a singing stage sensation following her split with Peter, while Peter was to have ended the film a professional failure, like Ravenal (Hammerstein, synopsis for *High, Wide and Handsome*, Paramount Pictures scripts, MHL).
79. Basinger, *The Movie Musical!*, 70.
80. Altman discusses the picturesque tradition in early folk musicals prior to *High, Wide and Handsome* in *The American Film Musical*, 296–98.
81. Arthur Hornblow to Rouben Mamoulian, October 5, 1936, *High, Wide and Handsome* file, RMP.
82. All these requests, and many others, can be found in the *High, Wide and Handsome* file in the RMP.
83. Late in life, Mamoulian wrote an article titled "What We Can Learn from the Animals" in which he listed life lessons that can be imparted to humans by twenty-six different animals, ranging from cats and dogs to spiders, butterflies, seagulls, and rattlesnakes (RMP).
84. Altman, *The American Film Musical*, 304.
85. Bland Johaneson, "Spectacular Story of Oil Fields," *New York Daily Mirror*, July 22, 1937, *High, Wide and Handsome* file, RMP.
86. Harrison Carroll, "Laud 'High, Wide and Handsome' Musical for Virility," *Los Angeles Herald-Express*, August 13, 1937, *High, Wide and Handsome* file, RMP.
87. This specific comparison to *Show Boat* and *San Francisco* can be found in Frank S. Nugent, "'High, Wide and Handsome,' A Story of the Oil Rush, Opens at the Astor," *New York Times*, July 22, 1937, *High, Wide and Handsome* file, RMP.
88. "'High, Wide and Handsome' Colorful Entertainment, Production Lavish, Mamoulian Scores," *Hollywood Reporter*, July 22, 1937, *High, Wide and Handsome* file, RMP.
89. Nugent, "'High, Wide and Handsome,' A Story of the Oil Rush, Opens at the Astor."
90. "Two-Fisted Operetta," *Evening Public Ledger* (Philadelphia), September 25, 1937, *High, Wide and Handsome* file, RMP.

91. "High, Wide and Handsome," *Daily Variety*, July 22, 1937, *High, Wide and Handsome* file, RMP.
92. Mamoulian, Columbia University oral history, 22.
93. Ibid., 25
94. Hannah Lewis similarly divides the concept of integration into aesthetic unity, and numbers that become part of the storytelling process ("*Love Me Tonight* [1932] and the Development of the Integrated Film Musical," 4).
95. Mamoulian, Columbia University oral history, 27.
96. Ibid., 28.
97. Ibid., 29.
98. Geoffrey Block, "Integration," in *The Oxford Handbook of the American Musical*, ed. Raymond Knapp, Mitchell Morris, and Stacy Wolf (Oxford: Oxford University Press, 2011), 99–102.
99. Lewis, "*Love Me Tonight* (1932) and the Development of the Integrated Film Musical," 13.
100. For "Mimi" and its tenuous relationship to narrative integration, along with a broader assessment of the film's integration between narrative and number, see ibid.
101. Mamoulian, interview by Becvar, Tape 2, p. 2.
102. Thomas Riis, "Musical Theatre, " in *The Cambridge History of American Theatre, Vol. 2: 1879–1945*, ed. Don B. Wilmeth and Christopher Bigsby (Cambridge: Cambridge University Press, 1999), 440. Block points out that trade-press discussions of integration—uncommon prior to *Oklahoma!*—became ubiquitous after this production (Block, "Integration," 102).
103. Ethan Mordden, *Beautiful Mornin': The Broadway Musical in the 1940s* (New York: Oxford University Press, 1999), 70–79; Denny Martin Flinn, *Musical! A Grand Tour: The Rise, Glory, and Fall of an American Institution* (New York: Schirmer Books, 1997), 225–29; Sheldon Patinkin, *"No Legs, No Jokes, No Chance": A History of the American Musical Theatre* (Evanston, IL: Northwestern University Press, 2008), 5–21.
104. Spergel outlines some of the most prominent squabbles in *Reinventing Reality*, 186–193.
105. Oscar Hammerstein laid out these aims in Hammerstein, "'Away We Go' Called a Labor of Love," *Boston Sunday Post*, March 14, 1943. Clipping from the *Oklahoma!* file, RMP. *Away We Go!* was the title of the production at the time of the Boston tryouts.
106. Mamoulian, in 1942, had finished his multi-picture contract with Fox and had no firm commitments to direct another film. In September 1942, Mamoulian found himself on the East Coast trying to get an army commission to make a film. Unfortunately, the commission fell through, and his efforts to direct two films—*Porgy and Bess* and the Gershwin biopic *Rhapsody in Blue*—were also fizzling (Kurt Jensen, "What Did 'Mamoo' Do?: The Rouben Mamoulian Papers and *Oklahoma!*," *Studies in Musical Theatre* 4.3 [2010]: 251).
107. Ibid., 252.
108. Mamoulian, Columbia University oral history, 96, 115.

109. Jensen, "What Did Mamoo Do?," 253.
110. The account of Mamoulian directing the songs comes from Theatre Guild head—and *Oklahoma!* producer—Lawrence Langner (Tim Carter, *"Oklahoma!": The Making of an American Musical* [New Haven, CT: Yale University Press, 2007], 179). Information on Mamoulian's rehearsal of "The Farmer and the Cowhand" comes from Agnes de Mille biographer Kara Anne Gardner (*Agnes de Mille: Telling Stories in Broadway Dance* [New York: Oxford University Press, 2016], 28–29). There are also many accounts of Mamoulian functioning as an autocrat on the set, even relegating de Mille to the basement for the choreography of the dances.
111. Jensen, "What Did 'Mamoo' Do?" 255
112. Altman, *The American Film Musical*, 306.
113. Jensen, "What Did Mamoo do?" 254.
114. "Script E" in the *Oklahoma!* collection, RMP. This idea may have inspired Rodgers and Hammerstein to feature a pig snorting rhythmically at the end of the opening number to their lone musical written directly for the screen, *State Fair* (1945).
115. This information, often cited in scholarship on *Oklahoma!*, is recounted by Mamoulian in an untitled document in the *Oklahoma!* file (Box 111, Folder 13) at the RMP.
116. Jensen, "What Did 'Mamoo' Do?" 255–56.
117. Mamoulian, interview by Oberstein, 45.
118. Ibid., 45.
119. Jensen, "What Did 'Mamoo' Do?" 256.
120. Spergel, *Reinventing Reality*, 189–192.
121. This staging was known as the "flying wedge" (Jensen, "What Did 'Mamoo' Do?" 256).
122. Mamoulian, interview by Becvar, Tape 3, p. 9.
123. Spergel, *Reinventing Reality*, 106.
124. Altman, *The American Film Musical*, 306.
125. E. C. Sherburne, "Mamoulian Back on Broadway," *Christian Science Monitor*, Boston, Friday, June 4, 1943, RMP file for *Oklahoma!*
126. In a set piece that Mamoulian added, zealous missionary Davidson subdues the natives by having them stop their drumming. *Sadie Thompson* playscript, March 1944, *Sadie Thompson* file, RMP.
127. Spergel, *Reinventing Reality*, 196.
128. Ibid., 197.
129. Mordden, *Beautiful Mornin'*, 86–87
130. John K. Hutchins, "About a Man on a Tightrope," clipping in the *Carousel* file, RMP.
131. Undated *Carousel* playscript, *Carousel* file (Box 102, Folder 8), RMP. Though undated, the word "final" is written across the front cover and the interior pages are signed by the entire cast, making it highly likely that this was the script used during rehearsals.
132. Undated *Carousel* playscript, *Carousel* file (Box 102, Folder 8), RMP.
133. Altman, *The American Film Musical*, 307. Altman is actually describing the function of the barker in the *film* version of *Carousel*, but it applies equally to the original stage version.

134. Mamoulian, interview by Becvar, Tape 3, p. 9.
135. Spergel, *Reinventing Reality*, 200–1.
136. The whistle ending appears in six *St. Louis Woman* playscripts, all undated, Box 120 Folders 8–11, and Box 121 Folders 1–2, *St. Louis Woman* file, RMP.
137. Memo from Rouben Mamoulian to John Mercer and Harold Arlen, "Outline of the Suggested 'Racing Scene' (Musical Number)," March 6, 1946, St. Louis Woman file, RMP.
138. *St. Louis Woman* playscript, undated, Box 121, Folder 3, *St. Louis Woman* file, RMP.
139. *Lost in the Stars* playscript, October 30, 1949, *Lost in the Stars* file, RMP.
140. Mamoulian's memo make scant reference to the 1935 dramatic adaptation of O'Neill's play—also titled *Ah, Wilderness!*—but Mamoulian owned a copy of the screenplay, and the filmmakers consulted this screenplay when adapting the work (*Summer Holiday* file, RMP).
141. Rouben Mamoulian, "Stage and Screen." Mamoulian's memos can be found in the *Summer Holiday* file, RMP. See especially Rouben Mamoulian to Harry Warren, Ralph Blane and Irving Brecher, "'Ah, Wilderness!' Memorandum #1," December 27, 1945, *Summer Holiday* file, RMP.
142. Ibid., 18.
143. Ibid., 18.
144. Mamoulian, "'Ah, Wilderness!' Memorandum #1."
145. Mamoulian, "Stage and Screen," 17.
146. Ibid., 17–18.
147. Mamoulian, "'Ah, Wilderness!' Memorandum #1."
148. For another assessment of how *Summer Holiday* fits within folk musicals from the period, see Desirée J. Garcia, *The Migration of Musical Film: From Ethnic Margins to American Mainstream* (New Brunswick, NJ: Rutgers University Press, 2014), 99–124.
149. Jane Feuer describes the "passed-along song" method in *The Hollywood Musical*, 2nd ed. (Bloomington: Indiana University Press, 1993), 16.
150. According to Turk, Minnelli "judged *Love Me Tonight* to be the perfect film musical" (*Hollywood Diva*, 119).
151. *Summer Holiday* screenplay, January 29, 1946, Turner/MGM scripts, MHL.
152. Altman, *The American Film Musical*, 284, 317–18.
153. Rouben Mamoulian to Ralph Blane, Irving Brecher, and Harry Warren, "'Ah, Wilderness!' Memorandum #4," January 24, 1946, *Summer Holiday* file, RMP.
154. *Summer Holiday* screenplay, June 13, 1946, *Summer Holiday* file, RMP.
155. Memo from Mamoulian to Frank Hall, Connell, and Brinkman, "Lighting," March 20, 1946, *St. Louis Woman* file, RMP.
156. Altman, *The American Film Musical*, 277.
157. Ibid.
158. Mamoulian, interview by Greenberg, T3/P136.
159. Altman, *The American Film Musical*, 277.
160. Mamoulian, interview by Greenberg, T3/P135–136.
161. Mamoulian also shot a musical number titled "Omar Khayyan" that would have included Grant Wood–style landscape shots, but the number was cut from the release version. For a description, see Mamoulian, "'Ah, Wilderness!' Memorandum #4."

162. Mamoulian, "Stage and Screen," 19.
163. Spergel, *Reinventing Reality*, 207.
164. For one of many analyses of the fantasy ballet and its art references, see Esquevin, "*An American in Paris*: Art on Film," http://silverscreenmodes.com/an-american-in-paris-art-on-film/.
165. Spergel, *Reinventing Reality*, 211. Mamoulian would later admit to an interviewer, "to tell you the truth, if I were asked to present my credentials at the gate of paradise, I would not even include *Arms and the Girl*" (Mamoulian, interview by Oberstein, 69).
166. Mamoulian expresses these feelings in "'Ah, Wilderness!' Memorandum #4."
167. For one example of this oft-told anecdote, see George Stevens Jr., *Conversations with the Great Moviemakers of Hollywood's Golden Age* (New York: Alfred A. Knopf, 2006), 182.
168. Rouben Mamoulian to Arthur Freed, Harry Kurnitz, Eugene Loring, and Hermes Pan, "Memo #4 Re: Dances in 'Silk Stockings'" August 30, 1956, p. 7, *Silk Stockings* file, RMP.
169. Rouben Mamoulian, "Memo #9 Re: Script of 'Silk Stockings,'" October 20, 1956, *Silk Stockings* file, RMP.
170. Mamoulian, "Memo #4 Re: Dances in 'Silk Stockings,'" 8.
171. Ibid., 9–10.
172. In a description resembling the choreography in the finished film, Mamoulian suggested that Canfield do "a few swift dance movements" with the women to encourage them to dance, and also "tap bottles, glasses, plates, the table, the chairs, etc. etc. as a rhythmic accompaniment to the dance." Mamoulian to Arthur Freed, Leonard Gersh, Eugene Loring, and Hermes Pan, "Memorandum #5 Re: Dances in 'Silk Stockings,'" September 18, 1956, 1–2, *Silk Stockings* file, RMP.
173. Mamoulian, "Memo #4 Re: Dances in 'Silk Stockings,'" 5.
174. For more on *Silk Stockings*' numbers and integration, see Todd Decker, *Music Makes Me: Fred Astaire and Jazz* (Berkeley: University of California Press, 2011), 68–69; and John Mueller, *Astaire Dancing: The Musical Films* (New York: Wings Books, 1985), 393–94.
175. Altman uses this term to describe certain Astaire/Rogers numbers in *The American Film Musical*, 162–77.

Chapter 5

1. Rouben Mamoulian, "Colors and Emotions," for *N.Y. Variety*, May 4, 1946, RMP 2.
2. Rouben Mamoulian, "What Color Will You Wear?," *Californian* 4.3 (October 1947): 28.
3. Tinting involved dipping the positive print in a chemical bath so that only the light portions of the frame became colorized, while toning involved dipping the film in a different chemical solution that colored only the dark parts of the image.

4. Joshua Yumibe, *Moving Color: Early Film, Mass Culture, Modernism* (New Brunswick, NJ: Rutgers University Press, 2012), 5–6.
5. Scott Higgins, *Harnessing the Technicolor Rainbow: Color Design in the 1930s* (Austin: University of Texas Press, 2007), 2–3, 23.
6. Richard Jewell, *RKO Radio Pictures: A Titan Is Born* (Berkeley: University of California Press, 2012), 102.
7. Ibid., 101.
8. Higgins, *Harnessing the Technicolor Rainbow*, 22–27.
9. Rouben Mamoulian, interview by David Robinson, 126.
10. The dates are all from Mamoulian's 1935 diary, RMP. The pneumonia detail comes from Allan R. Ellenberger, *Miriam Hopkins: Life and Films of a Hollywood Rebel* (Lexington: University Press of Kentucky, 2018), 107–8.
11. In a 1950s oral history, Mamoulian acknowledged both his lack of knowledge about color going into the production and his limited time to prepare the film (Mamoulian, Columbia University oral history, 114). In an interview after his career ended, Mamoulian was more explicit: "having done *Becky Sharp*, I got very excited about the potential of color, which to me was not totally fulfilled in *Becky Sharp*" (Mamoulian, interview by Steven Greenberg, T2/P57).
12. This argument is laid out especially clearly in Rouben Mamoulian, "What Do You Think of Color?," *The New Movie Magazine* 12.3 (September 1935): 16, 44–45. For the relationship between stylization and color, see also Rouben Mamoulian, "Some Problems in Directing Color Pictures," *Society of Motion Picture Engineers* 100.12 (December 1991): 971.
13. Mamoulian, "What Do You Think of Color?," 43. Rouben Mamoulian, "The Coming of Color on the Screen" (speech, 1937), 1.
14. Mamoulian, "Some Problems in Directing Color Pictures," 971.
15. Rouben Mamoulian, interview by Anthony Slide.
16. Edmund Jones, "The Crisis of Color," *New York Times*, May 19, 1935. Edmund Jones, "A Revolution in the Movies," *Vanity Fair*, June 1935, 13, 58. Natalie Kalmus, "Color Consciousness," *Journal of the Society for Motion Picture Engineers* (August 1935): 139–47. For a detailed examination of their theories, see Higgins, *Harnessing the Technicolor Rainbow*, 27–31, 39–47.
17. Higgins, *Harnessing the Technicolor Rainbow*, 48–75.
18. Rouben Mamoulian, "Colour and Light in Films from 1946 to 1956," for *Ararat Magazine*, no date, RMP, 6. For other versions of this comment, see Mamoulian, "Some Problems in Directing Color Pictures," 971; Mamoulian, "The Coming of Color on the Screen," 5; Mamoulian, "Colors and Emotions," 2; and Mamoulian, "The Psychology of Color," for Harrison Carroll's column, April 23, 1941, RMP, 3.
19. When the bonze announces that the couple has been married ("ye, newly married, go in peace!"), the spotlight emanating from the pagoda (located stage right) illuminates Thi-Linh and is extinguished after she collapses in grief (Annotation in *Congai* playscript, January 14, 1929, *Congai* file, RMP). *Congai* Light Plot, *Congai* file, RMP.
20. Annotation in *Congai* playscript, January 14, 1929, *Congai* file, RMP.
21. *Becky Sharp* screenplay, "Revised Final Script," December 10, 1934, 1, *Becky Sharp* file, RMP.

22. Mamoulian, "What Do You Think of Color?" 43.
23. Mamoulian, interview by Robinson, 126.
24. *Rio Rita* introduces color over an hour into the film during a musical number, which begins with seventeen seconds of a ship's captain—clad in black and white—singing in front of neutral curtains. The curtains are then raised, revealing dancers in a breathtaking array of red and blue costumes against a neutral background.
25. Higgins notes this brownish-red color in *Harnessing the Technicolor Rainbow*, 52.
26. Mamoulian, "Opera School," January 21, 1924, RMP.
27. Mamoulian, "What Do You Think of Color?" 45.
28. Mamoulian, "Controlling Color for Dramatic Effect," 262.
29. *Becky Sharp* screenplay, "Revised Final Script," December 10, 1934, 71, 75, *Becky Sharp* file, RMP.
30. Ibid., 76–77.
31. Ibid., 78–79.
32. Ibid., 78.
33. Ibid., 71.
34. For more on this grouping, see Mamoulian, "What Do You Think of Color?"; Mamoulian, "Some Problems in Directing Color Pictures"; and Mamoulian, "Colour and Light in Films from 1946 to 1956."
35. Higgins, *Harnessing the Technicolor Rainbow*, 61–63
36. Ibid., 62.
37. Ibid., 92–107.
38. Mamoulian, "The Psychology of Color," 1–2.
39. Mamoulian, 1937 diary, RMP.
40. Mamoulian, interview by John A. Gallagher and Marino A. Amoruco, 21. Mamoulian also briefly describes this level of color planning in Mamoulian, interview by William Becvar, Tape 3, p. 13.
41. I am grateful to Scott Higgins for providing me with information on the advisory service.
42. Kalmus had published a strategy in which her department would review the script and create "a color chart for the entire production," with an eye toward the "dominant mood or emotion" of a particular scene (Kalmus, "Color Consciousness," 145).
43. Mamoulian, "The Psychology of Color," 1–2.
44. Mamoulian, "Controlling Color for Dramatic Effect," 288.
45. All these quotations are from ibid., 263.
46. Ibid., 263.
47. Mamoulian, interview by Greenberg, T2/P57–58.
48. Mamoulian, "Controlling Color for Dramatic Effect," 263.
49. Mamoulian, "The Psychology of Color," 4.
50. Mamoulian, "Controlling Color for Dramatic Effect," 288.
51. Ibid., 288.
52. Rouben Mamoulian, *Dialogue on Film* (interview, 1972), 15–16.
53. Memo from Darryl Zanuck to Rouben Mamoulian, "Rushes on Blood and Sand," March 4, 1941, *Blood and Sand* file, RMP.

54. For Mamoulian's descriptions of these general aims, see Mamoulian, "The Psychology of Color," 1–3; Mamoulian, "Controlling Color for Dramatic Effect," 288; and Mamoulian, interview by Gallagher and Amoruco, 22.
55. Mamoulian, "Controlling Color for Dramatic Effect," 288.
56. Ibid.
57. Higgins, *Harnessing the Technicolor Rainbow*, 34–36, 183–86.
58. Mamoulian, "Controlling Color for Dramatic Effect," 263.
59. Annotations in *Blood and Sand* screenplay, January 24, 1941, 58–59, *Blood and Sand* file, RMP.
60. For indications of the importance that Mamoulian placed on the reintroduction of these red elements, see Mamoulian, "The Psychology of Color," 3; and Mamoulian, "Controlling Color for Dramatic Effect," 288.
61. Memo from Darryl Zanuck to Rouben Mamoulian, January 16, 1941, *Blood and Sand* file, RMP. Mamoulian's diaries indicate that he spent roughly a month in Mexico City to obtain this footage, leaving December 23, 1940, and returning January 21, 1941 (Mamoulian, 1940 and 1941 diaries, RMP).
62. Bad weather was partly responsible, but Mamoulian's slow pace and extensive camera angles—along with costs associated with set design—were primary culprits (Memo from Darryl Zanuck to Rouben Mamoulian, "Rushes on Blood and Sand," March 4, 1941, *Blood and Sand* file, RMP; Memo from V. J. Christensen to Darryl Zanuck, May 2, 1941, *Blood and Sand* file, RMP).
63. "Corrections on Technicolor Print of *Blood and Sand*," *Blood and Sand* file, RMP.
64. Though Mamoulian wanted the studio to make a new print of the film, Zanuck refused, claiming that the print could not be darkened further without making the image indecipherable in smaller theaters with lower projection-bulb brightness (Memo from Rouben Mamoulian to Darryl Zanuck, May 14, 1941, *Blood and Sand* file, RMP; Memo from Darryl Zanuck to Rouben Mamoulian, May 16, 1941, *Blood and Sand* file, RMP).
65. Mamoulian, interview by Greenberg, T3/P89.
66. According to the *Blood and Sand* screenplay, a planned close-range shot of the bull, "with banderillas placed," "panting" with "his tongue hanging out" had to be eliminated for the US release version (*Blood and Sand* screenplay, December 4, 1940, 127, *Blood and Sand* file, RMP).
67. "Blood and Sand," *American Cinematographer*, June 1941, 272, *Blood and Sand* file, RMP.
68. Rouben Mamoulian, "Memorandum #9: Color in 'Ah, Wilderness,'" May 13, 1946, p. 3, *Summer Holiday* file, RMP.
69. Mamoulian, interview by Robinson, 127.
70. In an interview, Mamoulian described the essence of O'Neill's play as a "nostalgic memory of [O'Neill's] childhood." Mamoulian, interview by Greenberg, T5/P208.
71. As James Dennis has demonstrated, such qualities did not adequately characterize Benton, Curry, and Wood's art, but these painters were widely described in these terms in the 1930s and 1940s (*Renegade Regionalists: The Modern Independence of Grant Wood, Thomas Hart Benton, and John Steuart Curry* [Madison: University of Wisconsin Press, 1998], 3–50).

72. Mamoulian, "Memorandum #6," 2–3.
73. Rouben Mamoulian to Harry Warren, Ralph Blane, and Joan Holloway, "Memorandum #6," April 20, 1946, *Summer Holiday* file, RMP. At the end of the memo, Mamoulian described his aim as follows: when the drunken Richard arrives home after this episode and exclaims, "'Ma! I feel—rotten!' he expresses our feelings too" (4).
74. See, e.g., Jeanine Basinger, *The Movie Musical!* (New York: Alfred A. Knopf, 2019), 354–55.
75. In production memo language, Belle is supposed to be made up like a "tart" (Rouben Mamoulian to Charlie Schoenbaum, Perry O'Brien, Wally Wersley, Johnny Greer, Ray Ramsay, and Stanley Campbell, "Memorandum #10: "'Ah, Wilderness' Bar Room Sequence [Camera, Lights, Costumes, Makeup]," October 5, 1946, p. 1, *Summer Holiday* file, RMP).
76. Ibid., 2.
77. Mamoulian spells out these lighting changes in ibid., 2.
78. According to Mamoulian's production memo, a somewhat similar effect was to have occurred earlier. Prior to this final transformation, when Belle calls, "Hurry up with those drinks, waiter," and the close-range camera shows the couple nearly kissing, a "rosy glow" was to have come into the shot, thanks to a red color gel held over the front light, before receding when the waiter comes in and breaks the spell (ibid., 3).
79. In his writings about color, Mamoulian obsessively tied red to passion. See Mamoulian, "Some Problems in Directing Color Pictures," 971; Mamoulian, "The Coming of Color on the Screen," 5; Mamoulian, "The Psychology of Color," 1; Mamoulian, "What Color Means in Wardrobe"; Mamoulian, "Controlling Color for Dramatic Effect," 288; Mamoulian, "What Color Will You Wear?" 29; and Mamoulian, "Colour and Light in Films from 1946 to 1956," 6.
80. Mamoulian, "Memorandum #10," 4.
81. Memo from Rouben Mamoulian to all departments, "Color Treatment, 'Silk Stockings,'" September 25, 1956, *Silk Stockings* file, RMP.
82. No author, "History of Stockings," 2, *Silk Stockings* file, RMP.
83. Mamoulian, "Color Treatment, 'Silk Stockings,'" 3.

Chapter 6

1. Rouben Mamoulian, interview by Lloyd Chelsey and Michael Gould, 148.
2. Rouben Mamoulian, *The American Film Institute Seminar* (May 27, 1981, RMP), 1TB/P35.
3. Rouben Mamoulian, interview by William Becvar, Tape 4, p. 5.
4. For a thorough examination of the US censorship situation from the late aughts through the 1915 Supreme Court decision, see Lee Grieveson, *Policing Cinema: Movies and Censorship in Early-Twentieth-Century America* (Berkeley: University of California Press, 2004).

5. Lea Jacobs, *The Wages of Sin: Censorship and the Fallen Woman Film, 1928-1942* (Madison: University of Wisconsin Press, 1991), 10, 28.
6. "The Production Code," in Stephen Prince, *Classical Film Violence: Designing and Regulating Brutality in Hollywood, 1930-1968* (New Brunswick, NJ: Rutgers University Press, 2003), 297. Donald Crafton discusses sound's perceived effect on impressionable audiences in *The Talkies: American Cinema's Transition to Sound, 1926-1931* (Berkeley: University of California Press, 1997), 471-79. See Michael Slowik, "Revealing Reality: Fan Magazine Rhetoric, Sound Technology, and Stardom in the Early Sound Era," *Journal of Film and Video* 70.2 (Summer 2018): 30-45, for an examination of how fan magazines treated sound as an added dimension of reality.
7. Crafton, *The Talkies*, 470. Richard Maltby, "The Production Code and the Hays Office," in *Grand Design: Hollywood as a Modern Business Enterprise, 1930-1939*, ed. Tino Balio (New York: Charles Scribner's Sons, 1993), 45.
8. Maltby, "The Production Code and the Hays Office," 45. Crafton, *The Talkies*, 467.
9. For a detailed discussion of the creation of the Code and its early enforcement, see Maltby, "The Production Code and the Hays Office," 37-52.
10. Jacobs, *The Wages of Sin*, 28.
11. For an examination of these weaknesses with respect to the fallen woman film, see ibid.
12. For thorough discussions of this function, see especially ibid., 33-35; and Prince, *Classical Film Violence*, 46-51.
13. Rouben Mamoulian, *Dialogue on* Film (interview with the American Film Institute, 1972, RMP), 34; Mamoulian, interview by Steven Greenberg, T1/P7-17; Mamoulian, interview by Becvar, Tape 3, p. 13.
14. "The Production Code" (in Prince, *Classical Film Violence*), 296-97.
15. Mamoulian, Columbia University oral history, 109.
16. Mamoulian, *Dialogue on Film*, 5.
17. Mamoulian, interview by Becvar, Tape 4, p. 5.
18. Mamoulian, interview by Chelsey and Gould, 148.
19. In O'Neill's play, for instance, the father advises his son that with a prostitute, "you just have what you want and pay 'em and forget it" (Eugene O'Neill, *Complete Plays*, Vol. 3 [New York: Library of America, 1990], 104).
20. Mamoulian, interview by Chelsey and Gould, 148; Mamoulian, interview by Greenberg, T5/P211.
21. Mamoulian, interview by Becvar, Tape 4, p. 6.
22. Rouben Mamoulian, "Time for Audiences to Do Their Part," 3.
23. Rouben Mamoulian, "The World's Latest Fine Art" (unpublished, 1965), 22.
24. Rouben Mamoulian, "History of the Motion Picture" (lecture, November 29, 1938), 22; Mamoulian, "Stage and Screen" (unpublished, 1946), 20.
25. Mamoulian, *The American Film Institute Seminar* (1981), 1TB/P36-38.
26. Rouben Mamoulian, interview by Thomas R. Atkins, 37.
27. Maltby, "The Production Code and the Hays Office," 44-48.
28. Letter to Walter Wanger, September 18, 1929, *Applause* Production Code Administration Records, Margaret Herrick Library (hereafter noted as PCAR, MHL).

Ruth Vasey, in *The World According to Hollywood, 1918–1939* (Madison: University of Wisconsin Press, 1997), identifies the author as Jason Joy (105).

29. Summary by James B. M. Fisher, October 9, 1929, *Applause* PCAR, MHL.
30. Robert C. Allen, *Horrible Prettiness: Burlesque and American Culture* (Chapel Hill: University of North Carolina Press, 1991), 243–48.
31. Summary by James B. M. Fisher, October 9, 1929, *Applause* PCAR, MHL.
32. Letter to Walter Wanger, September 18, 1929, *Applause* PCAR, MHL.
33. Ibid.
34. September 19, 1929, *Applause* PCAR, MHL. The supervisory tone of the letter and its contents suggest that it is likely a letter by Hays to Joy.
35. Summary by James B. M. Fisher, October 9, 1929, *Applause* PCAR, MHL.
36. Report to Colonel Joy by Maurice McKenzie, November 20, 1929, *Applause* PCAR, MHL.
37. According to a Western Union telegram from E. E. B. to John P. Hutchings, *Applause* passed without eliminations in New York "largely as a result of cooperation between board and studio during production." January 14, 1930, *Applause* PCAR, MHL.
38. Mamoulian, Columbia University oral history, 110.
39. Allen, *Horrible Prettiness*, 245.
40. Anonymous letter to Adolph Zukor, October 11, 1929, *Applause* PCAR, MHL.
41. *Applause* PCAR, MHL.
42. Ibid. The quotation comes from a report on the Chicago board dated January 20, 1930.
43. Mark Spergel, *Reinventing Reality: The Art and Life of Rouben Mamoulian* (Metuchen, NJ: Scarecrow Press, 1993), 102.
44. *City Streets* production file, MHL.
45. "The Production Code" (in Prince, *Classical Film Violence*), 295, 301.
46. Ibid., 294.
47. Ibid., 297.
48. The SRC file for *City Streets* includes a letter from a police sergeant in which he assesses how six recent gangster films—including *The Public Enemy* and *The Secret Six*, along with *City Streets*—might impact the public. Letter from August Vollmer to Will Hays, April 17, 1931, *City Streets* PCAR, MHL.
49. Mamoulian, interview by Chelsey and Gould, 120; Mamoulian, interview by Atkins, 40; Mamoulian, interview by William Hare, 131; Mamoulian, interview by Harry A. Hargrave, 263–64; Mamoulian, *The American Film Institute Seminar* (1981), 1TA/P20–22.
50. Tom Milne, *Mamoulian* (London: Thames & Hudson, 1969), 39.
51. Mamoulian claimed credit for the idea in later interviews, and this is certainly possible. The idea appears in the treatment, which was completed on June 11 (treatment by Percy Heath, Paramount Pictures scripts, MHL). Mamoulian had been under contract for the film since April 7 (*Dr. Jekyll and Mr. Hyde* production files, MHL). The treatment itself, however, is not credited to Mamoulian, but rather to Heath, who would later co-write the screenplay.
52. "Shooting Continuity as Dictated by Rouben Mamoulian," 1, *Dr. Jekyll and Mr. Hyde* file, RMP.

53. Mamoulian, "History of the Motion Picture," 9.
54. Percy Heath and Samuel Hoffenstein, *Dr. Jekyll and Mr. Hyde* screenplay, August 7, 1931, *Dr. Jekyll and Mr. Hyde* file, RMP.
55. Annotations in *Dr. Jekyll and Mr. Hyde* screenplay, August 7, 1931, *Dr. Jekyll and Mr. Hyde* file, RMP.
56. *Congai* playscript, January 14, 1929, *Congai* file, RMP.
57. According to Spergel, Menken wore "a body stocking intended to simulate nudity" (*Reinventing Reality*, 82).
58. Annotation in *Dr. Jekyll and Mr. Hyde* screenplay, August 7, 1931, *Dr. Jekyll and Mr. Hyde* file, RMP.
59. Rouben Mamoulian, "*Dr. Jekyll and Mr. Hyde*: Shooting Continuity as Dictated by Rouben Mamoulian," 34, *Dr. Jekyll and Mr. Hyde* file, RMP.
60. Ibid., 34–35.
61. Ibid., 35.
62. The Production Code expressed particularly concern that improper sexual desire might seem naturally attractive and thus needed to be handled with particular care ("The Production Code" [in Prince, *Classical Film Violence*], 299–300).
63. Letter from Jason Joy to B. P. Schulberg, December 1, 1931, *Dr. Jekyll and Mr. Hyde* PCAR, MHL.
64. Mamoulian, interview by Atkins, 40.
65. *Dr. Jekyll and Mr. Hyde* screenplay, August 7, 1931, *Dr. Jekyll and Mr. Hyde* file, RMP. Ivy's whispered line—and her superimposed leg—also appears in Mamoulian, "Shooting Continuity as Dictated by Rouben Mamoulian," 37–8.
66. This information is based on the files the SRC kept on what various boards eliminated (*Dr. Jekyll and Mr. Hyde*, PCAR, MHL). Additional information comes from a letter from Lillian Brind to Albert Deane, February 12, 1932, *Dr. Jekyll and Mr. Hyde* file, RMP.
67. Letter from Jason Joy to B. P. Schulberg, December 1, 1931, *Dr. Jekyll and Mr. Hyde* PCAR, MHL.
68. Mamoulian, interview by Greenberg, T2/P43–44.
69. Letter from James Wingate to Will Hays, May 20, 1933, *The Song of Songs* PCAR, MHL.
70. Note by Rouben Mamoulian, enclosed in a letter from A. M. Botsford to James Wingate, June 5, 1933, *The Song of Songs* PCAR, MHL.
71. For the SRC letter, see ibid. For the New York censor board letter, see A. M. Botsford to John Hammell, May 29, 1933, *The Song of Songs* file, RMP.
72. Note by Rouben Mamoulian, enclosed in a letter from A. M. Botsford to James Wingate, June 5, 1933, *The Song of Songs* PCAR, MHL.
73. Letter from James Wingate to William Wright, February 10, 1933, *The Song of Songs* PCAR, MHL.
74. *The Song of Songs* screenplay, January 28, 1933 (no author listed, but likely Leo Birinski and Samuel Hoffenstein), C-6, Benjamin Glazer collection, CYRL.
75. Letter from James Wingate to A. M. Botsford, May 18, 1933, 2, *The Song of Songs* PCAR, MHL.
76. Letter from "Rudy" to Rouben Mamoulian, May 31, 1933, *The Song of Songs* file, RMP.

77. Letter from James Wingate to A. M. Botsford, June 21, 1933. Letter from Botsford to Wingate, June 22, 1933. Letter from Harold Hurley to Wingate, July 1, 1933. Letter from Wingate to Botsford, July 3, 1933. All letters are in *The Song of Songs* PCAR, MHL.
78. Letter from James Wingate to A. M. Botsford, May 18, 1933, *The Song of Songs* PCAR, MHL.
79. Maltby, "The Production Code and the Hays Office," 56–57.
80. *The Song of Songs* screenplay, January 28, 1933, D-7, Benjamin Glazer collection, CYRL.
81. Ibid., D-8.
82. Memo from William Wright to Rouben Mamoulian, February 19, 1933, *The Song of Songs* file, RMP.
83. Jacobs, *Wages of Sin*, 16.
84. Note by Alice Ames Winter, circa May 1933, *The Song of Songs* PCAR, MHL.
85. Had Ames known it, she could have also pointed to the statue's dimensions, which were apparently Dietrich's own measurements, taken by sculptor Salvatore Cartaino Scarpitta (Mamoulian, interview by Greenberg, T4/P157).
86. Note by Alice Ames Winter, circa May 1933, *The Song of Songs* PCAR, MHL.
87. Milne, *Mamoulian*, 65.
88. *The Song of Songs* screenplay, January 28, 1933, D-9, Benjamin Glazer collection, CYRL.
89. Letter from James Wingate to A. M. Botsford, May 18, 1933. Letter from Wingate to Botsford, June 21, 1933. Both letters are in *The Song of Songs* PCAR, MHL.
90. Letter from A. M. Botsford to John Hammell, June 7, 1933, *The Song of Songs* file, RMP.
91. "The Production Code" (in Prince, *Classical Film Violence*), 299–301.
92. L.H.C., *Cinema*, September 6, 1933, 2, *The Song of Songs* file, RMP.
93. Unnamed author, "Marlene Dietrich Giving a Beautiful Performance in a Role That Is One of the Greatest Woman Characters in All Literature," *Kansas City Star*, August 20, 1933, *The Song of Songs* file, RMP.
94. Dan Thompson, *The Louisville Times*, July 22, 1933, 1, *The Song of Songs* file, RMP.
95. Intriguingly, Mamoulian did hold two work-related meetings with screenwriter Salka Viertel when she was working on the initial screenplay for *Queen Christina* back in late 1932 and early 1933, but there is no record of what was discussed (Mamoulian, 1932 and 1933 diaries, RMP).
96. By the end of July 1933 (well after Mamoulian's arrival), such Mamoulian staples as kittens and shadow play at the inn start to appear in screenplay revisions. Though they would eventually be dropped from the film, Mamoulian's handprint on the inn scene by this date remains clear (*Queen Christina* screenplay, July 28, 1933, MGM/Turner collection, MHL). It is at this same time that the room-touching scene first appears. Mamoulian would—in promotion for the film and later interviews—single out this scene as an important contribution, and the screenplay's description of Christina walking in "half-rhythmic accompaniment to the music" as she touches the objects is entirely consistent with Mamoulian's career-long obsession with rhythm in the arts (*Queen Christina* screenplay, July 31, 1933, MGM/Turner collection, MHL).

97. In a review of Salka Viertel and Margaret Le Vino's treatment for *Queen Christina*, for instance, staff screenwriter Jessie Burns advanced the concern that would preoccupy MGM for months. If romance was the catalyst behind Christina's decision to abdicate, Burns argued, the film needed a truly great passion in the film. Surely, Burns argued, Christina would have *already* experienced an ardent love affair. "The love that inspires her finally to abdicate should be a tremendous thing and should possess elements that we feel to be new in her life (as Robert Montgomery's freshness was new to Garbo in "Inspiration," for instance)." Burns, synopsis of *Queen Christina* treatment, July 29, 1932, MGM/Turner scripts, MHL.
98. Letter from James Wingate to Eddie Mannix, August 7, 1933, *Queen Christina* PCAR, MHL.
99. Internal SRC memo by James Wingate, August 11, 1933, *Queen Christina* PCAR, MHL. The memo affirms that Wanger felt the proposed adjustment would "seriously affect his picture."
100. "Rhythm on the Screen," interview with the *New York Times*, February 11, 1934, Section X, p. 5.
101. Rouben Mamoulian, "Importance of Rhythm on the Screen," *The Film Daily*, March 15, 1934, *Queen Christina* file, RMP.
102. The SRC agreed to suspend judgment until they learned about the New York censor board deletions (Joseph Breen to Louis B. Mayer, January 8, 1934, *Queen Christina* PCAR, MHL). Evidence of the SRC's dissatisfaction appears in a letter from Breen to Will Hays on December 29, 1933 that summarizes the censorship situation for many films, including *Queen Christina* (*Queen Christina* PCAR, MHL).
103. Memo from W. D. Kelly to Eddie Mannix, December 21, 1933, *Queen Christina* PCAR, MHL.
104. On January 3, 1934, Will Hays sent Nicholas Schenck a letter scolding him for holding public screenings of *Queen Christina* without approval by the SRC (*Queen Christina* PCAR, MHL).
105. Letter from Joseph Breen to Louis B. Mayer, January 8, 1934, *Queen Christina* PCAR, MHL.
106. Letter from Jason Joy to Earl Bright, January 11, 1934, *Queen Christina* PCAR, MHL.
107. Mamoulian, interview by Hare, 133–34.
108. Gregory D. Black, *Hollywood Censored: Morality Codes, Catholics, and the Movies* (Cambridge: Cambridge University Press, 1994), 206.
109. The information in this paragraph comes largely from the PCAR files in MHL for *We Live Again*; *Becky Sharp*; *The Gay Desperado*; *High, Wide and Handsome*; *Golden Boy*; *The Mark of Zorro*; *Blood and Sand*; *Rings on Her Fingers*; and *Silk Stockings*.
110. Letter from Joseph Breen to Louis B. Mayer, April 6, 1946, *Summer Holiday* PCAR, MHL.
111. Annotation in *Sadie Thompson* playscript, March 1944, Act II, 38, *Sadie Thompson* file, RMP.
112. *Sadie Thompson* playscript, undated, Act II 40–41, *Sadie Thompson* file [Box 119, Folder 9], RMP. Though this playscript is undated, it was clearly written after the March 1944 playscript, as changes penciled in the margins by Mamoulian from March 1944 have been typed up in this version.

113. For a detailed account of the film's trip through various censorship entities, see Black, *Hollywood Censored*, 94–99.
114. Stevens, *Conversations with the Great Moviemakers of Hollywood's Golden Age*, 184; Mamoulian, interview by Becvar, Tape 4, p. 6.

Conclusion

1. Rouben Mamoulian, *Dialogue on Film* (interview with the American Film Institute, 1972, RMP), 33.

Bibliography

This bibliography refers only to works cited in the endnotes. With the exception of Mamoulian's interviews, it does not include newspaper articles cited in the endnotes.

Archives

CYRL   Charles E. Young Research Library, University of California, Los Angeles
MHL   Margaret Herrick Library, Academy of Motion Picture Arts and Sciences, Los Angeles, California
RMP   Rouben Mamoulian Papers, The Library of Congress, Washington, DC

Articles, Books, and Interviews

Allen, Robert C. *Horrible Prettiness: Burlesque and American Culture*. Chapel Hill: University of North Carolina Press, 1991.
Allen, Robert C., and Douglas Gomery. *Film History: Theory and Practice*. New York: Alfred A. Knopf, 1985.
Altman, Rick. "Afterword: A Baker's Dozen Terms for Sound Analysis." In *Sound Theory/Sound Practice*, edited by Altman, 249–53. New York: Routledge, 1992.
Altman, Rick. *The American Film Musical*. Bloomington: Indiana University Press, 1987.
Altman, Rick. "Establishing Sound." *Cinémas* 24.1 (2013): 19–33.
Altman, Rick. *Film/Genre*. London: BFI, 1999.
Altman, Rick. "The Material Heterogeneity of Recorded Sound." In *Sound Theory/Sound Practice*, edited by Altman, 15–31. New York: Routledge, 1992.
Altman, Rick. "Sound Space." In *Sound Theory/Sound Practice*, edited by Altman, 46–64. New York: Routledge, 1992.
Altman, Rick. "The Technology of the Voice, Part I." *Iris* 3.1 (1985): 3–20.
Altman, Rick, with McGraw Jones and Sonia Tatroe. "Inventing the Cinema Soundtrack: Hollywood's Multiplane Sound System." In *Music and Cinema*, edited by James Buhler, Caryl Flinn, and David Neumeyer, 339–59. Hanover, NH: University Press of New England, 2000.
Arnheim, Rudolph. *Film as Art*. Berkeley: University of California Press, 1957.
Balázs, Béla. *Early Film Theory*. Translated by Rodney Livingstone. New York: Berghahn, 2010.
Barrios, Richard. *A Song in the Dark: The Birth of the Musical Film*. New York: Oxford University Press, 1995.
Basinger, Jeanine. *The Movie Musical!* New York: Alfred A. Knopf, 2019.
Belton, John. "Awkward Transitions: Hitchcock's 'Blackmail' and the Dynamics of Early Film Sound." *Musical Quarterly* 83.2 (Summer 1999): 227–46.

Berman, Anna A. "Scripting Katyusha on the Way to an Operatic Adaptation of *Resurrection*." *Slavic and East European Journal* 55.3 (Fall 2011): 396–417.

Black, Gregory D. *Hollywood Censored: Morality Codes, Catholics, and the Movies.* Cambridge: Cambridge University Press, 1994.

Block, Geoffrey. "Integration." In *The Oxford Handbook of the American Musical*, edited by Raymond Knapp, Mitchell Morris, and Stacy Wolf, 97–110. Oxford: Oxford University Press, 2011.

Bordwell, David. "Camera Movement, the Coming of Sound, and the Classical Hollywood Style." In *Film: Historical-Theoretical Speculations*, edited by Ben Lawton and Janet Staiger, 27–31. Pleasantville, NY: Redgrave Publishing, 1977.

Bordwell, David, Janet Staiger, and Kristin Thompson, *The Classical Hollywood Cinema: Film Style and Mode of Production to 1960*. New York: Columbia University Press, 1985.

Carnicke, Sharon Marie. "Rethinking 'Stanislavskian' Directing." In *The Great European Stage Directors*. Vol. 1, *Antoine, Stanislavski, Saint Denis*, edited by Peta Tait, 91–111. London: Methuen Drama, 2019.

Carnicke, Sharon Marie, and David Rosen. "A Singer Prepares: Stanislavski and Opera." In *The Routledge Companion to Stanislavsky*, edited by R. Andrew White, 120–38. London: Routledge, 2014.

Carroll, Noël. "The Specificity of Media in the Arts." *Journal of Aesthetic Education* 19.4 (1985): 5–20.

Carter, Tim. *"Oklahoma!": The Making of an American Musical*. New Haven, CT: Yale University Press, 2007.

Chion, Michel. *Audio-Vision: Sound on Screen*. New York: Columbia University Press: 1994.

Crafton, Donald. *The Talkies: American Cinema's Transition to Sound, 1926–1931*. Berkeley: University of California Press, 1997.

Decker, Todd. *Music Makes Me: Fred Astaire and Jazz*. Berkeley: University of California Press, 2011.

Dennis, James. *Renegade Regionalists: The Modern Independence of Grant Wood, Thomas Hart Benton, and John Steuart Curry*. Madison: University of Wisconsin Press, 1998.

Ellenberger, Allan R. *Miriam Hopkins: Life and Films of a Hollywood Rebel*. Lexington: University Press of Kentucky, 2018.

Esquevin, Christian. "*An American in Paris*: Art on Film." http://silverscreenmodes.com/an-american-in-paris-art-on-film/.

Feuer, Jane. *The Hollywood Musical*. 2nd ed. Bloomington: Indiana University Press, 1993.

Fischer, Lucy. "*Applause*: The Visual and Acoustic Landscape." In *Film Sound: Theory and Practice*, edited by Elisabeth Weis and John Belton, 232–46. New York: Columbia University Press, 1985.

Fleeger, Jennifer. *Sounding American: Hollywood, Opera, and Jazz*. New York: Oxford University Press, 2014.

Flinn, Denny Martin. *Musical! A Grand Tour: The Rise, Glory, and Fall of an American Institution*. New York: Schirmer Books, 1997.

Gabbard, Krin. *Jammin' at the Margins: Jazz and the American Cinema*. Chicago: University of Chicago Press, 1996.

Garcia, Desirée J. *The Migration of Musical Film: From Ethnic Margins to American Mainstream*. New Brunswick, NJ: Rutgers University Press, 2014.

Gardner, Kara Anne. *Agnes de Mille: Telling Stories in Broadway Dance*. New York: Oxford University Press, 2016.
Geller, Theresa L. "Dorothy Arzner." *Senses of Cinema* 26 (May 2003). http://www.sensesofcinema.com/2003/great-directors/arzner/.
Grieveson, Lee. *Policing Cinema: Movies and Censorship in Early-Twentieth-Century America*. Berkeley: University of California Press, 2004.
Higgins, Scott. *Harnessing the Technicolor Rainbow: Color Design in the 1930s*. Austin: University of Texas Press, 2007.
Higham, Charles. *The Celluloid Muse: Hollywood Directors Speak*. London: Angus & Robertson, 1969.
Horowitz, Joseph. *"On My Way": The Untold Story of Rouben Mamoulian, George Gershwin, and "Porgy and Bess."* New York: W. W. Norton, 2013.
Jacobs, Lea. *Film Rhythm after Sound: Technology, Music, and Performance*. Berkeley: University of California Press, 2014.
Jacobs, Lea. "The Innovation of Re-Recording in the Hollywood Studios." *Film History: An International Journal* 24.1 (2012): 5–34.
Jacobs, Lea. *The Wages of Sin: Censorship and the Fallen Woman Film, 1928–1942*. Madison: University of Wisconsin Press, 1991.
Jensen, Kurt. "What Did 'Mamoo' Do? The Rouben Mamoulian Papers and *Oklahoma!*" *Studies in Musical Theatre* 4.3 (2010): 247–59.
Jewell, Richard. *RKO Radio Pictures: A Titan Is Born*. Berkeley: University of California Press, 2012.
Kalmus, Natalie. "Color Consciousness." *Journal of the Society for Motion Picture Engineers* 25 (August 1935): 139–47.
Keating, Patrick. *The Dynamic Frame: Camera Movement in Classical Hollywood*. New York: Columbia University Press, 2019.
Koszarski, Richard. "The Greatest Film Paramount Ever Made." *Film History* 15.4 (2003): 436–43.
Koszarski, Richard. *Hollywood on the Hudson: Film and Television in New York from Griffith to Sarnoff*. New Brunswick, NJ: Rutgers University Press, 2008.
Kozloff, Sarah. *Invisible Storytellers: Voice-over Narration in American Fiction Film*. Berkeley: University of California Press, 1988.
Knight, Arthur. *The Liveliest Art: A Panoramic History of the Movies*. New York: The New English Library Limited, 1957.
Lecomte, Jean-Marie. "Rouben Mamoulian's *Applause* and the Birth of the Disenchanted Musical." *Studies in Musical Theatre* 2.2 (2008): 147–61.
Lerner, Neil. "The Strange Case of Rouben Mamoulian's Sound Stew: The Uncanny Soundtrack in *Dr. Jekyll and Mr. Hyde* (1931)." In *Music in the Horror Film: Listening to Fear*, edited by Lerner, 55–79. New York: Routledge, 2010.
Lewis, Hannah. "*Love Me Tonight* (1932) and the Development of the Integrated Film Musical." *The Musical Quarterly* 100.1 (2017): 3–32.
Luhrssen, David. *Mamoulian: Life on Stage and Screen*. Lexington: University Press of Kentucky, 2013.
Maltby, Richard. "The Production Code and the Hays Office." In *Grand Design: Hollywood as a Modern Business Enterprise, 1930–1939*, edited by Tino Balio, 37–72. New York: Charles Scribner's Sons, 1993.
Mamoulian, Rouben. *The American Film Institute Seminar*. May 27, 1981, RMP.

Mamoulian, Rouben. "The Art of Films." Lecture given to "History of the Motion Picture" class at Columbia University, Museum of Modern Art, December 6, 1939, RMP.
Mamoulian, Rouben. "Bernhardt versus Duse." *Ararat*, September 1957, 26–32.
Mamoulian, Rouben. "Colors and Emotions." For *N.Y. Variety*, May 4, 1946, RMP.
Mamoulian, Rouben. "Colour and Light in Films from 1946 to 1956." For *Ararat Magazine*, no date, RMP.
Mamoulian, Rouben. "The Coming of Color on the Screen." Speech for the Society of American Cinematographers, 1937, RMP.
Mamoulian, Rouben. "Common Sense and Camera Angles." *American Cinematographer* 12.10 (February 1932): 8–9, 26.
Mamoulian, Rouben. "Controlling Color for Dramatic Effect." *American Cinematographer* 22.6 (June 1941): 262, 263, 288, 290.
Mamoulian, Rouben. "Conversations with Mamoulian." Unpublished interview by Bennet T. Oberstein, August 1973, RMP.
Mamoulian, Rouben. *Dialogue on Film*. Interview with the American Film Institute, 1972, RMP.
Mamoulian, Rouben. "*Dr. Jekyll and Mr. Hyde*: An Interview with Rouben Mamoulian." Interview by Thomas R. Atkins. *The Film Journal* 2.2 (1973): 37–44.
Mamoulian, Rouben. "The Essence of Theatrical Art." Lecture delivered in Rochester (NY) 1923–1924, RMP.
Mamoulian, Rouben. "History of the Motion Picture." Lecture delivered to the Department of Fine Arts, Columbia University, November 29, 1938.
Mamoulian, Rouben. Interview by Anthony Slide, n.d. MH.
Mamoulian, Rouben. "Interview with Rouben Mamoulian." Unpublished interview by William Becvar, March 20–22, 1973, RMP.
Mamoulian, Rouben. "An Interview with Rouben Mamoulian." Interview by John A. Gallagher and Marino A. Amoruco. *The Velvet Light Trap* 19 (1982): 16–22.
Mamoulian, Rouben. "Interview with Rouben Mamoulian." Interview by Harry A. Hargrave. *Literature/Film Quarterly* 10.4 (1982): 255–65.
Mamoulian, Rouben. "Mamoulian First Used Camera at Eastman School, He Recalls." *Democrat and Chronicle*, Rochester, NY, February 11, 1934, RMP.
Mamoulian, Rouben. Oral History Transcript, Columbia University. New York, December 1958, RMP.
Mamoulian, Rouben. "Painting the Leaves Black: An Interview with Rouben Mamoulian." Interview by David Robinson. *Monthly Film Bulletin* 30.3 (Summer 1961): 123–27.
Mamoulian, Rouben. "The Psychology of Color." For Harrison Carroll's column. April 23, 1941, RMP.
Mamoulian, Rouben. "The Psychology of Sound: The Second in a Series of Papers Challenging the Realistic Conception of Art." July 1938, RMP.
Mamoulian, Rouben. "Rouben Mamoulian: An Exclusive Interview." Interview by William Hare. In *American Classic Screen Interviews*, edited by John C. Tibbetts and James M. Welsh, 131–46. Lanham, MD: Scarecrow Press, 2010.
Mamoulian, Rouben. "Rouben Mamoulian: Hollywood Innovator." Interview by Lloyd Chelsey and Michael Gould. *MovieMaker* 57 (Winter 2005): 118–21, 148.
Mamoulian, Rouben. *Rouben Mamoulian: Oral History*. Interview by Steven Greenberg. American Film Institute, May 1973, RMP.
Mamoulian, Rouben. "Some Problems in Directing Color Pictures." *Society of Motion Picture Engineers* 100.12 (December 1991): 970–72.

Mamoulian, Rouben. "Stage and Screen." Unpublished article intended for collection titled *Their Magic Wand*, edited by William Hawks, October 23, 1946.
Mamoulian Rouben, "Time for Audiences to Do Their Part." Unpublished, August 3, 1965, RMP.
Mamoulian, Rouben. "The Use and Abuse of Perambulation." Lecture given to the American Society of Cinematographers, July 19, 1932, RMP.
Mamoulian, Rouben. "Verbatim Interview with Rouben Mamoulian." Interview by Russell Birdwell. Undated, RMP.
Mamoulian, Rouben. "Visual Anti-Realism: The First in a Series of Papers Challenging the Realistic Conception of Art." July 1938, RMP.
Mamoulian, Rouben. "What Color Means in Wardrobe." *Brooklyn Eagle*, May 20, 1941, RMP.
Mamoulian, Rouben. "What Color Will You Wear?" *Californian* 4.3 (October 1947): 28–29.
Mamoulian, Rouben. "What Do You Think of Color?" *New Movie Magazine* 12.3 (September 1935): 16, 44–45.
Mamoulian, Rouben. "The World's Latest Fine Art." *Cinema Arts* 1 (1936): 21–22.
Milne, Tom. *Mamoulian*. London: Thames & Hudson, 1969.
Mordden, Ethan. *Beautiful Mornin': The Broadway Musical in the 1940s*. New York: Oxford University Press, 1999.
Mueller, John. *Astaire Dancing: The Musical Films*. New York: Wings Books, 1985.
O'Neill, Eugene. "Ah, Wilderness!" In *O'Neill: Complete Plays, 1932–1943*, 1–108. New York: Library of America, 1990.
Patinkin, Sheldon. *"No Legs, No Jokes, No Chance": A History of the American Musical Theatre*. Evanston, IL: Northwestern University Press, 2008.
Prince, Stephen. *Classical Film Violence: Designing and Regulating Brutality in Hollywood, 1930–1968*. New Brunswick, NJ: Rutgers University Press, 2003.
Riis, Thomas. "Musical Theatre." In *The Cambridge History of American Theatre*. Vol. 2, *1879–1945*, edited by Don B. Wilmeth and Christopher Bigsby, 411–45. Cambridge: Cambridge University Press, 1999.
Salt, Barry. *Film Style and Technology: History and Analysis*. London: Starword, 1983.
Sarris, Andrew. *The American Cinema: Directors and Directions, 1929–1968*. New York: Octagon Books, 1982.
Sarris, Andrew. "Notes on the Auteur Theory in 1962." In *Film Theory and Criticism*, 7th ed., edited by Leo Braudy and Marshall Cohen, 451–54. New York: Oxford University Press, 2009.
Silke, James R., ed. *Rouben Mamoulian: "Style Is the Man."* Washington, DC: American Film Institute, 1971.
Slowik, Michael. "Experiments in Early Sound Film Music: Strategies and Rerecording, 1928–1930." *American Music* 31.4 (2013): 450–74.
Slowik, Michael. "Revealing Reality: Fan Magazine Rhetoric, Sound Technology, and Stardom in the Early Sound Era." *Journal of Film and Video* 70.2 (Summer 2018): 30–45.
Spergel, Mark. *Reinventing Reality: The Art and Life of Rouben Mamoulian*. Metuchen, NJ: Scarecrow Press, 1993.
Spring, Katherine. *Saying It with Songs: Popular Music and the Coming of Sound to Hollywood Cinema*. New York: Oxford University Press, 2013.
Stevens, George, Jr., ed. *Conversations with the Great Moviemakers of Hollywood's Golden Age*. New York: Alfred A. Knopf, 2006.

Stinnett, Jack. "New Yorker at Large." *Enquirer*, Cincinnati (OH), August 11, 1937.

Turk, Edward Baron. *Hollywood Diva: A Biography of Jeanette MacDonald*. Berkeley: University of California Press, 1998.

Vasey, Ruth. *The World According to Hollywood, 1918–1939*. Madison: University of Wisconsin Press, 1997.

Whittington, William. *Sound Design and Science Fiction*. Austin: University of Texas Press, 2007.

Wollen, Peter. "The Auteur Theory." In *Film Theory and Criticism*, 7th ed., edited by Leo Braudy and Marshall Cohen, 455–70. New York: Oxford University Press, 2009.

Yumibe, Joshua. *Moving Color: Early Film, Mass Culture, Modernism*. New Brunswick, NJ: Rutgers University Press, 2012.

Index

For the benefit of digital users, indexed terms that span two pages (e.g., 52–53) may, on occasion, appear on only one of those pages.

Tables and figures are indicated by *t* and *f* following the page number

Academy Awards, 1, 79–80
actor movements and rhythm, 91, 94–95, 96
African Americans
    actors, 10
    bands in feature films, 112
    black culture in films, 10–11, 141–42, 144
Alibi (1929), 106
All Quiet on the Western Front (1930), 79–80
all-talking films, 55, 57, 58, 97
Altman, Rick, 4–5, 125–26
American Cinematographer, 1, 21–22, 193, 194–95
The American Film Musical (Altman), 124
American Society of Cinematographers, 21, 39
animal symphony, 156–57
annotations by Mamoulian, 3–4
Applause (1929)
    background sound manipulation, 72–73, 75–77, 78, 105–6
    camera angles, 31–33, 75, 125–31
    camera movement, 54, 60–67, 62*f*, 63*f*, 64*f*, 66*f*, 100
    censorship of sexuality, 205, 209–14, 212*f*
    direct sound, 60–67, 78
    dissolve transitions, 49
    editing rhythm, 100–5, 102*t*, 104*f*
    expressive sound, 54–55, 69, 73–77, 78, 106–7
    film style manipulation, 127–28
    flashback images, 82–83
    forced framings in, 31*f*, 31–34, 32*f*, 35*f*
    foreground voices, 69–72
    impact of, 17, 78–79
    introduction to, 1, 11, 16
    manipulation of film style, 127
    manipulation of sound, 72–73, 78, 129–30
    rhythm use in, 97, 98–105
    selective on-location sound, 73–77, 76*f*
    semi-sync sound in, 58–59, 78
    shadow play in, 25–28, 27*f*, 28*f*, 98–99
    as show musical, 125–31, 129*f*, 130*f*
    sound innovations in, 53, 54
    sound rhythm, 105–6
    sound theory and, 67–79
    sustained split-screen transition, 39–43, 40*f*, 42*f*
    voice-overs in, 107
Arlen, Harold, 161–62
Arms and the Girl (1950), 173
art and cinema philosophies
    dissolve-based transition, 39–51
    forced framings, 30–38
    identifying elements in, 20
    introduction to, 6–7, 17
    overview on, 18–23
    scene transitions, 39–51
    shadow play, 23–29
    summary of, 51–52
    symmetrical graphic match, 50
Astaire, Fred, 202
auteurism, 1–2, 3–4
auteur theory, 1–2
average shot length (ASL), 101, 106–7

background sound manipulation, 54, 68, 72–73, 75–77, 78, 79–80, 105–6
The Beating on the Door (1922), 9, 19, 91–92
Becky Sharp (1935)
    color design, 11–12, 180–82, 184, 185–86
    color theory and, 178–87
    introduction to, 1
    oozing into color, 181–83
    red (color) as drama, 183–84
    shadow play and, 29
    Technicolor use, 177, 178–84
Benton, Thomas Hart, 168–69, 195
Berkeley, Busby, 125
Bernhardt, Sarah, 18
The Big Trail, 82–83
Birinski, Leo, 15, 144–45
birth of Mamoulian, 9
black culture, 10–11, 141–42, 144

Black Narcissus (1947), 195–96
Blane, Ralph, 164
Blood and Sand (1941)
  color design, 1, 187–95
  forced framings, 35–36, 36*f*
  introduction to, 1, 12–13
  musical approaches to, 110
  music's rhythm-based functions, 116, 118–22
  sonic distortion, 87
  "speaking" objects, 88
  Technicolor in, 177, 187–95
Boleslawski, Richard, 6
booth-enclosed multiple-camera shooting, 56–57
Borzage, Frank, 51
bravura camera moves, 33, 60, 64–65
Brecher, Irving, 164
Breen, Joseph, 177–78, 241
Broadway (1929), 60
The Broadway Melody (1929), 135
Bulldog Drummond (1929), 98–99

camera, as essence of cinema, 21–22
camera angles
  Applause, 31–33, 75, 125–31
  Becky Sharp, 182, 185
  censorship of sexuality and, 233–34
  The Cocoanuts, 127
  High, Wide and Handsome, 150–51
  The Mark of Zorro, 117
  in show musicals, 125–31
camera movement
  Applause, 54, 60–67, 62*f*, 63*f*, 64*f*, 66*f*, 100
  bravura camera moves, 33, 60, 64–65
  High, Wide and Handsome, 150–51
  innovation in, 247–48
  Jekyll Dr. and Mr. Hyde, 214–24
  rhythm and, 100, 108–9
Capra, Frank, 17
Carousel (1945), 1, 159–61
censorship of sexuality
  Applause, 205, 209–14, 212*f*, 213*f*
  eroticism and, 110–11, 215, 224, 227, 234, 236–37, 245–46
  introduction to, 8, 204–5
  Jekyll Dr. and Mr. Hyde, 205, 214–24, 218*f*, 220*f*, 224*f*
  male gaze and, 237, 238, 242–43
  Queen Christina, 205, 237–43, 240*f*, 242*f*, 243*f*
  rhythmic stylization and, 239–41, 240*f*
  self-censorship by Hollywood, 8, 205, 206–7, 209, 235–36, 241
  Song of Songs, 205, 224–37, 228*f*, 229*f*
  summary of, 243–46

Check and Double Check (1930), 112
Chekhov, Anton, 19–20
Chicago (2002), 249
cinematic subjectivity, 107, 216, 222–23
City Streets (1931)
  cast shadows in, 29
  dissolve transitions, 49–50
  flashback images, 82–83
  introduction to, 11
  musical approaches to, 111–12
  rhythm in, 106–7
  sound innovations in, 53
  voice-overs in, 53, 79–84, 81*f*, 85–86, 88–89
Clair, René, 1
Cleopatra (1963), 14–15, 247
The Cocoanuts (1929), 60–61, 63, 127
color design
  Becky Sharp, 11–12, 180–82, 184, 185–86
  Blood and Sand, 1, 187–95
  color associations and, 180
  innovations in, 2
  sexuality and, 248–49
  Silk Stockings, 202
  Summer Holiday, 195–97
colored lighting in *Summer Holiday*, 198–200, 203
color restraint, 201–2
condenser microphone, 55–56
Congai (1928), 25, 181–82, 218–19
Cooper, Merian C., 178–79
Cukor, George, 1
Curry, John Steuart, 168–69, 195
Curtiz, Michael, 6

dance-action, 92, 136, 137, 153, 154
dance integration, 173–76
Danger Lights (1930), 79–80
dark privacy, 125–26
De Mille, Agnes, 155, 157, 158
DeMille, Cecil B., 1
dialogue director, 11
Dietrich, Marlene, 11
directional microphones, 68, 79
direct sound, 58, 60–67, 78
Dishonored (1930), 82–83
Disney, Walt, 178–79
dissolve-based transition, 39–51
The Divorcee (1930), 79–80
Dreier, Hans, 15
Duse, Eleonora, 18
dynamic shadow play, 98–99

Eakins, Thomas, 169–71
early sound techniques, 4–5, 11

Eastman, George, 10, 18–19
Eastman School of Drama and Dramatic
    Action, 10
Eastman School of Music, 10
editing rhythm, 100–5, 102t, 104f, 108–9
editing sound strips, 56
Eisenstein, Sergei, 1
eroticism and film censorship, 110–11, 215, 224,
    227, 234, 236–37, 245–46
expressive sound, 4–5, 54–55, 69, 73–77, 78,
    106–7, 204, 249

Faust (1923), 23–24
Fejos, Paul, 60
Film: The Liveliest Art (Knight), 1 2
film censorship. *See* censorship of sexuality
film director reputation of Mamoulian, 1–2
film musicals
    dance integration, 173–76
    fairy-tale musical, 153–58
    folk musicals, 141–73
    introduction to, 7–8, 124–25
    show musicals, 125–31
    St. Louis Woman, 160–62
    Summer Holiday, 163–73
film rhythm. *See* rhythm
*Film Rhythm after Sound: Technology, Music,
    and Performance* (Jacobs), 90–91
film style manipulation
    Applause, 127–28
    censorship of sexuality and, 204, 206, 208–9,
        224–26, 230
    innovation in, 8, 249
    Love Me Tonight, 132, 224–25
Fisher, James, 209
flashback images, 82–83
flashback voices, 85–86
Florey, Robert, 127
folk musicals, 141–63
forced framings
    Applause, 31f, 31–34, 32f, 35f
    Blood and Sand, 35–36, 36f
    The Gay Desperado, 37–38
    Golden Boy, 36–37, 37f
    innovation in, 6–7, 17, 30–38
Ford, Garrett, 55
Ford, John, 1–2, 3, 17
foreground sound manipulation, 69–72
foreground voices, 69 72
Freed, Arthur, 13–14
French New Wave, 22

The Game of Love and Death (1929), 35

Garbo, Greta, 11–12
The Gay Desperado (1936)
    as folk musical, 144–46, 146f, 147f, 148f
    forced framings in, 37–38
    innovations in, 124–25
    introduction to, 12
    shadow play in, 29, 30f
Gershwin, George, 10–11, 12, 142–44
Gershwin, Ira, 10–11, 12
Golden Boy (1939), 12, 36–37, 37f, 112–
    13, 115–16
Goldwyn, Samuel, 14
Goya, Francisco, 188–89
Gustafson, Esther, 92

Hallelujah (1929), 98–99, 149
Hammerstein, Oscar, 148, 155–56
*Harnessing the Technicolor Rainbow: Color
    Design in the 1930s* (Higgins), 180–81
Hawks, Howard, 1–2, 18
Hell's Heroes (1929), 81–82
Higgins, Scott, 180–81
High, Wide and Handsome (1937)
    camera angles, 150–51
    dissolve transitions, 50
    distorted images and sounds, 109
    as folk musical, 146–52, 151f, 152f
    introduction to, 4–5, 12
    sonic distortion, 87
    sonic subjectivity, 88
Hitchcock, Alfred, 1–2, 17, 247
Hoffenstein, Samuel, 15
Hornblow, Arthur, 148–50
Horowitz, Joseph, 3–4, 19

identity as an artist, 2
immigrant status, 6
In Old Arizona (1929), 57
intellectualism, 18–19, 197–98

Jacobs, Lea, 90–91
Jekyll Dr. and Mr. Hyde (1931)
    censorship of sexuality, 205, 214–24, 218f,
        220f, 224f
    distorted images and sounds, 108–9
    musical approaches to, 110–11
    rhythm in, 107–8
    sound innovations in, 53, 84–87
    sustained split-screen transition, 43f, 43–48,
        44f, 46f, 47f, 48f
Jones, Robert Edmond, 180
Joy, Jason, 206

Kazan, Elia, 1–2

Kelly, Gene, 173, 249
Kern, Jerome, 148
King Kong (1933), 86–87
Knight, Arthur, 1–2

Lady in the Dark (1944), 195–96
Lang, Fritz, 1
Langner, Lawrence, 93–94
Lasky, Jesse, 11, 144–45
The Last Laugh (1924), 23–24
The Last of Mrs. Cheyney (1929), 60–61, 64–65
Leonard, Robert Z., 88–89
The Letter (1929), 57
Library of Congress, 3–4
lip synchronization, 75
Litvak, Anatol, 6
Lost in the Stars (1948), 163
Love Me Tonight (1932)
    censorship analysis, 224–25
    as fairy-tale musical, 153–58
    film style manipulation, 132, 224–25
    innovations in, 124–25
    rhythm in, 107, 131–41, 139*f*, 140*f*
    shadow play in, 29
    sonic subjectivity, 87–88
    voice-overs in, 138–39
Lubitsch, Ernst, 1, 132, 134, 205
Luening, Otto, 92

Macgowan, Kenneth, 11–12
male gaze, 237, 238, 242–43
Marchand, Léopold, 132–33
Marco Millions (1928), 25
The Mark of Zorro (1940)
    camera angles, 117
    introduction to, 12–13, 15
    music's rhythm-based functions, 116–22, 119*f*, 120*f*
Mayer, Louis B., 6, 11–12
medium specificity, 6–7, 20–21, 22–23, 53, 58, 89, 93–94, 124, 126, 193
Meet Me in St. Louis (1944), 164–65, 169–71
Mercer, John, 161–62
Meredyth, Bess, 15
MGM, 11–12, 241–42
microphones
    mobility of, 56–57
    multiple microphone use, 70–72
    omnidirectional microphones, 55–56, 70
    selectiveness of, 68
Milestone, Lewis, 6
Milton, Robert, 6

Minnelli, Vincente, 164–65, 249
Moscow Art Theatre (MAT), 9, 18–19
motion paintings, 179–80, 189
Motion Picture Producers and Distributors Association (MPPDA), 206, 209–10
movement within the frame, 98–99
multiple-camera shooting, 56–57
multiple microphone use, 70–72
Murillo, Bartolomé, 188–89
musical approaches to non-musicals, 109–16
musical performances in film, 116–22
musical rhythm, 92, 112–13, 133–34, 136

narrative-number integration, 7–8, 19–20, 153–58, 159, 160–61, 164, 179–80, 203, 247–48
Newman, Alfred, 15
Newman, Azadia (wife), 11
New York Times, 25
noise symphony, 94
nudity as art, 224–37, 228*f*, 229*f*, 230*f*, 232*f*, 235*f*
Nugent, Frank S., 151–52

Oklahoma! (1943), 1, 13–14, 153–58
omnidirectional microphones, 55–56, 70
O'Neill, Eugene, 160–61, 163–73
on-location sound, 73–77
On My Way (Horowitz), 3–4
on/ off switch approach to sound, 72

pacing concerns, 96–97
Paramount, 210–11
Paramount Pictures, 11, 15, 20–21, 53, 55–58
part-talking films, 55
perceptual realism, 72–73
performer-spectator dynamics, 124–25, 131
personal truth in art, 22
Pioneer Pictures, 178–79
point-of-view camerawork, 85
point-of-view filmmaking, 216–17
Porgy (1927)
    introduction to, 1, 10–11, 20–21
    noise symphony in, 94, 135, 141–42
    rhythm use in, 94, 95, 135
    shadow play in, 23–25, 94–95
Porgy and Bess (1935)
    as folk musical, 141–52
    innovations in, 124–25
    introduction to, 1, 12
    symphony of noises in, 143
Porgy and Bess (1959), 247
Porter, Cole, 202
post-production sound manipulation, 53

Power, Tyrone, 12–13
Preminger, Otto, 13, 18
Production Code, 177–78, 205–7, 214, 221–22
psychological sound, 84–87
"The Psychology of Sound" (Mamoulian), 67–79
The Public Enemy (1931), 112

Queen Christina (1933), 8, 11–12, 204–5, 237–43

rapid editing, 101, 105, 248–49
Ratoff, Gregory, 6
realism
  censorship of sexism and, 209–11
  expressivity over, 185–86
  fantastic realism, 19–20
  folk musicals, 151–52
  musicals and, 127, 148–49, 151–52
  perceptual realism, 72–73
  shadow play and, 24–25
  sound manipulation, 68, 72–73, 78, 91–92, 109
  stylization *vs.*, 19–20, 21–22, 67–68, 93
  Technicolor and, 179–80, 185–86, 188–89, 191–92
red (color) as drama, 183–84, 191–93
Reinhardt, Max, 93
rhythm
  actor movements and, 91, 94–95, 96
  approach to drama, 22–23
  baton use, 106, 107
  camera movement and, 100, 108–9
  Carousel, 159–61
  in editing, 100–5, 102t, 104f, 108–9
  experiments in, 106–9, 248
  introduction to, 7, 90–91
  in *Love Me Tonight*, 107, 131–41, 139f, 140f
  metronome use, 107
  musical approaches to non-musicals, 109–16
  musical performances, 116–22
  musical rhythm, 112–13, 133–34, 136
  in narrative-number integration, 153–58
  screen rhythm, 96–105
  sonic rhythm, 95, 135–36
  in sound, 105–6
  sound rhythm, 8, 23, 105–6
  stage rhythm, 91–96, 97, 133–34
Rings on Her Fingers (1942), 12–13
Rio Rita's (1929), 182–83
Rochester American Opera Company, 10, 18–19

Rodgers, Richard, 124–25, 134–35, 155–56
Romance (1930), 82–83
Rosing, Vladimir, 10
Rouben Mamoulian Papers, 3–4
R.U.R. (Rossum's Universal Robots) (1930), 158
Russian Revolution, 9

Sadie Thompson (1944), 158–59, 163, 244–45
Sarris, Andrew, 1–2
scene transitions, 39–51
screen rhythm, 96–106
The Seagull (1898), 19–20
selective on-location sound, 73–77, 76f
self-censorship by Hollywood, 8, 205, 206–7, 209, 235–36, 241
Selznick, David O., 1
semi-sync sound, 57–59, 78
7th Heaven (1927), 51
shadow play
  Applause, 25–28, 27f, 28f, 98–99
  art and cinema philosophies of, 23–29
  censorship of sexuality and, 232
  City Streets, 29
  dynamic shadow play, 98–99
  The Gay Desperado, 29, 30f
  Love Me Tonight, 29
  Porgy, 23–25, 94–95
  realism and, 24–25
The Shakedown (1929), 60
Sherman, Lowell, 11–12
shooting without sound, 57
show musicals, 125–31
silent films, 64–65, 74
Silk Stockings (1957)
  color design, 202
  color restraint, 201–2
  dance integration, 173–76
  introduction to, 14
  sonic subjectivity, 88
  Technicolor in, 201–2
  voice-overs in, 88
singing in movies, 164–68
Sirk, Douglas, 3
Sister Beatrice (1926), 92–94, 133, 153
Song of Songs (1933)
  censorship of sexuality, 204–5, 224–37
  flashback voices in, 88
  introduction to, 8, 11–12, 15
  rhythm use in, 107
sonic distortion, 72–73, 87
sonic recordings, 84–87
sonic rhythm, 95, 135–36

sonic subjectivity, 54–55, 88
sound filmmaking
  background manipulation of, 54, 68, 72–73, 75–77, 78, 79–80, 105–6
  direct sound, 58, 60–67, 78
  expressive sound, 4–5, 54–55, 69, 73–77, 78, 106–7, 204, 249
  foreground voices, 69–72
  introduction to, 2–5, 6–7, 53–55
  manipulation of background sound, 72–73, 78
  need for innovation, 55–58
  selective on-location sound, 73–77, 76*f*
  semi-sync sound, 57–59
  shooting without sound, 57
  sound-on-disc editing, 56
  synchronized sound, 3, 7, 11, 54, 57–60, 68–69, 83, 205–6
  synthetic sound, 2, 7, 247
sound-on-disc editing, 56
soundproofing cameras, 55–56
sound rhythm, 8, 23, 105–6
"speaking" objects, 88
St. Louis Woman (1946), 160–62, 168–69
stage director reputation, 1–2, 10, 13–14
stage musicals, 124–25, 153–63. *See also* specific musicals
stage rhythm, 91–96, 97, 133–34
Stahl, John M., 6
Stanislavski, Konstantin, 19–20, 93
Sternberg, Josef von, 51
Studio Relations Committee (SRC), 177–78, 214, 217, 221–23, 224–43
Stull, William, 1
stylization. *See also* forced framings; rhythm; shadow play
  introduction to, 3, 4–5, 6–8, 10–11
  narrative-number integration, 7–8, 19–20, 153–58, 159, 160–61, 164, 179–80, 203, 247–48
  rapid editing, 101, 105, 248–49
  realism *vs*., 19–20, 21–22, 67–68, 93
  scene transitions, 39–51
  theory of, 19–23
  voice-overs, 2, 53, 79–84, 247–48
subjective color, 8, 177, 195–96, 199–201
Summer Holiday (1948)
  censorship of sexuality and, 207
  color design, 195–97
  colored lighting in, 198–200, 203
  folk elements in, 163–73, 170*f*
  Technicolor of, 177, 195–201

Sumurun (1912), 93
Sunny Side Up (1929), 60–61
Sunrise (1927), 74
superimpositions, 108–9
sustained split-screen transition
  Applause, 39–43, 40*f*, 42*f*
  Jekyll Dr. and Mr. Hyde, 43*f*, 43–48, 44*f*, 46*f*, 47*f*, 48*f*
swooping camera moves, 60
symmetrical graphic match, 50
synchronized dialogue, 57
synchronized sound, 3, 7, 11, 54, 57–60, 68–69, 83, 205–6
synthetic sound, 2, 7, 247

tableau vivant, 128*f*–29, 171, 173
Technicolor films
  Becky Sharp, 1, 177, 178–84
  Blood and Sand, 177, 187–95
  colored lighting and, 198–200
  color restraint, 201–2
  emotional impact of color, 179–80
  influence of painting on, 168–69, 170*f*, 188–93, 195
  introduction to, 4–5, 8, 177–78
  oozing into, 181–83
  red (color) as drama, 183–84, 191–93
  Silk Stockings, 201–2
  subjective color, 8, 177, 195–96, 199–201
  Summer Holiday, 177, 195–201
Theatre Guild NYC, 10, 20–21
The Son of the Sheik (1926), 223
three-strip Technicolor. *See* Technicolor films
Truffant, François, 247
Twentieth Century–Fox, 12–13, 187–88
two-track recording, 2, 7, 81

Vakhtangov, Yevgeny, 19
voice-overs
  Applause, 107
  beginning use of, 54
  in character's dreamspace, 138–39
  City Streets, 53, 79–84, 81*f*, 85–86, 88–89
  flashback voice-overs, 88
  introduction to, 2, 7
  Love Me Tonight, 138–39
  Silk Stockings, 88

Wanger, Walter, 11–12, 14–15, 209–10, 238–39
Warner, Harry, 6
Warner Bros., 15–16, 56, 57–58, 125, 126–27

Warren, Harry, 164
We Live Again (1934), 38, 112–15, 114*f*
Welles, Orson, 17
Wellman, William, 112
West, Roland, 106
Whitney, Cornelius Vanderbilt, 178–79
Whitney, Jock, 178–79
Willard, MacNeal, 171
Wings over Europe (1928), 95–96

Winter, Alice Ames, 233–34
Winter, James, 226, 228–31, 234
Wollen, Peter, 1–2
Wood, Grant, 168–69, 170*f*, 195
Wyler, William, 60, 81–82

Zanuck, Darryl, 12–13, 116–22, 187–88
Ziegfeld, Florenz, 210–11
Zukor, Adolph, 6, 145